OUT OF RUSSIA

AND BACK

To my Dear Sister Mary & Brother
Chobby with best wishes
and Christ. love,

Roya
4-8-17

OUT OF RUSSIA AND BACK

A Life of Surprises

RAYA ABADIR

TABLE OF CONTENTS

LIST OF FIGURES

FOREWORD

Writers cannot tell whether their writing is good or not. But as I read Raya's book, I kept saying, "How wonderfully said," and, "I hope my own writing is half this good."

Not only does Raya write well, she takes normal life and makes it a mysterious adventure. Best of all, she shows each of us how to make our own lives that way.

The amazing thing is that, though her life and mine never converged until the last few years and our paths are far from similar, I feel we are one. As you read, you will either find your own oneness with her or discover how easily you can have it.

Perhaps we have each reached Nirvana in our way. All may!

Though our paths could scarcely be more dissimilar, the reason we both write is to lay a few bricks atop the foundation our families and our differing heritages have left for us to build upon.

Within the first few pages, my wife and I were enthralled with this story. It only got better.

In a fit of rhetoric, I gasped, "I know not what other gems lie hidden, unpublished in closets, but this one must see the light."

Hilary Paul McGuire, author of:
Hopie and the Los Homes Gang: A Gangland Primer
Homeboys in College: Heralds of Progress
Tennis Saves: Stewart Orphans Take World by Racket
San Diego, August 23, 2015

PREFACE

Do you often find yourself wanting more in life but still do not feel gratified? When doing more for others, your blessings are multiplied. In this book, I will share with you some stories of how, through God's help, I was able to accomplish so much for others.

Charles de Lint wrote: "I don't want to live in the kind of world where we don't look out for each other. Not just the people that are close to us, but anybody who needs a helping hand. I can't change the way anybody else thinks, or what they choose to do, but I can do my bit."

In this memoir, I did my "little bit." I did not know God until I was 18 years old because I grew up in Russia during the Soviet Union Communist Regime and was a teenager during World War II. Now that I have retired, many church and neighborhood children call me Grandma Tiny, because my height towers at 4'6". With God's guidance, He has made my work mighty.

My desire is to share with you my travels and work that I did around the world. I wrote this book, not just as a memoir for my family, but as an inspiration for young people. A gentle reminder that by doing a "little bit" to help others, by lifting burdens and giving service to others, you will receive greater satisfaction and happiness.

As a missionary educator, I have enjoyed meeting people from all walks of life, associating with them, and learning their cultures and languages. In finding out what their needs were, I have been able to help them with the knowledge of God and healthful living and to inspire our youth to further their education.

Part I starts with my birth in the Union of Soviet Socialist Republics (USSR). The book continues with my travels, the hardships I had to overcome, and my missionary experience. May reading this book be a blessing to each of you.

ACKNOWLEDGEMENTS

This book is dedicated to my three children Daniel, Esther, and Ella; my two granddaughters Rema and Mimi; and all the youth of the world.

Above all, I thank God for guiding my life, sending me to the right place at the right time, keeping me safe in my travels, and for all His blessings.

My gratitude also goes out to my daughter Esther for spending countless hours many evenings entering my stories and words on the laptop. And my thanks also go to my son Daniel for his support during my retirement and while I wrote this book.

I appreciate my dear friends and family who helped me edit the book: Kimberly and Richard Kenyan, Morgan Brown, Rebecca Guzman, and my daughter Ella Abadir.

Many thanks to my friends, Phyllis and Hilary Paul McGuire, who worked on all the final edits to get this book published.

PART I: RUSSIA, 1926–1945

MY ANCESTORS

"Oh my God, why have you forsaken [us]? ..." Psalms 22:2

It was not always run by Communism, not always bleak and grey and lacking promise for those who desired to work hard. At one time, Russia was a glittering land of prosperity for some, a high society life filled with the arts, where wealthy businessmen raised knowledgeable children to follow in their ornate footsteps.

I was born to children of Persian merchants whose families had settled in Astrakhan, a port city in southern Russia, astride the Volga River just before it empties into the Caspian Sea. I'm not exactly sure how deep my ancestors' roots went, but I know they were there for many years and lived prosperous lives during the tsars' reigns.

My father had two older brothers, Aghajan and Ishmael, and one younger sister, Sara.

My uncles worked with my father as jewelers in Astrakhan. They had carefully built up a very successful business and together they owned a large house with a beautiful back yard. Their home included stables that were cared for by Tartar horse keepers. Horses and buggies at that time were as common as cars today. The stablemen's wives were the family's maids and they all lived in a little dwelling past the garden behind the main house. Life was going exactly as my family had planned.

COMMUNISM INVADES OUR LIVES

When the Bolsheviks took over the country, the new Soviet government felt it had a better idea of how life should be. Wanting to nationalize all the private businesses and properties, they sent notices informing my parents that they would be required to share their wealth equally with all the citizens. My father and his brothers understood the hidden meaning of this declaration. Rather than having to give up what my parents felt was rightfully theirs to the communists, my family decided that they would escape to the nearby country of Iran.

Their plans were carried out in stages due to the fact that my mother was pregnant with me. The adults all thought it would be better if my brother, two-year-old Abraham, traveled with his uncles and aunts to Iran first, especially Uncle Aghajan's wife Anay who had no children and loved Abraham as her own. Certainly, four adults could care for one small child and in this way alleviate the burden on my expectant mother. This plan also gave my father the opportunity to wrap up all the unfinished jewelry business. He was chosen to handle things because, though he was the youngest, he was the smartest of his siblings.

In the next stage, once everything was settled and after my mother was strong enough for the trip, my parents would be ready to follow my father's family to Iran. Of course, plans seldom work out the way they are supposed to in third-world countries, even if they are the plans of the wealthy.

It was a time when the government was so greedily sucking up everyone's belongings that people who refused to give in were sent away to die. My father was labeled an enemy of the people because he not only refused to give up his business but also would not reveal to questioning officials where the rest of his family had gone.

At last my parents started on their long journey by train. At every stop, the Soviet police would search the train and question male travelers on their citizenship; women were not disturbed quite as much. Each time this happened, my father would hide himself under my mother's blankets and belongings. Both of my parents knew full well that the government was searching for him since his siblings' escape. Meanwhile my mother, with her swollen, pregnant belly, concealed her frazzled nerves by feigning sleepiness.

The train route did not go directly south towards Iran but took them far east of the Caspian Sea. By the time it arrived in Tashkent, Uzbekistan, my weary, pregnant mother had endured extreme hardships in her travels. Labor pains had begun to torment her, and my father rushed her to the hospital where I was born two months prematurely on November 1, 1926. These days, with modern medical technology, two months early is not a great threat. However, in 1926, in the depressed economy of Uzbekistan, there were no baby formulas, heart rate monitors or incubators available for my care. My mother told me later that the hospital workers covered me with soft cotton and hot water bottles to keep me warm. They fed me by dropper until they were convinced I was out of danger.

Once the hospital was sure I would live, my mother had the responsibility of naming me. The hospital gave her a list of *government-accepted* names that would label me by my birthplace, Uzbekistan, which had become part of the Soviet Union in 1924. My mother studied the long list but only recognized one name: Mohabbat (Love).

"We can call her Mohabbat," my mother said reluctantly. She was feeling isolated from her culture and homeland while facing the prospect of raising her child in this foreign land. Hence, she rarely used that name for me and gladly abandoned it years later when my Uncle Habib renamed me Raya.

Weeks passed before my mother and I were released from the hospital. When they asked for the father's name for the birth certificate, they recognized him as one wanted by the Soviet government. Needing to keep himself hidden, my father did not join us when my mother took me to the home of my oldest maternal uncle in Uzbekistan. He had been sent by the Soviets to manage the hospital there. The new plan was that we would stay for several months until mother and I were strong enough to make the difficult trip back to Astrakhan by train, instead of continuing on to Iran. My father went back via the underground network to avoid capture.

Once we were back in Astrakhan, life became even more complicated for our little family. As a fugitive, my father was away for long periods at a time. Although we never knew for sure where or when he traveled, my father became skilled at utilizing an underground network of facilitators who could easily be bribed to let him cross borders. His talent as a jeweler kept him in work, even when he was an outlaw. Sometimes he would have a piece of jewelry commissioned to him. Other times he would have to secretly sell portions of his business in order to provide for our family.

Though I was only a child at this time, I could recognize that my mother was sad when he was away. With my brother Abraham gone, as well as my father's family, it was usually just the two of us surviving alone. We didn't even know if Abraham and my father's family made it alive to Iran.

In 1928, my mother gave birth to another baby boy. Precious Tofig was two years younger than I, though his life was cut short when he contracted childhood dysentery at the age of two. We were photographed together only once. On the same day, another photo was taken of him wearing an Uzbekistani costume. By the time we got the finished photos back, he had already died. The single pictorial memory of us together turned out a bit blurry and could never be retaken.

STRANGE VISITORS, 1930

Often, my mother and I would sit quietly in our home. A large fireplace, dividing four expansive rooms, would burn gently, keeping us warm. The Soviet Union regime restricted its people from any sort of religion. Without religion to give us hope, worry and sadness permeated the air.

Many times we would be scraping the bottom of the food barrels with little left to eat. However, the days when my father was home were joyous and filled with gifts of chocolate, toys, or new clothes.

One such day, I was running around the house, pleased with the return of my father. "Look Papa!" I cried, spinning and twirling for him. I vaguely remember tumbling in the great living room of our home. Large, ornate mirrors stretched toward the ceiling, and I loved to watch myself dance and turn in front of them. Then we heard a pounding at the door and my mother got up to answer it. Somehow, at that moment, my father was nowhere to be found. Soldiers stood in the doorway, demanding to search our home. The terror was obvious in my mother's face. I clung to her skirt, hiding from these strange men. The search did not last long; my father was soon found and dragged away from us.

Our life, the routine we were struggling to establish, was suddenly and permanently disrupted. My mother had no idea where her husband was being taken, but she knew that it was useless to argue with soldiers. Any dispute against authority could result in having me taken away from her as well.

Almost immediately my mother applied with the local government offices to find out where he was. When the news finally came, it was not good: My father had been sent to Siberia. Prisoners were exiled to concentration camps in this icy, north-eastern province. The tales of prisoners' hardships traveled back to us, increasing our worry, reducing our hope for my father's return. Had we known how to pray, perhaps the outcome would have been different. At the very least my mother and I would have had the peace of knowing that my father was in God's hands.

With no one to support us, my mother and I left our home in Astrakhan and traveled south along the west side of the Caspian Sea, to be near her family in Baku, Azerbaijan. Baku was part of the Soviet Union since 1920, so we did not have to cross any international borders on our journey.

Knowing that we could not be sure of what would happen to our belongings while we were away, my mother left valuables with trusted neighbors or relatives until she could return and claim them. We would periodically go back home, so that my mother could slowly collect our few belongings and care for our grand home as best as she was able.

On one such occasion, when we returned to our home, my mother was shocked to see that the whole house had been confiscated and was turned into a commune with different rooms assigned to families according to size. The parlor was given to a family with three children. In our large dining room lived another family, also with three children. The den was occupied by a family with two young children, and in each of the three bedrooms lived single-child families. Though the house had belonged to my parents, my mother and I were sent to live in the smallest room and endure this strange life amongst people we would never have even socialized with before the new regime.

Mother cried herself through her chores and homemaking tasks during the day and to sleep many nights, frustrated by the situation. My own six-year-old mind could not comprehend what had brought about all these sudden changes.

"Mama, who are these people?"

"They are no one to us, *melyamaya*, my dear."

"Why are they in our house?"

"They were sent here."

"Why don't you send them back, Mama?"

"I wish I could, *melyamaya*. I wish I could."

BAKU, AZERBAIJAN

Rooster knocked on Hen's door. "It is so cold out here, I have no place to roost, and I scarcely have the strength to crow. Can I please sleep on your doorstep? I won't bother you at all." So that night Hen let Rooster sleep on her doorstep.

The next day Rooster knocked on Hen's bedroom door. "The wind blew so hard, I could feel it creeping under the door and I scarcely have the strength to crow. May I please sleep under your kitchen table? I won't bother you at all." So that night Hen let Rooster sleep under her table.

The third day Rooster stood in Hen's room. "You have all the best places in this house. It is only fair if you share your little bed with me. I will sleep on one side and I won't bother you at all." So that night Hen slept on one side of her bed and Rooster slept on the other.

The next day Rooster pushed Hen out of the bed and shouted. "This bed is too small for both of us! I won't allow you to sleep here anymore!" He kicked her out of the room and out of the house and poor Hen was left outside in the cold.

~A Russian Folktale

Mother didn't like sharing the common kitchen and bathroom with all these strangers who were communists. With no one else to rely on, my mother decided to move to Baku permanently in 1932. Her brother, two sisters and her mother were living there, and we could be close to family. I fondly remember growing up in this quiet, peaceful, adult-filled environment, loved by everyone.

With seven children in their family, my grandmother's home was large, affectionate and happy. In my earliest memory of my grandmother, Babushka, as we called her, she is sitting cross-legged on her bed, amusing me with stories of a rooster and a hen. Like all Russian folk tales, this one ended tragically ever after. All the stories that I most vividly remember her telling me seemed to be symbolic of the government of that time.

Though she was quite old by the time we moved in, Babushka was still agile and active. My grandfather had passed away before I was born, and my grandmother lived as the matriarch of her adult children during this impressionable time in my life.

One day she just went away. I never knew where. I must have wondered, must have questioned others, but I don't remember ever getting an answer. There were just some topics that were grown-up and I was clearly left out of these conversations.

My mother's oldest sister was named Zina. She was a widow and eventually came to live with us. Because my mother worked out of the house, first as a seamstress for family friends, and later when she found a factory job, Auntie Zina was always close by taking care of me. I came to love my aunt dearly as she became a surrogate grandmother for me after my own *babushka* died.

My mother's oldest brother Sami was a doctor and already married to a young Russian girl and had a daughter. During the Soviet Union regime, when young people graduated from Moscow University, they were sent to work in other provinces where they were needed. As a result, the government sent him to Tashkent, Uzbekistan where he worked as the administrator of the only hospital in that city. He lived there his entire life, and unfortunately I never met him although I was born at that hospital. For the same reason, when my mother's merchant brother Taggi was sent to work in another province, I never had the opportunity to meet him either.

One of my mother's younger brothers, Habib, was an artist. He was a gentle and kind man who would sit at his easel and paint beautiful pictures, often times letting me watch. He had nicknamed me Raya, and I nicknamed him Diy-Diy. While he was painting, I would ask him, "Diy-Diy, why are you smiling?"

He would always give the same answer: "I like my painting."

My mother had two younger sisters, Galya and Sima. When I was in kindergarten, I recall my Auntie Galya taking me to and from school. This was convenient for everyone since she was the principal there.

The government provided our school lunches, and I was a slow eater. My Auntie Galya would tease and constantly beg me, "Raya, please eat faster. Eat faster, Raya! All the workers will think I am giving you more food than the other kids." To this day, I have never learned how to eat fast. I usually start a meal before anyone else but am still the last one at the table.

Eventually, both my younger aunts and my uncles got married and left home. Life was even quieter than before, with only my mother and my Auntie Zina home alone with me. I looked forward to the weekends when Auntie Galya and Auntie Sima would come to visit us in our home with their husbands, often taking me to parks, the mountains, or to the beach with friends.

On one of these trips to the Caspian Sea, my Auntie Galya decided she would try to teach me how to swim. After showing me a few strokes and breathing skills, she felt I was ready for more advanced swimming techniques. Supporting me at the waist, she murmured words of encouragement as she urged me to paddle my arms and legs. "Good job, Raya," I could hear her voice close by as I splashed in the water, safely within her reach. "Keep trying! You're doing great!" I eagerly splashed along beside her, or at least I thought I was beside her. Suddenly, I noticed that her voice sounded much farther away than I expected it to. "Keep going Raya," I could hear her calling from a distance now. In a panic I sputtered and flailed, helplessly sinking like a rock into the water I had believed I could conquer only moments before.

Though Galya dashed immediately to my rescue, I was never able to forget my fear of drowning. As an adult, I finally gained a love for the water, although that one experience prevented me from learning how to swim properly. Instead I have always taken to the water with a doggie paddle stroke, completely lacking grace, through lakes, rivers, and swimming pools.

I never really learned how to ride a bicycle. One day, my Uncle Habib bought one for my birthday when I was visiting his home. I recall him patiently trying to teach me, but I struggled so much. Not only was balance a difficult concept for me to accept, having been uncoordinated since childhood, but I quickly learned to distrust the safety of my two-wheeled vehicle. On my very first attempt, I broke my left ankle. The doctor had set it as best as he could, but nothing is as good as God makes it the first time, especially nothing recreated by the ill-equipped medical staff of a third-world hospital.

Once my leg healed and the plaster cast was removed, I made a second attempt at bike riding. Truthfully, the idea of owning a set of wheels gave me the promise of freedom which I could not resist. The world was mine if I could access friends' homes and school with the speed and ease I saw so many others enjoying. That promise was short-lived when, once again, I ended up in a plaster cast waiting for the same ankle to heal.

It took me a long time to get over that second fall, both physically and mentally. In spite of this, with the second cast off and enough time to help me forget the pain, I decided to give it another try. This time I succeeded, not in learning how to ride a bike but in breaking my ankle one more time. The doctor looked at me sternly.

"Give up the bicycle," he warned me. "If you manage another break to your leg you will be lame for life!" I remembered the difficult existence of my Uncle Ishmael, crippled as a child from a wrestling match with his older brother. I vowed that I would never sit on a bike once more. I quickly gave my bike to a friend and never touched it again.

ALONE IN BAKU

"God help the outcasts hungry from birth
Show them the mercy they don't find on earth
God help my people we look to you still
God help my people where nobody will."

-Esmeralda in Disney's *Hunchback of Notre Dame*

Every day from 1930 and for many years, my mother searched for word from my father. Many sickening stories of "heroic" government actions were printed in the newspaper. Occasionally, the media would publish long lists of Siberian prisoners who had died. This was how we finally learned that my father had passed away. There was no explanation of his death, not even a date on which we could mourn him. We simply read his name, printed carelessly among a long list of others who had suffered a similar fate. Life for us felt empty. We had no hope to cling to without even the promise of meeting my father again in Heaven.

People returning after their exile period was over would tell us that huge trenches, dug by the prisoners in Siberia, were used for mass burials in the concentration camps. This was an effective method of providing prisoners with work, while simultaneously intimidating them into cooperating with the authorities.

Political conditions started changing and my close-knit family began departing Baku, one by one. The first to go was my Auntie Sima, but she did not leave us because of any political unrest. Instead, she got tuberculosis and passed away. I knew my aunt had been sick, but as a ten-year-old, I simply expected her to get better. One day, I walked into my aunt's home after school and was surprised to find all the adults crying. I snuggled up to my mother, embracing her, trying to fix whatever was wrong. "Why are you crying, Mama?"

"My sister died today, *melyamaya*," she answered as she lifted the edge of the crisply ironed, white sheet so I could peer at the ashen face of my precious Auntie Sima. I had never seen her look that way. No color remained on her waxy skin. Her eyes were shut, as if she was sleeping. I had seen my Auntie sleep before, but this time she just didn't look right. Her mouth was closed but only slightly. I knew this face belonged to my Auntie, but I couldn't believe it was really her. A strange fear tugged at my gut and choked me while my legs seemed to propel themselves out, away, as far and as fast as they could go.

I never went back into that house.

When Auntie Sima passed away, she left behind a one-year-old daughter named Mina. Her sister-in-law took in the small child, raising her niece as her own child.

My Auntie Galya married a petroleum engineer. Because of his great depth of knowledge, the Soviet government feared he was an easy target for espionage. As a result, both he and my aunt were exiled, along with their ten-month-old daughter Toma to a concentration camp in Siberia.

Knowing the fate of my father, my mother was torn with grief for her sister's family. At that time we could only assume that the worst would become of them. Later we found out that while they were in exile, my aunt gave birth to a son, Nadir. Though the family was finally released many years later, I never saw them again as a child and never expected to meet this concentration camp baby.

Since my Uncle Habib was an artist, he was transferred to Moscow where he was employed in the Bolshoi Theater. There he married another Russian artist who worked with him as a stage decorator. For several years their occupations kept them living in an apartment near the center of the city. I remember visiting them during school vacations. They would take me back stage to watch musicals and ballets such as *Hunchback of Notre Dame* or *Swan Lake*. To this day, I love to go to the theater. Whenever I sit in the audience of a Russian-produced ballet, I am immediately transported back to my childhood, peering through the curtains to watch all the action from the most mesmerizing seat in the house.

In the 1930s, the government sent orders that citizens of different ancestry could leave the Soviet Union and go to the countries of their origin. My Uncle Habib and my Auntie Zina applied to go to Iran. But being Russian born, my uncle's wife was not allowed to leave the country. Since both had applied, it was too late for my uncle to change his mind and stay in Russia with his wife. The government would not let him remain and Uncle Habib was forced to leave his beloved wife behind.

With all of our family members gone, my preadolescent years became quiet and sad and lonely for both my grieving mother and me. For about ten years my mother and I remained in Baku alone. She must have been terribly torn as she faced her situation. On the one hand, she wanted to be near her family. Life was difficult enough for a single parent and having family around would have made her tasks much easier. But Mother did not want to go to Iran even though her great-great-grandparents were from Iran so it was considered her country of origin. Propaganda had thoroughly convinced her that I would not have a chance for education in any other country outside of the Soviet Union.

MISHKA

"Blessed be the Lord, who daily loads us with benefits, even the God of our salvation..." Psalm 68:19

Winters in Baku were especially cold and bleak. In fact, the city gets its name from *baadkoubeh*, which means "windy city" in Azerbaijanian. But New Year's 1938 held a particularly exciting celebration for children. All across the Soviet Union, every town would cut down a giant evergreen tree and carry it from the woods to be set up in one of the many communist youth halls. Hanging from every bough and branch were candies, brightly wrapped in papers depicting famous fairy tales.

The children would gather around these massive trees and sing adoring songs to celebrate the New Year. "The Forest bore an Evergreen Tree. In the forest it grew tall. All winter long and summer long it grew upright and strong." Looking back on these momentous days, it seems ridiculous now that none of the lyrics even mention New Year's at all.

After the singing had ended, some of the adults would pass small bags of candy and chocolate to the children. Sometimes hot tea or even cookies would be served to close the night. In the end, we would all blissfully return to our homes, full of happy tunes, memories, and grainy bland *Mishka* brand chocolate, the finest that Russia offered. I am certain that Russians put the "chalk" in chocolate. Even so, I loved these special treats. Although I don't know which I liked better: the bright Teddy Bear pictures on the wrapper, or the fact that the candies were such a rare luxury for us.

When I was about 12 years old, I had a gray, Persian cat. Her name was Mishka, which meant teddy bear. I chose this name because, with her wide round face and soft furry body, she resembled a stuffed toy. Loving and snuggly, Mishka would rub her head and neck against my legs, wrapping her long, soft tail around me.

One cold winter day, Mishka disappeared. My mother and I were worried sick about her. The day stretched into night and another day came and went without a sign of my precious cat. We were certain she was gone forever. What animal could survive the bitter cold of a Russian winter?

In the middle of the third night, I awoke to hear her meowing outside. When I ran and opened the door, there was Mishka sitting on our porch beside a large package wrapped with old newspapers and tied tightly with string. My mother and I brought our cat inside and showered her with affection. Our attention then turned to the mysterious package.

Carefully, we unwrapped layers of newspaper, saving the bits of string for a future use. Inside the box, we were shocked to find a chunk of beef bones and a small head of cabbage, just perfect for making borscht, our Russian soup (recipe at end of chapter). Onions, potatoes and beets completed the list of ingredients. We thanked Mishka for our food rather than thanking God, since at this time we had no knowledge of who God was or how to worship him.

With all these wonderful ingredients, we made a huge pot of borsht. We set the pot outside our window in the snow where it could keep cold since most people did not have refrigeration in those days even though we were living in the capital city of Azerbaijan. It was enough to provide us with supper for several days.

WORLD WAR II

"... There is a noise of war ... It is not the voice of those who cry out in victory, nor is it the voice of those who cry out in defeat ..." Exodus 32:17–18

In 1940, Hitler started his attacks on Russia. The media filled our ears with propaganda about the results of the war. Every house had a radio and the only station we could tune to was run by the government. With one-sided news stories blaring in every home, we were led to think that Russia's strength was causing us to overcome our enemies. Since Baku was a petroleum city, we were kept well protected from German attacks. Under curfew, with no other source of information, we had no reason to doubt our government, even when contradictory stories surfaced.

Still, those were very sad and difficult years. Food was scarce and we were rationed only 200 grams of dense, black bread every day. Occasionally, we would see a line forming and everyone would run to stand in a queue not knowing what they were going to find when their turn came. Sometimes we would find fresh produce such as potatoes, carrots, onions or cabbage. Often, however, we would get to the front of the line only to find that nothing remained to reward us for our wait.

Most of the time my mother and I would go to the commercial stores where she would trade her precious jewelry, handmade by my father and his brothers, for 100 grams of butter (less than one cup), a couple of eggs, flour or some other food items which could not be found in the government stores. These commercial stores were a convenient way for the government to collect the expensive belongings of citizens at a fraction of their true value.

Hunger was not the only way we struggled. None of us thought to question our lack of indoor plumbing. It was part of our daily routine to draw water directly from the well. Yet we believed our water system was quite advanced. We would merely pour the cool well water into a tin vessel which hung over our wash bucket. The vessel was fitted with a spout on the bottom that had a small ball stopper. When the ball was touched, water would pour out and we would wash our hands, faces or dishes. Our simple mechanics worked well in giving us the illusion of having running water. The dirty wash water would then be poured into our outhouse, where it could be used to clean the outdoor waste receptacle there. Everything that could be reused was.

CELEBRATIONS

"... And as he drew near ... he heard music and dancing." Luke 15:25

As my teen years approached, I began to enjoy many of the summer celebrations held in the city parks for adults. Adorable children would perform folk dances during the afternoon, providing entertainment for all those who attended.

As the evening drew near, people would pack onto makeshift dance floors built into the walkways while amateur musicians carrying accordions, guitars, and violins filled the air with songs. Famous waltzes, tangos, and foxtrots would draw out the dancers' talents and creativity. Onlookers cheered and clapped for those impromptu performances that were especially impressive, and everyone left the revelry feeling joyous.

I always enjoyed these festivities. Singing and dancing were the types of activities that united all of us under the "comrade" umbrella. But once the Second World War pressed in closer and closer everything around me started to change. People did not seem to feel much like celebrating anymore and moods were dampened. In time, the only festivities we encountered were parades to show off Russia's military skills.

One particular day, however, has never lost its importance among communists: November 7th, the anniversary of the Socialist Revolution. My family found this date a convenient way to celebrate my own birthday which actually fell on November 1st, "All Saints Day," as I came to know it many years later.

❖ ❖ ❖

As teenagers, our days were spent in military training and school lessons. Marching drills, designed to build our endurance, filled our time and we were forced to carry heavy sacks of sand in order to strengthen us, ten kilograms in each bag. The whole time we were marching we were commanded to chant, "*My ne khotim voyny, no my budem borot'sya, chtoby zashchitit' sebya* [We don't want a war, but we will fight to defend ourselves]! *Solntse, vozdukh i voda nashi luchshiye druz'ya* [Sun, air and water are our best friends]!"

We were also taught songs of praise and patriotism for our country. One of those songs went like this: "Wide is my dear country. There are many woods, seas, and rivers. I do not know any other country where so freely a person can breathe." Only later in my life did I realize that Russia designed these songs in order to brainwash her citizens.

OUT TO FREEDOM

"... All things God works for the good of those who love him ..." Romans 8:28

Evenings were quiet in our small home. Our light came from a simple oil lamp. Come morning it would be my responsibility to keep the lamp polished so that it could shine brightly again that evening. A simple, two-wick kerosene burner was all my mother had in order to prepare our meals, one dish at a time. Usually this dish only consisted of a meager soup made from millet, a few pieces of onion and potato with a lot of broth.

Late one spring evening in 1945, my mother and I were at home. I was studying for the next day's lesson while my mother was cooking dinner over our small kerosene stove. There was a soft knock on the door that disturbed our peaceful home. When I ran to open it, I was scared to see two young Russian soldiers standing before me. The same fear that had consumed me during my father's arrest resurfaced. I thought that surely they had returned to arrest my mother this time.

Seeing my concern, the soldiers assured me that they had good news and persuaded us to let them into the house; it wasn't safe for them to talk on the streets. "We were stationed in Tehran, Iran where we met your uncle, Aghajan," one soldier began, immediately easing our fears. "He has a big jewelry store in a prominent part of the city." My father's brother had befriended the soldiers, inviting them to his beautiful, grand home. His wife prepared a delicious meal for them and the men were given three watches. "One for you Raya, and one for each one of our wives," a uniformed man told me. But most importantly, my uncle had sent an invitation for me and my mother to join him in Iran.

Mother's first reaction was to object. "I want my daughter to be educated," she insisted. She had always dreamed that I would someday become a nurse. "If we leave the Soviet Union, there will be no schools for girls." Keep in mind, propaganda had led us to believe that life inside of our communist country was superior to life outside.

Knowing that they brought good messages from her brother-in-law, the young men gently persuaded my mother, speaking freely while lowering their voices. "Everything is so much better in Iran than it is here," they insisted, looking around at our deprived home. "Girls are free to study and learn, stores are plentiful, and your family is very wealthy there. You will be much happier in Iran."

Typically, people would never hear anyone say such things. We were warned that "the walls have eyes and ears." Many even felt they could not trust their own neighbors or family members. Full realization of the risk these men were taking for our sake finally set in. My mother acceded. The trip was scheduled as a family visit, but we understood that a new life was beginning for us.

Again if we knew at that time that there is a loving Father in Heaven who works for good to them that love Him, we would have knelt down and thanked Him. But the communists had taught us for many years that there is no God.

After we left the Soviet Union, we were afraid to talk about all that we had gone through, afraid they would take us back and kill us.

Now in Iran we would be free, thank God! No more captivity or fearful living. We would live in a wonderful country where we had freedom of speech, freedom to worship and freedom to write the truth about whatever we had endured.

Recipe for Borscht

Ingredients:

Some marrow bones of beef
1 onion, finely chopped
1/2 head cabbage, chopped
2 stalks celery, sliced with leaves
2 carrots, sliced
3–4 potatoes, cubed
4 fresh tomatoes, peeled, seeded and chopped

2 precooked beets, diced
1 green bell pepper, chopped
1 tsp allspice berries
2–3 bay leaves
2–3 cloves garlic
salt and pepper to taste

Directions:

1. Boil beef bones in plenty of water with salt, pepper, allspice and bay leaves until bones separate at joints.
2. Add onion, celery, carrots, cabbage and garlic.
3. Boil until all vegetables begin to get tender.
4. Add potatoes, beets, and bell pepper.
5. Simmer until potatoes are tender.
6. Serve hot with a dollop of *smitana* (sour cream), finely chopped parsley and a squeeze of fresh lemon if desired.

Note 1:

For New World style borscht, make sure bones have a generous portion of meat on them and use canned tomatoes or tomato paste rather than fresh. Mushrooms taste great, but are not found in any original Russian recipes I know of.

Note 2:

For third-world style borscht, make sure the bones are bare and the celery looks like pale, limp parsley. It also tastes more authentic if you have such a high proportion of cabbage, beets and water that very few of the other ingredients are recognizable in your bowl.

Figure 1 - Aunt Galya, a Friend, Aunt Sara; Mother's Father and Siblings
(Leila is second from right)

Figure 2 - Aunt Zina, Aunt Galya with Toma (back) and Nadir, Aunt Sima, Leila

Figure 3 - Abraham with Father and Aunt Sara before Leaving Russia

Figure 4 - Raya as a Child in Russia

Figure 5 - Raya in 6th Grade, Tofig and Raya, Tofig in Uzbek Costume

PART II: IRAN, 1945–1960

LIVING IN IRAN, 1945

"Stand fast in the liberty which Christ has made us free ..." Galatians 5:1

My mother and I packed the few belongings that we could take with us into one small, wooden trunk. Whatever we could not carry, we gave away, knowing there would be no way to return for our meager possessions. We boarded a Russian military ship and headed south on the Caspian Sea to the port city of Pahlavi, Iran (later renamed to Bandar-e Anzali, after the deposition of the Pahlavi Dynasty).

At that time, Iran was an ally of Russia. The Russian government, knowing that Iran was a Muslim country, only allowed male soldiers to be stationed there for fear females would be abducted and abused. Though there were women enlisted in the Russian army, they were not sent to any Muslim countries. Because of this, my mother and I were the only females on that ship.

As we pressed through the swarm of military men who eyed us curiously, I had no idea where this journey would take me. All of my life, Russian propaganda had pressed my limited mind into believing that our country was the most powerful, the most advanced, the wealthiest, and smartest. Doubts crept into my mind, and I'm sure the same doubts must have been nagging my mother. "Really, why are we even leaving? We have the best of everything here!" Somehow in our hearts we knew that none of these beliefs could have been true. Every morsel we ate was rationed. How could *that* be the best? How could the constant fear we lived in be normal?

From the minute the ship started sailing, I was extremely sea sick. For twenty-eight hours I lay in my cabin, sleeping continuously and waking only to vomit into a bucket, which my mother would periodically empty. For the duration of our trip, my mother sat, worrying over her sick child. Sometimes she would drift off to sleep and occasionally she would leave the cabin to get fresh air or to find out what news she could about our journey.

At last my mother came rushing into the cabin. "Rayichka, wake up and look outside," she exclaimed. We had arrived. As I dragged myself out of our berth, a sight met my eyes that I had never seen before. Though it was the middle of the night, all of the stores were open! We had known life only under the Black Curtain of Communist rule and the wartime curfew; this, we were told, would protect us from enemy attacks. An early curfew and lights out had darkened our streets and homes each night. Yet here, the streets were well lit. Even in my sick and weakened state, I was delighted to see how alive this new city was. Merchants anxiously awaited the hungry Russian soldiers who would come and buy their abundant produce.

A small gathering of family eagerly greeted us at the port. My father's brother, Uncle Aghajan and his sister, Auntie Sara were there to greet us with my brother Abraham, now 20 years old. They took us to Auntie Sara's house where we were given tea to quench our dehydrated mouths and delicious Persian rice and *khoresh* with rich flavorful sauce to fill our bellies.

We sat in the beautiful, expansive living room, talking until morning. It had been so many years since I had seen luxury that I could hardly remember living a wealthy life. I had grown sleepy but was still too excited to retire to my room.

Suddenly, we heard a loud cry, "*Allah ho akbar, Allah ho akbar* [God is great, God is great]!"

"What is that noise?" I asked, frightened. I had never heard anything like it before. The sound was so near that I thought someone was attacking us. Laughing, my family told me that the mullah, the Muslim prayer leader, was calling patrons to the Mosque for prayer. Sights, sounds, and even beliefs were so strange and new in this country.

I glanced around the room at my relatives' faces, and I was struck by a sudden realization: I did not actually know them, and my mother hadn't seen them for years. We knew almost nothing about them. "Does the Government force you to pray at this time?" I asked to their amusement.

"Nothing is forced here," Aghajan laughed.

"Do *you* pray?" I questioned them again with a mixture of awe and fear. In Russia no one ever spoke of prayer out of worry over severe corporal punishment. Yet, in this country, they not only prayed but proclaimed it loudly from the top of a minaret over the entire city.

Soon after arriving in Iran, my uncle Aghajan took Mother and me to Rasht, the capital city of the province of Gilan. Though inland, that city was much bigger than Pahlavi, the port city where my Auntie Sara lived. Their language and cultures were different as well. Here we were able to request Persian citizenship. My uncle immediately changed our surname to his name. He had long ago changed his own family name to Zarsahzi-Moghaddam (a fitting title meaning "prime jeweler") when he first escaped Russia. Now my own name once again matched his.

The plan was that I would be staying in Uncle Aghajan's luxurious, two-story home in Rasht where my brother Abraham was living. After years of living as an only child, I was most excited to get to know my one sibling.

Abraham was funny and spontaneous. One of the stories I loved to hear him tell was about when American tourists would visit my uncles' jewelry store where my brother worked. World War II was ending, and military families stationed in Europe took an occasional furlough to the Middle East. Anytime he saw some Americans, my brother would charm them saying, "Thank you, *bedeh* much!" This was his little joke. The women thought he was just having trouble with the English language, but Abraham was using a play on the Farsi word for "give me a kiss."

Even though I loved spending time with my brother, with no children of her own, Aghajan's wife Anay was not very pleased to have Abraham's birth mother and sister around. She had raised my brother from childhood and considered him to be her own son.

Also, my uncle and aunt knew that they would need someone to eventually take over the family business. Aghajan wasn't getting any younger. Fortunately for them, Abraham was not interested in leaving his aunt and uncle's family. He thought of himself as the rightful heir and approached his life and the family business with that assumption.

I soon realized that I was viewed as a burden to my uncle's family. His wife tolerated me only out of loyalty to my deceased father. Feeling the tension in her brother-in-law's home, my mother left to visit her family in nearby Langarud, Iran. I was still waiting for finalization of my citizenship before I would be allowed to have a job. I struggled through several months with nothing to relieve the tension in my uncle's home and looked forward to working and thus to start gaining my independence as a young adult.

WORKING AT SHILAT, 1945

"... I will make you fishers of men ..." Matthew 4:19

While visiting me in Rasht, my mother noticed how unhappy I was living with my Uncle Aghajan. She decided that I should go and stay with my Auntie Sara. My aunt was a very gracious host. She and her husband always made me feel welcome, and their four-year-old daughter, Adeleh, was thrilled to have a teenager around to be entertained by and to boss around.

One day Auntie Sara's husband, Sattar, came home with a whole whitefish for dinner. I had never before seen an entire fish. In Russia, the only fish we had ever eaten had been purchased frozen, in small chunks, or pickled. In fact, it seemed that everything we ate in Russia was either frozen or pickled. Even when cantaloupe or watermelon was available, we could only find the fruit pickled. The fresh quantities of food available in Iran fascinated me.

Intrigued, I followed Uncle Sattar out to the patio where he began to prepare the fish. He showed me how to use a sharp knife to gently scrape the iridescent scales from the flesh. When I asked to try, he quickly relinquished the knife and whitefish over to me. "Why don't you fix this up nicely," he suggested. "This type of meal is delicious fried." I was excited to do something to help my generous family.

My uncle went back inside to relax after a hard day's work and I set out to carefully prepare the evening's dinner. I cleaned every scale from the surface of the fish. Using the outdoor water pump, I washed and patted the fish dry. Then I carried the fish inside to fry it up, as Uncle Sattar suggested. I had not bothered to remove the head or tail from the fish, since he had commented that he considered the head a delicacy. Instead, I laid the fish into a pan of hot oil, where it sizzled and browned. I carefully turned it, appreciating the golden color of the crispy skin.

The smell of frying fish soon drew my young cousin, Adeleh, into the kitchen. "Go call your parents," I said proudly. "Dinner is ready." I set a platter of rice, leftover from lunch, onto the table. A bowl of tangy pickles and my steaming hot fish rounded out the meal. I had never prepared anything by myself and though, truly, my Auntie Sara had made the rice, I felt I had accomplished a great deal by cooking my first dinner.

Everyone eagerly gathered around the table. Auntie Sara seemed so pleased to have a night off from her usual duties. "It smells delicious," she commented as her husband prepared to serve us. "You may have a new job as the family chef." But as soon as the first cut was made, we realized that I would not be holding any such position.

"Raya," my uncle said, in dismay, "did you forget to clean out the fish?" A coiled mass of black intestines revealed that the internal organs had not been removed. Little Adeleh wrinkled her nose, disgusted.

"I didn't know I was supposed to remove the insides," I defended myself, though I had to admit that I had never seen cooked fish look like that before. "You just told me to clean off the scales and this was my first time cooking anything!"

"It's OK," my aunt soothed, quickly. She picked up the tray and carried it back into the kitchen. "I'll just clean it out now and it should be just fine."

It really wasn't as fine as she had promised. Even with the innards removed, the fish looked dirty. The bitter gall bladder had exploded and the process of separating the cooked flesh made it crumbled and messy. But the worst part was the taste. "You didn't use salt?" Uncle Sattar was laughing at me now. "This is the most interesting meal I have ever eaten," he gently teased. I was disappointed. I had wanted to contribute something to the generosity of my aunt and uncle, but the meal was ruined.

Since we now knew that my domestic abilities were not going to sustain me, my aunt arranged for me to work as a typist in the office of a nearby fishery called Shilat. Auntie Sara was employed as the treasurer for the same company. Being situated on the Caspian Sea, the Shilat fishery was jointly owned by both Russia and Iran. Contrary to what we believed, my mother and I did not need to fear our new identities being discovered by the Russian government. In fact, my Russian background made it possible for me to acquire the position since I was required to type in Russian.

Auntie Sara and her husband hired a Persian tutor to help me learn the local language quickly. Since I already knew Russian, Tartarian, and Azerbaijanian, I found it quite easy to learn to speak Farsi. However, the alphabet was entirely different, so learning to write took much more discipline.

By this time, my mother had returned to Auntie Sara's home to live with us. She took on small jobs as a tailor and dressmaker for family friends in order to earn some wages. Her precise and detailed work led to other small jobs. Soon, between our two incomes, my mother and I were able to rent a two bedroom apartment and live independently. Life quickly settled into a comfortable routine.

In Pahlavi, due to its highly transient nature, we soon developed a companionship with many other foreigners. I met a darling young lady named Clara, who quickly became my best friend. She was bright and friendly, drawing me into her cluster of Russian speaking friends.

Periodically, a group of us would get together at the home of Javid, our director at the fishery. Javid not only held a prominent position in the fishery, but he was also a generous host. Because Javid was an avid hunter, parties in his home were filled with roasted deer, wild boar and pheasant. Clara's mother was an excellent baker and we would feast on the pastries she sent with us to the gatherings.

Later, as food was served, the music would start and we would all enjoy dancing. Pahlavi was strongly influenced by many other countries. We all learned the foxtrot, tango and waltz. Girls, wearing their finest party dresses, would line up on chairs along the wall of Javid's expansive living room. It was up to the young men to ask us to dance. As the songs would change, another potential partner would approach with an invitation. Dancing was my favorite part of our evenings together. Although the food was richer than we would customarily enjoy and the home was more affluent, it was the expression through movement and a chance to socialize with pure abandon that drew me to these monthly events.

Eventually Clara and Javid married. Although Javid had been married and widowed with a young son in tow, this union seemed very predictable. Both were naturally friendly and bighearted. Clara was a sweet and caring new mother to Javid's loveable son. The innate relationship grew as she became the only mother the little boy knew.

NEW FRIENDS, NEW LANGUAGE, NEW BEGINNINGS

Redeemed! How I love to proclaim it/ Redeemed by the blood of the Lamb/
Redeemed through His infinite mercy/ His child and forever I am!
Fanny Crosby (1820–1915)

One day in 1945, a young worker stopped into our office. "An American family was planning to go to Russia to be Missionaries, but the Russian Government refused them an entry visa," he said. "As long as they are here, they are offering to teach free English classes if we will listen to their Bible stories." I didn't know what Bible stories were, but I knew I liked all stories. Besides, it would be a chance to learn one more language! English seemed very exciting and strange.

It didn't take long to consider this opportunity. I decided to study with the Americans, and about twenty of my co-workers joined me. Our teachers, Daniel and Gladys Kubrock, were a lovely, young couple with two little children. Four-year-old Martha and three-year-old Charles were delightful children. The couple had studied the Russian language at Pacific Union College in Northern California, thinking they could do the most good by sharing their faith and Christian beliefs with Russians. Although at the time I knew nothing about their Seventh-day Adventist religion, this was the beginning of a new life for me.

English seemed easy to learn, and I was advancing very fast. For me the Bible stories sounded like fairy tales at first. I had never heard of God while I lived in Russia, and my family in Iran never spoke much of their beliefs. I didn't find out until countless years later that my Auntie Sara practiced Islam like many others in Iran. I never knew when she'd started her religious life; I never recall seeing her observe that way of life when I was in her care. But at some point I just came to the realization that somewhere in her life she had picked it up.

Although Iran has long been considered a Muslim country, religion was not enforced in the 1940s. It wasn't until decades later that the Ayatollah would take over and make the practices of Islam mandatory to everyone living in or visiting Iran. I would be long gone by then.

Sometimes, the Kubrocks would host parties in their home. Though these events were developed to improve our conversational English, the young couple would make our time together more than a learning experience. Games, stories and American food, such as vegetarian casseroles, filled our time and helped us to pass the hours on a rainy afternoon.

The Kubrocks were vegetarian, eating only foods that came from plant sources. One of the earliest lessons they taught us was about living a healthy lifestyle, free from alcohol, smoking and animal products. Vegetarianism was unusual in Iran where, typically, even vegetable dishes were prepared with meat or meat broth.

Despite their health message, there was one animal product Gladys could not stay away from: *Silotka* (pickled herring). "This is my *dessert*," she would say, gobbling up the tiny salty fish she kept in a large barrel. I loved to see how they mingled with others, never judging us, just the way Jesus did in the stories they taught me.

My favorite lessons were on Saturdays, the day that Mr. Kubrock reverently called the Sabbath. On those days we would all gather on the shores of the Caspian Sea. Mrs. Kubrock would play her accordion while we sang soothing hymns that they taught us from small books. I began to feel closeness to this warm family.

I loved the songs and the stories we were learning from our English language teachers. My favorite hymn was called "Redeemed! How I Love to Proclaim It." Even at home I would skip and dance around the house as I sang the song. The brisk 6/8 timing in the song reminded me of the waltz rhythms I had enjoyed with Clara and my group of work friends.

Within a few months, word of our American teachers had reached the Russian government. Because Shilat was co-owned by the Russians, and the Iranian Government wanted to maintain their allied relationship, new rules were set in place at the fishery.

Those of us who were attending the missionaries' lessons began to hear rumors that Shilat would lay off any employees who were associating with the Americans. More than that, we were also told that the Kubrocks were believed to be American spies. I knew these claims were false. How could anything bad come from such wonderful people? But others were not so sure. One by one our class dwindled down until I was the only student who remained. Even so, my faith in the new beliefs I had learned continued to grow. After six years of working in Iran, even with only one small follower to claim, the Kubrocks felt their trip was a success. Often, Mrs. Kubrock would remind me, "You are our treasure," assuring me that they appreciated our time together.

The fishery never fired me. Perhaps since I was the last student attending classes, my company did not feel quite as intimidated. Or perhaps the threats had just been a part of idle gossip, with nothing to substantiate them. It is also possible that Javid's or Auntie Sara's influence within the company helped protect me. Regardless of the motive, I was content to continue studying the English language and learn more about my American friends' love for God.

MOVING TO TEHRAN

"... Make every effort to add to your faith goodness ... knowledge ... self-control ... and perseverance." II Peter 1:5, 6

After two years studying with the missionaries, the Kubrocks suggested that I should go to Tehran. It was 1947 and they were being relocated south to Isfahan in central Iran. I would be alone again, but the Adventist missionaries had a boarding academy in Tehran and Mrs. Kubrock told me I could study while working as an assistant teacher. In exchange for teaching I was provided room and board as well as free schooling. Even though I had completed high school in Russia, this different culture and milieu made a second high school education worthwhile. Mrs. Kubrock sent a letter of recommendation to Kenneth Oster, the president of the mission.

My job would include teaching English to the Oster children as well as to the children of Principal Paul Boynton and his wife Ruth. Once several of the wealthy Persian families and ambassadors in the area found out about the academy's English language program, they enrolled their children in the school as well.

I found that I loved teaching little children in first and second grades. The Boyntons and the Osters were wonderful people to know and work with. Mrs. Boynton was tall and elegant, her long brown hair always wound neatly into a bun on the top of her head. Dorothy Oster was more athletic, always directing the more physical games and activities for the children. Even as she grew old, Mrs. Oster did not seem to grow frail. Many years later, at the age of 89, she would still be found diving and swimming every day near her home in Northern California.

The responsibility of morning and evening worship services would alternate between Mr. Oster and Mr. Boynton, with one of their wives on the piano leading the song services. Music played a key role in our lives at the academy. When we were not singing songs of worship and praise, we would sing folk songs that were common in the United States. "Oh! Susanna" and "Old Black Joe" were favorites with all the students.

Although Mr. Oster had been born and raised in Iran by his own missionary parents and despite the fact that we were still centered in the heart of Persia, I learned much about American culture and Christianity from the fun activities these families hosted.

We celebrated American Thanksgiving with special programs in which the children would perform. These activities were remarkable to me. We were living in a time when Iran did not have televisions or computers, so the memorable holidays were brought to us for the very first time by our leaders. The reenactments were a great way to learn about life in the United States and its history.

At Christmas time, Mr. Oster would dress up as Santa Claus and distribute gifts to the students. The children stared in awe at this large, generous stranger, barely understanding why he was giving them presents. None of the children recognized our principal under the snowy beard and red velvet suit.

One favorite activity outside of school was skiing in the Al Borz Mountains, just north of Tehran. Though learning languages came easily for me, physical activities did not. I was extremely uncoordinated and found myself traveling backward more often than forward. My skis would tangle and I would tumble hopelessly down the hill, a growing ball of snow and poles. Fortunately for me, these trips did not occur more than a handful of times while I lived in Tehran. Still, it was fun to try something new and have the chance to get away from the school and the city every once in a while.

FAMILY CELEBRATIONS

One afternoon I received good news from my Uncle Aghajan's home. My brother Abraham announced his engagement to a lovely young lady named Effat. My mother and I eagerly made plans to attend the elegant affair in Uncle Aghajan's home.

My young cousin Adeleh, Auntie Sara and Uncle Sattar's daughter, had grown much since I saw her last and was anticipating the wedding with all the giddiness of a young girl. Her brother Keyoumarce was barely a toddler and had no idea why there was so much commotion in the family. Still, he was happy to follow his sister around during the festivities, feeding off of her excitement.

Uncle Aghajan's enormous home was overflowing with family, friends, and every possible dignitary the city knew. Musicians filled the place with traditional Persian selections and tables were full of *koreshts*, sweet wedding rice (recipe at end of chapter), meats, *pahlava*, nuts and fruits. I had never seen so much food served at one time.

A FIRST OF MANY COMMITMENTS

"If anyone is in Christ, he is a new creation; the old has gone, the new has come!"
2 Corinthians 5:17

Once I returned to the mission in 1948, my mother moved in with me. I continued to work for the Osters for three more years. About the same time the Tudeh Iranian Communist party began to cause uprisings in vital areas around the country. These insurgencies were suppressed as often as possible by a Muslim extremist party, but many borders were closed and travel became more difficult as Iran suffered from her own form of a cold war.

The more time I spent with my Adventist mentors, the more I became aware of the Holy Spirit moving in my own heart. I began to feel the urge to do God's work.

So, when Mr. Boynton offered a baptismal class to prepare anyone who had made that decision, I was one of the students who made the commitment to be baptized. "But I want Daniel Kubrock to baptize me," I said. Without the Kubrocks I would never have known about the Adventist church.

"I am sorry, Raya," Mr. Boynton said, "Daniel has left for Isfahan. He can't come back just for this event." Instead, I joined the other students in our mission swimming pool to be baptized as a group. I felt blessed to be among so many others who believed as I did, but I also felt melancholy that my dear friends couldn't witness the celebration.

A few years later, a coup deposed Iran's Prime Minister, Mosaddegh, and the missionaries found they would no longer have freedom to educate Iranian Nationals. Sadly, I said goodbye to my friends, the Osters and the Boyntons, as the two families evacuated to America and I found myself living alone with my mother once more.

It didn't take long for me to figure out what to do once my missionary friends left. The Persian and wealthy foreign families I had been teaching begged me to maintain a school for their children. One family offered their ten bedroom home, which we converted into a school. I hired two Iranian teachers who had studied at the Adventist Middle East College in Lebanon, and we used the standard Adventist school books left behind by our Missionary friends.

Looking back I realize what an impact we made on these families. Most of them were Zoroastrians and Israelis, yet they insisted that their children attend our small Christian school where they could study English.

In order to maintain the level of music and activities that our students were accustomed to, I also hired a Turkish couple to be our musical directors. The wife taught the choir and led the children in their plays and dramatic activities. Performances with children acting out the roles of flowers and snowflakes or dancing to traditional Russian Folk tunes would entertain parents and families at school functions.

During the performances, a local photographer, Makhnel, approached me with an offer to record these events and provide pictures which the parents could later purchase. It seemed like a great idea because the parents appreciated the great quality of the photos, my students' events were recorded for posterity, and Makhnel was able to earn extra income through the arrangement.

Many years later, I found out that Makhnel was a distant relative, the brother-in-law of my dear Auntie Galya. But while we worked together, we did not know of this acquaintance. In fact, our friendship grew, and Makhnel asked for my mother's permission to propose to me. I think my mother was relieved at the opportunity. I was 27 years old by this time, and she was beginning to worry that I would end up old and unmarried.

However, I could not even consider marrying the young man. My first concern was that he did not have the same religious beliefs that I did. Having been raised knowing no God, I found I was craving the solid grounding I felt now that I had become an Adventist. But more than that, this sweet friend was just too short. "If we get married our children will be Lilliputs," I objected. "He barely stands taller than me, and I am shorter than any women my age that I ever met!"

We decided to remain friends and business associates, and he did not pursue a relationship beyond that any more.

WORLD YOUTH CONGRESS

The choir director continued to lead her own musical group outside of our small school several nights a week. This original choir consisted of young adult singers who enjoyed sharing music with others.

In 1953 our choral group was invited to Bucharest, Romania, to perform for the World Youth Congress. This would be an amazing opportunity for all of us since we were able to acquire visas to travel throughout many provinces of the Soviet Union.

When we crossed the border, Soviet officials met us for a briefing. "You may not travel alone," they instructed us, assigning several representatives to accompany us.

"I don't need a companion," I insisted. "I know my way around the Soviet Union very well, and I want to visit my family in Baku." My requests fell on deaf ears.

"This is standard procedure," the official told me. "You may visit your family, but one of the agents must travel with you." Of course, the government officials made it sound like they were just concerned about our safety, yet I remembered very clearly the oppression I had lived under as a youth. I knew that the Soviets wanted us to have guides so that we would not be able to influence the locals we would come in contact with.

As a result, I found myself and my "tour guide" seated in my Cousin Mina's home several days later. She and I reminisced about her mother, my Auntie Sima, now long gone from her struggles with tuberculosis. She died when Mina was only one year old. Mina never had a chance to know her own mother who had been one of my childhood heroines. Our conversations were brief since they were censored by the official who accompanied me.

As I was leaving Mina's home, I realized I did not have a gift to give her. I looked through my belongings. I hadn't brought much with me since we would be traveling through various countries by many different modes of transportation. My hands brushed against the nylon fabric of a blouse I had sewn. The lightweight fabric had been perfect for traveling since it did not crush or wrinkle. I knew it would be difficult to obtain the rare material again, which had been a gift from Mrs. Boynton before she left for the United States. Still, I remembered only too well, how difficult life in Russia was. It gave me greater pleasure to give my cousin the blouse as a small token to remember me by, than to keep it for myself.

Once I was reunited with my choral group, we traveled the Black Sea through Armenia and Georgia by ship. Dusk and dawn on the Black Sea provided the most beautiful sights. The water appeared as spilled tar beneath our ship, smooth and dark in the faint moonlight.

In every port city, our ship was received with welcome and celebration. Kabobs, rice, rich sauces and wine were served to us. We performed for the locals as they did for us. Everyone communicated in the Russian language, the most commonly known by all.

We were as excited to have the opportunity to travel through these countries as they were to welcome us. Since the Soviet Union was tightly contained within their Iron Curtain regime, it was extremely unusual for these young people to have visitors. We gladly exchanged talents, gifts, and ideas with the friendly people.

From there we went on to Romania, our final destination. It was here that people from around the world congregated to perform in the World Youth Congress. Each group bore the flag of their country. Our flag was Iranian, although we had a varied representation of young adults from many different countries. Since the colors of our flag were red, white and green, people often confused us with the Italians.

"No," we would explain, "the Italian flag has the same colors, but their bands run vertically." Our stripes ran horizontally.

The event in Romania was a great exchange of cultures and traditions. Each group would give small gifts and mementos to their new friends, small souvenirs that symbolized each country. Between each of the meetings and concerts we found plenty of opportunities to shop for gifts to take home to our families as well.

Typically, it can be expected that a return trip is a big letdown after all the exhilaration that was enjoyed. However, our trip seemed to only get more exciting. Our ship traveled along the Volga River to the Don River. These two water ways were connected by a manmade canal, put in place by the Soviet government in order to hydrate the more arid space between them. Though this area should have been dry and desolate, it was lush, green and beautiful around the canal.

In order to move from one section of the route to another, we would travel by locks along the passage. As our ship neared the next portion along the way, hydraulic pumps would fill the locks with water beneath us, raising our entire ship to the next level. We would continue on until again, we came to the next lock where we waited for the next surge of water to elevate us. The whole experience was fascinating to watch.

When we returned to Iran, the coup had ended in a bloody insurgency and a new regime led by Prime Minister Zahedi was already in place. We had been gone only a short time but had been too far removed to know what was happening in our homeland.

The new government had no documentation that we had ever been granted permission to travel to the Soviet Union. We were immediately arrested and detained for three days and two nights under the suspicion of communist activity. Every one of us was frightened for our lives and I prayed fervently that we all would be returned to safety. Fortunately we were allowed to stay together as a group with our two leaders. Upon our arrest, they had confiscated our souvenirs, clothes, anything we were not wearing. Even once we were let go, *none* of our belongings were returned to us. We had nothing but memories left from our trip.

LITTLE GOAT

School started again in the fall of 1953, bringing an abundance of students and new, fun times to share together. Persian and Russian families customarily gift their teachers on the first day of school. Typical presents are flowers or fruits that are difficult to obtain, but on this particular year, I was given a very unusual present by the parents of one student: a small, white baby goat.

I gleefully brought the precious little hoofed creature home and showed him to my mother. "His name is Kozleonic [little goat]. Isn't he adorable?" I fussed, stroking his soft fur and gazing into his amber eyes.

"But Raya," my mother objected, "he will not stay this small! A kid will grow into a goat! Where will you keep him?"

"Oh Mama," I insisted, "You worry too much! How much trouble can a small goat be?"

I would soon find out. At first it seemed perfect for us to let Kozleonic graze in the garden. We no longer needed to weed or trim the grass and the small pellets he left behind acted as fertilizer.

When I would come home, I immediately let him into the house where he would follow me around, nuzzling his velveteen horn buds against my thighs while I worked. However, as Kozleonic grew, the garden could not contain him. No longer was he content to nibble the grass. Now he found tastier, delicate buds, leaves and flowers as he grew taller and his eye level was higher. Every afternoon I would come home to find my mother annoyed at yet another one of his antics.

"Kozleonic has found a way to sneak into the house," she would complain.

"Oh Mama! Why do you insist on banishing him to the garden anyway?" I asked, pulling a cloth napkin from his mouth as discreetly as possible. "Just keep him in the house while I'm gone. He'll be fine," I insisted.

Kozleonic actually wasn't fine in the house either. I came home one afternoon to find my usually patient mother looking very irritated. "Go look in your room," she directed me.

"Where's my satin quilt?" I asked, poking my head back into the kitchen where my mother continued her day's work.

"He ate it," she answered, factually. Her tone was cool and I barely perceived her unspoken message: "I told you so." She continued by saying, "I had noticed that the house was too quiet, so I went to search for him. I found him chewing your quilt."

"Fine, so he chewed up a piece of it," I answered, indifferently. "Give me the rest and I'll sew it into a lap blanket or some pillows."

"No, Raya," she insisted. "He shredded it all. There's nothing left of your quilt."

"Nothing?" I couldn't believe that such a small creature could destroy such a large quilt. "He may get sick," I agonized.

"Only if we are lucky," my mother said under her breath.

We followed Kozleonic around for an entire day to be sure that any digested pieces of the quilt would pass safely. In the end, I had to agree with my mother, we were not meant to be goat herders. I finally let him go to live on a small farm nearby.

BRIEF ENGAGEMENT

"Take me to a place where there is only God's light, you and I.
Take me to a land where there is warmth and no sadness in people's hearts,
Where kindness and hope fills their hearts."
from a Persian melody

One day in 1955, some family friends invited me to a party. "We are inviting another friend as well," they mentioned casually. "His name is Aram." I thought nothing of it at first, but when I met him we got along immediately.

Aram, whose name means "calm" in Farsi, truly was a peaceful spirit. He was well-educated and, like me, had a love for nature. We were both teachers, sharing our passion for education with the youth of our country. While I worked in a private elementary school, he worked in a public secondary school.

Later that summer, Aram and I planned a trip to Ramsar on the Caspian Sea in northern Iran. The mother of two of my students approached me at the end of the school year. "Raya, I know it is your summer vacation, but my husband and I need to go to Israel to visit my ailing mother and it will be difficult to travel with the boys," she pleaded. "Would you mind keeping them for a month?"

"Not at all!" I said. "We are going to travel too, and the boys will have fun with us." I knew that traveling to the sea would be much better for them than being stuck beside their mother while she tried to care for their grandmother.

Aram was not only open to the idea but embraced it. He came up with fun games and activities to keep the boys entertained along the way. With no air-conditioning, no radio and no I Spy games, we needed as many distractions as possible for the four-hour-long journey.

On the way our car started shaking loudly. The boys looked excited about having an unexpected adventure. I was not as thrilled. "What is that noise?" I demanded in alarm.

Aram eased the car toward the shoulder and got out to look. "A flat," he explained, pointing to the misshapen tire. "Everybody out!"

The boys and I jumped out of the car with the intent of stretching our legs while Aram changed the offending tire. Well, the boys jumped, but it seemed I more or less tumbled out, badly spraining my ankle in the process. The longer I waited for the tire to be fixed, the more my ankle swelled and throbbed.

Poor Aram! Now not only did he need to take care of the car, but he had to help me as well. Using the least dirty strips of rags he could find in the trunk, Aram bandaged up my leg into a makeshift splint. I eased back into the car, elevating my leg as well as I could for the remaining trip.

As we drove past rice plantations with workers wading up to their knees through the watery fields, I knew we were getting close. I well remembered visiting Ramsar with my cousin Adileh, who by that time was married to a man named Houshang. The scenery was becoming familiar and I excitedly pointed out various landmarks to the boys, briefly forgetting my inflamed ankle.

We arrived at the beautiful beach city of Ramsar after several more rest stops along the way. Small, flat-roofed cottages facing the seashore welcomed our car as we drove into town. Farmers worked to maintain the vineyards stretched randomly between territories. The brothers were delightful, playing together nicely and enjoying the warm summer sun at the beach.

When Aram and I returned to Tehran, it seemed natural for us to get engaged. I was excited to find a man I could love. Aram was dependable, peaceful and well educated. Plus, I wouldn't end up an old maid which was a big relief to my mother. Aram's parents invited me to their home with my mother, his sister and her husband. We had a small family celebration to commemorate the occasion. Aram gave me a ring, an heirloom piece from his own family, as a token of our commitment to each other.

MIDDLE EAST COLLEGE, LEBANON

The Kubrocks returned to Tehran and Daniel became president of the Iran Mission in 1956. I was overjoyed to be reunited with my friends.

With them came Gladys' mother, Ella May Robinson. The dear old woman took me under her wing and encouraged me to pursue my degree at Middle East College. After three years of teaching and improving the minds of children, I began to feel like I needed to be challenged by improving myself.

"Our church has a lovely college in Lebanon," Gladys agreed with her mother. "You are a natural teacher, Raya. You should go there to refine your skills and continue your education."

I remembered hiring fine young teachers from that very same school so it was an easy decision. My own mother was thrilled. Of course, it wasn't the nursing degree that she had always hoped I would get, but she was still happy that I would be able to receive a formal education.

Perhaps it was because of my non-Adventist background, or maybe because of my diminutive size, but the adults at the Iran mission seemed to be extremely protective of me. I knew they did not approve of my engagement to Aram. Mrs. Robinson gently encouraged me to break off the engagement and seek a fellow Adventist in order to be "equally yoked," as the Bible recommended. I smiled, humoring her, but I knew that Aram was a fantastic man. In my mind we really were equally yoked.

On the other hand, the prospect of advancing my education was more intriguing than getting married just yet. Since I would be gone for four years, Aram decided to take time off from work in order to continue his education in Paris. We were both excited and nervous about our life changes at the same time. With each of us heading off in different directions, we could better focus on our studies. We parted on a friendly basis, both of us believing that we would see each other again soon. I wonder if we would have been as ready to spread our wings if we knew then that we were going to be separated by more than just miles.

And so, it was settled. I packed up my belongings, said goodbye to my family, my students, the Kubrocks, and Aram, and headed to Middle East College. I had no worries about leaving and knew the school would be in good hands. The Iran Mission, run by my former teachers, Gladys and Daniel, would be taking over my responsibilities.

In order to travel to Lebanon, I was required to pass through Iraq and Syria. Because this would be an intense trip, the Kubrocks recommended that I travel with two other students, Davoud and Sonya. We boarded a rickety bus and left Iran through the southern city of Abadan on the Persian Gulf. This might seem to be far out of the way, but there was no direct route of travel to the west.

In Baghdad we got off the bus during a scheduled rest stop and stretched our legs, weary from the long trip. "Let's go down by the seashore," Davoud suggested.

"Do you think we can?" Sonya asked, hopefully.

"Of course!" I was certain. "We only need to tell the driver not to leave without us."

We checked for our next departure time and, stopping long enough to buy some roasted potatoes and chestnuts from a vendor on the way, we happily went on to the nearby Persian Gulf.

After being crammed into the ancient bus for so long, it felt liberating to be able to walk along the shore. We stepped through waves that danced along the sand. A small fishing boat was anchored along a pier and the fishermen were squatting over the coals of a low burning fire. The tempting smell of freshly grilled fish floated toward us, stirring up our appetites.

Quickly, we negotiated a price with the merchants and sat down to enjoy our meal of steaming-hot fish, potatoes, and chestnuts. The whole scene reminded me of the Bible stories Gladys had taught me years before. Even with my limited knowledge of Christ, I imagined Jesus walking on this very same strip of sand and approaching the fishermen who would eventually become his followers.

We caught our ride just in time and finally arrived in Beirut, Lebanon. As we traveled up a long road, into the grounds of our college, and to the top of St. Mary's Mountain, I stared around, amazed at the beauty of this small campus. It overlooked the Mediterranean Sea and had beautiful gardens and citrus trees.

Once on campus, I could tell my life had been vastly different from all of the other students. Most of these young people had been raised Seventh-day Adventists from childhood, while I did not even learn about God until I was an adult. And they were all five to ten years younger than I was, since they had come to college directly out of high school, while I had worked for several years between.

Despite these differences or perhaps it was because of them, I soon found that I had a great appreciation for my new life in college. I participated in every single event I could, taking piano lessons, joining the choir and worshiping with others. As a student for the first time in years, I embraced my new life.

CAMPUS WORK

During my freshman year, I worked as a Literature Evangelist. That required walking through various neighborhoods from door to door promoting the books and pamphlets written by our church founder Ellen White or by the Adventist General Conference. Popular books for adults included Ellen's *The Desire of Ages* and *Steps to Christ* while books in the series *Uncle Arthur's Bedtime Stories* were usually chosen for children.

Most of the students who took on this job used the opportunity to tell homeowners about our beliefs and spend a few minutes in prayer for them.

I was a natural for this occupation. Perhaps it was my competitive spirit, or it could simply have been my pure belief in the religion I had come to embrace, but I excelled as a literature evangelist.

It wasn't easy. First we had to navigate the mountainous streets of St. Mary's Hill near our school on foot and in the heat of summer! The next challenge was just getting people to open their doors to us. Add one more factor: I did not speak Arabic *or* French, the two primary languages of Beirut. It wasn't until later on in college that I learned to speak Arabic and I never learned the French language.

Yet I had always loved telling others about my beliefs, and now I was getting paid to do it. The situation couldn't have been more perfect if I had designed it myself. That summer I had the opportunity to witness to countless people, inviting them to visit our church services. As a result, my Adventist book sales topped even the students who spoke the native Arabic language.

My next assignment was teaching English to the new arrivals. Students came from all around the Middle East to study and all our classes were in English. Because I had prior experience in teaching English, this job was a natural fit for me.

During the summers, a few other advanced scholars and I stayed in the dormitories to teach English to new students. This proved to have two benefits: those who taught were able to help pay off their tuition at double time and the non-English-speaking students would be able to communicate once the school year started.

By the end of my freshman year, our assistant dean had graduated and his job opened up. I immediately applied and was extremely excited to get the position. This would be my occupation throughout the remaining college years at Middle East College.

ROOMMATES AND BEST FRIENDS

In the women's dormitory, I was introduced to my new roommates by our dean, Miss Williams. Latifa was from Egypt and Florence was from Iran, both the daughters of ministers. Already best friends themselves, these enjoyable and sweet young ladies became like sisters to me.

With classes underway in 1956 and my job as assistant dean, there was little time for socializing. Yet somehow I managed to make a special effort for extracurricular activities.

Because of my position, I was often the last one to retire for the evening, even when I was not mingling with others. Many nights would find me sneaking into our darkened room to undress as quietly as possible. Having no covert skills to speak of, I would usually awaken my roommates as I knocked into a bedpost or stubbed my toe on a dresser. Then morning would come and I would struggle awake long after Latifa and Florence were up.

Finally, my roommates could not bear it. They put a simple plan into action. Late one night, they pretended to sleep as I made my usual, noisy entrance. Lying in the dark, they must have had to stifle giggles into their pillows as they listened to me stumble around the room. Once my sheets were no longer rustling and my breaths became long and even, Florence and Latifa slipped quietly out of bed and headed toward my sleeping form. With each of my roommates working on one side of me, the two of them soundlessly sewed me into my sheets!

The next morning, in my hazy state of mind, I thought I must have had a paralyzing stroke during the night. I struggled against my bedclothes but was unable to move more than a few inches, if at all.

Florence and Latifa couldn't help but laugh at the panicked look on my face. "I hope this teaches you a lesson," Florence chastised gently as they left for breakfast. "'Early to bed, early to rise,' can be translated into 'Late to sleep, get sewn into your sheets!'"

Somehow I did not find their little lesson as amusing as my roommates did. But I must admit I rarely snuck in late after that night.

COLLEGE LIFE

School days were enjoyable, keeping us busy with so much new knowledge. There were strict rules which we were all expected to obey: be on time and well prepared for classes, participate in class discussions, and stay out of unstaffed classrooms.

One day I arrived at my history class and found all the students waiting outside of the room. "Why don't you go in?" I asked them.

"Dr. Keough hasn't gotten here yet," one of the boys replied, slumped against the brick wall as he tried to seek out shade from the hot spring afternoon. We waited several minutes more, each of us melting under the sun.

"Well, it doesn't make sense for us to wait out here," I remarked as I walked around the side of the building. I carefully wedged myself between the bushes in order to get closer to the ground floor window. I pushed gently on the pane and the window swung open. Moments later I had climbed through and unlocked the door for my classmates.

No one really knew what to do at that moment. The rules were clear, but the students were much too uncomfortable outside to resist. After a moment's hesitation they filed in, certain we would all be in trouble.

We were all seated and class should have been underway for fifteen minutes before Dr. Keough arrived. Puzzled, he looked through the open door.

"Who let you in here?" he demanded. The other students were only too glad to use me as the scapegoat. Several fingers pointed in my direction.

"Raya, how did you get in?" He asked, shocked.

I cringed, knowing I was in trouble. "I climbed through the window," I answered, sounding much more confident than I felt.

"Good job," he exclaimed, surprising us all. "Raya, you get the award for problem solving today!"

The other students objected, their own comfort now forgotten. "She broke the rules when she climbed through that window," one girl exclaimed.

"And yet you all benefitted from her actions," Dr. Keough could not be swayed. "It's typical for foreigners such as our little Russian student here," he tapped me on the shoulder, "to find ways to adapt to any situation. I hope you all will learn to think quickly whenever you are presented with a dilemma from now on."

WEEK OF PRAYER

Each year our school would host a Week of Prayer event, inviting one or more pastors or conference leaders to enlighten and motivate us. One particular speaker inspired us with his discussion on leadership roles. After so many years, I don't even remember the pastor's name, but his lessons certainly left an impression on me. The man was massive, especially from my four-foot-eleven-inch point of view! I sat in my usual front row spot listening to his talk, straining to peer up at his towering image.

At first the discussion seemed inspiring as he described the various personality types and how to identify them. All of us stretched our minds to imagine ourselves in leadership roles, guiding souls to the Lord who may otherwise have been eternally lost. However, I began to take offense at the man's opinions.

"As you go from church to church, you will find that the prime leadership roles are filled by people who have the loftiest stature," he theorized. "It makes sense since a tall person is naturally easiest to look up to."

I was stunned. Here I had such high hopes of being a quality leader in my church, and I believed that God had immense plans for me as well. Yet this man was basically telling me it was too much of a tall order to fill. I couldn't believe that I was getting the short end of the deal.

My stewing psyche suddenly landed on a verse from Zechariah which I paraphrased in my mind. "'Not by might, nor by power, nor by height, but by my spirit,' says the Lord of hosts." If God wanted to use me in leadership roles, He certainly could.

Years later, when I was given a title longer than I was tall, I remembered that long-ago speaker. By that time, weak bones and old age had reduced my already short stature to only four feet nine inches. "I'm the Associate Director of Education of the Euro-Asia Division of Seventh-day Adventists," I thought to myself. "I guess God found a way to make little old me into a leader for His work after all!"

TRAVELING TO BETHLEHEM

In my sophomore year my group of friends included a young man from Bethlehem named Fayez. That spring of 1957, in anticipation of his graduation, Fayez arranged a trip for several of us. Seven students traveled with him to visit the Bible Lands around Israel.

Piled into his large but badly-beaten car, we headed past Haifa then through Nazareth and finally into Bethlehem. For twelve hours we drove on, singing songs or telling stories to help our driver stay awake on the winding roads. At that time there were no border limitations in the Middle East. Travel was fast and unrestricted with each of the countries being about the same size as many American states.

Once we arrived in Bethlehem we were welcomed into Fayez's large house by his gracious parents and loving grandmother. Here we feasted on platters of rice, sauces made from vegetables, and salad before we slumbered for the night. The boys were ushered into Fayez's room and all the girls gratefully collapsed into a guest bedroom to rest after the long day's travel. The next few days would be packed with sightseeing.

Our tour of Bethlehem took us to the Church of the Nativity, jointly owned by all religious faiths. Inside the church was a small shrine which, according to the tour guide, had been the birthplace of Jesus. We walked along the Jordan River at the point of history's most famous baptism and had the chance to see the small tomb that held Jesus for only two nights after his crucifixion. Because it was Easter time, we even had the opportunity to watch a reenactment of Jesus' life. I felt uplifted, as if I was in the presence of holy beings.

One afternoon, as we traveled through the mountains surrounding the Dead Sea, Fayez pointed out a small cave opening where a young shepherd boy had recently made a great discovery. While absently tossing rocks into the cave opening, he heard the crash of pottery breaking. Frightened, he ran in to find out what he could have broken. He found large pottery vessels that looked as if they had been hidden there for centuries among the rocks.

At the time, their mystery had not yet been unraveled by scholars. Many years later, after I was retired and living in San Diego, I went to the Museum of Natural History with my church to examine the contents found in those very same vessels, now known as the Dead Sea Scrolls. They were on exhibit from Israel and took up the entire lower level of our expansive museum. Fortunately, the scrolls were translated, since none of us could read the Hebrew, Aramaic, or Greek language in which they had been preserved. Staring down at the miniscule printed scrolls, spread out under the protection of glass, we were able to see stories of the Old Testament in their original language.

The next day we traveled to Jerusalem. It was fascinating to be walking on the very ground that Jesus once trod. We viewed areas reported to be the same places where Jesus and his disciples healed the sick, the blind, and the lame. Now that I had deeper roots in my religious faith, I found the whole experience to be refreshing, firmly grounding me in my new beliefs.

We leaned our heads against the Wailing Wall, built by the Israeli Jews who wanted to offer prayers for their ancestors. We also enjoyed a picnic on the Mount of Olives. Here we rested under the shady trees, heavily laden with olives as we ate our lunch.

Our weeklong visit with Fayez and his family also took us to the Pool of Bethesda where Jesus healed the lame man and the synagogue where he had healed the blind man. We enjoyed a swim in the Sea of Galilee and toured the Dome of the Rock where a ram had been sent to rescue Isaac from sacrifice. Our meals were taken on the road from vendors or at restaurants in the cities we visited.

At the end of the week, we thanked Fayez's parents, said our goodbyes, and headed back to college. After our firsthand tour of biblical history, it was time to return to the daily routine of work and lessons.

ENGAGEMENT SUMMER

"The Lord has been mindful of us: He will bless us ..." Psalms 115:12

"Who can tell me where to find the description of Daniel's dream with the six headed beast?" Dr. Vine asked in our Bible class. Even though we all scrambled to find the correct verse, I knew, without looking up, who would answer first.

"Go ahead, Lotfy," our professor prompted as the tall, young man quickly stood up. My desk mate and I exchanged surprised glances. I had not even gotten to the correct book of the Bible, let alone found the specific verse.

I listened to Lotfy reading and wondered how someone so young could know so much about the Bible. Having come from an atheistic background, I was intrigued by the wealth of stories and lessons which were in the Bible. I was still struggling to learn everything I could about it, and Lotfy seemed to have the entire Bible memorized.

Lotfy was also the first one to offer prayer or to lead Bible study groups during chapel or on Sabbath afternoons.

As Seventh-day Adventists, Saturday was our day of worship. On Sabbath, once church was over, we spent the day hiking and scouring the woods which encircled our campus. Often, a group of students would travel into the nearby villages for missionary activities. Small group meetings were held within a church member's home. Theology students would provide the stories for a sermonette and everyone else would join in as hymns were sung. As education majors, some of the other students and I would gather the children of the neighborhood together for songs, stories, and activities.

It was the hot summer months in 1958, with their long lazy days, that provided an opportunity for me to get to know Lotfy better. Once my music practice was completed, my lessons and books had been put away, and my duties as the dean's assistant were fulfilled, the remaining time was my own.

Usually, the school would take tours to Cyprus. The wooded mountains there were a popular site for visitors who wanted a peaceful day away from their responsibilities. Our college provided a picnic for the students and we would lounge against the fragrant cedar trees, cooling ourselves with glasses of water, fresh fruit, and sandwiches made from flat bread and feta cheese. Since Lotfy and I were among these students, we would often find ourselves chatting the afternoon away.

During our second school year, Lotfy and I found many more chances to get to know each other. On Friday evenings, our school would celebrate the incoming Sabbath with Vespers in the chapel. Participating in chapel services where I performed skits or choral events and Lotfy did Bible readings required us to put our heads together to coordinate upcoming programs.

I grew to admire this young man who was so excited about the church and so familiar with the Bible. I understood now what Mrs. Robinson's concerns were when she told me I should marry an Adventist. It made sense to share my love with someone who shares a love for God.

When Aram sent me a melancholy photo of himself from Paris, I received it with mixed feelings. I had shared a brief but enjoyable history with him. Now I knew that my path was taking me closer to God. Aram and I had slowly grown apart and our engagement dissolved as a result of it.

After remaining single until my early thirties, I did not want to rush into another engagement so quickly. Instead, Lotfy and I announced that we intended to marry; we just didn't really call it an engagement. That was our sophomore year.

Most people have romantic stories about romantic reasons leading up to their marriage. My reasons were simply practical.

I was very mindful of my choice as I selected Lotfy to be my husband. First of all, like me, he had entered college at a much later age than most of the other students. Since I was so much older than any of the students, I knew that the twenty-nine-year-old Lotfy would be closest to my age of thirty-four. Besides, every year the gap between the new students' ages and my own would just keep increasing. If I was going to act, it had to be now.

Secondly, my husband had to be tall. He at least had to be taller than I am! I had known that for a fact when I turned down the photographer Makhnel's proposal years before. I was short, and Lotfy did manage to tower over me.

Most importantly, my husband would have to love God the way I had grown to. I believed that this final characteristic was the biggest draw toward my relationship with Lotfy. I also believed that any man who loved God would act respectfully in all matters and that was important to me. Besides that, he was the only Adventist man who had ever asked me to marry him.

Shortly after announcing our intention to marry, Lotfy and I decided to celebrate in town. As I remember it, Lotfy had the idea. Students were allowed to leave campus only when accompanied by a staff member. "You are the assistant dean," he rationalized. "Doesn't that make you part of the staff?" I really couldn't deny that.

"And we both teach summer school lessons," I agreed with him. "That's like being with two staff members."

With our reasoning settled and our minds made up, Lotfy and I headed for the marketplace of Beirut. Small open tents shaded the cafés where hot tea and sandwiches could be purchased. Though all our needs were provided for on campus, even poor students like us found these simple treats an inexpensive indulgence.

We chatted the afternoon away, reminiscing about our childhoods as we strolled through the small shops in the narrow streets. "Your mother died when you were just a child?" I gasped when Lotfy told me of his early loss, wondering how I would have survived without my own quiet, loving mother to raise me. It had been difficult for me when my own father was sent to Siberia, yet the thought of having my mother die gripped me even more.

During one of these afternoon excursions, Lotfy and I picked out the ivory fabric and pattern that I would use to make my wedding dress. The heavy silk had fine golden threads woven through it. I wished that my mother could design the dress. All my life, she had made the most beautiful and stylish clothes for me. Sadly, after numerous phone calls and mailed letters announcing our wedding, the Iranian government declined her visa, and she was not able to visit.

Word eventually got around school that Lotfy and I were spending time alone together. This was completely unacceptable by Middle East College standards in the 1950s. We were immediately assigned to the Russells, our Bible teacher and his wife, who would act as our chaperones.

It was ironic that Mr. and Mrs. Russell were considered our chaperones. Truthfully, even in their small faculty home, Lotfy and I were usually left alone; typically, we had the place to ourselves. Still, the school officials were content believing that they maintained control over the students.

Regardless of our perceived freedom or lack of it, we knew well enough to conduct ourselves responsibly. Any time that Mr. and Mrs. Russell walked into their home, they could find us sitting at their kitchen table, studying or making plans for our wedding the following summer.

A WARNING FROM DR. GERATY

One afternoon Dr. Geraty, our college president, asked me into his office. "Raya," his tone was grave as he began, "I want to warn you about a relationship that is unequally yoked."

"But Lotfy is Seventh-day Adventist, like me," I objected, recalling Mrs. Robinson's earlier warnings concerning my relationship with Aram.

We spoke for more than two hours as Dr. Geraty explained all the ways that Lotfy and I were so vastly different. Having previously visited the impoverished area of Upper Egypt, Dr. Geraty knew firsthand the meager conditions my future husband came from. He also pointed out the immense cultural differences between Russia and Egypt.

I thought I had already come to understand all of this from my recent discussions with Lotfy. Besides, I argued, being equal in our Adventist beliefs makes us equally yoked. "After all, didn't Boaz marry the Moabite woman?" I quoted from the Old Testament book of Ruth.

Finally, realizing that I could not be dissuaded, Dr. Geraty advised me to be cautious. Lotfy's temper had gotten him into trouble in the past. Dr. Geraty, who was like a father to me, was just looking out for my well-being.

I assured him that we would be just fine. "I have lived in so many different environments, with such a broad range of people, that I am sure I will be able to adapt," I promised.

WEDDING BELLS

I married Lotfy Abadir on June 12, 1959. The whole campus seemed to be anticipating our wedding day, just as we had looked forward to weddings of other students. The ceremony was performed by my future brother-in-law Abadir who was an Adventist pastor in Cairo. In Egypt, it is very common for someone to have a first name that is the same as his last name.

The campus chapel was adorned simply with white crepe paper bows and streamers running down the aisle as well as two large bouquets of gladiolas in front of the stage. Our wedding was basic and minimally decorated, nothing at all like the luxurious Persian wedding my brother had given his wife a few years before.

Despite this, I loved every minute of it. All the other weddings I had seen my previous years at the college had been just as simple, yet full of the love and warmth shared between good friends. Only one thing prevented me from having the perfect day; my mother was absent and I had no true family representation there.

Two of my friends, Mary and Jeanette, stood up for me as bridesmaids. Each of them wore a pink dress they had chosen on their own, thus eliminating my need to spend hours deciding the perfect outfit for them and probably reducing the number of useless garments in their closets.

Two faculty children were our flower girl and bible boy. Lotfy's friends, Habib and Mokhtar, stood up for him as groomsmen. Special music was provided by my own choir teacher, Miss Soper, and a fellow student, Najlah. Each of these ladies sang a beautiful song for us. And when the "Wedding March" began, it was Dr. Geraty who walked me down the aisle and gave my hand to Lotfy.

The faculty had decorated the rooftop of the administration building for the reception. White and pink crepe paper ribbon adorned the walls around the area. Our initials, L and R, made up the centerpiece over the beautiful lace tablecloth lent to us for the occasion by a faculty member.

We did not provide an elaborate banquet for our reception. Instead, our guests enjoyed punch and a beautiful little three-tiered cake made by our school cafeteria's chef.

Dancing was not accepted because of our school's strict Adventist beliefs, so our guests sat in chairs which circled the empty floor as they laughed and chatted through the evening. We enjoyed more special music as well as the beautiful gifts and well-wishes from those who attended the celebration.

Our honeymoon was spent in our new bungalow, the housing that was provided to married couples. The married student homes were fully furnished, just as our dorm rooms had been. Though the college usually reserved two-bedroom homes for married students with children, Lotfy and I were fortunate to be able to acquire one of these as well, since we were expecting my mother to join us during our last year in college.

MARRIED LIFE ON CAMPUS

We stayed on campus for the next couple of years to continue our student teaching over the summer, rather than take the time for a vacation together. All these decisions seemed practical.

Life with Lotfy began as a constant emotional struggle because of our vastly different cultural backgrounds. Lotfy was demanding and temperamental. I hoped that a child would bring us closer and ease the tension, but I also feared that I would be too old to bear children.

I quickly realized that I should have listened to the advice of Dr. Geraty, but I was almost 34 years old by the time we married and I really wanted to have children. Besides, I knew it would be extremely difficult to find anyone else with a similar background to mine. Although I had never been at a loss for friends, I had spent most of my adult life feeling like a minority in every situation.

Mealtime was the biggest chore for me. While I had always loved food, I never really learned how to cook. For one of our first breakfasts together, I set some eggs into a shallow pan of water to boil while I finished getting ready for the day. I quickly made the bed, dressed, and fixed my hair before Lotfy and I sat on the couch for our morning devotion.

Suddenly, an explosion in the kitchenette reminded me of the eggs I had forgotten. Lotfy and I ran in to find bits of egg yolk and shells all over the floor, walls, and ceiling of our small kitchen. Though we scrubbed everything as quickly as we could, the slight sulfur smell clung to our home for days.

It soon became evident that I used the smell of burning food as a kitchen timer. Having come from a home where food was scarce, Lotfy did not complain when my meals did not turn out as planned. Nonetheless, I was used to being able to do all things well and I was certain that I would be able to master this skill quickly.

I was thrilled when, one month after our wedding, my mother was finally granted permission to join us. She eased our work load by preparing meals, calling us to the table with her approximation of an English phrase, "Ready bready."

Now Lotfy and I would come home after a long day of classes and work to find that our lunch or dinner was already prepared for us. This was a huge benefit since we had already established that I was not much of a chef.

While I appreciated not having the task of cooking, it was also evident that Lotfy appreciated my mother's excellent culinary skills. Once dinner was over and the kitchenette was clean, my mother would join us with a smile on her face, ready for us to answer her questions about a God that she had never known in her childhood. This was the highlight of her day.

Having lived around the Osters and the Kubrocks in Iran, my mother was familiar with the tunes of the Christian hymns they had taught me, though she did not know how to sing the words. She would whistle "Nearer My God to Thee" or Fanny Crosby's "All the Way My Savior Leads Me" beautifully while she worked. I won't say that I was exactly jealous of my mother, but it never seemed quite fair that she could whistle so well, while I never could learn.

Since I had translated the hymns for my mother when we lived in Iran, Lotfy and I used them, as well as stories from the Bible and our quarterly Sabbath school lesson books, to teach my mother about Christianity.

Before the start of the new school year, my mother was baptized into the Seventh-day Adventist Church. Everyone on campus walked down to a quiet cove in the Mediterranean Sea on a Sabbath afternoon to watch the ceremony. Pastor Vine gave a brief prayer, and Miss Soper directed onlookers in singing a hymn. Then, supporting my mother's head, he dipped her beneath the warm, blue water. As she rose, a bright smile lit her face. My mother had found a new family to call her own.

ENTERTAINING ON CAMPUS

One of our favorite things to do as a married couple was to entertain guests in our small bungalow. This was much easier with my mother living with us. She would bake *perogies* stuffed with cabbage and potatoes and seasoned with lots of fried onions or garlic. Many of the Persian girls on campus would stop by our home during the day to chat with my mother in Farsi. She always appreciated these visits and reciprocated by filling their tummies with her good, homemade food.

Just as often, the three of us would head to the cafeteria to celebrate festivities with the school. Thanksgiving, Christmas, and Easter would bring students together for holiday meals. No one really decorated for the holidays or passed out presents. The days were merely marked by a special dinner together. We never saw an Easter Bunny, or had an Easter egg hunt until we arrived in the United States many years later.

Though my mother joined the students for these meals, she was more likely to stay at home than take advantage of bigger outings, such as trips to the mountains or the beach. These outings, as well as chapel time and brief walks around campus or into town, were the only opportunity for Lotfy and me to spend time together as a couple.

GRADUATION

1960 marked the end of my senior year. Only two tiny things stood between me and graduation: first was that every graduating student needed to be a Master Guide in our youth organization, the Pathfinders. It is similar to Girl Scouts and Boy Scouts. There are investiture services once a year when the Pathfinder leader from the conference comes and gives honors and promotion pins. In order to be a Master Guide, I had to complete several honors demonstrating my learned skills in such life altering areas as nature studies and home economics.

Second was the fact that I had never attended an American-accredited high school. Although Middle East College was in Lebanon, it was run by the General Conference of Seventh-day Adventists. This meant that I was required to pass the high school exam for my General Equivalency Diploma before I could be eligible for my bachelor's degree.

This prerequisite seemed even more ridiculous to me than the need to fill a sash with tiny honor badges. I had already completed high school in Russia and had even taken advanced classes in the Iran Training School. Fortunately, I managed to successfully pass my GED test just weeks prior to graduation. This enabled me to march with the rest of my class and finally receive my college diploma in 1960.

Recipe for Persian "Jeweled" Wedding Rice

Ingredients:

1 lb Basmati rice

1/2 cup almonds, thinly sliced

1/2 cup green raisins

7 Tbsp extra virgin olive oil

water

1/2 cup orange marmalade or peel, thinly sliced

1/2 cup dried barberries, thinly sliced

1/2 cup pistachios, thinly sliced

2 tsp saffron

4 Tbsp sugar

salt and pepper

Directions:

Dissolve the saffron threads in 4 Tbsp. boiling water and set aside to soak. This will go on top of the rice once the rice is prepared and ready to be served.

Place Basmati rice in large bowl and fill with water. Rinse 2–3 times by draining water and filling bowl with water again. Add 1 Tbsp. salt to the water and rice. Set aside for 2–3 hours.

After 2–3 hours, fill a non-stick pot halfway with water and bring to boil. Drain the rice and add it to the boiling water. Pour in 1 Tbsp of olive oil and continue to boil for about 10–15 minutes.

In the meantime, in another pan, heat 2 Tbsp. olive oil, add sugar, and heat until dissolved. One by one, add barberries, almonds, pistachios, and raisins side by side so they don't touch. If needed, use two pans. This is important for the presentation later on. Cook on low heat just to heat each item. Warm marmalade or orange peel in microwave for 1 min. on low heat.

Drain rice in strainer. Place pot back onto medium heat and add 1 1/2 Tbsp. olive oil to the bottom of the pot. Add drained rice back to the pot and add the 1 1/2 Tbsp of olive oil on top of rice.

Cover the lid of the pan with a cloth and cover the pan tightly. On medium heat, steam rice for about 30–45 minutes or until rice is completely cooked and soft and a golden rice crust forms at the bottom of the pan. Make sure you don't overcook the rice or burn the bottom crust. Monitor rice at this point.

Once rice is cooked, carefully ladle it into a large serving tray. With a spoon or ladle, start adding the saffron mixture to the rice in a horizontal or vertical pattern. Then one by one add barberries, almonds, pistachios, raisins, and orange peel in a similar vertical/horizontal pattern so every ingredient on top of the rice is lined up side by side. The presentation of this rice is extremely important for Persians as this is usually served at large celebrations so the rice should be very beautifully designed.

Once complete, in a small pan heat the remaining 1 Tbsp. olive oil. Pour over the rice. This gives the additional "jeweled" look to the mixtures on top of the rice. Serve immediately with cooked chicken breast, leg, or thigh.

Figure 6 – Abraham's Daughters Roya, Lida; Abraham and Wife Effat; Raya and Abraham, Daughter Mitra; Uncle Aghajan, Aunt Anay, and Abraham

Figure 7 - Raya as a Teen in Iran, Raya with Cousin Adeleh, Feasting on Fish in Bagdad, Raya (Wearing Blouse She Gave to Cousin Mina) and Mother in Iran

Figure 8 - Mr. Oster as Santa, Teachers at Iran Mission Boys High School

Figure 9 - Iran Mission School Teachers and Raya with Students

Figure 10 - Iran Mission School, 1955; Students with Raya

Figure 11 - Caspian Sea (Raya: front center), Skiing Al Borz Mountains, Esfaahan Ruins, Train in Iran

Figure 12 - Iran New Years, Picnic, Sheep in Esfaahan, Esfaahan Ruins

Figure 13 - Javid and Clara, Worked in Irano-Russian Fishery; Raya and Clara; Clara and Her Mother

Figure 14 - Oster Family, Aram, Dr. Geraty

Figure 15 - Kubrock Family, Boynton Family

Figure 16 - Pathfinders, Middle East College Class, Raya and Lotfy - Graduation

Figure 17 - Raya, Abadir, and Lotfy at Wedding; Ella Mae Robinson and Raya (on right); Raya at Her Baptism

PART III: EGYPT, 1960–1962

DON'T LET THE BEDBUGS BITE!

"Trust in the Lord always ..." Proverbs 3:5

As soon as we graduated from Middle East College, Lotfy and I received a call to work for the Nile Union Academy in Gabel Asfar, not too far from Cairo. This academy was for high school boys only, because most schools were not co-ed at that time. In fact, most girls did not have the opportunity to study beyond the eighth grade. Because of this, all the other teachers were male; I was the only female. As if that were not enough, I was also the only foreigner.

Lotfy was hired as a Bible teacher, as well as the boys' dean. My job would be to teach music, most specifically just choir. It was not a fancy music program and had no instrument lessons of any kind. I was also to be the cafeteria matron, a job I would quickly learn to hate.

When we first entered our apartment, located on top of the boys' dormitory, we were very pleased with the building. The light-filled rooms were big and spacious, adorned with large windows.

Our apartment had been nearly empty when we moved in. The only things that were provided for us were our beds, a table, and chairs. Lotfy and I did not have any furnishings of our own. But within a week my husband had created beautiful and functional shelves, flower planters, and storage chests.

My inspection of our apartment kitchen proved to be a shock and disappointment. As soon as I opened the oven and the refrigerator doors, cockroaches swarmed around the room. Always the one to bravely face a stressful situation, I ran out of the house and refused to go back in until every last cockroach was gone.

To combat our unwanted house pests, Lotfy pulled out all the electrical fixtures and sprinkled them with DDT, a very poisonous powder, which was banned in the US in 1972 and many years later in most parts of the world. With that task completed, we locked up the doors and went to stay in the home of one of my bridesmaids while we waited for the chemicals to take effect.

When we returned to our apartment, our kitchen floor was like a battle field covered with all sizes and colors of dead cockroaches. Fortunately, we had my mother with us. It took the three of us two full days to clean up the mess. As a result, my mother and I became compulsively clean. We would not allow a single dish to remain in the sink, and crumbs seemed to vanish from the room before they even landed on the floor. We lived in that house for two years and not one cockroach was ever seen again.

Our own apartment was not the only place we waged a war against grime. We found that bedbugs were common in the boys' dormitory. These we combated by pouring boiling water between the wooden slats to destroy the eggs of the bedbugs before they had a chance to hatch. Every time new students came to the academy from Upper Egypt, we would boil their clothes, killing off any possible lice, bedbugs or cockroach eggs before they ever came into the dormitory.

SHOPPING IN EGYPT

Shopping for groceries in the early 1960s required a bit more effort in Egypt than it did in Iran. The majority of our purchases required a twenty minute bus trip into Cairo where we would walk from shop to shop buying necessities. Sights and sounds, and especially smells, in Cairo were often overwhelming.

Everywhere we went, shoeless children were pawning useless items while old men clothed in *galabias* (long, dress-like clothing) were begging for *zakat* (alms that made up an Islamic charity tax). Cars pushed themselves along the narrow roads and pedestrians were fearlessly crossing the roads. No one was afraid of dying on these dangerous streets, though many often did.

Men could be heard calling out their goods as we neared them: freshly roasted corn, steamy fragrant falafel, and any fruits in season. Fruit was especially plentiful in Egypt. Prickly pears, bright red watermelon, and the most fragrant, juicy mangos could be purchased on almost every street corner of the city by peddlers pushing heavily-laden carts. Dates were so abundant that a song was even made about the fruit. "Dates, dates, wonderful dates. Brown dates, black dates, yellow dates, won't you buy my sweet dates?" (This song rhymes in Arabic.)

The bakery was an amazing sight to see. Small, dry pita breads were baked at such a high temperature that they puffed open into elliptically-shaped balls. These semi-orbs were stacked from the dusty floor to the ceiling along the wall, near the register. Flies, abundant in the city, would land on the counters, the bread, or even the workers with no fear for their lives.

My mother and I would select the cleanest loaves we could find, an adventure in itself. Taking them home, we would wash them in hot water sanitized with a drop or two of detergent. Though it seems crazy to look back on it, this would not only make the pita clean but also soften the brittle bread.

In addition to our city shopping, every couple of weeks my mother and I would walk into the villages near the Academy to purchase milk. Along the way we would usually pass women carrying large jugs of water, balanced precariously on their heads, as well as the long, dense bones of a camel, left behind after a slaughter for food.

"That would make a delicious meal," I would joke, sarcastically.

"Yuck," mother would wrinkle her nose in disgust as we scurried through the alleyways, away from the massive carcass.

We would arrive at the tent of a family that owned a buffalo. No cow's milk for us! And no chance of purchasing pasteurized or refrigerated milk in a carton or even in a glass bottle. Instead, the man would take the container which we would bring with us and pour the rich creamy buffalo milk into it from the spigot of a wooden barrel.

Occasionally, as roosters and chickens would run in and out of the tented room around us, a generous woman would offer us a drink to quench our thirst after our long trek. She would pour water from a tall clay pitcher sitting in the corner of their small, arid room. You only needed to taste this sweet, cool water once to know that it was worth its weight in gold. "How do they keep it so cold in this hot village?" my mother would wonder every time we enjoyed it. Somehow, the earthenware jug kept the water freshly chilled.

Once we took the buffalo milk home, the first thing we would do was to boil it, then let it cool in the refrigerator. It would take about a day to cool. By the time that happened, the milk had separated and the rich, heavy cream had solidified, floating on the top of the jar. This dense, flavorful cream was the perfect ingredient for my mother's desserts.

Careful not to leave even a drop of the thick emulsion in the jar, my mother would whip the cream together with sugar, eggs, and flour creating one of her tempting pastries. The sweet dough was filled with various indigenous fruits such as dates or guavas. The aroma of the sweets wafted through the whole dormitory as they baked. Other staff members loved coming to visit our small apartment whenever my mother had baked treats. Soon we noticed a growing pattern of visitors the week following our buffalo milk shopping days.

EXPECTING

One morning I entered the cafeteria to supervise the boys at breakfast. As the fragrant smells drifted toward me from the kitchen, a wave of nausea almost knocked me over. Lotfy was concerned as were the other teachers on campus. They insisted that I seek medical help. A smelly, rattling bus trip to the doctor confirmed my suspicions: I was pregnant.

For three months, I was plagued with nausea. Unfortunately, my morning sickness was triggered every time I entered the cafeteria where I was required to work. Even my favorite food, the sweet, fragrant guava which grew in an orchard on campus would make my stomach churn. Unable to keep most foods down, I ate only boiled potatoes or plain yogurt through that entire first trimester. Because I was fatigued from lack of nourishment, my duties as a music teacher also suffered.

SINGLE INCOME

Shortly after my morning sickness ended, I encountered another problem. I received a notice from the Board of Education that I was no longer permitted to work in Egypt. The Egyptian laws had changed and no foreigners would be allowed to earn an income if another citizen was available to do it.

With unemployment rates rising and the population rapidly increasing, it was easy to see why the government would make this law. Egypt had no shortage of available people to take my job. In fact, there were plenty of other teachers whose wives would have appreciated the added income.

Of course, I did not think the new law was fair at all, and the school was upset as well since they had spent time preparing and training me. Now the academy would have to train another teacher.

Lotfy had an excellent solution for our dilemma. "Let's go have you sworn in as a citizen," he said, eager to retain our dual income.

"No way," I exclaimed. I had already gone from calling myself a Russian to calling myself an Iranian. I did not need another citizenship, especially in a land where I could barely speak the language. Besides, we were not happy in Egypt. Lotfy was continually arguing with me and with Dr. Lescher, the headmaster. There was nothing that could convince me to change my mind.

My decision did not please Lotfy and he became irate. He had gotten used to having both salaries. Though my job was only part-time, we would now have to make some adjustments in order to maintain our lifestyle.

VISITING THE GRAPEVINES

Toward the beginning of my third trimester, I was suffering much less and had plenty of free time now that I could no longer work. However, my belly was beginning to look enormous protruding from my tiny frame. Though it was spring, the weather already felt unbearably hot and our second story apartment was like an oven. "Why don't we go down to the vineyards?" I suggested to my mom one afternoon.

The grapevines climbed a trellis just outside of the boys' dorm. In season they yielded sweet, juicy grapes, just enough to feed the staff and students for a few meals. At that time of year, there were no grapes yet, but the shade provided by the fruitless vines offered a brief interruption from the stifling heat.

Awkwardly, I slid to the ground beneath the trellis and closed my eyes to enjoy the cool shadows. I then rested my head against a sturdy vine.

"How are you feeling, Rayichka?" My mother's voice was soothing as she sat beside me on the sand beneath the vines.

"Much better these days," I replied, though I was still wiggling to settle in. "I never thought I'd feel comfortable again."

She looked at my swollen belly and laughed. "Enjoy it while you can," she suggested. "You will soon be so heavy and round that you won't be able to eat or sleep or even breathe from the discomfort!"

I squirmed slightly to adjust my skirt, noticing a prickly sensation where my leg rested on the sand. I could almost imagine the pressure of the baby's weight causing me pain. In fact, leaning down to scratch my other leg, I realized that I was already uncomfortable. I squirmed again.

"Are you sure you're OK?" My mother was laughing at me as I wiggled and scratched at my legs and waist. Her laughter stopped abruptly as I lifted the hem of my dress to find out what was bothering me. My legs were completely covered with tiny sand fleas, so thick that it looked as if I was wearing pants.

"Raya, you're covered in fleas!" My mother was always good at pointing out the obvious.

"What should I do? What should I do?" I asked, struggling to stand while my enormous stomach pinned me down.

My mother scrambled to her feet and hoisted me up. "Run upstairs to the shower," she commanded. I am not really sure how anyone would expect a short, heavily pregnant woman, covered in fleas from the waist down to run, but my mother had faith in me.

I waddled toward the door and pulled myself up the two flights of stairs to my apartment. My mother was close behind me. As I tried to undress, she stopped me. "Just get in with your clothes on," she instructed. "If you try to take your dress off, the fleas will go all over you and all over the house."

I stepped into the shower and turned on the water. Standing fully clothed and soaking wet, I watched in amazement as a blanket of the black insects washed onto the tiles beneath me.

I itched for over a week from those bites and had large red welts covering my legs. After that day, no matter how hot the apartment seemed, my mother and I never felt the urge to visit the grapevines again.

BABY SHOWER

Two weeks before the baby's due date, we made a temporary move. Since travel through Egypt was so tedious and time consuming, it would have been too great a risk for me to stay so far away from the hospital. Instead, following the instructions of my doctor, we would spend our remaining fortnight in the guest house that our church conference owned in Heliopolis. This way, we would be nearer to medical care once the contractions started.

My mother, Lotfy, and I climbed onto a stinky, overcrowded bus and headed for the city. Since it was already the beginning of July, most of the boys had returned to their homes for the summer. The few who remained were left under the care of the assistant dean.

Lotfy came and went during these two weeks, working for a few days and then spending a couple of days with us. Most of the time my mother and I were alone, but we would fill the void by shopping or visiting friends around the city.

Mrs. Lescher, the wife of the Nile Union Academy Principal, took advantage of the occasion to host a small baby shower. This was a new concept for me since babies in Iran were usually given gifts of flowers or jewelry by visitors, and that was *after* the birth. Even in Cairo, this practice was so unique that only the American women attended.

I loved the idea of having a layette provided for me. I was even more thrilled when the other conference wives arrived bearing gifts that they had purchased in the United States. Imagine, my baby would be wearing tiny, precious clothes from America! My mother examined the details of the sewing and fabric carefully with her well-trained eye. The gifts of soft cloth diapers, undershirts, and nightgowns were so small that I wondered if the child would even fit into them.

My mother had many ideas for the tiny outfits she planned to make once the baby was born. Russian superstition and a general sense of impending doom meant these garments could not be prepared ahead of time in case of some misfortune to the unborn child.

Toward the very end of the pregnancy, Lotfy and I missed each other so much that he decided to spend the last few days in the city, by my side.

The baby was reluctant to leave the comfort of my womb. My mother was gripped with fear as she listened to my cries and watched my agony. "Please, deliver baby quickly," she begged the doctor in her broken English, then repeated her requests to induce me in Farsi, Russian, and even in Turkish, hoping that somehow this woman would understand and save her daughter from what she was sure would be certain death.

"Your daughter will be fine," my doctor replied patiently in her strong Greek accent, trying to sooth my mother's worry.

In between the jarring contractions and waves of exhaustion, I would try to quiet my mother's fears, assuring her that my doctor was excellent. Though female doctors were the norm in Egypt, where most of the women were conservative Muslims and unwilling to be seen by a man, I was surprised and pleased to find the Greek doctor. I had immediately felt confident in her capabilities when I had met her nine months before.

Still, my mother's worries could not be pacified. She was certain that her daughter's life would end in this primitive, third-world country. Fearful that she would be left alone and unable to communicate with anyone, my mother continued to plead with the doctor in every language that she knew.

On July 13, 1961, after twenty-eight hours of suffering from labor pain, our sweet little girl, Ella, finally came into this world. We chose her name as a tribute to my precious friend Ella May Robinson, the mother of Gladys

Kubrock, who, with her husband Daniel, introduced me to Christianity. When at last I had a chance to rest after the difficult night, the nurse brought my baby to me. "What a very good baby," the nurse praised me. "She is so sweet and she never cries."

I peered into the blanket where my sleeping child lay swaddled in my arms. Alarmed, I noticed that my baby's head was unusually narrow and long. By the time my doctor came to check up on us, I was in tears.

"Something is wrong with my baby," I cried out, pointing to the child's distorted head. "And that is not all! She doesn't even know how to cry! The nurse told me she didn't cry for them, and the baby hasn't cried for me either!"

"Hmm, you're right! A baby who can't cry would be very unusual," the doctor replied with a mildly sarcastic tone. Then, reaching under Ella's blanket, she gave the baby a quick pinch before I could object or even knew what was happening. My baby let out a scream. "See? She's perfectly normal," my doctor reassured me, shouting now, to be heard above the baby's wailing. "And as for the head, don't worry. After few days it will look just like you would expect it to—round!"

Later, alone with my child, I admired all her perfect fingers and toes. Everything added up, everything seemed intact. Ella had thick, straight, black hair and beautiful, big, black eyes.

Lotfy and I thought she was a darling little gift from God. My mother, who had never had the opportunity to be a grandparent to my brother Abraham's children, adored her precious new granddaughter. Ella was certainly received with joy and love by all.

As soon as my mother returned to our apartment, she could start on her happiest tailoring task. She adorned her granddaughter with exquisite little dresses and coats, handmade and finely detailed with love.

By the time Ella was eight months old, we received a call from the Iran Mission of Seventh-day Adventists. President Oster wanted to inform me that they needed teachers for elementary school in Tehran. I was thrilled since Lotfy had been pressing me to obtain my Egyptian nationality and resume working.

I applied to teach at the Mission school in Tehran and was accepted immediately. Without delay, Ella, my mother, and I left for Iran. Lotfy continued teaching in Egypt until the Nile Union Academy had their next summer vacation and he could join us. As we headed back to the country that had welcomed me as a young adult, a new chapter in our lives started.

Figure 18 - Nile Union Academy in Egypt; Ella; Raya with Lotfy, Ella, and Leila

PART IV: IRAN, 1962–1967

BACK TO TEHRAN

"... He is a shield to those who put their trust in Him." Proverbs 30:5

Our new apartment in Tehran was on the fourth floor of a small, squat building. It was perfect for us, with its two bedrooms and little kitchenette. The best part was the rooftop that we were able to use as a patio. Laundry was hung to dry there, and mealtimes could be enjoyed under the moonlight on warm summer evenings.

Although I missed my larger apartment in Egypt, I was glad to be near my relatives and friends. We spent every holiday and special occasion with my Auntie Sara's family and other cousins, sometimes in my tiny apartment or at the much grander homes of my family. It was a treasure to reconnect with everyone once again.

While I worked as an elementary school teacher, my mother was very busy at home. From the time that Ella could sit up, my mother was training her to sit on the potty. On the day of my daughter's first birthday, we took off her diaper for the very last time. From that day forward, Ella was potty-trained.

After the school year ended, Lotfy joined us at the Iran Mission. He was employed on probation under the condition that he learn the Persian language. This task proved to be very easy for him. As an Arabic speaking person, he quickly realized that the majority of the Persian vocabulary is made up of Arabic words. Usually, the main difference was a slight modification of the pronunciation. Within six months, Lotfy had mastered Farsi and was employed full-time by the Iran Mission.

In September of 1962, with the school year underway, our apartment building began to shudder with a sudden jolt and dishes crashed to the floor from the kitchen shelves. I jumped up, thinking something had hit the side of our building. Running to the window, I was amazed at the flood of people rushing out of their houses and swarming into streets.

Quickly, my mother reached over to turn on the radio, hoping for some report of what had happened. The news reporter was urging people to leave their homes immediately. Tehran was under a mandatory evacuation notice due to a massive earthquake.

Lotfy and I looked at each other in dismay. My mother's pinched nerve had been misdiagnosed by the Persian medical doctors as arthritis which had disabled her. She was unable to manage the walk on her own and was in constant pain.

"I cannot possibly carry your mother down the stairs," he confided in me. "She's too heavy."

"What should we do?" I wondered out loud. "We can't just leave her!"

"We have no choice but to stay here," he decided. "Even if we managed to get out of the apartment, we don't have a car to carry us away from Tehran. We would never make it on foot with a small baby and a disabled woman."

Throughout that day, with the streets abandoned, my mother, my husband and I stayed in our apartment. We had no idea how we would survive. We hoped that the majority of the damage had been done, and that we would remain safe in our home.

With no other possibility for help, we turned to our faith to get us through safely. We prayed continuously that God would work a miracle for us.

Every time there was an aftershock, we braced ourselves for possible destruction. The view from our apartment window was terrifying at these moments. The whole building seemed to rock and sway as each new tremor seemed stronger than the last one. Finally, the earth stood still. One by one, people began returning to the city to assess the damage in their homes. With our nightmare behind us, we could breathe a prayer of thankfulness to our God who carried us to safety.

SHEMRAN, 1963

After two years in Tehran, Lotfy and I were invited by the General Seventh-day Adventist Conference to move to the Iran Training Academy in Shemran. This suburb of Tehran had tall walls guarding the residences of political figures. The area was so renowned that even the Shah of Iran had his summer palace there. The school grounds were like a park with the property bordered by a cherry grove and vegetable gardens. Scattered around the property were the small homes of other faculty. Lotfy would be working as a math teacher in the high school, while I taught the overseas missionary children.

Those were the best years for us. Lotfy was happy in his work, and our employers were pleased with him as well. In the past, he had been harsh and impatient. But now, even Lotfy's overbearing behavior had softened. I wasn't sure if it was because he was no longer in his own country, and so thought it best to be careful, or if it was due to his job contentment.

Either way, we settled into one of the teachers' apartments with a beautiful courtyard surrounded by gardens. It was tastefully but simply furnished with a large kitchen, so my husband had no need to put his carpentry skills to work.

Across the courtyard from our apartment lived my former teachers, the Osters. My friendship with Mrs. Oster was so different from the one I had with Mrs. Kubrock. Where the Kubrocks filled our time with stories, songs and laughter, Mrs. Oster was all business. Somehow all our conversations centered on class work, students, and the music lessons she taught.

FOUR SEASONS, 1964

During our first spring in Shemran, Ella walked out of our house and exclaimed, "Mommy, Mommy, it snowed!" Surprised, I looked up to see that the whole cherry orchard behind our house was bursting in blossoms. Ella's little two-year-old mind associated the white flowers with snow.

By the time Ella was three years old, my dear mother's health was getting worse and worse. Her osteoporosis had completely paralyzed her. Though our lives had been comfortable, we were still in a third-world country and medical care was not advanced enough to help her. We were told that her condition was incurable, and shortly thereafter, my mother, Leila, passed away very peacefully in her sleep. She was only 56 years old.

I had gone into her room to wake her for breakfast but found that my mother could not be awakened. I called my husband, and he rushed to my side. Lotfy came in to find me sobbing over her body. He grieved with me also. My mother had been the only mother Lotfy had ever known. Quietly, we covered her head and, composing ourselves, closed the door to her room. I did not want Ella to walk in and find her grandmother's body.

I quickly called my cousins in Tehran; Adeleh came to help me. By this time she had married Dr. Hushang Dowlatshai and had a child of her own. Ella was so thrilled to have her cousin Haleh to play with that she did not even notice the flurry of activity in our home—nor her grandmother's absence.

But Ella had been very close to her grandmother, and now Lotfy and I were faced with the difficult decision of what to tell the child. As the days passed, Ella began to ask where her *babushka* was. "She is resting," we would say, hoping to quiet her questions.

However, Ella was not satisfied with that answer. Running into her grandmother's empty room she persisted, "Where is my *babushka*?" Her desperate questions would break my heart each time. I knew my little girl would miss my mother as much as I would. Still, we found it difficult to discuss the issue of death with our young child. Eventually, her mind was filled with other people and activities, and Ella stopped asking.

As she had requested, we buried my mother in a Christian cemetery. In later years, the Shah of Iran was dethroned and exiled to Egypt. The new ruler Ayatollah Khomeini turned that same cemetery into a park, plowing over the bodies resting there. Sadly, we do not know where my dear mother's bones are now, but I look forward to the day when The Lord comes to take us home. I know He will find my mother and many others whose bodies were lost in different wars, disasters, and even the concentration camps as my father's was.

DRIVER'S ED

By 1964 Lotfy bought a small Volkswagen Beetle to make the commute into town easier. Since I was busy caring for our home as well as a young child, Lotfy ran most of the errands and drove me anywhere that was necessary. When I finally decided to take a turn behind the wheel, it was my husband who taught me.

Standing by the road, Lotfy would wave me into a parking space as I nervously watched him through the rear view mirror. "What are you doing?" he would holler at me. "You can't drive while you're looking at your own face!"

I tried again, this time with him beside me as we drove down the narrow country lanes. "Watch out! Watch out! Watch out!" he yelled anxiously as I neared an approaching car. I realized that I would have to endure the stress if I was going to learn to drive.

Finally, Lotfy deemed me ready to take my driver's test. Once I passed, I noticed how much more enjoyable driving was without my instructor beside me. At last, I had my freedom.

Unfortunately, my freedom was surrounded by four tires, a windshield and a metal frame. I quickly learned that tires pop, windows crack and metal bends and dings whenever they are hit. Driving was not my forte.

The streets of Iran have deep drainage ditches running alongside them. On rainy or snowy days, I would find myself skidding across the road and landing nose first in one of those ditches. I would climb out of my vehicle and flag down a passing motorist. Soon two or three men would come by and pull my tiny car out of its imprisonment and I would be safely back on the road, at least until the next severe weather day.

Whenever I arrived home with a scratch on my bumper or a dent in the door, Lotfy would fume about my lack of consideration for the nice things he bought us. My unwillingness to counter his attacks only seemed to increase his rage.

Lotfy would often stand by the front of the house while I was preparing to leave for the day and call to me, "*Yallah!* Let's go!" This phrase greatly irritated Mrs. Oster who complained that he was taking the name of the Lord in vain. *Allah* is the Arabic and Farsi word for *God* and it is very similar to the Arabic word for "let's go." This was the only objection she had concerning him, but soon other complaints arose.

Whenever some of the high school students did not obey Lotfy, he would resort to corporal punishment. Our students came from very wealthy and influential homes in Tehran and Shemran. Although hitting the students proved effective, it also angered the parents to learn their children were receiving such harsh punishments. Soon, the school board requested that the Mission president send them another teacher to replace Lotfy.

Fortunately, the Iran Mission Church needed to replace their pastor. Since Lotfy had double majored in secondary education and theology, he was also qualified to be a church pastor. He got the job and we moved back to Tehran where I was able to teach in the Mission School.

ESTHER'S BIRTH

Several exciting events were happening in our family in the mid-60s. First, Abraham had been selected as the jeweler who would create the golden key to Rasht. This was a great honor for my brother because he was invited to meet the shah and to give him the key when he visited that city after his coronation ceremonies. Mohammad Reza Shah Pahlavi became the shah of Iran in 1941, but in 1967, he crowned himself as "King of the Kings" (emperor of Iran).

Secondly, my sweet Uncle Habib received a tribute of his own during the same time period when he was commissioned to sculpt the twin lions that would guard the entrance to the shah's palace near the Caspian Sea.

We were all very happy and proud of their accomplishments, but the most exciting news for me came when we found out that our tiny family would finally be growing.

My precious Ella had started complaining that all the children in our church had brothers and sisters and she had neither. Every day she began to pray for a brother. As a five-year-old child, she didn't understand that her father and I had been trying for several years to conceive. I had gone to doctors in Egypt, but no one could give me an answer about my infertility. Busy with a young child, sick mother, and full-time work, I had abandoned any hopes for more children. However, my daughter's prayers and pleading prompted me to look into the problem once again.

In Tehran, I visited a new gynecologist who had been trained in the United States. He recommended a procedure I had never heard of before, a D&C to clean out my uterus. I consented and, once I had this procedure done, immediately became pregnant.

As the school year progressed, my stomach grew bigger and bigger. Every day the students would race home to tell their mothers how fat their teacher was getting. When parents came to get their children's report cards on the last day of school, every one of them understood why my weight gain had been so noticeable to their kids.

"When is your baby due?" they asked me countless times. Every time I answered, "Tomorrow," surprise would register on their faces. Everyone wanted to know what we were hoping for and I told them that Ella had been praying for a brother.

Sure enough, the next morning, June 16, 1967, I started having contractions at eight o'clock in the morning. Lotfy had already left to go mountain climbing with our friend Dr. Kayvan and several of her friends. Anxiously, I paced the floor of my apartment between contractions, worried that my husband would not make it back in time. With no cell phones and very limited forms of communication at that time, I had no way to contact him.

As the pain started recurring at closer and closer intervals, I knew I couldn't wait any longer. I called my neighbor and asked her to take me to the hospital.

After my mother had died, my Auntie Zina had come to help me with Ella. Before I left for the hospital, I went and found my child playing in her room. "Baby is knocking!" I told Ella, placing her hand on my belly to feel the kicks following an intense contraction. Her large black eyes widened. "It's time for the baby to arrive," I explained.

Ella jumped up and started dancing with anticipation. "Baby's coming! Baby's coming!" She exclaimed, hopping around me.

My aunt came running into the room to find out what the commotion was about. "Baby is on the way. I'm leaving for the hospital," I explained to her in Farsi.

As Ella settled down from her excitement, she looked at me soberly. "Mommy, I don't want a baby brother," she said.

"Why, Ella?" I asked, surprised at her sudden change of heart.

"A brother will go and play with all the boys and I will be alone again," she reasoned. "I want a baby sister."

I told her that Jesus will give us whatever will be the best for all of us. We had a quick prayer together and I was whisked away to the hospital.

I was relieved as soon as I saw my doctor. "I don't want to feel a thing," I reminded him. "Knock me out, do whatever you have to, but I am not going to endure another twenty-eight hours of heavy labor!"

"Don't worry, Raya," he patted my arm reassuringly as the anesthesiologist prepared to put me under. "You're going to be just fine."

The medication took effect and the room seemed to spin around my head. I did not feel another thing until I awoke after the birth.

"Congratulations, ma'am," the nurse was gently shaking me awake. "You have a beautiful baby girl."

"A girl?" I asked, still hazy from the medication. "Is she OK? When was she born?"

"She was born at ten," the nurse surprised me with her answer, "and her only problem is that she's hungry!"

Ten o'clock. Only two hours after I had first arrived at the hospital. I was amazed that the delivery had gone so easily.

I nursed the baby peacefully. A short time later, the room filled with sweaty, noisy men and women, just returning from their hike.

"Oh Raya," Dr. Kayvan exclaimed, "I can't believe we took Lotfy away on such an important day!"

"Of course, you can never be sure with these things," I told her, "but the doctor did say she was due today, and he was right!"

Lotfy picked up his second baby girl, carefully bracing her head with his arm. We named her Esther, after the historical Queen of Persia who saved her people, the Children of Israel, from being destroyed.

A FALL OFF THE LEDGE

Ella was very excited to have her baby sister come home. She seemed to believe that the new baby was a live doll for her to play with. As a result, Ella had a hard time keeping her hands off of our fragile infant.

Every time I would finally get the baby fed, diapered, and asleep in her room, Ella would come running to tell me that baby Esther just woke up. I could not understand why my child was not sleeping until I caught Ella nudging her slumbering sister awake.

Our home had a large shaded balcony with plenty of fresh air. A ledge, approximately three feet high, was built onto the apartment wall. It was there, just high enough to keep the baby out of Ella's reach, that we kept Esther's bassinette. The idea seemed perfect at first. The baby was able to rest for longer than ten minutes at a time, and I was finally able to do simple things such as shower and dress without being disturbed.

One afternoon, while I was working in my room and the baby was resting, I heard a loud crash. My aunt and I ran to the balcony to see what had happened. What we found nearly stopped our hearts. Ella was on the floor with the baby basket on top of her. A toppled, broken stool nearby was evidence of what had transpired. Ella had climbed up to take a peek at her sleeping sister and, reaching too high on the rickety stool, fell down. She had pulled the baby down with her.

Frightened, we checked the children over. Ella was badly shaken but otherwise unhurt. Baby Esther was still asleep, swaddled in her bassinette. How God protected my children that day completely amazed me for years to come.

Figure 19 - First Car in Iran, Abraham with Key to Rasht, Uncle Habib with Sculpture for Entrance to Caspian Sea

PART V: FORT BRAGG, NC, 1967–1970

A MOVE TO THE US

"... He who trusts in the Lord, mercy shall surround him." Psalms 32:10

Esther was two months old when one of our friends from Middle East College called us. He was now working at the Command Language School located on the Fort Bragg military base in North Carolina and wanted to let us know that there was an opening for Russian and Farsi teachers. Since Lotfy now spoke Farsi fluently, there were positions available for both of us, if we were interested. Who would refuse such an opportunity? Everyone living in the Middle East believed in the American Dream. The chance to move to the United States was an enormous privilege.

So on August 18, 1967, we packed up four suitcases, leaving behind most of our worldly belongings. Ella carried only one toy, her favorite stuffed monkey named Zip that I had ordered through the Sears catalog when we lived in Tehran. I carried Esther in her bassinet and we boarded a Lufthansa airplane in Tehran.

The flight would last many hours. Ella was fidgety and excited over the new experience. Her large black eyes watched everything so seriously, recording the memories in her sharp little brain. Questions poured out from her every time she noticed something new, while baby Esther slumbered peacefully throughout the entire trip.

At one point during the flight, Ella, who had been sleeping, woke up. She glanced around at her unfamiliar surroundings and I rubbed her sleepy head trying to soothe her back to sleep, but it did no good. She was wide awake now, suddenly back in tune with all the fascinating things going on around her.

Ella sat up and leaned toward the window beside her. "Mommy, look!" Surprise was evident on her sweet face as she pointed to the fluffy white clouds floating below our plane. "There's snow everywhere!"

"That's not snow, Ella," I tried to explain. "We are high above the clouds now." But Ella would not believe me. How could clouds, which always floated so high in the sky, suddenly be lower than she was? She watched suspiciously, waiting to prove me wrong as we soared swiftly to our new country.

We finally landed in New York City's John F. Kennedy Airport. Ella's fascination with the clouds was nothing compared with the sights and sounds which greeted us in this busy metropolis. Her first amusement came when she discovered the airport's automatic doors. She kept running back and forth across the sensor pad, watching the huge doors open and shut, bursting into giggles every time.

We were lucky that she was so easily occupied since immigration would take quite a long time for us. Even so, it was nothing compared to what many new immigrants go through these days. Our documentation was sufficient to grant us green cards and working permits as soon as we arrived.

After the legalities were taken care of, we boarded the smallest and most rickety little plane I'd ever seen to take us to North Carolina. Lotfy and I exchanged nervous glances. "I thought things are supposed to be *better* in America," I whispered to him. I had not flown much before arriving here, but I had never seen such a questionable form of transportation before. Somehow, the plane managed to carry us safely to Fort Bragg where we would begin our work as civil service workers for our new country.

LIFE DOWN SOUTH

For a while after arriving in North Carolina, we stayed with our college friends. Though this was convenient, Lotfy and I knew that we had to get out and find our own home. With an active six-year-old and an infant, we would quickly wear out our welcome.

We had been fortunate to set aside a comfortable savings during our work in Egypt and Iran. Every day after work and every weekend, we searched the neighborhoods around the military base, looking for the perfect piece of real estate. Finally, we found a tiny two-bedroom home close by in Fayetteville. We would live in that home for the next two years during our contract.

As if the excitement of being homeowners for the first time was not enough, we found that our neighbors were friendly and caring, the perfect example of southern hospitality. We came home from church on our first Sabbath to find an enormous welcome basket from an anonymous giver, a surprise that made us feel truly welcome.

Both Lotfy and I enjoyed teaching on base. The officers and enlisted men were eager to learn foreign languages. We always thought our command of the English language was excellent. Yet we found that we were truly challenged as we listened to our southern neighbors and students speak in their soft twang, so new for us. Over and over we would ask them to repeat themselves. Their deep drawl would become more pronounced and the volume of their voices would escalate as they tried to make themselves understood.

As the school year began, we registered Ella in the first grade of a public school not too far from where we worked. When she came home on her first day of school, I asked her the burning question that every mother has for her children, "How was your day, dear?"

"It was good," she answered.

"And how did you like your teacher?"

Ella responded, "She was good, but we did not see her."

"What?" I was shocked. I could not believe that American schools would allow their students to stay in a classroom without a teacher supervising! "Ella, what do you mean you did not see her?" I pried.

"We only saw her eyes and teeth," Ella said in her effort to describe her new teacher's dark skin. She had never seen an African American before, so her teacher was a whole new experience for her.

Ever since college, Lotfy and I had held positions within whatever church we attended. Always eager to participate, we usually conducted Pathfinder worship services, acted as treasurer, or taught study classes. After several weeks in our new church, though, we quickly noticed that no matter how much we offered to help, the nominating committee refused us.

Finally, Lotfy and I sat down with some of the board members and expressed our interest in serving the church. "I'm sorry," the Pastor explained, "We do think that you would be an asset to us. However, we are a conservative congregation."

"That's fine," Lotfy urged them. "We are conservative too!"

"But you see," the Pastor answered, "you are wearing jewelry." He stared pointedly at the wedding ring on my finger.

"This is just a symbol of our unity," I objected.

"But it is still jewelry," the Pastor was adamant.

Once home, Lotfy and I faced each other with the question that had been on our minds the whole drive. "Should we take off our rings?" I had worn mine continuously since we married eight years before. Yet I knew that my desire to help the church weighed more than my need for a golden representation of our marriage. Lotfy agreed. We removed our so-called jewelry and began our service to our new church.

ESTHER'S DEATH, 1967

The church was close to our home in Fayetteville. In order to keep the church service quiet, all the mothers would take turns watching the very young children in our Cradle Roll classroom. "Cradle Roll" is the age group of infant to toddler. Each family signed up for a different week to supervise the babies as they napped or played quietly. This way all the other parents had the chance to enjoy the service.

Before Esther was five months old, we began to take advantage of this service. One week, when it was not my turn to watch the children, I left Esther sleeping peacefully in the Cradle Roll room. I had laid her on the floor where I knew she would be safe should she wake up and decide to roll over.

After church, while we were talking to our friends in the foyer, Ella skipped over to the classroom to check on her little sister. When she got there, the lights were off and no other children were in the room. Fear gripped her as she searched the room for baby Esther. She soon discovered a fallen flower trellis in one corner. Our baby was pinned under it.

Frightened, Ella came running to us. "Mommy! Daddy!" She tugged my arms urgently. "Hurry, come quickly! Esther is hurt!" We rushed after our daughter into the Cradle Roll room.

Lotfy lifted the trellis and I sank down beside our infant, carefully scooping her into my arms. Her body was cold and her lips were blue. Hearing the commotion, people got word to the two physicians who attended our church. They came running to help.

Time seemed to stand still. One of the doctors tilted Esther's head back. "Her tongue is lodged in the back of her throat," he confided. "Airway obstruction," the other doctor concurred, quickly sticking his finger in the baby's mouth to clear her air passage. The two doctors worked furiously doing artificial resuscitation, but still she remained blue and limp. Meanwhile, all the church members who had stayed behind now circled around us, praying and pleading with God to bring life back to our child.

The doctors looked grim. "There's not much hope," they admitted as I sobbed beside my child's still form. We had no idea how long she had lain under that trellis before Ella found her. "There's a hospital two miles from here," one doctor suggested.

My husband picked up Esther and hurried her to the car, with Ella and me close behind. We rushed off, knowing that our church family stayed behind to keep praying, just as I was praying continuously in the car.

By the time we arrived at the emergency room, a startling thing had happened. Esther took a deep shuddering breath, pulling air into her previously still lungs.

After the strain and shock of finding her sister injured, Ella was now so excited to find Esther sitting up. She laughed and danced around the emergency room chanting, "My sister is all well! Jesus made my sister all well!"

Esther didn't understand what the excitement was about, but she loved to watch her older sibling acting so happy. When the doctor walked into the exam room, she was sitting on the examining table, cooing and laughing at Ella as if nothing had happened.

"What seems to be the problem?" The doctor looked puzzled as he glanced over her chart.

We explained our story to him, choking with the thought of the near death we had witnessed. "She was completely blue, and we don't know how long," I said, blinking back the tears. "I know she was dead."

The physician regarded me skeptically as he examined the child on my lap. "How did her mouth get scratched?" he demanded.

"It must have happened when the doctor pulled her tongue out of her throat," Lotfy answered.

"If all that you are telling me is true," the doctor still did not seem convinced, "we must do an EEG to make sure that she does not have brain damage."

"The Lord would not revive our child from the dead and then leave her with brain damage," I answered optimistically. Nevertheless, we agreed to all the tests he suggested.

An hour later, when the doctor returned to our small examining room, he confirmed that the test results were perfect as we had expected. We smiled, both with relief and satisfaction that our God had delivered her through this crisis, just as we had known He would.

DANNY'S BIRTH, 1969

During the second year of our work in America, I found out that I was pregnant yet again. All that school year, I continued teaching at Fort Bragg. If that had been my only responsibility, my life and my pregnancy would have been easy.

Struggling to chase after a busy toddler and play games or answer the many questions of a bright seven-year-old, I found myself exhausted most of the time. Still, I would return home from work only to find that I needed to cook the meals and clean the house for my family.

When my phone rang one afternoon, I was thrilled to take a break from my tiring day. It was my darling friend, Gladys Kubrock.

"How are you, Raya?" she asked me, tuned in to the weariness in my voice.

"I miss my mother," I answered truthfully. I didn't mean to complain to her, but I probably sounded like I was grumbling. Fatigue had been consuming me with this pregnancy.

"Raya," Gladys suggested, "Daniel, and I are going to be returning to the Iran Mission and my mother will be staying alone in the States. Why don't we send her to help you out?"

"Would she do that?" I couldn't believe my good fortune. To have another surrogate grandmother for my children would be wonderful.

And so it was settled. Ella Mae Robinson came to stay with us while I was in my sixth month of pregnancy. It was a joy to have her around again.

Ella Mae helped me so much with the children and the house work! Being a child of the depression, she was a very creative cook. Nothing was thrown away; even the vegetable skins and potato peelings were used to make broth.

Having grown up poor and hungry ourselves, Lotfy and I had a great appreciation and respect for our tiny, elderly friend. And as it turned out, God's timing in this situation could not have been more perfect.

Within one month of her arrival, I woke up from my sleep, drenched in the sweat and pain of a contraction. "The baby," I gasped, shaking my husband awake.

Bleary eyed, he stared at me in surprise. "What baby?" he asked rolling over and dozing off again.

"Baby is coming." I struggled to speak through the contractions.

"Too early," Lotfy mumbled sleepily. "Can't be the baby."

Even though it was true that the baby was not due for two more months, it seemed evident that he or she was not going to wait. And after the brief amount of time I spent in labor with my second child, I did not want to risk waiting to find out.

"Do you want to drive me to the hospital," I panted through my contractions, "or should I do it myself?"

This got his attention. Lotfy sat straight up in bed. "I'm coming, I'm coming," he was finally beginning to respond. I struggled to stand and waddled toward the door.

Nothing was packed. We were not prepared at all, yet we made the eventful phone call to my doctor and informed Mrs. Robinson that we were leaving. She also knew that something was wrong. "I'll be praying for you," she assured me, though I would have expected nothing less.

Normally, when something exciting is happening, people say "time seemed to stand still." But in our case, it seemed to flash by especially quickly. We barely had an instant from the moment we arrived at the emergency room until precious baby Daniel was born, named after my friend and teacher, Daniel Kubrock and Daniel in the Bible.

Our tiny infant was immediately attached to the life-saving cords and tubes of an incubator before I even had a chance to see him. The doctor had grim news for us. "I want to warn you that there is not much hope for your son," he said, facing me and my husband. The doctor went on to warn us that Daniel's skin was not fully developed, and his breathing was abnormally fast. I felt my stomach do a flip at the thought of losing my child.

Distraught at being away from him, I wrapped myself up in a hospital robe and made my way slowly and painfully down the corridor to the nursery. Daniel looked so weak and frail.

Surprisingly, our little son was not below the average birth weight. In fact, he was so large for my petite frame that I ended up with a double hernia from the seven months that I had carried him. I couldn't believe this was happening to him. I always mentioned being born prematurely as the excuse for my small stature and I felt so sorry to think that my baby boy had the same fate ahead of him *if* he even managed to live.

Once again, we turned to our Fayetteville church family to rally for us in prayer as another child's life was threatened. The doctor did not want us to get our hopes set too high. I was advised against breast feeding since it was expected that our new child would need to stay in the hospital for too long. Still, we continued to pray.

After only a week, a surprised doctor came into my room. "Daniel is stable now. It looks like he will be all right," our doctor said with amazement in his voice. "You should both be able to leave the hospital within a couple of weeks."

With God's help, we finally went home.

NEW JERSEY

At the end of our second year in Fort Bragg, we received a call to go to New Jersey. Lotfy and I would both be working for our church school again and we were happy for the opportunity. This was to be a very short period in our lives and one that we would strive to forget.

Barely two weeks after we moved there, Ella and Esther were sitting in the driveway, rolling a ball back and forth to each other. Danny was napping and I was working on the next day's lesson plans.

I could hear the girls giggling through the open window as I enjoyed the late autumn afternoon breeze. I would periodically look up smiling from my work to watch them. Ella was such a helpful and caring older sister. The ball bounced out of reach and Ella jumped up to grab it before it rolled into the street.

I then heard a car door slam, followed by an engine turning over. The sounds puzzled me since they were very near. I watched, paralyzed as the next scene unfolded before my eyes. Lotfy was backing our car down the driveway toward my precious toddler. Without her bigger sister beside her, Esther's small head was too low to be seen as he backed out, and she was too young to understand the grave danger she was in.

Frantically, Ella shouted and waved at her father to stop. Thinking she was waving goodbye, Lotfy smiled and waved back without stopping. The car rolled directly over my child's small body. Ella burst into tears, frightened for her sister's life. I suddenly realized I had a phrase running repeatedly through my mind. "Lord, save my child!"

Finally noticing Ella's distress, Lotfy stopped the car, but it was too late. We all rushed toward her helpless form and I scooped my limp child into my arms, still praying for a miracle.

The movement jarred her enough to make Esther gasp suddenly for the breath which had been knocked out of her. The bellowing wails that ensued were evidence that God most certainly had been watching over our child.

We were too shaken up to do more than rock our frightened toddler as we took turns kissing her and hugging each other with relief. A large bruise quickly formed on her head and Lotfy carried Esther into the house to put ice on it. Ella would not leave her sister's side for one second.

When we finally returned to Lotfy's abandoned car, we stared in wonderment at how closely the child had come to death. Rather than crushing her beneath the tires, his car had merely knocked her over as the wheels rolled past her on each side without even grazing her.

Our little miracle was the only way we seemed to sense God's presence in New Jersey. After leaving the generous hospitality of the South, our cool and unwelcoming new church was a shock to us. I had not felt so unwanted since I left my uncle's home many years before.

Lotfy and I had never before seemed at a loss for friendships until we joined this new community. It was evident that racism ran deep here; an Arab and a Russian are most unwanted in such a profoundly white neighborhood. In those days, the government did not require employers to follow equal opportunity guidelines. Even if it had, we were sure that the small church we found ourselves in would have worked around them. We knew we needed to make a move.

Figure 20 - Esther, Lotfy, Ella, Raya, and Danny; Ella and Esther; Esther

PART VI: THE BIG APPLE, 1970–1976

"... With God all things are possible" Matthew 19:26

Within months of arriving in New Jersey, Lotfy and I placed a request with the New York Conference and were immediately offered new positions in Yonkers. A small, two-room school had just lost their principal and Lotfy would take over that position as well as teach grades five through eight.

The younger students in grades one through four were currently being taught by a woman who was intending to return to her family in Trinidad. Until that time, I could substitute as needed and eventually take over the lower-grade classes.

It was January, 1970 when we arrived in New York. The snow was deep on the ground and Ella was excited to play in the drifts with her young siblings.

The school was in the basement of our local church, and some teachers rented the parsonage next door. We loved our new neighborhood and soon made friends with a young mother of two living across the street from us. She offered to babysit, providing an ideal situation for my work. During the day, I would be able to check up on Daniel if need be. Esther was already enrolled in a Catholic preschool nearby.

Our small school had no office and a tiny playground. It was situated on Broadway Avenue, a busy street. At recess time, weather permitting, we had to walk about a block to a nearby park where the students could exercise and release some energy. Otherwise the students could play in the church's attic or slide down the hill behind the school.

THE NEXT BABE RUTH

My first day of school did not come until that spring. I told my students that in other countries where I taught lower grades we used to play "Flying Dutchman," "Last Couple Out," and "Hide and Go Seek." "Which game would you like to play at recess tomorrow?" I asked them.

"Baseball! Baseball!" they chanted unanimously.

I had never even heard of baseball in any of the Middle Eastern countries where I had lived and taught. Still, I did not want to allude to the fact that I had no clue what the students were talking about.

"OK," I said. "Do you have all the equipment you need?" I figured this would reveal the nature of the game to me in case it was similar to something I had learned in the past.

"I have a bat!" one boy exclaimed. Immediately the image of a night-flying mammal popped into my mind and I could not imagine what type of sport they were talking about.

"I can bring the bases and home plate," another boy offered, confusing me even more. One girl offered to bring the ball and, to my surprise, several kids said they could bring mitts. I decided not to ask why oven mitts and plates would be required since I was already perplexed by the need for winged mammals.

"So, then it is decided?" I asked much more hesitantly than I had earlier when I thought *I* would be the one teaching *them* something new.

The students were very excited about the following day's recess. Meanwhile, I still did not know how to play this mysterious game.

That night after supper and family worship, I put my children to bed and told Lotfy that I needed to go to the library. The narrow streets were dimly lit as I drove to our nearby branch. Once there, the librarian pointed out the easiest books that would teach me how to play baseball. I sat late into the night studying, reviewing all the steps of the game. Occasionally I would close my eyes to picture the methods until everything was absolutely clear to me.

I wasn't very concerned once I understood the concept. We would need two teams, and my classroom had just enough students to fill the required positions. The next day, though, I realized that there was something I hadn't anticipated.

As lunch time approached, the students became more and more excited. We packed up our lunches and headed off to the park. One of the students was absent that day and along the way, I overheard a boy saying that the teacher could just take his place. "That's *me*," I thought. My heart started pounding in my chest as I mentally reviewed the steps I had learned the previous night.

A Bible verse came to mind. "Fear not, for I will be with you. I will never leave you nor forsake you."

"Even in baseball, Lord?" I wondered. Determined, I clung to that promise and somehow found the courage to accompany my students to the park.

As our two teams formed, I was the last batter in my group. I hoped that our team would be out before it came to my turn but no such luck. I held the bat the way I had practiced in my mind the night before and took a deep breath. As I watched the ball spin toward me in the air, I swung with all my might and felt the ball connect with the bat. I threw the bat down and ran as fast as I could to first base.

I didn't bother looking up as I ran to the next base and then to another. When I reached home plate, my whole class erupted into screams and cheers. "At last we have a teacher who can play baseball!" they chorused excitedly.

On the way back to school, I asked my students why they were so excited about my homerun. "We never had a teacher who would play baseball with us," the kids replied. One girl explained that before Lotfy and I came to their school, the upper-grade teacher/principal was a Frenchman and the lower-grade teacher was from Trinidad. Neither of them would participate at recess.

I recalled the first thing I had read in the encyclopedia under the heading: "Baseball is considered the all-American sport." I pointed out that each one of us had come from countries where baseball is never played.

"But you hit a home run," the students defended. They could not believe that I had never played the game before that day.

It is amazing how our brains work. I told the children that it is never too late to learn new skills. "If you have the desire, plus the perseverance, you can accomplish anything," I said. "And remember, the Bible tells us that with God all things are possible."

Recess times remained a joyous time for the students. And the neighbors whose homes surrounded the park often commented on how well-behaved our classes were.

A LANGUAGE LESSON FOR TEACHER

One afternoon, I received a phone call from the mother of one of my students. "Raya," she implored, "please let me know whenever Georgie uses bad language. We do not want that behavior to go unpunished." Georgie was a high-spirited boy in my class and his sister, Maria, was an upper-grader in Lotfy's class.

"Oh, Georgie is such a good boy," I defended. "He never uses bad language!"

"But Maria told us that she has heard him swearing in front of you during recess and you have never done anything about it."

I paused now, trying to recollect what she could have heard. "Maybe I just don't know the bad words," I admitted. After all, my English language classes had never taught me to swear!

"Why don't you tell me the words so I will recognize them next time," I suggested.

"I can't say those words," Georgie's conservative mother was shocked at my suggestion. "They are very bad!"

How would I be able to reprimand a child for swearing if I couldn't distinguish the language? "I know," I proposed. "You can just point them out to me in the dictionary."

"Raya, you won't find *these* words in the dictionary," she said.

It's amazing to me that *now* every form of slang and swear word actually *is* in the dictionary.

Finally, Georgie's mom decided to write the words down so I could be familiar with them when I heard Georgie swear. Armed with my new knowledge, we soon put that behavior to a stop.

SWING LOW, 1971

One afternoon, we stopped at a park for a picnic lunch on our way home. All of us were happy to get out of the car and stretch our legs. We happily devoured the meal I had packed before the children ran off to play on the swings and explore the garden.

"Push me, Mama," Danny begged.

"No, Danny," I told my two-year-old son. "You are too small to swing by yourself." Swing sets in those days did not have safety straps to keep young children on them. But Danny begged me to push him and I finally agreed. Danny giggled and squealed as I rocked him, barely making him move. He loved throwing his little arms up in the air, thinking it made him swing faster.

"Higher, Mommy, higher!" Danny commanded.

"No, Danny," I said firmly. "I want you to be safe."

"Peeese Mommy," he begged, "peeese higher!"

"Danny, I'm sorry, but you keep letting go and that's not safe," I explained. "I won't push you higher as long as you keep letting go."

But my little boy could not be appeased. "Peeese Mommy, peeese higher," he continued to plead with me.

"Danny," I thought my voice was stern as I finally agreed, "If you promise not to let go, I will push you higher."

"I pomise Mommy," he assured me as sincerely as a little boy could.

Against my better judgment I ignored the mischievous twinkle in his eye, grasped the chains tightly and instructed, "Now hold tight Danny. Don't let go." I pulled the swing toward me and released it, letting it arch just a bit more than it had before.

"Higher!" Danny shouted excitedly. Noticing that he had not let go this time, I pushed again, stronger this time.

"Wheee!" he cried out as the swing swept upward. Suddenly Danny forgot his promise. His little arms flew upward and I gasped, unable to reach him as the swing moved swiftly away from me.

Danny tumbled off the swing and I immediately ran to him. I picked up my crying child as Lotfy and the girls came running over to find out what the commotion was about.

"He said he wouldn't let go," I repeated over and over, nearly in tears myself as Danny's wails grew louder by the minute.

We loaded the children back into the car and Lotfy rushed us off to the hospital. Once there, we sat through x-rays and examinations until we learned the inevitable. "Your son has a fractured femur," the doctor told us. "He will need a cast for at least three months. Don't let him walk on it, and don't let it get wet. No tub baths, no showers, no swimming," he instructed us sternly.

I wondered how I was going to keep an active two-year-old child from walking on his cast for three months. It wasn't easy. Danny's favorite pastime was entertaining family guests and visitors with a silly boogie around the living room. Now that he had a clunky cast on his foot he relished the new, noisy dance that he loved to perform on the living room coffee table. He not only walked on the broken leg, he ran, hopped and danced on it, heedless of my warnings.

❖ ❖ ❖

After a month, Danny began to complain that his leg itched, but with a trip to the doctor we found out that this complaint was normal. We were sent away with no remedy for his discomfort. A few weeks later, my little boy began to complain more.

"It's hurting, Mommy," he fussed. His limping was more pronounced now. I wondered why he would suddenly have pain when he should be healing. We took another trip to the doctor.

"Well, it could be that the leg is growing too big for the cast," our doctor guessed. "Or it's possible that his leg has healed already. The best way to find out is to remove the cast and have another x-ray."

What we found was totally unexpected. In an attempt to soothe the itching he was enduring, Danny had stuffed every imaginable object between his skinny leg and the cast. Coins and dollar bills that he had pulled off his father's dresser, paperclips and pencils from our desk, and even pins that he had confiscated from my sewing kit fell out of the cast as the doctor sawed it open.

Realizing that Danny could not be contained any more than his leg could, the doctor decided that his femur had healed as much as it needed. The annoying cast could stay off.

LOTFY'S SCHOOL PROBLEMS, 1971

While I assumed that all my students were extraordinarily well behaved, Lotfy seemed to believe that his students needed stricter discipline. The sounds of constant yelling drifted from his classroom into mine. Several parents began to complain that Lotfy was striking the children's hands with a ruler whenever they had trouble learning a lesson.

At home, I begged him to remain calm in the classroom, fearful that we would both lose our jobs. Unfortunately, defending the students only resulted in having my husband turn his wrath toward me.

Shortly thereafter, Lotfy was asked to resign from our school. We felt fortunate that a local public school was looking for teachers at the same time. He was thankful to have a job.

LINCOLN TERRACE

Lotfy took our savings and purchased a home on a quiet, dead-end street that was backed up by woods and an old aqueduct leading to the Hudson River. He quickly put Ella to work helping him build a large deck in the backyard. I felt sorry for my child who was only ten years old. While her brother and sister were running and playing, she was laboring in the dirt, carrying heavy wooden beams back and forth with her father. Standing up for her only resulted in shouting fights between us, and Lotfy, believing that the complaints were coming from Ella, would only push her harder.

Shortly after we moved into our new neighborhood, I sent Ella and her siblings down the hill to the local market to buy a few groceries. Although it was just two blocks from our house, the neighborhood changed drastically in this area. Past our small, quiet street, the main road was full of activity with more commercial buildings and fewer homes.

The children set off down the street, money in hand, happy to walk together in the late autumn day. Taking a shortcut through the aqueduct, they resurfaced into the parking lot behind the store. Just then, three teen boys surrounded our children.

Looking Ella in the eye, the oldest one demanded, "Give us all your money!"

Though she was intimidated, Ella immediately replied, "No! I'm not giving you anything!"

Another boy stepped behind her and pulled something out of his pocket, jabbing it into Ella's ribs. "I've got a knife here, so you better do what he said," the boy threatened.

Ella rolled her eyes. "I saw you pull a comb out of your pocket," she answered a lot more coolly than she felt. "I'm not giving you anything." She grabbed her siblings protectively by the wrists, pulling them toward the heavily populated street. "I'll give you the change after I get the milk my mom needs," Ella called out over her shoulder as she ran into the store.

Once inside, Ella took her brother and sister directly to the store manager. Trembling from the encounter, she asked him to call her home. Hearing the story, Lotfy immediately drove the two blocks to retrieve our children. Thanks to Ella's quick thinking, they remained unharmed but badly frightened by the day's excitement.

LOST LOVEY

Our church had various programs for the children and the families. One activity was ingathering. Members would go door to door, collecting funds for third-world countries and disaster areas. It gave us a chance to go into our community and share information about our church with others. One such afternoon, as the parents and I were preparing to go ingathering, Ella and her friends came to find us.

"We want to go out alone, Mom," Ella implored. I knew that being ten years old, Ella was striving for more independence. I gave her permission as long as they promised to stay together.

A few minutes later, four-year-old Esther approached me, begging to be allowed to join her sister. Since Ella typically watched her siblings, I told her to go ahead but to be sure and listen to whatever her big sister told her.

Esther went off in the direction that the older girls had headed. I took Danny's hand and we headed off toward another area. Danny loved to collect money with me. He would stand as straight and tall as a three-year-old could, holding up the can for the neighbors to fill. As the coins would fall into his can, he would smile brightly, shaking it noisily until we approached the next home.

On this day, we stood at the first house and I recited our request for financial help.

"Oh, what a sweet little boy," a woman said, answering the door. This was a typical response, which was one of the reasons I enjoyed bringing the kids along with me. She stepped inside and returned with a few dollar bills which she stuck inside Danny's collection can. Giving it a quick shake my son only heard silence. He burst into tears, perplexing us both.

"Danny, what is the matter?" I asked, sinking to my knees in front of him.

"I want money!" he complained, loudly.

"But sweetie, she gave you money," I insisted, getting rather embarrassed in front of the lady.

"I want jingle-jingle money!" Danny shouted through his tears. The lady and I tried to explain that the money she gave was much better than noisy coins, but a three-year-old's mind does not change easily. I finally had to carry him off as I apologized profusely to the bemused neighbor.

Once we finished our collections for the day, we returned to the church to wait for the others to return. As the afternoon wore on, groups of people began to trickle in. The other deaconess and I busied ourselves with the task of counting our money. Soon, Ella and her friends came in with cans that were not quite as full as we had expected.

"Where's your sister?" I asked distractedly counting another pile of cash.

"What do you mean?" Ella sounded worried. "I told her to come back and stay with you!"

"When was that?" I was now worried too.

"I don't know," she said. "We didn't even get very far when I heard her calling and I told her go back with you."

"Why wouldn't you just take her with you, Ella?" I was surprised. Most of the neighbors were much more receptive when they answered the door and found a small child amongst the group of ingatherers.

Ella burst into tears. "We wanted to go to the park, but we were afraid that Esther would tell on us if she came," Ella sobbed. "So I sent her back and now she's lost!"

My stomach clenched and my heart pounded. My four-year-old daughter had been missing all afternoon and none of us knew it. Frantically, we asked each of the other parents if they had seen her, but no one had. In desperation I called the police.

My hands trembled as I dialed the number on the school's rotary phone. I could sense my fellow church members praying around me and my mind was racing through pleas of safety for my child. When the precinct answered the phone, I realized that my voice was quivering from fear. As calmly as I could, I told them that my child Esther was missing, describing her outfit and the time of day we believed she had gotten lost.

I held my breath, listening through the pounding in my head as I waited for his answer.

"I'm sorry, ma'am," the officer said. "I wish I could tell you that we have your daughter, but there is no little girl here by the name of Esther." Tears burned behind my eyelids. I was prepared to thank him and hang up, but my voice choked. "Strange thing, though," he continued, "another little girl who fits that same description was brought in. She can't be yours. She gave us a different name."

"Lovey!" I shouted into the phone. "Everyone calls her Lovey! That's her nickname!"

"Yes!" The officer sounded as pleased as I was. "You're right! She said her name is Lovey!" I took the address of the precinct and Lotfy and I sped off to pick her up.

Once there, we were met with another surprise. The experience of being away from her family all day should have frightened Esther, and we expected to find her weeping and inconsolable. Instead, she was skipping around the desks at the station, happily chatting the ears off of any officer who would smile her way. I called out to her and she came bounding toward me. The front of her dress was covered in ice cream, and chocolate was smeared across her face. She smacked away at chewing gum, another treat we did not often bestow on our kids, and I later found out that she had also enjoyed chips and soda that day.

But who could blame them? My child was happy and had felt safe from the moment they had gotten her. We sat down to exchange stories with the officer so that he could file his report. Lotfy and I were surprised to hear that it was not the police who had first found Esther wandering, lost on the streets. Rather, it was a drunk, elderly man and his wife. I hugged my child closer to me, realizing that something terrible could have happened to her that day.

Several days later our telephone rang. Lotfy was surprised to hear the slurred words of an older gentleman. "S'Lovey there?" he mumbled.

"Lovey is just a child. Who is this?" my husband wanted to know.

"I know 'oo she is. I'm th' man 'oo brought 'er to the police," he slurred.

"How did you get this number?" Lotfy demanded.

"I jus' called th' station an' told 'em who I am," he answered.

Lotfy stayed on the phone, talking to the man about the harmful effects of alcohol abuse and listening as the gentleman praised our little girl. He ended the call by thanking the man for taking care of Esther for us, and saying a prayer. For quite a long time after that day, we would receive a phone call periodically and have the same, slurred conversation with the man. We never told him not to call. Instead we hoped that our brief talks and prayers would eventually have a positive impact on the man's life.

BERRIEN SPRINGS, MICHIGAN

It was 1972. Lotfy and I decided to further our education. He would be studying for his master's degree during our summers off from work, while I took selected classes which the conference required for me to upgrade my current credentials. Since the conference paid for me to attend Andrews University in Berrien Springs, our lessons would be conducted there.

Each year, a couple of days before we were to check in at the school, Lotfy and I would pack up the car with anything we might need for the summer. Early in the morning before the sun had risen, we would coax Ella from her bed, then lift Danny and Esther up, piling the three sleepy children into the back seat of our family car. They would continue resting while the miles rolled on ahead of us.

When the children began to wake and the morning sun was shining brightly, I passed out sandwiches, cut fruit and drinks. Soon happy chattering and, yes, sometimes bickering, could be heard from the back seat of our car. Of course, we knew it was inevitable that one of the children would ask, "How many more minutes till we'll be there?" I would start some traveling songs or one of the car games, like "I Spy" or "The ABC Game" to pass the time. Eventually, we knew that we would hear it again: "Are we there yet?" After nine long hours we finally piled out onto the campus.

Most years we would stay in the dormitories with all of us crammed into two rooms separated by a bathroom. One year we stayed in an on-campus apartment that is usually reserved for married couples. That first summer our apartment was like a zoo of wild animals that Danny had "rescued" from the field outside our building.

During the day he would be on alert, squatting outside of a selected hole in the ground until a furry little head would pop up. Then, quick as a flash, he would bag the unwitting creature and bring it happily upstairs to show us. By the end of that summer term he had an impressive menagerie of frogs, field mice, and chipmunks, though when he brought up a field snake, I put my foot down and limited what type of animals were permitted to live with us.

The campus had plenty of amenities to keep the three children happily entertained while we were busy. A museum, playgrounds, and wooded areas, as well as other children whose parents were studying during the summer months, kept Danny, Esther and Ella content all term long. But then everyone's favorite activity was swimming.

The university boasted an indoor, Olympic-size pool that was used to train the swim team during the school year. My children loved the afternoons when I could escort them over to splash and play during the free swim period.

The first time we entered the pool, little Danny, only four years old, treaded water beside Esther and me, carefully watching all the activity. College students swam laps or dove off one of the two diving boards while families splashed happily in the open areas. Danny finally resolved himself to take action. "Mommy, I am going to jump off that board," he proclaimed, pointing to the high dive. From where we were positioned, that diving board towered over 12 feet above us.

"Oh no, Danny," I gasped. "You can't go up there, you can't even swim! You'll drown!" I knew that I would not be able to help him. I could barely doggy paddle from one end of a pool to the other. I always stayed safely in the shallow end where my feet were firmly grounded.

But Danny was adamant. "Don't be afraid, Mommy," he assured me as he climbed out of the pool and scampered toward the queue waiting to jump. "I won't drown."

"Oh please!" I called over one of the lifeguards, "Help my son! He has never swum before and he wants to jump off that tall diving board." The two of us watched his little, sun-bronzed body make its way to the far end of the big pool. The lifeguard walked toward him, assuring me that she would be on alert in case he needed her to intervene.

I held my breath and prayed. "Maybe the other divers won't let him on." But instead, they made room for the adorable little boy, allowing him to cut directly to the front of the line. He scaled the ladder effortlessly, then, barely pausing at the end of the board, stepped off. His body dropped to the water with a giant splash! I waited, still holding my breath until his little, brown head bobbed to the surface. Danny thrashed to the edge of the pool and hoisted himself out before I allowed myself to exhale.

Watching him run back, dripping wet, to the line at the diving board, the lifeguard smiled and shook her head. She squatted down beside the pool where I remained frozen, clinging to the edge and assured me, "I don't think he'll need my help today."

Danny spent the rest of that afternoon tirelessly queuing up near the diving board, jumping off and swimming back to the edge. He quickly made friends with the older kids who braved the deeper end of the pool.

Since Lotfy and I were locked in our classes most days, Ella was responsible for watching her younger brother and sister. Every afternoon, I would come back to the apartment where Ella would give me a rundown on all the misdeeds of "the babies." One day I came back to the apartment, surprised to find Esther alone and crying.

"Ella and Danny went to play with their friends and my friends all left," she sobbed. But being left alone was not the problem. Esther had quickly grown bored of playing on the swing set while she waited for everyone to return, so she started exploring other parts of the playground.

The merry-go-round made her dizzy, and the metal slide was too hot from sitting under the scorching sun all morning long. The wooden see-saw would have been perfect if only Esther had a partner to play with. Since she was alone, she decided to use that particular equipment as a slide. One trip down the wooden see-saw helped Esther understand why she had never seen anyone use a see-saw in that manner before. The pain in her bottom alerted her to the fact that something was not right.

Crying, Esther had staggered around the block several times, unsure of the direction to our apartment and growing more frantic with each passing moment. She had just barely found her way inside when I got back.

I walked my sobbing child across campus to the clinic. She was immediately put at ease by the nurse and doctor there. I was quite sure that my adventurous child liked having all this attention, though I didn't mention it aloud. By the time the visit was over, the campus doctor had pulled a fat splinter, nearly one inch long, from her bottom. Even if he hadn't given her a stern warning not to slide down the see-saw again, Esther wouldn't have. In fact, it took her nearly a week to sit anywhere comfortably again.

By the end of the summer session, one of the faculty had noticed Danny's intense interest in the animal kingdom. "We have a guinea pig and we won't be able to keep him any longer," she confided in me. "Do you think your son would like it?" She didn't have to ask twice. I negotiated with Danny to release all his captive field animals in exchange for a real live pet. Danny spent the last two weeks of our time there, happily loving on his new fat, furry friend.

One of our family traditions was to visit the site of the Seventh-day Adventist founder, Ellen White's estate in Battle Creek, Michigan. On this particular year, our schedule had been so busy that we were unable to manage the tour until the very last day. Lotfy was anxious to get on the road, so we had checked out of the apartment and the car was packed with all our belongings before we made our way to the estate.

Knowing that we had several perishable items in the car, Lotfy selected a parking spot sheltered by a tall willow tree. We all piled happily inside of the museum and wandered around for over one hour, asking the knowledgeable docent questions and listening to stories of what life must have been like a hundred years before.

When we finally emerged from our explorations, the sun had moved and the shade of the tree no longer protected our car. "Ugh, the car is going to be so hot now," I thought, dreading a nine-hour ride baking in the late summer heat. But a hot car ride and perishable food was the least of my worries. During our long visit to the Estate Museum, we had completely forgotten that Danny's precious guinea pig was inside. We found the little animal stiff, dead from the heat of the car. Lotfy buried the creature along the side of the road. We set off with Danny quietly mourning his lost pet.

BIRD ON A WIRE FENCE

While shopping one day, the children convinced me to take them into a pet store. We entered the shop, filled with the smell of cedar wood shavings and pet foods. Noisy birds chirped and puppies yipped while the kittens stretched in their cages. Danny and Ella bounced from one cage to another, reaching in to pet the hamsters and guinea pigs. But Esther was drawn to the birds. She would have happily stayed by their cages for hours if I had been willing to leave her. However, chores called us away and I dragged my adventurous child from the pet shop.

But Esther could not forget our trip to the pet store. Every day, she chatted blissfully about how wonderful it would be to own a birdie. I had very little interest in a pet, though. No matter how small, it would be one more mouth to feed, one more room to clean, and one more responsibility for my already busy life. "Why don't you pray for it," I suggested. "If Jesus wants you to have a bird, He will bring you one."

Shortly after our visit to the pet store, Esther was playing in the small kiddy pool we kept in our tiny back yard. I could hear her happily splashing and singing as she soaked. Suddenly, she cried out to me, "Mommy! Come quick!"

Alarmed, I raced through the house to the back of the apartment. I was immediately relieved to find that she was not hurt. "Look Mommy," she whispered. "Jesus sent a birdie to play with me!" I followed her pudgy finger to the place she was pointing and sure enough, a small, green parakeet sat perched on the wire fence behind her.

Without another thought about the trouble of pet ownership, I stepped cautiously, attempting to be stealthy as I approached the bird. As soon as he noticed my movement, he flew to a nearby branch, just outside of our reach. Little Esther was heartbroken. She was sure that her God-sent bird was gone forever.

"Esther, you prayed for a bird once and Jesus sent it to our yard, why don't you pray again," I suggested. So my little girl knelt, dripping wet in her kiddy pool, and requested that Jesus help us catch the parakeet. Opening our eyes, we watched in amazement as the small green form fluttered back down to our fence. I knew the pressure was on for me to perform.

Breathing a silent prayer, I once again moved as quietly and slowly as my nerves would allow. Minutes passed as Esther squirmed with anticipation in her small pool. I stepped closer still to the tiny, green bird. He seemed to tilt his head and regard me questioningly, but he didn't move. When I knew I was close enough, I stretched my hands at an achingly deliberate speed. Still the bird did not move. Finally, I cupped both of my hands swiftly but gently around his small form.

Jumping up from her pool, Esther squealed with delight. "You got him, Mommy! You caught the birdie that Jesus sent me!" Inside my cupped hands I could feel the bird's small heart beating rapidly as he squirmed trying to get away.

Quickly, Esther and I ran into the house. Though I was mindful of the water she was dripping everywhere, I knew there was no time to worry about it. I instructed her to open a hat box in my bedroom closet and I gently placed the bird inside, shutting the lid as fast as I could before he flew away.

We punched some holes into the lid of the box so Esther's bird could get sufficient oxygen and went in search of a birdcage and food. I remembered one of our church families telling me that they had an empty cage which they no longer needed. I was as happy to relieve them of the habitat as they were to give it to me, but no one was more pleased than Esther.

Later on, one of our friends gave Ella a yellow parakeet. Ella was thrilled to have a companion for Esther's bird. The two got along well when they were caged. They were tame enough for us to let them fly around the house.

Often, when Ella or Lotfy were sitting still enough, one or both of the birds would perch on their shoulders or head. This would make Esther and Danny giggle and plead for us to put the birds on their own heads, but the younger children would wiggle and squirm with excitement and were never still enough for the parakeets to stay with them.

On cleaning day, I would confine the birds to their cage knowing that we would be in and out of the door often. Still, Danny could not stay away from his small, chirping friends. It was a chore for me to keep him from letting them loose around the house.

Because of this, I found it prudent to get as much done as possible while he was outside playing. On one such day, I had the doors open wide as I was shaking off some area rugs in the back patio. I did not hear Danny enter the front door. As was his custom, he went directly to the cage and freed the birds so they could fly around the house.

When I returned indoors, I was surprised to be greeted by a fluttering of bright green and yellow wings. I rushed to close the door in time, but Esther's little parakeet flew out of the front door before I could reach it.

Poor little girl. Esther grieved for her lost bird, unable to understand why it would leave her. I finally told her that maybe God sent her pet to answer another child's prayer, just as he had answered her own. This seemed to make her feel a little better, though she still missed her parakeet.

One afternoon, Danny came home with a kitten wrapped around his neck. "Mommy, can we keep him?" he begged.

I looked at the adorable, playful feline and knew that our home could not contain both a cat and a bird. "I'm sorry, Danny," I said honestly. "We already have a parakeet here. A cat might eat the bird."

"But Mommy," he negotiated, "this isn't a *cat*, it's only a *kitten*!"

"Danny," I laughed, "kittens grow up to be cats and it wouldn't be safe." But Danny begged relentlessly. I finally convinced myself that by growing up with birds around, the kitten would only think of the parakeet as another member of the family, not as a meal. Besides, it only seemed fair that Danny have a pet, since Esther and Ella each had one in the past.

Unfortunately, I couldn't convince the kitten that he belonged to the same family as Ella's bird. We came home one afternoon and found feathers and bones scattered around the cage and kitchen table but no parakeet. Danny refused to believe that his pet could do anything as dishonorable as eat another living, breathing being, so he went through the house, calling for the bird to come out of hiding. But soon even he had to admit that Ella's bird was really gone.

READY TO MOVE AGAIN

Two school years had passed and Lotfy's attitude of gratitude for his job at the local school in Yonkers seemed to diminish. During that time, we had stopped attending our local church. Too many bad feelings remained between Lotfy and several of the parents. Instead, we drove twenty miles through traffic to another church in the Bronx. Finding parking in the city streets was a chore, and Lotfy would circle the block over and over. By the time we would arrive, one of the three children would be nauseous, which

Lotfy blamed on my breakfast and I blamed on his driving. Danny and Esther loved having this excuse to sip on a Coke, a treat that was normally excluded from our diets.

I tried to make the journey a happy one, singing songs with the children and playing car games on the way. But Sabbath mornings soon became another source of stress for our family. The children missed their friends in the Yonkers church, though they were able to make more. And all of us hated driving so far each week. Only Lotfy insisted on attending those services.

Finally, one day in 1973, Lotfy announced that we were returning to the Iran Mission. He had been told of an opening there and, remembering only the good times from those years, had reported to the conference that we would take the position. My heart sank. Although I had enjoyed my time in the Middle East, we were settled into our new life in America and I did not look forward to taking that step backward. Ella had already adjusted to living in New York, and it was the only home that Esther or Danny had ever known. "Not my will but yours, Lord," I prayed.

I knew that I had no say in the matter. Lotfy was not happy here in Yonkers and, as his wife, it was necessary for me to support his decision. Sadly, I resigned from my position in our small church and, as the school year came to a close, said a final farewell to my students and their families.

We packed up our belongings and prepared to leave our home. But before we left, we learned that the Middle East Conference had found out that Lotfy had been asked to resign from our school in New York and we soon received a notice that the position was filled by another candidate. We would not be moving back to Iran. I should have known that God had everything under his control.

Lotfy was able to get a job in a public school teaching English to the students who had come from the Middle East, and I quickly reapplied with the Greater New York Conference. I was hoping to reclaim my job, but the position was already filled. Disappointment overcame me. How could all my doors be slamming closed so suddenly? Once more, I turned to God to fulfill our needs.

One day we received a surprising call regarding a job that was fortunately still close enough for us to remain in Yonkers. I would be teaching first grade for a large Adventist church school in the Bronx, called the Bronx-

Manhattan SDA School. The location was less than desirable—even today teachers tend to avoid inner city schools—and I had a long commute by bus and subway in order to get there. Ella went with me, but Esther, just entering kindergarten, was too young for the long journey each day. Instead, she attended classes in her father's public school.

The majority of students I would be teaching came from inner city homes. Many of these families did not speak English. I had already been warned by our principal, Mrs. Alvarez, that the Hispanic children, mainly from Puerto Rican and Cuban homes, would be struggling to learn the language. None of the children knew English before they entered my class. It was my job to get them ready for first grade graduation, but I would have the huge language barrier to overcome first. I was not intimidated by my new challenge.

Two weeks before the school year began I headed out on my long journey to the Bronx-Manhattan School in order to set up my new classroom. Two other teachers would be traveling with me through the city streets and we appreciated the sense of safety we drew from each other.

I stepped off the bus, chattering happily with the two other teachers as we made our way toward the subway. Suddenly, a bottle came plunging towards me out of a tall, high-rise building. I did not have time to react. The ladies gasped as glass shattered at my feet, showering my heels with sharp fragments.

Somehow, none of the shards cut me, but the other teachers and I were badly shaken up. "What if the bottle had hit my head instead of my feet? What if something like this happens while Ella is with me?" The possible scenarios frightened me as we ran toward the safety of the subway.

That evening I told Lotfy that it would not be wise for us to allow Ella to travel through the dangerous city streets every day. Yet our options were limited. With both of us working long school days, we would not have anyone to drive Ella to another school. She begged to remain at the Yonkers school with the friends she had already made. We soon realized how inconvenient the arrangement would be so Ella joined me at the Bronx school. We simply needed to place our lives and safety in God's hands.

In the meantime, I resubmitted a request to the Greater New York Conference to be transferred back to the Yonkers school, located in a safe, suburban area. I had heard that one of the teachers was not working out there. Unfortunately, my new principal would not approve of the transfer. She quickly recognized that I had the dedication and determination needed to improve the student's English skills so she was not willing to let me go easily.

We finally came to an agreement. I would remain in her school for the entire year, I would develop a program for the first grade class that could easily be followed by subsequent teachers, and I would have a real graduation for my students.

The last requirement seemed trivial, but the principal was adamant. "We have never had a nice first grade graduation," she insisted. "Most of the students are still struggling to keep up with their lessons, so we hold them back a year. If you can improve the class, I will sign the recommendation for your transfer."

BRONX–MANHATTAN ADVENTIST SCHOOL, 1973

In my classroom, I incorporated art, music, poetry and physical activities to improve the children's English. The students were strictly forbidden from speaking any Spanish in my presence, even amongst themselves. Many of the songs I taught them could be used for school performances in front of the parents, but more importantly, I understood that by using various forms of media, the children would have a deeper understanding of the English language.

Each school day started with worship and songs. One morning I led the children through a new song that I had not taught them before. After I sang the words to the first verse, I picked out a portion of the stanza to go over with them. "Boys and girls, this song talks about sharing your faith," I began. "Do you know what it means to share your faith?"

Excitedly, one little boy raised his hand. "I know, teacher, I know!"

"Yes, Angel," I called on him.

A superior look spread over the little boy's face as he began explaining the meaning of our song to his fellow students. "Every morning my father uses share cream to share his faith in the bathroom," he explained. His pudgy hand grasped an imaginary razor and made long strokes against his smooth round cheeks.

I struggled to suppress my laughter. "No, Angel," I explained. "That is shaving your *face*. Sharing your *faith* means teaching others how much you love and trust in God." I could tell that this school year was going to be my biggest challenge yet.

❖ ❖ ❖

With twenty-four precious children in my class, all who struggled to learn a new language as well as their curriculum, I was kept very busy. Yet I noticed that these children were very different from the students I had taught in the past. Some of the children did not bring lunch to school. I would bring plenty of extra food in order to share with them. Every day brought a new excuse. "I forgot," or "I lost it," and some even told me outright that they only ate two meals every day. I did not question them. It could be possible that the working mothers were too busy to prepare a meal, or perhaps they did not have the money to afford lunch.

One other difference I noticed was the hygiene of some students. Some of the children had an odor that I was not used to. When I questioned them on their bathing routine, I found out that many of them would only shower once a week. As a result of the new knowledge, I soon incorporated personal hygiene into my science lesson, teaching them to use a washcloth and change their underpants between showers.

Saddest to me was when a child was left behind at school. These children waited anxiously, watching every student leave for the day. One by one a parent would arrive, and one by one the students would leave. It always broke my heart to see the anxiety in the little face of a child who realized that, for whatever reason, he or she had been forgotten.

Locking up for the day, Mrs. Alvarez would comment at how late I was staying. Sometimes I would spend the afternoon making phone calls, trying to find the whereabouts of parents or guardians. Eventually, I would take the student home with me and bring him or her to school the next day. The student would enjoy playing and studying with my children and didn't seem to feel neglected with the excitement of a slumber party. After baths, the student would put on one of my children's clean pajamas and I would wash his or her clothes to prepare for school the next day.

Thirty-eight years later, I had the chance to talk to one of these students. That trip to my house was etched brightly into her mind. "You were like a ray of light to many of us," she admitted. "We came from such sad homes and we all saw you as a kind family member." As she and I talked, reconnecting all those years that had passed between our teacher-student relationship and the present time, we realized that God had sent me to that school for a specific purpose. I unwittingly was bringing hope to several neglected, and perhaps, abused children.

The school year ended with a beautiful graduation for the first graders. It would be the first year that the inner city school had such a successful turnover with so many bright young children ready to enter the second grade. My curriculum was well established and an incoming teacher would have no problem following it. As promised, the principal wrote a letter of recommendation for me to return the very next school year to the Yonkers church school, close to my home and my heart.

CAMP MEETING, 1974

Every summer our church set up Camp Meetings for a week in the Berkshire Mountains. This trip required us to pack almost everything in our house that was not nailed down and cram it into our family station wagon. The drive would take no less than four hours but, almost immediately, one of the children would begin to ask, "Are we there yet?" Once there, we would all meet and reconnect with friends.

The eventful week was focused on the Bible. It was a great getaway from the usual rush of life. Some families would put up tents, and others would stay in cabins or bring their own RVs. Our family would usually stay at the hotel, a multistory building surrounded by views of the mountains and campgrounds which had originally been part of a resort. The five of us would bunk together in one of the tiny rooms for the week.

Regardless of where we decided to reside, insects feasted happily on the soft flesh of our children all through the week. Every year we could guarantee that Danny would wake up with one eye swollen completely shut from a mosquito bite. When I would observe the smooth, unmarked faces of the other children in camp, I was sure that my son must be the sweetest boy around. At least the bugs seemed to think so!

Camp Meetings are high energy places, packed with enough activities for the old and young to stay busy all day. Nature hikes, boat rides and swimming in a large pool were the most popular events, though horse riding was also available for those skilled in that area.

Meetings took up the majority of the day. Adults met in the Big Tent, seated on hard benches and swatting flies or fanning themselves with the cardboard fans that were passed out by white-gloved ladies. Children and youths were split up into smaller tents, each within their own age groups. Here they could sing songs, listen to stories, and do crafts for a few hours each day.

Ella attended the junior tent with her friends while Esther and Danny stayed together in the one designated for kindergarten age children. Because camp was so family oriented, we never seemed to worry about who was watching the children. Either Ella or I would drop the younger ones off in the morning and pick them up in time for lunch.

One particular day, we did not seem to coordinate schedules well enough. Esther and Danny finished their meeting and sat in the tent waiting to be picked up. Seven-year-old Esther was entranced by all the toys and crafts in their class tent. She loved to play in the large dollhouse that was used to demonstrate stories and songs, so she was content to wait for her older sister once the room cleared up.

Danny, on the other hand, had too much energy to remain still for very long. Dollhouses could not hold his interest, even if Esther tried calling it "a fort" to entice him to play with her.

"I think Mommy forgot us," Danny fretted one day.

"Mommy wouldn't forget us!" Esther insisted.

"Yeah, but Ella would! What if she forgot us and we're gonna starve here! Let's go to the room, Esther," he begged. "I'm so hungry!"

"I don't know the way," Esther resisted.

"I do! C'mon!" And with that he headed out. Esther had no choice but to scramble off after him, just as worried that they would get into trouble for leaving their post as she was that they had, in fact, been forgotten.

Having no real sense of direction herself, my adventurous child Esther was surprised when her younger brother found his way to the hotel. As he had expected, Danny was able to let himself into the unlocked room. "Let's eat! I'm starved!" he called to her.

Esther looked around the room but could not imagine what he was going to find to eat. Chips and other snacks were not kept by our family and anything else would require cooking. "There's nothing to eat here, Danny," she complained.

"Don't worry," he consoled her. "I watched Mommy and Dad make eggs lotsa times. I can do it!" In fact, eggs were probably the first food to come to his mind as a food that a *man* can make since it was the usual food their father prepared for the kids on the rare occasion when I was not home at dinner time.

With his new plan in mind, Danny pulled two eggs out of the cooler. He cracked them open into a Tupperware bowl, leaving a trail of sticky, gooey egg whites behind. Next, the five-year-old boy with no cooking experience turned on the hotplate. Everything was going well up to this point, so Esther wandered over to the window to watch for any sign of their family.

Meanwhile, Ella had arrived at the Big Tent without her brother and sister. I immediately knew something was wrong. "The babies weren't there," she explained, upset, knowing that she would be blamed for their absence. All three of us set off in search of the missing children.

Back at the hotel, Danny had set the Tupperware bowl onto the hotplate. Soon smoke started streaming out from under it. "Oh man, oh man!" Danny exclaimed while frantically stirring the ingredients with a fork. He could not understand why his parent's eggs had never smelled this way when they cooked, but he was sure that his persistence would pay off. Soon, the semi-liquid eggs started dripping from a hole in the melting bowl and onto the hotplate as well.

Esther was frantic. Smoke was beginning to fill the room, tipping her off that something might not be right with Danny's recipe. It was at this moment that we burst into the room to find our son swatting away at the smoky fumes and Esther cowering in a far corner of her bunk.

Lotfy rushed in and shut the burner off as I opened the windows. We scrubbed the hotplate and threw out the remnants of the meal, but the stink of burnt eggs and plastic hung around our room for the remainder of the week.

As Camp Meeting came to a close, Lotfy and I began the difficult task of repacking our car for the long trip home. Ella ran off to say her final goodbyes to friends while Esther and Danny hung around to "help" us. Finally tired of all the questions and chattering, Lotfy sent the two younger children into the car to wait for us, though he gave them strict warnings to sit still, stay in the back seat, and not touch anything. With only a few more loads to carry down, we were almost ready to leave.

Sitting still is not a skill that Danny had ever learned well. He soon hopped over the wide bench seat, making motor noises as he played with the steering wheel. Beeping at passersby, he would laugh when they jumped from the noise, then scramble back into the backseat any time Lotfy or I carried something down.

On one of his swift returns into the backseat, Danny's foot bumped against the gearshift, knocking it into neutral. I stepped toward the street to find the car rapidly rolling down the hill with the doors open and my children inside. Thinking quickly, my emergency instincts kicked in and I screamed, "Aahhh! Save them! Oh Lord! Please save my children!"

Ella and her friends were just returning at that time. One of the young Schwartzer boys jumped into the car before I could even set my box down. He quickly maneuvered the car toward the curb as he slammed on the brakes, stopping it suddenly.

I ran to the car, afraid of what I might find there, but both children were safe. Smothering them in hugs and kisses, I told Danny and Esther to sit quietly on the curb. No matter how enticing the idea of driving may have been, both kids were too shaken up to get behind the wheel again—at least that week!

We returned from our trip to Camp Berkshire safely despite the younger children having two close brushes with death. Ella seemed to be my only child who survived the camp without any issues. At least it seemed that way until two days after we had settled back into our home. A rash of red, watery welts started spreading around her face and hands.

"I think I have poison ivy," Ella complained, scratching and rubbing at the rapidly spreading irritation.

"Oh Ella, how would you get poison ivy?" I wondered. We did not seem to have any in the woods nearby our house, yet she was certain of what was ailing her.

"I must have touched it at camp," she admitted. So Ella had not survived unscathed after all.

Another day passed and the rash seemed to be quickly covering every area of her body, despite the calamine lotion we attempted to slather over her sensitive skin. Her eyes burned and I noticed that the little bumps of poison ivy were even coating her lips and mouth.

"It almost looks as if you ate the stuff," I said, suspiciously.

"Well ..." Ella was hesitant to respond.

"Ella!" I gasped. "You didn't really eat the poison ivy, did you?"

"Mom, the boys dared me and I couldn't let them call me a chicken," she exclaimed defensively.

"But Ella, it is called *poison* ivy for a reason! You might get really sick!"

Ella assured me that her friends had tried some before and they hadn't gotten sick from it. But I had to remind her that they did not demonstrate their faith in the safety of the plant by tasting it with her. For over a week after the rash began, Ella could only eat cool yogurt and applesauce as her mouth and esophagus healed. Nothing could soothe the itchiness she was made to endure from her small act of bravado.

RETURN FROM WASHINGTON

During summer vacation in 1974, while Ella was in middle school, Lotfy and I took the children to Washington, DC. The kids were excited to see the capital of the United States while Lotfy and I were excited to reconnect with some old college friends.

Ella, Esther, and Danny were used to visiting museums. With two teachers as parents, it was a regular pastime for our family. The old aqueduct behind our Yonkers home, which was now a long, wooded pathway, led directly to a small, yet impressive planetarium, science museum, history museum, and art gallery right on the Hudson River. This was our favorite retreat during the long summer months when I desired to instill a little more culture in the children than they were getting by playing on the streets with their friends.

As commonplace as our trips to the museums were, we had no idea what to expect when we arrived in Washington. We visited the Smithsonian Museum, the Jefferson and Lincoln Memorials, the Washington Monument, and the Aerospace Museum. In each place, we were amazed by the vastness of knowledge and by the displays we encountered.

Out of all the many tours we took, the family favorite was the White House. We were so impressed by the vaulted ceilings and enormous chandeliers that we barely heard anything the docent said. Esther stared in awe at one of the dining room tables that appeared to be fully decorated for a banquet that night.

Though Lotfy was an immaculate gardener in our home, and we enjoyed beautiful varieties of flowers, bushes, and even the best peach tree ever, nothing could compare to the grounds of the White House. With hedges neatly clipped, tulips and roses brightening the garden, and the immense lawn trimmed to perfection, Lotfy's yard paled in contrast.

We stayed in the area over a week, enjoying a visit to the Tomb of the Unknown Soldier and live reenactments of both the Revolutionary War and the Civil War. Danny loved the smelly, noisy shows and wanted to touch everything. I was fairly sure that if we left him unattended long enough, my son would be dressed like one of the Red Coats and carrying a rifle.

After so much time away, we were ready to return home, regardless of how much fun we may have had. On any return trip I would always say, "East or west, home is best!" a quote that was sure to get groans from my children. But this trip home was not to be a pleasant one.

As we were loading up the car, I noticed that Ella was not herself. Usually one to charge into any task with vigor, she was barely moving. "Ella, pick up those bags," her father commanded. "Don't you want to go home?" But Ella just sighed, moaning softly at the thought of moving her body.

Soon, Ella began to complain of achiness. I touched my lips to her forehead. "Lotfy!" I gasped, "This child is burning up!" He paused in his packing for a moment, questioning my reaction.

"Lotfy, maybe we should wait until after lunch and see if she gets any better," I suggested.

He scowled and teased us about trying to get more vacation time out of him, but Lotfy looked worried too. Ella gratefully crawled back into bed, shivering under the covers. She and I spent the rest of that quiet morning in the cool darkness of our hotel room while Lotfy took Esther and Danny out to the city. I poured cold water from the tap onto a starchy white washcloth and then laid it on her forehead, hoping to bring the fever down. But by the time our family had returned, Ella was nauseous, waking from her feverish sleep to vomit into a garbage can I left nearby.

Lotfy looked dismayed when he returned to the room. "We have to take her to the hospital," he agreed with me.

At the emergency room, Ella was immediately placed on a stretcher and wheeled into a private treatment room. We were shocked to find out how high her temperature had soared.

The nurses quizzed us on all the places we had visited, anything we had eaten and anyone we came in contact with during the past week. The list was immeasurable. Being tourists in the city we could not even begin to count all the attractions we had been to.

"She has a virus," the Doctor said as he passed us the papers admitting her into the hospital's intensive care unit. "We need to get her into an ice bath right away to get her temperature down." I blinked away the tears that burned the back of my throat and filled me with fear. I was certain that Ella's condition was grave. In every fiber and every cell of my own body, I could feel the pain she was experiencing.

For the first twenty-four hours, the medical staff kept her immersed for short periods of time in a tub of ice. Ella would whimper from the discomfort of a severe fever, compounded with the ice bath. Once that was over, I waited by her bed in a constant vigil, continuing to pray night and day for her recovery.

Lotfy would sometimes give me a break and send me out to get a drink or to choke down a meal in the cafeteria. Because Ella's condition could have been contagious, Danny and Esther were not allowed in the room. Instead, they would wait in the hallway while their father and I switched responsibilities.

After one month, Ella was allowed to transfer out of ICU and into a non-critical medical unit. She had asked to the nurses to let her sleep all night with heavy blankets and without any disturbances. That night, two Seventh-day Adventist pastors from the Washington, DC area prayed and anointed her with oil.

Miraculously, the next day, her temperature was under control though she was still in a weak state from the fever and dehydration she had experienced. Now our prayers could be those of thanksgiving. Day by day, Ella was getting stronger. Still, I sat with her for long stretches of time each day, although I felt more confident leaving her while I cared for the rest of my family.

MUSIC HEALS THE SOUL

Ella's school year had already begun when we were finally able to check her out of the hospital and bring her home. Her illness had affected her heart and made her too weak for the amount of energy required at school. Because she was already behind, the state assigned her a private tutor. While Lotfy and I worked and "the babies" attended their classes, Ella sat home alone, except for the three hours that her tutor was with her.

One afternoon, I returned home to find Ella sitting at the piano we had bought when she first started taking lessons. She had been only six years old at the time and was very excited to learn. However, time took its toll, and soon Ella loathed practicing, begging me to let her quit, while I insisted that she continue. But today something was different about Ella. Here she was sitting on the cool wooden bench, gliding her fingers gently over the keys.

"Ella, are you sure you feel well enough to be sitting like that?" I asked her.

"I'm fine, Mom," she said, deliberately running though scales and arpeggios. "You know, Mom," she said, following me into the kitchen, "I want to thank you."

"Really?" I was surprised. "Whatever for, Ella?"

Her answer shocked me even more, "I really wanted to quit piano so many times before, but you never let me. Now when I'm home alone and everyone is at work or at school, music is my only friend. Thank you for pushing me to keep learning the piano."

A RETURN TO YONKERS CHURCH SCHOOL

Luckily, we returned from DC in time for the first day of school at Yonkers Church School where I returned to my old post as the elementary teacher. Ella would be attending the upper grades with me once she was well enough. Danny stayed with a local babysitter. Our concern was with Esther. She would be entering the first grade, one of the four grades I taught. We discussed our options back and forth, and then finally decided that it might be much easier for both of us to concentrate if she was taught by someone who was not so emotionally involved with her. Esther would return to the public school where her father taught.

The decision worked out well for us. It was a comfort to know that Lotfy was able to take our daughter to and from school. This was especially helpful when the public school had short days, while my school still had full sessions. On the other hand, I was responsible for taking Danny to his babysitter and Ella, of course, came to school with me.

A STREAK OF LUCK

It was the middle of the 1970s and the hippie era was in full swing, though we felt immune to it from the protective bubble of our Adventist Church community. Occasionally our family would take short excursions on the weekends to a nearby community park called Untermyer. Here we would watch free concerts, puppet shows, and plays during the muggy summer days.

One afternoon, Lotfy and I drove our children to Untermyer Park with the intention of picnicking before the evening concert. Stepping over and around the denim clad couples lying openly on blankets, it was challenging to conceal this unusual lifestyle from our children. "Why are they just sleeping there Mommy? Don't they have a house to sleep in? Are they kissing? Is that little boy naked?"

We made our way to a quiet area where Esther and Danny could run and play while Ella, Lotfy and I watched from our picnic blanket. The day wore on and Lotfy suddenly remembered the concert. Checking his watch, he realized it had stopped. We had no way of knowing the correct time.

Lotfy set off to find someone with a watch. With the children gathered and our belongings packed up, we followed behind him.

There was a unique characteristic to hippies; "peace" and "love" were in their vocabulary but "time" was not. We could not seem to find anyone to help us as we made our way to the outdoor performance.

Finally, from a distance, Lotfy noticed two figures with long blond hair tossing a Frisbee to each other. The closest one was facing away from us and had beautiful thigh-length wavy, golden locks. Esther said she had never seen such long hair in all her life.

My husband noticed the person was wearing a watch and, always eager to strike up a conversation with lovely women, scrambled over to them. "Do either of you pretty girls know what time it is?" he asked beaming, as he approached the nearest one. The young Frisbee player spun around to face him. His full beard and muscular chest made us realize immediately that *she* was a *he*.

"Eh?" Lotfy took a step back in astonishment, though his smile did not fade from his face. "I am so sorry sir," he said, trying to recover from his surprise. "I only saw your beautiful, long hair and I just thought …"

"It's cool, pops," the younger man said, tossing his golden waves over his shoulders. "What's up?"

"Do you happen to know the time, uh … son?" Lotfy asked again.

The man looked at his watch momentarily. "Four-thirty," he answered, unsmiling.

"Thank you, young uh … man," my husband muttered, still recovering.

"No problem, pops," the boy replied again, turning back to his Frisbee game.

"Why does that man have such long hair?" Esther wanted to know.

"Why does he keep calling you pops, Daddy?" Danny asked.

"Did you know him before?" Esther guessed, but Lotfy was already pulling them toward the performance area and I was still in too much shock to respond.

❖ ❖ ❖

The evening's concert was a collection of opera solos performed by a soprano artist. Danny, Esther and Ella fidgeted as the woman sang one piece after another, occasionally pausing between songs to give background information on their origins.

As the sun set, I encouraged Esther and Danny to rest their heads on my lap, but their bright eyes remained open. Suddenly, during an exceptionally high note in the final song, a streak of pale skin passed directly in front of our seats. Murmurs and gasps waved from the viewers on the right side of the stage across to those on the left.

"What was that, Mommy?" Danny asked sitting up quickly. From the look on Ella's face as she tried to suppress her giggles, I knew that she had seen what everyone else did.

"That was a streaker!" she whispered excitedly to her brother and sister. The soloist had not missed a beat of her song, though her eyes flew wide open as the man sailed passed her.

"A what?" Esther asked, sitting up as well and looking around.

"It's a naked man," Ella explained, as if the occurrence was so commonplace that she should know about it. I tried to change the subject, but Ella, Esther, and Danny kept bringing it back up.

Oh great, I thought to myself. It's going to get all around the school that Raya and Lotfy took their kids to a concert with a naked man. I could just imagine how that story would get blown out of proportion.

The song ended and the musician smiled apologetically. "I should be jealous that his performance drew more excitement than my whole evening," she said, drawing laughter from the crowd. "For those of you in the back who may not know what caused all the commotion up here, let me just say that there wasn't much to see," she joked. Thanking everyone for attending, the now flustered singer dismissed us for the night.

We made our way back toward the car, keeping the children as quiet as we could, but Esther and Danny could not stop asking their sister questions about the streaker, and Ella was only too happy to fill them in on any details they might have missed.

NATURALIZATION

By 1975, it was evident that we were settled into the United States for good. I took a trip to White Plains, NY and enrolled in a course to prepare me for my naturalization. Lotfy had already become a citizen several years before but did not feel it was necessary for me to do the same. I, on the other hand, had been anxious to feel fully grounded as a part of society.

Once I completed my course, I happily answered all the required questions at the local immigration office. "Who is your president? What colors can be found on our flag? Please recite the Pledge of Allegiance. Congratulations, Mrs. Abadir, you are now a citizen."

At the next election, I proudly voted and have never missed the opportunity to express my right to vote since then. I also finally insisted on having my own bank account. Before that, I never even saw my own paychecks.

When it was payday, Lotfy had immediately taken my paycheck and deposited it into an account in his name only. I had been working just as many hours as he was, yet I did not even know how much my paychecks were worth each month. I would come home from eight or ten-hour days and then have to help the children with homework while I prepared the evening meal and cleaned up. Most nights Lotfy stayed away from the home, working on repairs in the apartment buildings he had purchased to supplement his income.

I CAN DRIVE

One summer afternoon, Lotfy and I were busy with chores around the house. Believing that I was giving 14-year-old Ella a break from her usual, laborious work, I asked her to watch her younger brother and sister for the day. "Just keep them out of trouble," I directed.

Hours later, I resurfaced from a tiring day's work to search for my children and call them in for supper. I was pleased at how quiet they had been all afternoon. I stepped out of the front door and called, "Ella! Danny! Esther!" But none of them came. The yard was empty and I did not see any of their friends around. I was just going to knock on a few neighborhood doors when I noticed that something else was missing as well.

"My car!" I exclaimed. "Someone stole my car!" My heart was pounding with worry. Whoever had stolen my car must have kidnapped my children as well. The thought barely ran through my mind when I saw my car rolling slowly towards the house. I blinked in surprise, frozen in my place. Navigating it from behind the wheel was Ella. Her brother and sister sat happily in the back seat. Beaming, she parked the car and greeted me as if nothing was unusual.

"Ella! Where were you?" I demanded.

"Esther and Danny were bored and it was so hot out, so we went to play in the park," she answered candidly.

"But," I sputtered, "you are too young to drive! You should never do that! What if you had been in an accident or stopped by the police?" I insisted.

"Oh Mom," Ella brushed me aside, "You worry too much. Nothing happened and the babies had fun!"

"Ella, you must never do that again," I commanded sternly. "Even if nothing happened this time, it is still against the law." I could only hope that I was able to impress the severity of the situation on her, but knowing how harshly he would respond, I did not tell her father anything.

MRS. MOMMY

When Esther was in the second grade, she entered Yonkers Adventist School. For the first time I would be teaching my own child. I did not believe the situation would be any different from my other school years. I would treat everyone equally, regardless of whom I was teaching.

I soon discovered that there really is a difference when the student is your own child. One day, needing my help with a classroom assignment, Esther called me from her seat, "Mom? ... Mommy? ... Mom?"

I was busy assembling a display for the classroom and her voice fell on deaf ears. Deciding she needed a different title for me, Esther tried again. "Excuse me, Mrs. Abadir?" I heard a child call sweetly from behind me.

"Yes," I replied promptly, spinning around from my work to find that the student was my own Esther. She smiled smugly at my surprised expression. "Esther, why are you calling me Mrs. Abadir?" I had to ask.

"Mommy, I've been calling you for five minutes and you never answered," she said in exasperation. From that day on, Esther would call me "Teacher" or "Mrs. Abadir" any time she could not get my attention right away.

WHOOPING COUGH

As the school year marched on, so did the long list of performances, activities and, of course, standardized testing.

The week prior to the standardized tests, I prepped my class on healthy living. "Eat a nutritious breakfast and get plenty of rest," I warned them. I did not want any of my students getting sick and missing the statewide exams.

The first day of testing began uneventfully. I read the directions aloud to the students, instructing them to keep absolutely silent and stop at the end of each section when prompted. Then I sat at my desk to work quietly on my lesson plans while the children worked.

From the beginning, I could see that things were going well. My class was well prepared and even excited about the unusual format of this exam. Rather than the hand written, mimeograph copies I usually gave them, these test booklets were neatly typed, with little boxes to fill out. This would be no problem.

All was fine until just before lunch when I looked up to find that my daughter had her head down on the desk. Though she had been coughing throughout last evening, I believed she would be better by morning. Now

Esther's face was enflamed and her eyes were glassy. When she did cough, it sounded like she had swallowed a kazoo.

Normally, I would have thought that my adventurous child was just stressed from the testing or trying to avoid the work. But looking at her, I knew that these symptoms could not be faked. I walked her into a quiet hallway and instructed her to lie down on a cot while I finished my class. Then, at lunchtime, I took Esther to the doctor while a substitute took over my class.

"Whooping cough," the doctor informed me, checking her rapidly worsening symptoms. "Esther will have to be admitted immediately into the hospital." I couldn't believe it. Here I had been instructing my students to stay healthy for the testing, and my own child was so sick she would be hospitalized and placed in a vapor tent for her recovery.

THE PURPLE COAT

Styles were changing in 1975 and Ella was tired of the drab clothing her father insisted on buying her. Lotfy was a magnet for anything inexpensive. Unfortunately, buying clothes due to a good bargain does not ensure that one will be dressed fashionably.

Ella pleaded with me for a long purple plaid coat that was in style at the time. I sighed, knowing that my meager salary went directly into the children's schooling. "Ask your father," I suggested, but we both knew the answer.

Lotfy replied by yelling. "Why would anyone be so ungrateful about the beautiful things she has? People in my country would love these clothes! Who is putting these foolish ideas into her mind?"

Of course, I was blamed. But it did not matter to me. Frustrations in our marriage had been increasing. Lotfy was not only frugal on clothing expenses but also with food and other household necessities. He would buy whatever was on sale and I would have to make do with our inadequate groceries. I was also embarrassed and would cringe every time my college friends saw me and commented about how attractively I *used* to dress, implying how drab I looked now. My hair was falling out by the fistfuls from a cheap perm, and I'd resorted to shaving it completely, then wearing a wig to cover my baldness. To make things worse, Lotfy would frequently complain about my inability to have more children.

Eventually I gave in to Ella's wish for a new coat. I carefully cut corners and skimped on a few items here and there in order to buy my daughter the coat she wanted. Ella was so excited, proudly twirling around the room as she modeled it for her brother and sister.

Esther murmured, "You look so beautiful!" But she would have thought her older sister was beautiful even if she had been wearing rags. Little did we know, that was exactly what would happen.

Lotfy came home that evening and found Ella still wearing the coat she had longed for so badly. He immediately flew into a rage, aggressively yanking the coat off her. Ella cried and pleaded as she grabbed for the coat, but her father was too fast and too strong.

"See what happens when you love material things so much? Everything turns to garbage!" he shouted. With those few harsh words, Lotfy tore the coat to shreds. Ella sobbed, running into her room. Danny and Esther cowered in the living room, shocked and surprised that such a lovely thing could cause so much anger. It was obvious that Lotfy would control us any way he could.

KINGSWAY COLLEGE, ONTARIO, CANADA

In the summer of 1976 we visited our college friends who were working in Canada's Kingsway College. Ella loved the campus and soon found out that the college choir traveled to England each year. Though she was only a freshman in high school, Ella was invited to join the choir when the choral director heard her beautiful singing voice.

She did not need to be asked twice. I worried that my daughter would be too young to live in Canada so far away, but our friends, the Watsons, encouraged her by allowing Ella to live with them for the year. Besides, I knew that Lotfy took out most of his wrath on our oldest daughter. It seemed she would be safest if she remained at a distance from her father.

Barely a month into the school year, Ella called and told me that she needed a choir dress. All the other girls had learned to sew in college, but Ella was still in high school and had not yet studied home economics. She pleaded with me to help her sew the dress. I really wanted to provide this simple service for my daughter. Because it would mean a trip to Canada, Lotfy would not hear of it.

"Why can't she do it herself? We don't have the money! Besides, I need the car," he complained. Really, he didn't need the car since he worked close enough to walk each day. Though he had nothing to substantiate his arguments, Lotfy refused to listen to me. Yet I could not bear to let my child down.

All that night I did not sleep. Lotfy was used to me working late into the night, so my work did not disturb him. Quietly, I packed the car with food and clothing for a short journey. Sometime after midnight, while Lotfy slumbered deeply, I carried Esther and Danny from their beds and loaded them into the car. As I navigated the car through the darkness, I prayed for our safety.

The miles rolled on with Esther and Danny resting peacefully in the backseat. The long monotonous roads were unfamiliar through the dark of the night, and my eyelids became heavy as I struggled to stay awake. It was after four o'clock in the morning when we crossed the border into Canada.

Blinking my dry, tired eyes, I rolled down my window for some fresh air. "Lord, keep us safe," I continued to pray, knowing it would be nothing short of a miracle just to stay awake.

Crash! A massive jolt spun my car out of control. In a flash, I saw the offending automobile speed past mine as I steered my damaged car toward the side of the road and jumped out, hoping to catch a glimpse of the runaway vehicle.

I paced back and forth, waiting for someone to find us. But the dark road was empty at that hour. Though Esther and Danny had been jolted by the impact, they remained unhurt. Now the children were wide awake and agitated by all the excitement. It was half an hour before the first set of headlights appeared in the distance. I frantically waved my arms at an oncoming big rig in an attempt to flag him down. "Hit and run! Hit and run!" I shouted, jumping up and down.

Shocked and dismayed, I watched as the truck rushed past us. We were alone again. "How could anyone leave a stranded car along the road? What will happen to us here?" I wondered. Little did I know, but the driver of that truck had a plan. When he saw us stranded at the side of the road, he radioed ahead to the nearby police station since his own schedule did not permit him to stop.

Before the police even got out of their driveway, they found the runaway driver, drunk in his now disabled car. They had him in custody before they made their way down the road to find us.

Relief flooded over me as I saw the police lights approach. I gave the officer a statement of the incident as clearly as I could, but everything had happened so quickly. Occasionally, I would blurt out, "I can't find my glasses! They fell off and I won't be able to see or drive." As the early morning light began to dawn, the kind policeman walked up and down the side of the road, then pulled all our belongings out of the car to search for my eyeglasses, but they did not appear.

Later that morning, the policeman drove me to an optometrist who provided me with a temporary new pair. My car was still drivable; only the trunk was damaged and partially gaping open. The children and I were back on our way.

It was lunch time on Sabbath when we finally arrived at Kingsway College. Ella and our friends, the Watsons, had been so worried by our delay, but once we were all reunited, everyone was happy again.

After lunch, Ella excitedly showed us around the dormitory and introduced us to all her college friends. She rolled her eyes exaggeratedly whenever one of the girls admired her siblings, "Oh Ella, they're so cute!" But I could tell that Ella was as happy to have Danny and Esther with her as they were to be there.

That evening, once the sun went down, Ella and I started working on her dress. I measured her and cut the appropriate fabric out. The sewing would have to wait until morning when the light was better.

As soon as we awoke, Ella and I began sewing and piecing the material together. Slowly, painstakingly, we watched the dress begin to take form. Nargis Watson walked in and out of the room occasionally to see how we were doing or even just to gossip with me about the trials we both shared of living with an Egyptian husband.

The job had taken us hours to complete, but we were so pleased when it was finally finished. As Ella tried the garment on one final time, I stretched my aching back and shoulders. I was dreading the long trip home, yet I knew I needed to leave soon so the children would have a restful night before school the next day. Then suddenly I realized that I hadn't heard Danny or Esther for hours. I poked my head out of the room and called my friend, "Nargis, have you seen the children?"

"They were playing outside most of the day, but I think they're now in Sammy's room," she answered from the kitchen.

Confused, I looked in her son's bedroom, right next to the one we had been working in. Sure enough, Danny and Esther were sitting cross legged by Sammy's bookshelf, playing with some trick coins stashed there. I had completely lost track of time, yet they had not fussed once. Nargis then peeked into the room. "I can't believe how good your children are," her comment echoed my thoughts. "They played so quietly without fussing or fighting. Children don't do that, you know," she added.

From that day on, her remark stuck with me. I repeated that story to my oh-so-perfect children many times after that. Especially whenever I would see other people's children fighting with each other.

When I returned home with Danny and Esther, Lotfy was irate. He screamed and raged for hours, storming around the house. "No more car for you!" he shouted.

"But Lotfy, I have to *work*," I rationalized. I thought surely he could see the logic in that. I was wrong. Lotfy did confiscate the car. As a result, the children and I had to walk two miles to school each day throughout the next month of school.

Meanwhile Ella remained at Kingsway College with the Watsons. Unaware of the plight which had resulted from our visit, she was more thrilled than ever to be there. Every phone call home relayed her excitement about the upcoming concert tour to England.

Unfortunately, school funds ran short. After a few months, Ella called me full of disappointment. "We're not going to England this year," she complained.

"But Ella, I thought they toured England every year," I said, surprised.

"This year they can't afford to," Ella replied dully. "They're going to *New England* instead."

"Oh Ella! I'm so sorry." I tried to sound sympathetic as I suppressed a chuckle. The Canadian students would not mind the modified plans. New England was still a change of pace for them. But Ella had been to New England countless times with our family. This trip would be a huge let down for her.

A ROOM UPSTAIRS

One year, Lotfy remodeled the attic into a separate studio apartment. The apartment opened up at the top of a tall stairway and boasted such luxurious amenities as a two-burner hotplate, a sink, and a cramped bathroom in the one-room dwelling.

As Ella reached adolescence, she fell in love with the tiny apartment. She had never gotten along with Lotfy and it offered her the independence she longed for in order to be away from her father. The studio also provided the privacy she needed but could not have while sharing a bedroom in the converted garage with her younger sister. As soon as the room became available, she begged Lotfy to allow her to live there.

At first he suggested that she might be able to, if the apartment did not get rented out. Hoping for a favorable outcome, Ella began to decorate the room with some abstract items. She used some old x-rays which had been donated to my class by a doctor's office (to be used for crafts), as well as several sheets and beaded curtains and hung them all over the room. Somehow, she managed to create a teenage wonderland for herself which was the envy of all her girlfriends.

Unfortunately for her, Ella's apartment was soon rented out to an elderly church member, Viola Baker who had just moved from South Carolina. Lotfy insisted that we needed the extra income. Though I promised her that "the babies" could share a room and she could take Danny's, she was frustrated at having to go back downstairs. Ella grudgingly peeled her precious decorations off the walls in preparation for our new resident.

Viola Baker and I quickly became friends, and at first Lotfy seemed to care for her too. She was heavyset, jolly and generous. The children all loved her, but without a doubt, Danny was her favorite. Any time he came into her view, Viola would immediately burst into song. Her blue eyes twinkled and heavy jowls quivered as she sang out her own version of "Danny Boy" time and time again.

Though she could have prepared meals in her own room, Lotfy and I usually invited her downstairs to eat, worship, and visit with us as part of our family. In the evenings, after the day's meals and chores were done, Danny would often beg to go visit "Aunt Viola." He would return hours later, with lips stained red or blue or green.

"Danny! What have you been eating?" I would ask, to which he always answered, "Aunt Viola gave me goodies!"

One day, jealous that her brother got all the attention, not to mention all the sweets, Esther followed Danny up the stairs. She was shocked to find our plump, older friend sitting on her rocker watching Danny eat an entire package of candy.

"You can have some too," Viola offered in her southern drawl, "but y'all gotta promise to spit all that red out into the sink. The red candy is no good for you." Esther was, of course, only too happy to oblige and soon she too could be found sporting a colorful ring around her lips.

VIOLENCE IN THE HOME

Though they started out as friends, Viola and Lotfy soon learned exactly how to get on each other's nerves. Her long prayers, punctuated by, "Oh, and P.S. Lord," angered him, ending worship time in a fight. Lotfy thought she meddled into our family life too much. Viola rebuked him for his quick and harsh temper, especially when he turned it towards her precious Danny Boy.

With his impish grin and playful spirit, Danny could bring laughter into any room. But just as often, the child's mischievous and curious nature caused Lotfy to turn his wrath against my little boy. Usually, Lotfy would furrow his eyebrows and lower his head as he stormed over to correct Danny for any misdeed. As soon as his father placed his hand on a belt, Danny knew what was coming.

"Oh please, Daddy, I'll be good! I promise, Daddy! I'll never do it again!" Danny would beg for forgiveness as he backed away from the irate man towering over him. Sometimes the pleading would result in a reduced sentence, but usually Danny would endure severe beatings for his mistakes.

Often Ella would bear the brunt of a punishment for the sole fact that she was the eldest and should have kept "the babies" from any trouble. Somehow Esther managed to escape the majority of Lotfy's fury, though not all. On occasion, Esther was just as easily struck as her siblings. But since she usually managed to avoid punishment, Esther would sit outside of the bedroom sobbing and sucking her thumb as she listened to her little brother's or older sister's cries. If Viola or I tried to intervene, the spankings would only be more severe.

One night, Lotfy's temper was worse than usual. He spanked Danny and bound his feet and hands. After several minutes the man stormed out of the room, shouting at me to stay away from my son. Lotfy then sat brooding in front of the TV for half an hour while Danny remained tied up in his room. When Lotfy returned, his temper had still not cooled. He struck our young son several more times while the girls and I cowered as far away as possible.

The children were not the only ones to suffer from Lotfy's rage. Throughout our marriage, there were many occasions when he would release his frustrations on me. He was unhappy with his work in the public school district and my inability to have more children. He also wanted to make sure I obeyed his wishes and that he had full control of all decisions made. Sometimes he would throw items at me, such as a full pan of food or nearby dining room chairs. Other times, he would be incredibly forceful in bed with his towering body, many times inflicting pain on my tiny frame. But I was his wife and therefore expected to be his submissive servant in every way.

The more she observed Lotfy's anger, the more Viola began to stand up for us. This only increased my husband's rage. Often, her comments to him would result in more broken plates as things were thrown against the wall. Soon, as our advocate, Viola disclosed our turmoil to the pastor. Although I had never complained to anyone about our difficult life, the conference became aware of the situation.

One Sabbath day, ignoring Lotfy's command that we would attend the Bronx church, I took my children back to our old congregation in Yonkers for a special event. Ella was excited to be around her close friends again and the two younger children were thrilled as well. As far as I was concerned, I felt as if I was back at home.

When Lotfy discovered that we had gone to Yonkers against his wishes, he barged into the church service, yelling at anyone who would get in his way. Then grabbing me roughly and shouting for the children to follow him, he dragged me out. I felt frustrated and ashamed of my husband's violent behavior. After all my years of trying to disguise our suffering from the eyes of my peers, Lotfy revealed his true nature to our entire congregation.

Soon the conference intervened. During a phone call from my education director, it was suggested that they transfer me out of Yonkers to a place where the children and I would be safe from Lotfy. "What would I do? How would I live?" I wondered, trying to imagine raising three children on my own. But the director was patient with my indecision. He recommended a trial separation, just one year at a good school in Elmira, New York. The support of my church, the only family I knew, was overwhelming to me. Divorce in those days was unconventional to say the least, so my director must have recognized the grave danger my children and I could have faced. The job offer in another city provided me with the motivation I needed to face such a drastic change in our lives.

BRONX MANHATTAN SEVENTH DAY
ADVENTIST SCHOOL

Mrs. Abadir - Grade 1

1972   1973

Figure 21 - Bronx Manhattan School

Figure 22 - Esther and Danny; Ella and Danny; Raya; Kids in Yonkers Home

PART VII: THE BIG D, 1976–1980

THE SEPARATION

"Seek first the kingdom of God and His righteousness, and all these things shall be added to you." Matthew 6:33

After being settled in Yonkers for more than eight years, I uprooted my small family and moved to Erin, New York, just outside of Elmira. Lotfy made sure that the transition was as difficult for everyone as possible. Every chance he got, he took the children aside and asked why they would leave him when he had loved them so much. On one occasion he even chased our car down the street in his *galabia*, the traditional cotton robe that men wear in Egypt. Even if every interaction the children had with him wasn't entirely painful, Lotfy's temper began to escalate beyond the usual tirades that had caused us so many traumas.

As though the emotional abuse was not enough, I soon learned that I would be leaving my home with nothing more than a few personal belongings. I petitioned to the family court system to help me retrieve the money Lotfy had taken from my paychecks when he invested in properties around the city. I was shocked to find that not one of the apartments, not even the home I had lived in for the past several years, was in my name. In fact, Lotfy had transferred them all from his own name to his brother's name.

With growing trepidation I packed my children and a few suitcases into our rusted Buick. The conference sent a moving truck to carry off any furniture and personal articles we would take. We pulled out of Yonkers and into a new era of our lives.

❖ ❖ ❖

After the hustle of the big city and the pain of a broken marriage, Erin was a haven. It was a peaceful, friendly, and very simple little town. Our church was located ten miles away in Elmira, and was filled with generous members, several from the nearby farming community. Before we had finalized the transfer, I visited the church for my interview and talked to the chairman of the school board about teacher housing. It was immediately suggested that we rent from a member who owned a vacant farmhouse.

Once we arrived in our new home, the children were thrilled. Our landlord had planted a large garden on the property filled with vegetables that he generously let us harvest, as needed, for our own use. This would take care of many groceries we might not have been able to fit into our meager budget. I spent the harvest season canning, jamming, freezing and drying any of the produce we were not able to immediately use. These items would take us through the long, cold farmland winter. Even better than the free food was the vast playland Esther and Danny could make use of. Trees to climb, a creek to wade in, and a small red barn to use as a fort were some of the many rural amenities we found on our new property.

As usual, Danny was the first to make friends. Coincidentally, the boy who lived across the road was also named Danny. The two of them were inseparable most afternoons. Danny De Fillipo, the only child of a well-to-do family, lived in a genuine amusement park for children. His home, yard, and garage were filled with all the expensive toys any boy, and even most girls, would want to play with. A pinball machine, snow mobiles, a pool table, and many more amenities entertained the boys when they were not out exploring the sixty-some acres that came with our own house.

It was a blessing that outside of the walls of our house, the children could find so much pleasure because the inside was sorely lacking. That is not to say that our actual home was unpleasant. With Ella's eye for visual appeal, we had filled the spaces as comfortably as possible. Yet the building was old and drafty and even with the most pleasant of furnishings, it still felt dark and tired.

My bedroom was the only room downstairs. A small kitchen and a large living space occupied the rest of the lower floor. Across from my comfortable bedroom was the sole bathroom. This room was probably the brightest in the house, equipped with a white porcelain toilet, a pedestal sink, and an old-fashioned claw-foot tub—no shower. At the far end of the long, dim living space, one could scale creaky stairs to the attic. These attic rooms, with their deeply slanted ceilings had been more recently refinished. Where the paneling downstairs was antiquated and so dark it was almost black, the paneling in these rooms was a brighter, honey hue, warmed by small windows facing the road. The stairs opened directly into Esther's room and one had to walk through the first room to get to Ella's door in the back.

Notice I didn't mention a room for Danny? When we first moved to Erin, the space seemed perfect for us. It was early summertime and Danny begged to be allowed to sleep in the large glassed-in porch that wrapped around two exterior walls of the house. He loved the freedom of sleeping under the stars so close to the nature he cherished. We did have to warn my little boy that he should never undress in that room. The last thing we needed was to be chastised by the small, rural community for indecent exposure.

By the time we discovered how cold and drafty the glass porch would become in the winter, Ella was away at Union Springs Academy, about 70 miles to the north. Danny was able to move temporarily upstairs into her room.

T'WAS THE NIGHT BEFORE CHRISTMAS

"Yet he sets the poor on high, far from affliction, and he makes their families like a flock." Psalms 107:41

During our first winter after the separation from Lotfy, we were still living in the drafty, old farmhouse in Erin. Christmas approached and school was released for winter break after a big celebration. Each of the parents had brought treats for the students to enjoy as we exchanged Secret Friendship gifts around an evergreen tree the school had set up in our multipurpose room.

Since we did not have extra money to spare, I decided to take the school's Christmas tree home on our last day. Years later we would call this recycling, but at that time my children just called it pathetic. That poor little tree would have made Charlie Brown's Christmas tree look luxurious in comparison.

By the time we brought it home, those needles that remained on the tree were mostly brown. The tree leaned precariously in one direction, no doubt due to the school boys tackling each other when they were too close to it. Ella, home from the academy, turned the tree in every direction she could to conceal the bald patches. Yards and yards of tinsel proved to be a very effective decorating tool that year.

Despite the modest greenery, Ella, Esther, and Danny were very excited about our first Christmas on our own. I took them shopping as soon as we were able and gave the children a few dollars to spend on each other. Two of the tires on my car were completely bald as well, so I stopped by Sears to purchase a couple new ones. A fresh snowfall gave the promise of a beautiful white Christmas.

When we arrived home with my trunk full of shopping bags and new tires, we found our driveway completely submerged in snow. Nine-year-old Danny, still pumped from the excitement of vacation combined with holiday shopping, offered to help.

"You stay right here, Mom," he assured me. "I'm the man of the family, and I'll get us in." He jumped out of the car while the girls and I sat huddled to keep warm. I watched as my son stomped over the deep, white drifts toward our house. Much more snow had fallen than we realized and it took him several minutes to make his way up our long driveway.

Picking up the shovel from inside our porch, Danny got to work digging a path from the front of the house to the street. He started out vigorously tossing heaps of snow over his shoulder. Soon the heaps became smaller, his work slowed, and Danny finally slumped over the handle of the shovel, exhausted. "There's too much," he panted when I jumped out of the car to be sure he was alright. "I can't do the whole thing."

I chuckled at how quickly Danny had burnt out from his chore. "Don't worry, honey," I consoled him, "just finish off this pathway so the girls and I can walk in. We'll keep the car on the street for tonight and hopefully we can all work on the driveway in the morning."

The next day was Christmas Eve. We awoke to a clear, sunny morning. Danny and Esther were excited to explore the nearby countryside now covered by a façade of snow. My little man was pretty sure that he could convince Danny De Fillipo to take them all snowmobiling that afternoon.

"But first we have to finish the driveway," I reminded them. Danny's face fell immediately as he recalled the hard work he had already endured the night before. I knew I was in for some objections, but Ella assured everyone that she would take the first turn. I bundled her up in a coat, scarf, hat, boots, and gloves and my daughter stepped onto the porch. She shut the door behind her, but not before a gust of icy wind forced several snowflakes in. Less than one minute later, Ella walked back through the door, followed by several more snowflakes. Danny smirked up at her from his place in the kitchen.

"Too tough for you, huh?" he pestered, ready to taunt her for being such a wimp.

"It's finished," Ella said, somewhat incredulously. Danny's jaw fell open.

No doubt he wondered how his sister, a mere girl, could finish something that he could not. Esther and I ran to the window and looked out. Sure enough, the entire driveway was plowed clear down to the gravel. We later found out that Mr. Stewart, a church member who lived in the next town, had brought his plow over and cleaned our driveway before the sun had even risen. Once again we felt blessed to have a wonderful church community to support us.

Later that morning, Danny raced out to bring all the gifts inside from the car so we could start wrapping them. A moment later, he too had run back inside in shock. "Everything's been stolen!" he sobbed, throwing himself down on the couch. "They stole our whole Christmas!"

"Don't be silly, Danny!" I reprimanded as I thought, "Surely no one could be so cruel as to steal gifts on Christmas."

Ella and I raced outside where the large heavy trunk sat gaping open. I could feel my stomach sink, as if I had swallowed lead with my breakfast. "Is this a joke?" Ella asked in dismay. But we knew it could not be a joke. Both tires and every one of the little gifts had been taken from our trunk during the night. I did not have a single present to offer my children the next day, Christmas Day, and the fifty dollars I had spent on tires was more than I could afford before my next paycheck.

Somehow we moved through Christmas Eve in a daze. I phoned the Stewarts and thanked them for helping us with the snow. "It was the best gift we got this year," I said, truthfully. I felt hollow inside, needing to share our misfortune with others, but didn't want to bother anyone. The children must have beaten me to it, but I would not know until later.

I called my attorney asking if Lotfy could send more child support this month in light of what happened. Lotfy was unwilling to spare a few extra dollars. But my attorney knew about an organization called Toys for Tots and made a request. That day we received two bags of toys for Danny and Esther. Then, later that evening we found a large box on our porch filled with food, gifts, and $50 in an envelope marked "tires." So, the word had spread. We never found out which of our church members had saved Christmas for us, but we thanked God for placing us in a caring community family.

PATHFINDERS

After leaving lifetime friends in Yonkers, Danny and Esther were pleased to find out that our new church in Elmira would have an abundance of children to befriend. Thankfully, all the families were highly active and participated in several events together. This gave the children plenty of opportunity to develop friendships in our new community.

A favorite activity was the Pathfinder Club. One night each week of the school year, this club for boys and girls took over our classrooms. Strong leaders within the church, headed up by Mrs. Wascisco, volunteered to teach the children skills and help them to earn their honors, for which they received small badges they could sew onto their sashes.

For a change, I could sit back and let others do the teaching, although I must admit, I did participate more than once, offering short-term classes on trees, flowers, and shells. Sewing, carpentry, cooking, and many other skills were taught by several of the other church members.

Camping events taught the Pathfinders important skills. During our first year in Erin, Mrs. Wascisco, prompted by a family friend, decided that winter camping would be a fun learning experience for the kids. One of our church families, the Stewarts, owned a large property in Horseheads, just outside of Erin. We would be camping for one night in the Stewarts' spacious multi-acre "yard," near enough to the house in case of an emergency.

Our cars climbed up the mile-long driveway onto the family's property and everyone tumbled out of the vehicles into the brisk, cold air. With steamy-white breaths billowing out, the children and adults enthusiastically stamped patches in the snow where we could pitch tents and set up campfires around the site. The Stewarts had two dogs that ran between us licking hands and wagging their tails over all the excitement.

In order for the students to qualify for a winter camping badge, all the main activities needed to be conducted outdoors: cooking three meals, sleeping, and even cleaning after the meals. Thankfully, that evening, the Stewart family did invite us indoors for a brief break from the cold. We warmed ourselves over hot chocolate and popcorn as we sang songs by the fire and petted their large, friendly dogs. After the enjoyable and unexpected treat, the children marched back to their tents and zipped up in sleeping bags for the night.

Early the next morning we awoke to the dogs barking and a sharp, pungent smell. The dogs had been sniffing around our tents, still excited by their new visitors, when they came across a surprise that none of us had foreseen—a skunk! The astonished animal quickly sprayed his potential predators. Unfortunately, the dogs had been positioned extremely close to the boys' tent. The girls laughed and teased the boys who had been sprayed. No one wanted to get near them.

DEER IN THE HEADLIGHTS

I always said that Elmira was like a salad bowl. The small community, only a ten-minute drive from one end to the other, sat in a valley completely surrounded by lush, green mountains. When we first moved there, the Aspens, maples, and oaks were bright green. They changed to fiery reds, oranges, and yellows in the fall. In winter they would sparkle white with frost, snow, and icicles.

In order to drive out of the Elmira area, it was necessary to scale those steep mountains in my rickety, old Buick. Even in the best of times that car was a sore sight to see. Patches of rust had grown until they consumed most of the car's exterior. The ice and salt of New York's harsh winters had eroded a pie sized hole in the floor on the driver's side of the car. It was so bad that one year we lost a pet cat through that hole. But that is a story for another book.

This story is really about something else that took me completely by surprise. One evening in 1977, I was returning home very late from a teachers' in-service meeting. The kids had stayed back in town at the home of another church member so I was probably pushing the beastly machine harder than I should have in order to get back to them.

The engine groaned as my car approached the crest of the steep mountain bordering our little town. I was giving my car all the acceleration it could take as I climbed the slope. The rest was downhill, as they say. I never expected to see a pair of eyes glaring at me from the middle of the road. But as my car started to descend that mountain, a small doe stood blinking in my headlights, right in the path of my car.

I veered to miss her, but she skittered away in the wrong direction. Unfortunately, she ended up running straight into the path to which I had redirected my enormous Buick. I slammed on my brakes, but the corner of my car still hit the poor animal. Before I could swerve to the edge of the mountainous road, the deer was dead.

Cautiously now, I continued my descent into Elmira. My car was still drivable, though barely so. I drove it, first to pick up the children, then finally home as I maintained a slow, deliberate speed until I crawled into our long gravel driveway. Inspecting my car the next day, I found out that the hood was completely smashed. On my salary, finding the $500 to have it fixed would be a miracle. Thankfully, a kind mechanic did the work and gave me a discounted price I could afford.

CHURCH ACTIVITIES

In the Elmira church, ingathering was more fun than in any congregations we were ever part of. Typically, churches have each family pledge to raise a certain amount of funds for the Adventist Development and Relief Agency (ADRA) during the specified time period, which could be a day or weekend or even a week or month.

The students were excited about ingathering. Two or three leaders would coordinate a large bus full of caroling children. The leaders went from door to door asking for donations with the pleasant sound of singing in the background.

Homeowners opening their doors on a blustery winter evening were much more likely to give money to our cause when they heard our off-key though enthusiastic songs of Christmas. And students were more likely to participate if they were not required to do the actual door knocking and donation asking.

At one particular home, our upper-grade teacher gave his usual speech: "We are collecting funds for the Adventist Disaster Relief Association to help those needier than we are."

When the man who answered the door heard Mr. Skinner's speech, he quickly replied, "Did you say Adventist?"

"Yes," Mr. Skinner answered.

"Just a minute," the man responded, quickly shutting the door and leaving the collectors out in the cold. The singing children paused briefly to find out what the hesitation was about, and Mr. Skinner turned to us and shrugged, demonstrating his own confusion. Most people either replied with "No, thank you," or by digging in their pockets for some change. A few people may have put in bills as large as a $10 or $20, but no one had shut the door on us with the expectation that we should wait.

When the homeowner returned to Mr. Skinner, he thrust a sizable check into the waiting teacher's hand. "Thank you!" Mr. Skinner said, gasping at the amount written.

"I just want to thank you and your church," the man said.

"Are you an Adventist?" Mr. Skinner asked.

"No, but some time ago, I took your Stop Smoking program. It was the only thing that ever helped me to quit. My life is better now because of what your church has provided."

Before the door had even closed, the children were chirping like little birds. "How much did he give you? What did he say?" Mr. Skinner shared the story with the waiting children and adults before we went on to our final homes. The one hundred dollar check was more than we had expected from our whole night and the children had the chance to observe first-hand the blessings our church provided to the community.

Piling into the bus for our return ride, the singers were giddy with the excitement of songs, snow, and the sizable donation. The boys began making silly rhymes for the standard carols, their voices competing to rise above each other.

"Danny Boy," I exclaimed, "you have the best singing voice!"

"That's your opinion," one of the seventh graders mumbled under his breath, causing the other boys to break out into teasing giggles.

"Oh Mom!" Danny's embarrassment was evident. Still, I was proud of the children, especially my son!

Back at the church, we had the most enjoyable part of the evening. Several ladies had stayed behind making enormous pots of steaming soup: vegetarian chicken noodle, mock beef barley, vegetable minestrone, and always, always, Mrs. Beamesderfer's thick and creamy potato soup. Best of all was the bread. If there is anything an Adventist can make well, it is fresh, hearty whole wheat bread. Many of us preferred the simple indulgence of a conservative smear of margarine on the crusty brown rolls. Being a rich animal product, butter was never used by a good Adventist, but margarine worked well when you didn't know any better. The food warmed our bodies and listening to the results of our fundraising efforts warmed our hearts.

IMPOSSIBLE PIE

Saturday afternoons were the perfect opportunity to connect with other church members. Every Sabbath we were either invited to someone's home for lunch after church or we would do the inviting and have people over. Since I was a single mom, it seemed prudent for me to invite two families over at a time. This way, the men could keep each other company while the children played and the women helped me prepare lunch in the kitchen.

As a working mom, I became skilled at impromptu meals. I never prepared food ahead since my job and other obligations consumed so much of my time. As with most good Adventist homes, our pantry was always stocked with plenty of Worthington brand vegetarian meats made primarily from gluten and soy. With a can of stewed tomatoes and sautéed onions, one of these staple foods could become a savory sauce to pour over steamy rice or noodles. Making the dessert for our instant Sabbath lunches became a breeze when one church member introduced us to Impossible Coconut Pie (recipe at end of chapter).

POPCORN AND APPLES

Because most Adventists ate a large, heavy lunch on Sabbath afternoons, our Saturday Night activities required a much lighter fare. Many times, the children and I were invited to people's homes for game night and we were served popcorn and apples. During a hayride we would also be served popcorn and apples. For Saturday night birthday parties we had popcorn and apples. And on movie nights ... well, you get the picture.

At least once each winter, everyone in the church was invited to the Ziegler's home to ice skate on their pond. The elderly couple's home sat on top of a hill overlooking a sparsely-wooded area. Beside these woods was the small pond where the children and many adults wrapped in multiple layers of wool, cotton and nylon would all don a pair of skates and brave the frigid air for some fun.

When we would tire from the cold and exercise, we could head up the short hill to the Ziegler's home to warm ourselves in front of the fire with a cup of hot chocolate and, you guessed it, popcorn and apples.

THE PINK HOUSE ON GRAY STREET

"True abundance is an absolute knowing that everything you need will be supplied."
Dr. Wayne Dyer

After our first drafty year on the farm, the next spring we decided to move into the town of Elmira where my school was located. There would be no more long, single-lane roads to skid across as I drove home in the winter, no more drafty, cold farmhouse that seemed too dark, even in the middle of the brightest summer day, and no more needing to haul our trash to the dump. City life was full of conveniences.

But that also meant no more fresh produce that we could pick from our garden and no more long walks for the kids through the hills and the creek behind our house.

At least one of these problems was soon taken care of by our church family. We learned in Elmira, perhaps more than at any other time of our lives, that God takes care of our every need. Perhaps that is because our needs were so great at this time of our lives.

It seemed as if all the families in our church were related to at least one other family in some way. Very few had such an uprooted family tree as ours did. One of my students' grandparents, the Simkins, had a small farm on their property richly abundant with tomatoes, peppers, eggplant, and melons. We were invited, along with the rest of the community, to harvest any of the fresh produce we could use.

Now that we had left our little farmhouse in Erin, this new offering would prove to be very helpful. Once a week I would bring out empty Ball jars and lids and carry the huge, black ceramic cooking pot into the kitchen in order to begin the grueling task of chopping, sterilizing, and canning our summer and autumn harvest. My fingers were so used to the years of scalding hot water that I could often pluck the jars out of the boiling water without even using tongs. As I got older, and my nerve endings further lost their sensations, my younger friends would gasp in horror upon seeing me handle hot items. And, indeed, I did endure my share of burns on my forearms. But somehow my hands could tolerate even the hottest of water.

I was also very good at finding pick-your-own farms on our return trips from Michigan's Fruit Belt each summer. They would supply a bushel basket and the apple trees for a nominal fee as long as we filled the basket ourselves. Danny loved scaling the trees and would even offer to climb into the higher branches of other trees for people picking nearby us. I soon found peach orchards, strawberry fields, and blueberry farms that provided the same deal. We drove home, our trunk weighed down with freshly picked fruits of late summer. Once the produce was canned, frozen, or dehydrated, it would last for many months.

With many kids on our new street, Danny and Esther made friends easily. The address was simple: 9 ½ West Gray Street. It was the only time we had an address like that, first because we never lived in a duplex again, and second because from there, the house numbers just kept getting bigger and bigger. By the time we finally ended up in California on a street with only fourteen houses, our address was 10784. Imagine needing to give such long and complicated numbers to a street with so few homes.

We loved our little "half" house that was close to everything we needed. The downstairs consisted of the kitchen, dining room, and a small, stuffy parlor which was only opened when company came to visit. On the second floor were the three bedrooms and the bathroom. Far above those rooms, under a steeply sloping roofline, was the attic where the children could play and watch the excitement on the street below.

Danny and I took each of the small bedrooms while the girls shared the master bedroom. In most households, the adult should have the master bedroom, but it only made sense for the girls to be less cramped and have the extra space. As the lone adult, I was comfortable having my own smaller room. If anything was odd with our living situation, it was the fact that the only bathroom in the entire house resided in the master bedroom.

DANNY SLEEPWALKING

Being a single parent of young children can be a challenge. Ella was sixteen, Esther was ten, and Danny was nine years old. Even though my children were old enough to carry out their basic needs alone, there were moments when having a man around would have helped some. The ones that pop into my mind are those when my son would inevitably fall asleep on the way home. I would tug and pull at him trying to lug his limp form out of the back seat.

"Stop it, Esther!" Danny would scold me, swatting my hands away.

"Get up, Danny," I would coax, tugging just a bit more firmly. "I am your mom, not Esther!"

"Esther! Get out of here!" He would continue to complain but without opening his eyes.

"Let me try, Mom," Esther would suggest. Then, sweetly, quietly she would lean over Danny's sleeping form. "Danny Boy!" He grunted in his sleep. "Get up, Danny Boy!"

"'K, Mom," he would immediately reply, dragging himself up by his own freewill and stumbling up the stairs, blind with sleep.

Danny's sleepwalking didn't seem like much until late one autumn night. Esther and I stayed up late, sewing some clothes in my room far into the night. My door was slightly ajar and Danny's bedroom light was on. We assumed he was still up, tinkering with some gadget or another.

Suddenly, my door burst open and Danny stumbled into the room. Esther and I stared at each other in surprise. Before either of us could say a word, he staggered into the closet and started a battle with my hanging clothes. "Get off me, Esther!" We could hear his sleep induced shouts muffled through the closet doorway. "Esther! I mean it! Get off me!" Then silence, nothing but silence. We continued to watch the closet door guardedly. Esther finally got brave and stood up to investigate. There lay Danny, tangled in all my clothes, fast asleep on the closet floor.

CALIFORNIA HERE I COME!

Our first summer in Elmira was filled with many milestone celebrations, literally and figuratively. The very day Ella turned 16 she went immediately to the DMV and got her driver's license. That year we also planned a trip to Hollywood in California to visit my cousins who were Aunt Sara's children.

I knew that my beat-up old clunker would never be able to make a 3000-mile trip, so I bought my very first, brand new car. I selected a hunter green 1977 Toyota Corolla with monthly payments I could manage. The car smelled brand new, with its velvety soft beige interior. We circled around and around the car in the lot, admiring ourselves in the high gloss shine of dark green paint and chrome. This car seemed to have it all: smooth ride, comfortable seats that I could adjust to fit my small frame, and even air conditioning! Imagine that—no more drab, faded paint that was more rust colored than its original black.

The kids were giddily excited with my new purchase. Though they had never complained about our old car before, the new one would certainly be much less embarrassing to ride in. The dealer showed me how to care for all the small daily maintenance and usage details, and I nodded thoughtfully, wondering how I would remember them all. No one seemed to be listening to him, but I would soon learn that Danny could figure out anything that had moving parts. Ella became the driver of our new car. As he got older, Danny became the mender.

This car would be a far cry from the toy cars Danny had tinkered with and figured out as a child. When he was about five years old, he had taken apart a new toy car track in an attempt to find out how its gas-pump-shaped battery charger held the fuel that made his tiny cars race around the track. Since then he had "fixed" toasters, lamps, radios, and toys all around the house. Any leftover parts would get thrown into his desk drawer to be used for another purpose. I was hopeful that my own car would fare better than his toys and our household items had when he attempted to fix them.

So we loaded up the car with luggage, food, a AAA TripTik®, and a pup-tent and strapped ourselves into our new purchase. Then, with Ella driving very capably, we headed west to California. We had no obligations, just 3000 miles of open road ahead of us.

Several well-wishers showed up to cheer us onward at the commencement of our voyage. We waved at friends as their faces grew smaller the further away we drove until finally, rounding a corner, we could see them no longer. The children settled back in their seats to enjoy the ride. That lasted approximately one hour. Soon Danny and Esther began to bicker from the back seat, "Mo-o-om! Danny's [book, shoe, thumb, knee, etc.] is on my side!" Or, "Esther took my game, but she didn't ask me!" Meanwhile, their arguments were peppered with, "Are we there yet?"

Ella continued to drive, seemingly oblivious to anything that may have distracted her from her duties. And I did my best to amuse Danny and Esther with car games and songs. Fortunately, the TripTik® was a great resource for entertainment.

"Oh Danny Boy," I suggested. "I think you would like to see this!" I said as I pointed to a train museum on the TripTik®.

"No, Ma! I do not want to see any more museums."

"Of course you do! Ella, why don't we stop at the next exit?"

"What do you mean, Mom? No! I can't keep stopping like that! We're already so far behind schedule!"

"Don't be silly, Ella! We can't pass this. It's a historic site! We will only stop for half an hour. Believe me!"

After several of those stops they no longer believed me. Our trip took a week and a half in each direction.

TORNADO WARNING

We entered Nebraska and traveled through most of the state without passing many other cars. No campsites were recorded on our TripTik® and I had suggested that we try to stay at Union College, belonging to our church. The children whined and complained, tired of my attempts to educate them on the wondrous schooling our church provides.

In the middle of our debate, which I was quickly losing, grey skies began to darken and the air took on a heaviness we had never experienced before.

Earlier, Ella had turned on the radio to distract us with some music. Now storm warnings filled the airwaves: "Tornado Warning! This is not a test. Persons within the southwest vicinity of Nebraska should take shelter immediately. Please be advised that it is not safe to remain on the road at this time."

"That's impossible," Esther declared from the back seat. "I thought the only place that has tornados is Kansas."

Ella pulled over and consulted our map. Sure enough, we were right on the edge of the area the radio was issuing warnings for. "We should go somewhere," Danny wisely advised from the back seat. We peered out of the car windows. There was nothing in sight; open roads and flat, barren fields spread in every direction from our car. We did not even know which way to travel in order to find safety and shelter. Ahead of us, in the distance, lightning flickered from heavy, black clouds.

"Why don't we drive that way?" Esther asked, pointing to the road behind us, the way we came. "It was safe back there."

"Because, a tornado can change direction at any time," Ella explained. "We might back track and lose all the distance we've already made, just to end up in the middle of the storm anyway."

"What are we going to do, Mom?" The children's questions were an echo of my own thoughts.

I came up with my best plan. "Let's pray," I suggested.

The children groaned their protests, not believing that prayer was, in fact, the answer to every single problem. But eventually they gave in.

"Lord, we know you have brought us safely this far, and we thank you for it," I began. "Now we are facing a storm like one we have never known before and we ask you to please take care of us again. Keep us safe as we rest here by the side of the road. Send us help if there is anyone around."

We snuggled down in our car, covering up with sleeping bags. We reclined the front seats as far as they could go so Esther and Danny could sleep there. Ella and I took the back. Using luggage to cushion the gaps where our feet would normally go, we created a makeshift "bed" for me to stretch out on while she slept beside me on the seat.

It's ironic that I use the term "sleep" to describe how we passed the night. Truthfully, no one rested at all. I was consumed with worry and drifted in and out of sleep several times to continue praying for our safety there on the side of the road. Positioned closest to the driver's side of the front seat, Danny kept bumping the horn, jolting everyone awake at intervals ranging from several minutes to half an hour. Even when I did manage to doze off, I would be startled awake by the noise.

No one came to our rescue. That does not mean that our prayers were not heard or answered. At dawn, we all tumbled out of the car, stiff and groggy from remaining cramped and sleepless all night. Folding up the makeshift bedding, we crawled back into the car to resume our journey. Despite the brightness of the new day, our car rolled past random patches of destruction and the rubble remains of the storm that had raged the previous night. It really was a miracle that we stayed alive, untouched by the deadly storm.

TWENTY-FOUR-HOUR SOMETHING OR OTHER

Our cross-country meals had simply been nuts, fruits, vegetables, bread, and cheese. We occasionally prepared a hot meal over the campfire but then ate the leftovers cold for several meals afterward. Russians are brilliant at maintaining a reliable stash of food to get them through any situation, whether it is a trip to the gas station or a trip across the United States. Being a post-World War II Russian, I was probably more talented than most in this area. We did not go hungry for a single day along our journey. In addition to the food I had hoarded, the Lord had provided so much more along the way.

Though I had been prepared to share the responsibility, Ella insisted on driving the entire 3,000 miles. For the most part, we drove eight hours each day, stopping at campgrounds in the evenings to sleep. By the time we arrived in Wyoming, Ella had driven herself to exhaustion. She burned with a fever and her bleary eyes had trouble staying focused on the road. I insisted that she pull over.

We drove through a small town but found nothing open. Every hotel and motel had their "No Vacancy" signs lit up, the blaring neon red, yellow, or green lights turning us away. I never knew Wyoming was such a popular vacation destination. "Please Lord," I prayed, "you know how badly Ella needs to rest. Help us to find a room somewhere."

"Pull in here," I directed her when another motel appeared into view.

"But Mom, it says, 'No Vacancy,'" she complained. Not taking "no" for an answer, I insisted. Ella finally complied.

I walked into the lobby and asked for the manager. "Sir," I pleaded, "we desperately need a place to stay."

"Sorry, ma'am," he said shaking his head. "There's a rodeo in town and every room has been booked for at least six months."

"Please sir," I persisted. "We only need one bed. We can share, but we are exhausted from our travels and my daughter has gotten sick. She just needs a place to rest. We didn't make any reservations because we've been staying at campsites all along our trip, but I can't expect a sick child to stay in a tent."

"Have a seat, and I'll see what I can do," the man said. But I could see the tiredness in his eyes too. I sent up another prayer that he would be able to help us.

I sat down momentarily, then stood back up and walked out of the small lobby to check on my children. Ella's eyes were closed and her head rested on the seat behind her while Danny and Esther entertained themselves by gathering small rocks, leaves, and insects from the bushes around the driveway.

Shortly, the man returned and motioned me back to the desk. "We don't have any more rooms available," he repeated. I sighed, unsure of how we would go on. "But there is a single bed in the groundskeeper's unit that we never rent out. You can stay there if you'd like. Your daughter can have a bed to sleep in, and I guess you can just use your sleeping bags for the rest of you."

"Oh, thank you, thank you!" I exclaimed as he slid the paperwork across the desk for me to fill out. I took the key and rushed to get my children unloaded. Ella staggered into the room, darkened the windows and went directly to sleep. Danny and Esther excitedly changed into their swimming suits.

"This place has a *pool*, Mom!" Danny shouted, slamming the door on his way outside with his sister. The two of them splashed and played blissfully for the remainder of the day while I went in and out, first checking on my swimming children, then checking on my slumbering child. Danny, Esther, and I ate a simple dinner, while Ella slept on, oblivious to any sounds around her. Then, as darkness spread outside, we rolled out our sleeping bags and crawled in to rest.

The morning was an echo of the previous evening. Ella was still sleeping soundly while Danny and Esther got in a few more precious moments of pool time until I finally returned to the room to find Ella sitting up in bed watching TV.

"I feel all better," she said. "Must have been a twenty-four-hour flu." I fed her a piece of bread, which she did not have much appetite for, and then went back out to bring Danny and Esther in from swimming.

The children burst into the room and immediately began protesting. "Why do we have to go? I want to swim more! How come she gets to watch TV?" We scurried around, taking one last shower and packing up our belongings while Ella seemed to regain her strength minute by minute. By the time we got back on the road, she was fine again and insisted on taking the wheel as before. That night was our only night in a hotel room for the entire trip.

SALT LAKE CITY

I wanted my children to learn about the history of each state we visited.

They discovered that pillories were used as a form of public humiliation and posed, smiling, with their heads and hands firmly clamped in the rings that held prisoners more than a century ago. They observed the salt mines of Utah and the Grand Canyon in Arizona. But all the children were interested in seeing was Hollywood movie stars. And the only things they wanted to learn were the lines of famous movies. Our trip was taking far too long for them.

Most nights we stayed in one of the many campsites along our route. Occasionally we were able to connect with friends and former church members who eagerly invited us to stay in their homes. Looking back on it, I realize that it was quite amazing the way that people reached out to us. Families of friends were just as welcoming as our own friends.

We pulled into Salt Lake City, Utah on a Friday afternoon. I enthusiastically searched for my former classmates, Zaki and Hasmiq from Middle East College. When I tried their number, the telephone operator said that all their phone calls were being temporarily redirected to another line. I tried the alternate number and reached the local Adventist Church.

The polite man who answered the phone introduced himself as Jack and told me that Zaki and Hasmiq were teaching English in Saudi Arabia. "But you are welcome to stay in our home," he quickly offered.

"Thank you so much," I said, "but I have my three children with me and that would be too much trouble for you."

"I insist!" he said. "My sister is also in town from Loma Linda University, and we have plenty of room."

Ella objected when I told the children of the offer. "But we don't know them!"

"They are our Adventist family," I explained. "Why should we stay at another campsite when these people are offering their hospitality to us?"

Convinced that we were going to inconvenience the family, Ella persisted, but it was too late. I had already accepted the man's generous offer.

He had given us directions to the church and we met up with him there. Jack then took us on a short tour of the salt mines, the Morton Salt Company, and a copper mine. We viewed the beautiful Mormon temple, though only from the outside since their law did not permit any non-consecrated Mormons to enter.

After a long day driving and sightseeing, we finally arrived at their home. The house greatly exceeded our meager expectations. After a week of staying in campsites and even our overnight experience sleeping in our car during the Nebraska tornado, Jack's house looked like a palace.

We soon learned that Jack was a builder. His home was certainly a reflection of his talent. Wide windows and doors led out to patios that overlooked their spacious property. His talented wife had wallpapered the walls of her children's rooms with sheets to match their bedding. Everything was precisely decorated and immaculately clean.

But best of all were the large, roomy guest quarters in the basement. Two single beds, as well as an oversized couch and chairs, filled the space. We were probably all wondering who would get the beds when Jack opened the couch *and* one of the chairs to reveal hide-a-beds within the furniture. Their basement was more comfortably adorned than any place we had ever stayed.

Since the following day would be Sabbath, our hosts suggested that we remain an extra day with them. We attended their church, ate lunch together, and then took a nature hike around the woods on their property. In the evening, Jack's sister Ellen had a special treat for us. We went into our basement room, the darkest area of the house, and she had each of the children sit in turn on a chair in front of her. She then turned off the lights and directed the beam of a desk lamp toward them. Then, very carefully, using only a sheet of black cardstock and her sharp, precise scissors, Ellen snipped and cut to reveal a profile cameo of each of my children.

I had never seen anything like that done in front of me. I was amazed at how talented she was. I must have expressed some admiration for her skill, because Ellen was soon demonstrating how I could do a similar project by tracing the profile onto a piece of paper taped to the wall behind the model. This tracing could then be cut out in the same manner. I took that craft idea back with me. For the next several years, my students and I would work together making cameos as gifts for their parents.

Once Sunday morning came, we bade farewell to an amazing family and new friends that we would never forget.

HELLO CALIFORNIA!

When we finally rolled into Hollywood, the children, star-struck and dazzled, gaped at the broad, six-lane boulevards lined with lofty western palms. "It looks like everything in California grows tall and skinny," Ella sighed, as we watched one more lean, bronzed couple walk in front of us.

My cousin Fahimeh and her husband Mohsen welcomed us warmly into their home. Within moments the children had formed a fast bond with

Fahimeh's girls, Avid, Azin, and Nazanin. For two weeks we trailed our extended family to the small French grocery store they co-owned with Fahimeh's younger brother Keyoumarce (Que). During that time, we also visited Que, his lovely wife Acram, and their 3 children: Fedra, Leila, and Sheila as well as Adeleh, her husband Dr. Hushang Dowlatshai, and their children Haleh and Kian. We toured numerous famous sights around Los Angeles as the days spun past in rapid succession until it was finally time for us to leave.

Of course, a return trip would be incomplete if it was uneventful. Ours went well until our air conditioning broke—right in the middle of Death Valley. We decided to brave the heat as we drove an entire day before coming to a reputable-looking repair shop along the route. As we rolled into the small desert town I glanced over at Danny, slumped on the front seat beside me, tongue lolling and sweat pouring down his thin, shirtless frame.

"Should we try to go a little farther?" I suggested hopefully.

"No!" the children shouted in unison. The Lord was kind and led us to a repair shop that was able to fix it in a few short hours.

NOSOCA PINES RANCH

One summer, the university I attended for my master's advertised a need for teachers for their summer camp at Nosoca Pines, which was located in a beautiful area between North Carolina and South Carolina. I volunteered to teach math, Danny was registered to study remedial reading, and Esther took a math class. Ella was at an age when she no longer joined us on family trips.

At this camp, there was a big lake with a little tiny island in the center of it. The campers could row boats to it or swim across. One day Esther insisted that we swim to the island. She stressed the fact that this lake was not a deep one. So I started my doggy paddle with her swimming beside me. Suddenly I realized my short legs could not touch the bottom of the lake. I started panicking and screaming "Help, help!" Esther thought I was joking and started laughing. Fortunately, someone else heard me as they were crossing the lake and came to my rescue. Without his help, I would have drowned that day.

Now in my 80s, I paddle laps every day at the gym, even in the 12 ft. deep section. Though I may not have the long strokes of a professional swimmer, I am no longer frightened of the water.

❖ ❖ ❖

When we had decided to attend Nosoca Pines, it seemed logical to call our dear old friend, Aunt Viola Baker, who used to rent the room upstairs in our Yonkers home. By that time she had moved to Kingstree, just north of Charleston, South Carolina, and we had not seen her for several years. Viola was more excited than we could have imagined to be reunited with us.

We sat on her porch, fanning ourselves and sipping on icy cold Coca-Cola from glass bottles to keep cool. I had never allowed my children to drink caffeinated sodas, so they were thrilled that the deep Carolina summer heat gave them an excuse. Viola's blue eyes twinkled and soft layers of chin and belly and cheeks quivered as her laughter rumbled out. "Ya'll know Ah nevah drank these dahk dranks, but it's so hawt out heah, we don't have much choice," she drawled, her lips curling into a pleased smile.

We were purposely situated on the front porch in order to have a better view of the street. "Ah called the paypah and they ah sendin' a reportah to meet ya'll!" She was so thrilled to be sharing her long ago friends with her small town. Viola scanned the cross street and sighed as two cars crawled along slowly, not turning toward us. "He must be stuck in awl that traffic," she decided. Danny and Esther looked at each other and giggled. That set off Viola's rumbling laugh. "Naw, Ah know what ya'll ah thinkin'!" She exclaimed. "Ah've lived in New Yawk and Ah know this ain't real traffic. But to these here folk, this is real heavy traffic and they don' know how to drive it!"

At that moment, a long town car pulled into the street and parked in front of us. "Miss Bakah? Ahm the reportah ya'll called fo."

We strained to comprehend the foreign sounding language the reporter spoke to Viola. Even her southern drawl had amplified since moving back. Ironically, one of the first comments the reporter had when I started speaking was about my own Russian accent!

We sat and chatted late into the afternoon, swatting flies and fanning ourselves until he proclaimed that he had all that he needed. The next day, much sooner than we had expected, the front page headlines proclaimed, "Russian Who Found God Visits Kingstree!"

DYSLEXIA

As a child and well into my adult life, I always struggled with reading and spelling. I never had issues with math and learning new languages, but my inability to comprehend words was troublesome. To compensate for these problems, I decided to take an evening speed-reading course in Elmira College.

According to the class description in the brochure, I should soon be able to read an entire book in ten minutes. Sadly, what I discovered was that, although I no longer mixed up letters within a word, I was now mixing up the meanings within entire paragraphs! All that "speed-reading" helped me to accomplish was getting my reading up to the speed of a normal person. I eventually learned that students with dyslexia compensate by using learning styles that are uniquely their own.

Now, as a senior citizen, I have undergone cataract surgery, replacing my old, worn out lenses with new ones and improving my vision so much that I can now read print tinier than anyone half my age. My children tell me I have "bionic eyes." Yet when I try to read anything, sometimes the words and letters still get jumbled up in my brain. Even my memory of spoken words get mixed up and to this day my kids giggle at my numerous spelling errors.

Studying for my master's degree seventeen years after obtaining my bachelor's in elementary education was very difficult, especially with my dyslexia. When I first started back to school at Andrews, I found that I could make friends easily with other students. This was a skill I used to my advantage. These friends were happy to help me out by lending me their class notes. In this way, I was able to condense long assignments into shorter, more comprehensible material to study from. With the help of my fellow classmates and my own copious note taking, I successfully completed several summer sessions and was another step closer to earning my master's.

A DAY IN THE LIFE

With Ella away at the academy, I needed afterschool activities to keep Esther and Danny busy. I found that I was often the last one left working late into the evening in order to complete grading and lesson plans. Once I discovered I had dyslexia, I understood why the tasks took me so much longer than any of the other teachers.

One night a week, we had Pathfinders. As a single mom working late every evening, I needed to cover four more weeknights. To solve this issue, Esther and Danny each took up a musical instrument. Esther chose the flute and Danny the trumpet. Unfortunately, the music teacher gave private lessons during the day at the school, which didn't help my dilemma much. Still, I could make them practice which would eat up at least an hour each day.

Although the trumpet provided some diversion, I realized that with Danny's energy, it would be more worthwhile to enter the children in some type of sport. I found a gymnastics school near the laundromat in town and enrolled Esther in it. Danny begged for karate. Between the two activities, I had three days a week where I could take the kids to their classes, do a quick load of laundry or do some grocery shopping, then rush back and pick them up.

By the end of our second year in Elmira, Esther discovered the guitar. One of her friends, Pam, had been taking lessons from a young lady in town, conveniently located near the gymnastics school. We went to the music store and picked out a small acoustic guitar for Esther to use and started one more music lesson. With piano lessons from the principal's wife, the kids were able to build on the lessons they took back in Yonkers. Since Danny was also playing the recorder, this totaled three instruments for each kid.

And if that was not quite enough to keep them entertained, I also talked one of the new moms in church into leaving her children with Esther for an hour each day after school. Theoretically Danny could be using that time to study, but more often than not, he would find a way to run off with the local kids and get into some kind of mischief.

ELLA HAS A SURPRISE

Ella was enjoying her independence and last year of high school at Elmira Free Academy. Although her grades had much improved, she made many new friends which did not meet my standards of approval. The girls were not from Adventist homes and I didn't know their families.

When Ella would go out with them, I never knew what they were up to. Often, when the girls would come to the house, I would give them religious pamphlets from the church. Some of them had messages about Jesus' love for us and others contained our Adventist health message about abstinence from smoking, drugs, and alcohol. For some reason, Ella did not appreciate it when I shared my beliefs with her friends.

Then one day Ella announced that she had a boyfriend. My first question was, "Is he an Adventist?" This immediately upset Ella. She listed all the faults that she perceived in Adventist men and ended with the fact that my marriage to an Adventist man was disastrous. She highlighted all this before stating, quite emphatically, that her boyfriend was not, in fact, an Adventist.

Jerry McConnell was tall, blond, and soft-spoken. He arrived at our home for dinner one evening and sat awkwardly through a guarded conversation with me in our stuffy, rarely-used living room while Ella sat proudly beside him, holding his hand protectively. After dinner they rushed off for a date, though why they needed to go out again was beyond my comprehension.

After a couple years of dating, Ella came home with another announcement. "We're getting married!" she exclaimed, showing off the dainty diamond on the fourth finger of her left hand.

"Ella! You are too young to get married," I insisted. "You're only nineteen." That was not an effective argument in her eyes. As far as Ella was concerned, she was more of an adult than anyone else she knew. Besides, they were in love. My heart fell and I'm quite sure it crashed into my stomach on the way down.

It seems that all the ladies in the church were more than happy to dive into the wedding plans and help me out. Onalee Hartman took over the bulk of the work, organizing other ladies into various work groups. The wedding itself would be held at a local Lutheran church, far outside of the limits of our little town, and the reception would be at the fire station hall.

Lotfy arrived in time for the rehearsal dinner. Danny and Esther piled into his car to drive to the church, excited to have their dad around and enjoying the peaceful circumstances with him for a change. Lotfy approved of Jerry's family immediately, though it would not have mattered one bit to Ella if he had disapproved of them.

Though the McConnells owned a trucking company and were much wealthier than we were, they lived a simple country lifestyle. They had several children younger than Jerry and he would continue to work for his father's business after he and Ella married.

Danny and Esther immediately started to enjoy their new extended family as they ran in and out of the house chasing after or followed by the rest of the McConnell clan. Mrs. McConnell took one look at my two younger children and gushed, "Raya, you have three beautiful daughters! I never knew you had twins!"

"I'm a boy!" Danny exclaimed. His hair was quite a bit longer than we normally let it grow and Esther's was cut short, no doubt causing the two to look a lot alike.

"Oh, what a sin," she sighed, staring at Danny's large black eyes. "Lashes like those should never be wasted on a boy, but too often they are!" The next week I would walk in to find Danny ready to trim his lashes with a pair of paper scissors! That happened immediately after he tried taming the part in his hair, by cutting it into the direction he wanted it to fall.

The wedding day was filled with the usual last minute jitters and stress, although Ella was very excited about her new life. Lotfy seemed to have more than child support on his mind when he gave Ella and Jerry his blessing. He used this opportunity to contact me about reinstating our marriage.

In the final moments before the father of the bride should be escorting his daughter down the aisle, Lotfy and I were having an argument in the church basement. Lotfy insisted that we end our separation. Esther, dressed in a long sky-blue junior bridesmaid gown, was sobbing, heartbroken about the ruined wedding so I quickly sent her out to line up with the other girls.

"This is not the time or the place." I finally suggested that the two of us meet for counseling, in order to find out if our marriage could be salvaged.

In the end, Ella had a lovely wedding. Although I did not concede to reuniting with him, Lotfy finally walked her down the aisle, both of them smiling as though nothing had transpired. Esther betrayed the stress of the day with a fresh flood of tears splashing down the front of her dress as she watched her sister and father interact. Fortunately for us, everyone misunderstood the source of her tears. Well-wishers hugged Esther in the reception line and assured her that she was not losing a sister but gaining a brother.

IT'S OFFICIAL: THE DIVORCE, 1979

As I had anticipated, the counseling sessions were fruitless. Lotfy spent every session raging to the therapist about my sins and shortcomings. I sat dumbfounded through three sessions, not even capable of standing up for myself, let alone bringing his actions to light.

The end result of our counseling sessions was to terminate our marriage. I received the official letter at school but waited for all of my students to leave for the day before opening it. As I stared at the divorce papers, a feeling of remorse and grief washed over me. After almost twenty years, I knew that a life with Lotfy would never be healthy for me or my children, but this deep sense of failure, loss, and disappointment in myself and in him could not be denied.

I covered my face in my hands and wept for the life I never intended to create. As is often the case, God sends someone to strengthen and comfort us in our darkest hour, even when we do not think to ask. Another teacher, Gloria Spielman, was working late that afternoon and happened to walk into my classroom and found me a complete wreck. She listened and soothed me as I released all my anger and frustration. I cried, I raged, and I vented while Gloria consoled me.

Months later she would come to me for comfort and healing. Being the only divorced woman she knew in our tiny, conservative community, Gloria would then need me to identify with her when her own family life became less than bearable for her. But for now, Gloria was the ear and the arms and the heart I needed in a dismal time of my life.

OCTAGON SOAP

I had made some very creative lifestyle changes and sacrifices since the divorce. One thing I did to economize was to start using Octagon Soap. This detergent in a tall, bright yellow container was not only dirt cheap but also a very effective cleanser. From dishes to delicate laundry to my children's hair, we used Octagon for everything!

Thursdays at our school were pool days. In the mornings, each class took one-hour turns at the local YWCA where we had swimming lessons.

After swimming in the highly chlorinated pool, I undertook the responsibility of ensuring that all my students thoroughly washed all the pool water out of their hair. Nothing would work better than Octagon. The older students were shocked. "Wait, isn't that for cleaning dishes?"

"So? If it gets dishes clean, why not your hair?" I asserted, while Esther shrank into the corner of the locker room, hoping not to be noticed.

ELLA MAKES A HOME

Through the hectic year-end craziness of school, we rarely had time to visit Ella in her home. She had graduated from Elmira Free Academy and was living with her husband. We all missed her, even Esther and Danny while they were away at Spring Camporee. So when Ella's birthday rolled around, we took advantage of the opportunity and paid her a visit.

When we got there, we were in for a huge surprise. Like everything else that Ella touched, she had transformed that little home into a lovely, modest haven. We found the place immaculate, as neatly organized and tastefully decorated as their newlywed budget would allow. We dined on pasta and the kids sat happily in the living room listening as Ella entertained us with stories about neighbors, work, and school.

As I listened to my children interact, I settled back into the couch and found something pressing into my thigh. I lifted the cushion next to me only to find a book on baby names. "Ella!" I exclaimed, "Are you pregnant?" She looked up at me from the kitchen sink and stalked over to where I was sitting, snatching the book away from my hands.

"Mom, why are you digging through my stuff?" Ella evaded my initial question as she rushed to stash the book away in a drawer.

"I'm not digging," I defended myself. "The book was digging into me. And it really hurt me!" I returned to my job as matriarch of the family by continuing my prying. "So, you're pregnant?"

"I never said I was pregnant, Mom," Ella replied.

"Then why would you have that book?" I asked. I was torn by this possible revelation. On the one hand, Ella had just graduated from high school, and at eighteen, was far too young for motherhood. On the other hand, I had waited far too long to become a mother and I didn't mind being a grandmother at all.

"Mom, I'm not talking about this anymore."

"You haven't talked about anything yet!" But Ella was already distracting her brother and sister with another story, this one involving an accident on the way home from work late one night.

"... so I was just lying there and my car was flipped into the bushes when a policeman came and tapped me. But I was passed out so he woke me up and I said, 'Leave me alone, I'm dead!'"

Esther and Danny burst into giggles at the thought of someone not knowing that they were in fact alive. "So then what happened?" Esther asked eagerly.

"So the policeman started to ask me all kinds of questions, you know. It was late at night and I was confused, so he thought I was drinking. I told him, 'I don't drink,' but he didn't believe me and he kept bugging me so I said, 'I told you, I'm dead!'" Ella's animated story inspired more laughter from her siblings and, of course, worry from me.

"Ella, were you really in an accident?"

"Yeah, Mom," she answered.

"What happened to your car?"

"It's in the shop. I'm driving Jerry's van when he's on the road, and he drives me around when he's home."

"Ella, why didn't you tell me you were in an accident?" I demanded.

"Mom, it's nothing. Anyway, the hospital called Jerry. He came out. It's his responsibility now."

Somehow the people we love the most are the ones who know exactly the words with which to hurt us.

Ella and Jerry eventually moved into an apartment near our house so the children and I could visit more frequently. A picture of Jerry's Corvette sat propped up on the mantle. "He sold that to buy a van," she said as she watched Esther scrutinizing the photo. We all knew that Jerry had customized his van the year he planned to take a road trip to Florida. Meeting Ella had derailed his plans, but the couple seemed happy about the changes they had encountered in their life together.

Then one day I returned from work to find Ella at our house. "What happened?" I asked.

"I'm done with him," she said through her tears. "I caught him at a bar with another woman. I don't need to live for 18 years with a man who will betray me in the end." I knew that Ella was referring to my own marriage to her father. She moved back in and, after only a couple of years, her short-lived marriage was over.

WATKINS GLEN – FALL BEFORE MOVING

Since leaving my husband, I had petitioned with the conference to move me to California. The only family I had in the United States lived there, and I really wanted my children to be able to develop roots. No matter what tactic I used to express my desire to move, the conference would not approve it. Making an interstate transition was fairly easy for them to handle. But a 3000 mile, cross-country change of address took a lot more coordination.

First of all, the receiving conference should want me. Typically, a conference tried to employ from within their own teacher list before dipping into others. Also, as in any industry, it's not always *what* you know but more often *who* you know that matters. Since I knew no one anywhere in California, other than my cousins who were most definitely not Adventists, I did not have the connections that would allow the move to happen.

With my third term in Elmira coming to an end in 1980, I received a notice from the conference that I would be required to change schools before the next school year. My children dreaded the thought of leaving their first real home town. It did not take much to notice that many roots were firmly established within the Elmira city limits. Generations of families lived and worshiped together in this small town. But our family tree would not take root here.

Springtime inspired a field trip for my class and I arranged for a tour of Elmira's nearby outdoor attraction: Watkins Glen State Park. Parent volunteers and I packed my sixteen students into two cars. It would be prudent to mention that I was not breaking any transportation laws of the time. Seatbelts were much more of a recommendation and much less of a perceived necessity in the late 1970s. As educators, we recognized that the value of an off-site educational experience was of far greater importance than safety, although to have both would have been ideal. So I found myself packed like my students, along with lunches, jackets and anything else we thought we might need, and headed out on a 45-minute drive on a beautiful spring morning.

Watkins Glen is comprised of a series of steps and walkways climbing over, under, and around trees, flowers, and waterfalls. After a long morning's hike, we found a grassy field to spread our picnic blankets and enjoy a leisurely lunch. The children romped around as we adults rested in the sunshine.

When it was time to finish our tour of the state park, I blew my whistle and waved the students over. They came running back and lined up ready to go. With the warmth of the day, as well as the energy of the children, we were soon panting and sweating on our hike. The heat could not have gotten much more unbearable.

Before long I heard a child cry out, "Pool!" I looked in the direction we were heading and saw what the student had pointed out. A large swimming area was filled with groups of people enjoying the cool water on the late spring day. I shushed the students who, by this time, had begun to bounce around excitedly, anticipating the option of splashing away the dirt and the day's high temperatures in the clear blue water.

"We can go to the pool," I promised them, "but you still need to walk in an orderly fashion." Turning back toward the pool, I missed the next step and stumbled forward. Fortunately, I was able to break my fall momentarily, but I used my ankle to do it. I felt a sharp pain and a snap in my left leg that my weak, Russian-bred bones could not withstand.

I tumbled to the ground and cried out in pain. The other parents rushed to my side and my students swarmed around me, their little faces pinched with concern. A young couple passing by helped me as I struggled to stand, but I could not put any weight on my leg.

In a blur of events, I was sent to the first-aid building, then to the Schuler County Hospital, close by the park. I had sustained yet another break to my weak left leg. Remembering the stern warning of my childhood doctor, I mourned that I would spend the rest of my life disabled.

When I shared my concern, the emergency room physician assured me, "No one ends up disabled from a simple broken leg!"

"But that was what my doctor in Russia had told me," I insisted.

"You are not in Russia any longer!" He promised. As my leg began to heal over the coming months, I soon came to understand how far superior American medicine was to anything the Soviets had offered.

Recipe for Impossible Coconut Pie

Ingredients:

3 eggs
3 tbsp. butter or margarine
1 1/2 c. milk
Pinch salt

1/4 c. and 2 tbsp. Bisquick®
1/2 c. sugar
1 tsp. vanilla
3/4 c. coconut

Directions:

1. Grease four 9-inch pie pans
2. Mix eggs in a blender
3. Add Bisquick® and butter and blend again
4. Add remaining items and blend well
5. Pour into pie pans and bake at 350° for 45–50 minutes

Figure 23 - Pathfinders in New York

Russian Who Found God Visits Kingstree

VISITORS—Posing with Viola Baker on the steps of her home are her visitors from New York. Back row, from left, Ella Abadir, Mrs. Raya Abadir, Miss Baker. Front row, Esther and Daniel Abadir.

Miss Viola Baker had guests last week—a family that has traveled a long road to get to America, a land they say is "the most wonderful place to live."

Raya Abadir, a native of Russia and Iran, sat with her three children in Miss Baker's home Thursday, explaining her background in a nation under the dictatorship of Stalin, where religion was banned. Her conversion to Christianity and adherance to the Seventh Day Adventist faith came when she moved to Iran after World War II.

At a Seventh Day Adventist mission in Iran, Mrs. Abadir was introduced to God and Christ. "I loved the faith and accepted it," said said. During Stalin's reign in Russia, parents could not teach their children any religion, she added.

She learned English at the mission, and taught a school of 75 children of ambassadors. For 20 years she has worked for the Adventist Church in Iran, Lebanon, Egypt and North Carolina. Today she teaches in Yonkers, N.Y., and is planning shortly to move to Elmira in upstate New York.

Mrs. Abadir speaks six languages—Russian, Turkish, Tatarian, Persian, Arabic and English—and her husband, also a teacher, is in Who's Who in the United States.

Mrs. Abadir's oldest daughter, Ella, 16, was born in Egypt and is named for the missionary who converted Mrs. Abadir, Ella Mae Robinson. Her second daughter, Esther, was born in Persia. The 10-year-old's Egyptian name is Hiam, meaning "love." Her son Daniel, 8, was born in North Carolina.

The children have enjoyed swimming in Black River during their stay in Kingstree. As Mrs. Abadir and family prepared last week to return to New York—and an imminent move to a more rural environment—the devout woman reflected on her journey from Communist Russia to the U.S., saying, "We thank the Lord for bringing us out of bondage."

Figure 24 - Newspaper Story Prompted by Viola Baker

PART VIII: NEW YORK'S CAPITAL, 1980–1982

"The Lord is my shepherd, I have everything I need." Psalms 23:1

One thing the emergency room doctor could not help me with was my impending move. I would have to endure it with a cast on my leg. I hobbled around as Ella packed boxes and hauled furniture from room to room in preparation for moving to Albany, NY. "Mom, sit down," she insisted more than once. "Mom, you're getting in the way again! I'll take care of it."

She certainly did. When the moving truck arrived at our new home, I found out exactly how Ella had managed to pack us up so efficiently.

"Ella, where is my sewing mannequin?" I asked searching through my belongings.

"Oh Mom, you never used that!"

"Didn't I have two black trunks?" I searched through the tall stacks of boxes for my large steamer trunks but could only find one. Surely these were far too large for one of them to be hiding.

"One of them was just filled with junk so I left it with the mannequin upstairs."

"Where upstairs?" I knew I had taken a final walkthrough before the truck pulled out and I hadn't seen anything in the bedrooms.

"I left it in the attic," she said. "And I left all those smelly fabrics you never used."

"Ella, those would have made a beautiful quilt!"

"Mom, they stank like mothballs and you're lucky I got rid of them!" Luck did not seem like the appropriate word, but there was no use in grieving my lost belongings. Instead, I turned to the task of meeting my new church family and decorating our new home.

It was 1980 when we arrived in Albany with no actual place to stay. Fortunately, the church allowed us to temporarily move into the school building. Tri-City Junior Academy boasted a large gymnasium, an enormous kitchen and, best of all, the two bathrooms had showers. The children and I took over our new makeshift residence.

This situation, though temporary, seemed perfect for us. I was able to work almost endlessly setting up my new classroom, while Esther spent many afternoons "helping" me arrange books on the shelf. Truthfully, she spent more time reading the books than shelving them.

Eleven-year-old Danny preferred the outdoors, happily using my car to spin donuts on the property's empty field, although he could barely see over the steering wheel. He also loved searching through the wooded area behind the building. While climbing trees and scouting trails, he discovered an amazing treasure one afternoon and came running in to show it to me. "Mom! Mom! Check out the beehive," he sputtered, as he and a friend dragged an enormous nest through my door. The boys carried it between them, hanging from a large branch, as the children of Israel may have transported the Arc of the Covenant ages ago.

"Danny! Where did you find that?" I gasped in amazement. "Are you sure that it's empty?" The rich, sweet smell of honey still clung to the comb.

"It's empty, Mom," he assured me, dropping specks of leaves and twigs around the classroom. The mess he made was evidently not sufficient so Danny attempted to shorten the branch which was holding the waxy bee hotel.

"Danny, Danny, leave that alone now," I ordered. "Help me hang it in this corner so it won't break." We pushed and pulled and propped it in every conceivable direction, but the giant beehive was just too big to hang.

The principal stopped in one day to set up his classroom and I asked him for any ideas. "I can bring you some fishing twine," he suggested. So, with several strands of the strong, nylon cord, my beehive was finally, securely hung. For three years it was perched from the corner of my classroom until we finally moved. And every year after that, with every move to a new city, I anticipated that my fragrant, golden beehive would travel with me and reside in my classroom, a source of awe for all who saw it.

One evening, a bouncy jazz beat drifted down the hallway to my classroom. I had already been forewarned that a neighbor rented the gym to teach a jazzercise class. I could hear her counting out the rhythm and calling movements as legwarmer-clad women bounced around among the echoes of the high gym walls.

Little did I know that my adolescent son had discovered this group of leotard-attired women and sat on the gym stage watching their every move. "Shouldn't you be going home?" the instructor asked.

"This *is* my home," Danny boasted, his interest never wavering. "I live here!"

The class continued, but I was later asked to assist with ensuring the ladies' privacy in the future.

Shortly after moving into the school, we received word that our church would be letting us rent the parsonage in Latham. The home was to be rented to our pastor, but he and his wife lived alone and did not need such a large space for themselves. Once they purchased a smaller home, the conference let us know that the Latham home could be ours as long as we remained in Albany.

We were so excited to move into the new neighborhood! Never before had we lived in such a spacious home. The children all had separate bedrooms which left one extra room that we rented to single men or women in the church. The small fee helped to offset our monthly expenses and I could be sure that someone trustworthy was almost always at home. Even so, it wasn't always entirely comfortable having non-family members living with us.

We soon learned to adapt to many different lifestyles and became acquainted with the most unusual people. One of our renters never let us waste any food. Now, I come from a third-world country where we learned to live without many things. Waste does not occur around me if I have any say in the matter, although I must admit that this young man had me beat. Anytime he shared a meal with us, he would scrape the children's leftovers onto his own plate and devour every crumb. The first time this happened, my daughter hesitated in passing her plate to him, but he assured her saying "I'll finish off anything for anyone! I do this at Pizza Hut too!" He went on to tell us that whenever he ate out, he would have the waitresses bring him the leftovers from nearby tables after the patrons had finished.

"Remind me never to go to Pizza Hut with him," Esther mumbled under her breath as she cleared the remaining dishes from the table.

Regardless of our interesting renters, our new home was beautiful and fully furnished with lined tapestry drapes and carpeting in every single room. Even the bathrooms and kitchen had carpeting. "What kind of person puts carpeting in a bathroom?" Ella wanted to know. But I didn't care. To me, our home was just perfect!

A FORT

We moved into our new neighborhood in the fall of 1980 and the woods, creeping up to our back windows, had already lost most of their autumn leaves. Danny was thrilled with the prospect of exploring the forest just as he had done in the wooded area behind our school. He created a live animal trap and lured squirrels into it before snapping the doorway down behind them. Then, always the animal lover, Danny coaxed and fed and finally trained a wild squirrel to come to him, eat from his hand, and even curl up, silky-soft on his shoulder, her bushy, auburn tail coiled around his neck. I had always wondered what was happening to the nuts I was buying from the local health food co-op. His demonstration of creature care made the answer clear.

One afternoon I noticed my son running back and forth from the house through our yard and into the woods. A moment later he would appear to rummage around in the garage, then disappear back into the woods. "Danny, what are you doing?" I asked as he ran back in to vandalize the garage once more.

"I'm building a fort, Mom," he said. "I found the best tree for it and it already has a floor! I just have to build a ladder, and some walls, and maybe a roof. Do we have a roof in here?"

"No, Danny, how would we have a roof in our garage?" I scanned the house protectively. I had seen how my son could disassemble anything in an attempt to make something better.

"Anything, Mom," he suggested. "Some plywood or boards or how about an old bookshelf?"

"Danny, do *not* use my furniture to make your fort!" I exclaimed. "And don't use any of *your* furniture either! Maybe we can look around the school, or ask one of the church members," I suggested.

Later that week, using lumber he had begged, borrowed, and hopefully not stolen, Danny completed his tree house. He had nailed a hodgepodge assortment of wooden planks ascending the tree trunk in a ladder fashion and reinforced the "floor" of his fort with a wall on one side and a six-inch rim around the base where the remaining walls should have been. A long rope hung from one of the lower branches, supporting a wooden plank. "I can use this rope to escape, if I need to, or to just swing on if I want," he demonstrated.

I noticed that it was nearly impossible to swing without slamming into the trunk of the tree. I contemplated the likelihood of him injuring an eye or bruising an arm on one of the ladder rungs protruding from the trunk.

"Danny, please be careful out here!" I cautioned, knowing that I would never be able to dissuade him from using his newly-created play space.

"I will, Mom," he waved me off impatiently and went back to banging against the tree trunk.

My son obviously does not know the meaning of the phrase "Be careful." Not one week had passed since the construction of his new fort before he managed to demonstrate his recklessness to us perfectly.

Noticing the quiet stillness of my home, I questioned Esther. "Where's Danny?"

"I don't know," she looked up from a book she was reading and gave her typical answer. If Cain had not coined the phrase, "Am I my brother's keeper?" I am sure that Esther would have.

With some prompting from me, my daughter went out to look for her brother but came back shortly without him. "Why don't you ride your bike around the neighborhood and look for him," I suggested. I needed to run to the store and I always felt better knowing that my younger children were safe inside before I left.

Esther sighed and grumbled, but she complied. Feeling certain that they would be tucked safe inside when I returned, I dashed off for the store. When I arrived back home I was met with an amazing surprise. Not only were both of my younger children at home, but an enormous fire truck and several firemen were there as well.

I struggled to stifle the panic I felt as I dashed from the car. I couldn't smell smoke and I saw no flames. "What else could be wrong?" I worried. The story soon unfolded.

Pulling her bike out of the garage, Esther had thought she could hear a voice behind her. She glanced around our tiny back yard but found no one. Turning back to her bike, she was certain she could hear a voice calling her.

"Danny?" She called back, hesitantly.

"I'm back here," her brother's faint voice sounded stronger now.

"I can't see you," she called back, stepping into the woods.

"Keep coming," his voice was barely audible and hoarse.

"Danny, this had better not be a trick," she warned him.

"Esther, please! I'm hurt!"

She then panicked, rushing back to his fort, but Danny was not there.

"Danny!" She called out to him again.

"Over here," his voice came from another direction but still up above her as she expected. Esther finally found her brother in one of the highest branches of one of the tallest trees of our little wooded patch.

"What are you doing there?" she demanded. "Get down!" But Danny could not get down.

While attempting to scale the massive tree, his support foot slipped beneath him. By the time Esther had found him, Danny's leg was bent and firmly wedged between two branches. His other leg dangled helplessly behind him. The awkward angle made it impossible for him to gain enough traction to push himself up. Pinched tightly beneath him, his leg had lost all its sensation. Danny had struggled to pull himself up with his arms and, when that did not work, had shouted himself hoarse, hoping that someone would hear him and come to his aid.

Esther did what any concerned sibling would do. She raced off to call the operator and to be connected to the nearest fire station. Admittedly, this was not before she burst into nearly uncontrollable laughter at her brother's predicament.

Just as the firemen were pulling my son out of the tree, I returned home. Hours later, Danny was still complaining that the feeling had not returned to his foot. He sat around and moped. Despite Esther's sisterly teasing, she showed enough concern for him that she was willing to be his caregiver and gofer, bringing him drinks and meals as needed, while I alternately soaked his foot in hot and cold water to help him regain his circulation.

ATARI

Our street was lined with basketball hoops in front of every home, standing guard to protect the inhabitants from boredom. Danny and Esther would spend hours playing one-on-one with other kids in the neighborhood or riding their bikes up and down the street to have fun at each other's homes. The houses on either side of ours had children the same ages as Danny and Esther, making it easy for them to remain entertained.

A brand new fad was shaking the nation, and its name was Atari. Any home that was worth anything had an Atari system in it, and Ella made sure that I got one for our home. Not that she had any interest in it, but knowing it would be important for her siblings, she made it important for me as well. Every afternoon I could find one of my younger children sitting in front of the TV, eyes bloodshot from watching the blinking white ball track across the screen as they attempted to knock it back to the other side. When "Pong" lost its thrill, there was "Battlestar Galactica," then "Pac-Man," and finally "Ms. Pac-Man."

Once again looking out for her siblings, Ella decided that Esther needed a new bedroom set. White princess furniture is something that Ella had always wanted as a child but that we could never afford. Each week, after Esther babysat, Ella took a portion of her earnings and set them aside. At the end of one summer, Esther had almost half of the money she needed to fulfill Ella's dream. Ella made the rest happen. The two girls drove to the furniture store together and picked out the perfect set.

For my part in Ella's plan, I was commissioned to create a Holly Hobby bedspread and curtain set for the room. By the time we were finished, Esther's room was pink and white and fluffy. And Esther was nearly ready for high school, far too old for a pink and white Holly Hobby room. Still, the set functioned for many years, even after graduation. In fact, Esther had married and moved out of the house before she was able to leave the set behind.

LIFE IN ALBANY

Like in Elmira, we made friends with a farming family in the Albany school. Just as we had experienced before, this family was generous with their crops, sharing them readily with me and my three children. But this was where the similarity seemed to end.

Unlike in Elmira, our school was divided into several different churches. There was the highly energetic inner city church that Esther's best friend, Sharon, attended. Though the services ran from early Sabbath morning until late in the night, Esther often enjoyed spending Friday nights at her friend's house so she could visit the church with Sharon's family. Song service was the most entertaining part of this mostly black congregation, with arms raised high, people swaying back and forth, and, "Praise the Lord!" emitting from every mouth.

Another church was held in the school itself. We never found an opportunity to visit this one, maybe because we already spent so many hours each week within the building's walls.

Our own church, made mostly of older families, took place in a small, musty, two-story building. Other than the family of Star, a mildly-slow and severely-obese young girl, the only family that had children the same age as

Esther and Danny was the Hudaks. This family was made up of two very mischievous boys and their younger sister. The children were raised by their patient, albeit strict, father.

At a weekend Pathfinder Camporee, we watched an exciting video of an amazing woman who lived a normal life, though she had no arms. The children watched in fascination as the young lady shopped, cooked and dressed while using nothing but her feet.

"Can you imagine," I asked the children assembled around me, "how much more each of you can do if *she* can do all this?" The video was truly inspirational, and it reminded Esther of the only time we had ever gone into a movie theater.

"Remember Joni, Mom?" Esther asked, recalling the story of a young girl who had suffered a terrible diving accident as a teenager. "She couldn't even feel her arms or legs, but she could draw like crazy." I couldn't remember Joni, and I probed Esther for more information, getting the words "movie theater," "Elmira," and "quadriplegic" to prompt my memory.

"How do you remember all these things?" I asked her in amazement.

"Mom, when you live your whole life being told at church that if you go to the movies, your angel waits outside for you because movies are a bad influence, then suddenly the whole church goes to the movies together, you're not going to forget it too quickly," Esther answered. Maybe it was because I had never lived in a church-going community that stressed the evils of the movie world, but I really had completely forgotten the whole experience.

The school in Albany was entirely different from the one in Elmira. Since our previous church school had been full of warm and friendly people, we were not prepared for the small, two-room schoolhouse. Though our principal, Mr. Landa, did an excellent job with the upper-graders, the whole feel of our new city was just not as friendly.

My classroom was located right next door to Mr. Landa's classroom, which also had an adjoining door. Whenever a student needed to be disciplined, all I needed to do was knock on that connecting door. Mr. Landa would send over one of his upper class students to watch over my classroom while another student watched over his. Then we would take the offending student to Mr. Landa's office.

Though the misbehaving child never enjoyed being reprimanded, the other students clearly made the best use of their moderately supervised time. Mr. Landa would know if his students had not been working at least most of the time he was away, just by the amount of class work that remained once he returned. So they would work as much as they needed to in order to continue to be left unattended. I later heard stories about some of these students sneaking off to run through the woods just outside of their classroom's back door, but I still don't believe that.

On the other hand, my students knew that their student supervisor was clearly much more liberal than their teacher and they could therefore be more mischievous than usual. As a result, the supervising students devised a checkmark system to keep their little charges in line, but this system was only loosely enforced. Perhaps the most effective deterrent was that the students believed that even through the walls and the closed door I could hear and see everything that went on. They were right! Or at least I let them think so.

A SUMMER OF STATISTICS

Each summer, I had continued my studies at Andrews University in Michigan. It was not easy being a single mom, but the few classes I had taken had already moved me closer to my master's degree and so it seemed silly not to complete the remaining courses.

That summer, as usual, I planned on attending classes, but this time at Atlantic Union College in Lancaster, Massachusetts. Ella had recently moved out and become roommates with a nurse's aide at the retirement home where they both worked. Her new roommate was a lovely Persian girl named Sherri. Esther would be staying at home for the summer since she had a full-time babysitting job in the neighborhood as well as several part-time jobs. My only concern was what to do with Danny. I knew that it would not be a good idea for my two younger children to stay at home all summer together. I could only imagine the trouble Danny would cause. It was not that he was a troublemaker, but trouble just seemed to follow him.

I finally decided to take Danny with me to Atlantic Union College. I enrolled him in various summer clubs and classes around campus, and the two of us headed off for college life. Ella had already agreed to check in on Esther several times each week, and I would make the three-hour drive home every weekend.

One class I needed to take before earning my master's in teaching administration was statistics. This was a required class in my curriculum. "No problem," I thought, "I'm great at math, so this will be easy." I soon discovered how wrong I was.

I struggled through assignments, studying the notes and examples every day. I stayed late after school to be tutored by the teacher, but still, I had only a C. The minimum grade that I needed was a B- in order to earn my degree.

I organized study groups and dedicated more time to reviewing the materials. Still, I could not raise my grade. In desperation, I sought out the teacher after church one day.

"Raya, I really can't talk about this now," Dr. Pope insisted. "Let me check with my wife. If we don't have plans Sunday, you can come over." This, I discovered, is the benefit of studying on a small campus. At most other colleges, rarely would one find a professor inviting a student over for tutoring on a weekend.

The next day, armed with my books, notes, and pencil, I showed up on the Pope family's doorstep. Then I showed up again on Monday evening and on Tuesday evening. By Wednesday, his wife was inviting me to dinner. From that time on, that man could not get rid of me. Today, it might be called stalking, but I am sure that my professor and his wife both knew that my sole intention was to pass my statistics class.

I shadowed him every evening but still seemed to struggle with my lessons. On the last day, I turned in my final exam with a sigh. "I leave it in God's hands," I said, though the sick feeling in my stomach betrayed my uncertainty in the outcome.

A month later, when my grades finally arrived from that summer, I opened them with trepidation. Tearing into the envelope, I discovered that my grade was exactly 82%, the very minimum I could get in order to graduate. I knew that it had been more of my perseverance than my actual command of the subject matter that had earned me that grade!

In 1986, four years after I had received my master's degree, Esther attended Atlantic Union College. As chance would have it, when she took statistics she ended up with the very same professor. "Are you Raya's daughter?" he quizzed her when he saw her name on the class roster.

"Yes," she hesitated, no doubt concerned that she was in some kind of trouble. "How do you know my mother?"

"I taught her statistics class several years ago," he said. "She certainly is a hard worker!" Based on that comment, Esther decided that he probably passed me to avoid having to teach me another summer.

"You're right," I answered when she confronted me about it. "His wife was probably tired of feeding me too!"

SHAKER HIGH

Although it was common for our church members to send their kids to boarding academies, I worried about sending Esther away when she started high school. "I think you're just too young," I explained though Ella had been the same age when she first went away to live in Canada. Unlike Kingsway College, I did not have a close childhood friend with whom Esther could stay anywhere near our local boarding schools.

Instead, I decided to keep Esther at home and send her to the local public school. She could catch the school bus right outside of our home and at the end of her school day, be dropped off at the same location.

The church parsonage which we were renting was in one of the finer neighborhoods surrounding Albany, so I felt Esther would have a great opportunity in her new school. One thing I had not accounted for was the fact that though the children in that school came from wealthy homes, they were not as sheltered as I had expected.

Having graduated from a school with only 24 students spread over eight grades, then being thrust into a larger educational system encompassing over 3000 students in four grades, it was easy to understand how Esther got lost, both physically and emotionally every day for the first two weeks.

When she finally adjusted to the layout of the campus and her new schedule, she noticed how different life was in public school. One teacher must have been an alcoholic. Esther complained of a sickly sweet-sour odor that hung around him, especially when he was sipping from his "coffee" mug. Another teacher was intolerant and rude, calling the quiet students to the front of his class in order to publicly ridicule them.

Dances were being held on Friday nights and football games on Saturdays. It was difficult for me to explain to Esther that she could not participate in these activities with the other students. I had to explain it to the teachers as well. Esther was in the band but was not allowed to perform with the marching ensemble on Saturdays. This put a strain on her relationship with her instructor who treated her differently from the other students. When her PE teacher asked her to join cross country, Esther found it easier to say, "I don't like to run," rather than, "I'm not allowed to race on Saturdays."

The school also had a high rate of drug and alcohol use among students, something Esther had been sheltered from. Everywhere I traveled around the world, I had tried to eradicate cigarette smoking, yet this school allowed it within designated areas.

Only a few months into the school year I realized that it had been a mistake to keep Esther home. Where her sister had thrived in a public school setting, Esther fared poorly. Her grades slipped and I could tell that the choices she was making were not consistent with her upbringing. One day I confronted her about a pack of cigarettes I found in her dresser drawer. "They're not mine," she insisted, and I truly wanted to believe her. My kids would never do something so unhealthy; but if not hers, then whose? Esther would not confess. In the end, I decided to put her in Union Springs Academy the very next year.

PAPER ROUTE

During the winter of 1981, on his birthday, Danny made me take him to the local newspaper office. At only 12 years of age, he needed a work permit and permission from his parents in order to apply for a job as a paper boy. Once the job was finally his, Danny set off excitedly as the world's best paper boy.

By 5 AM every morning, Danny would have already crossed the woods behind our home and begun delivering papers throughout the next neighborhood. In a perfect situation, he would have been delivering papers in his own neighborhood. Since another friend of Danny's had already cornered that route, Danny needed to settle for the next closest route that he could find.

I was amazed with the job he could do. For a young boy in New York, delivering papers was not very easy. During freezing winters, sweltering summers, or the rainy days of spring, Danny had to wake up every single morning before the sun was up to make his rounds.

Every one of his customers loved him, and on collection days, he seemed to really clean up on tips. One day he came back from collections nearly in tears. I calmed him down enough to find out that he had lost the envelope with all the money he had gathered. "Mom, I went back to every single house, but it wasn't there! Someone must have picked it up and now I'll never be able to pay for the papers."

"Don't worry Danny," I assured him. "We'll pray and Jesus will help us find your money." The two of us knelt down and pleaded with God to help Danny remember where he lost the envelope.

Since it was a school day, I sent Danny up to change his clothes and get himself ready. He had just gotten to the top of the stairs when the phone rang. I picked it up, already certain we would have good news.

"My name is Mr. Peters. Is this the home of Danny Aba-Abadir?" An older man struggled with our last name. I assured him that it was and that I was Danny's mother. My heart was already soaring.

"Did your son lose something today, ma'am?" he asked.

"Oh yes! He lost the money he had collected for his paper route!"

"Well, I found it under my stairs when I picked up my paper this morning," he told me. "Your son can pick it up any time today."

I conveyed my thanks to him. Then, hanging up the phone, I raced up the stairs to tell Danny the good news so we could thank God together.

ELLA'S 20TH BIRTHDAY

By Ella's twentieth birthday, she had moved out of the house. Still, I wanted to make the day special for her. Twenty years was quite a milestone, and I felt we should acknowledge it somehow. I'm sure having a chance to check up on how she and all her friends would be celebrating her birthday was also a small reason to have everyone over.

Esther cleaned the house, Danny mowed the lawn, and I spent the whole day cooking all of Ella's favorite foods. Cooking was always more of something I did to provide nourishment than to provide pleasure. In fact, I regularly told my children that I loved them so much, which was why I served them burnt offerings. I'm really not sure how I even knew what Ella's favorite foods were.

I do recall frying up an entire onion or two. I think my original intention was to caramelize the onion, but somehow, once I had managed to place the onion on the stove, the burner was set too high and all that was left was a plate full of tiny blackened bits. "I made these for you because they're your favorite," I told Ella, piling some onto her plate.

"They are?" She looked surprised. "I wonder why I hadn't known that."

"Of course they are. They always have been," I reminded her as I scooped a generous portion onto each of her friends' plates as well.

"Mom, maybe you better let us serve ourselves," Ella suggested, no doubt thinking that her friends probably were not very interested in having a plate full of charred onion bits. I later learned that it was actually fried onion *rings* that Ella liked, not chopped up greasy specks of scorched onion.

Still, in her favor, I never heard her complain even once, at least not about the meal. But as we were serving up the cake (I know I got that right;

Ella always loved Carvel ice cream cakes!), she and her girlfriends started to complain about their age.

"I feel so old," Joanne moaned, rubbing her arms.

"I can hardly feel my thighs," Ella agreed, shaking her head in disappointment.

"Old! How can you feel old?" I asked them.

"We worked out yesterday," Ella explained, stretching her back and groaning.

"For two hours!" her friend Pina exclaimed.

"Nonsense," I replied briskly. "I exercise every day and I never get sore!"

I proudly gloated as some of Ella's friends praised me on my strength and vigor, until my daughter set them straight.

"Mom," Ella corrected me, "we were lifting weights and doing aerobics. We weren't playing 'Tag' with a bunch of third graders!"

Those third graders are pretty fast. Still I didn't have the nerve to correct her in front of her friends. Let Ella complain about her workout. I still knew that I was fit!

LENNY AND SQUIGGY

Danny, with his love for any living creature, decided he needed a pet. "Mom, can I have a dog?" he begged.

"Sorry, Danny, we are not allowed to have dogs in this house," I reminded him again as I had done several times since we moved in. "No dogs, no cats, no chickens or ponies and no wild creatures," I listed off the typical requests he had bid for over the past several months.

"Well, what does that leave me with?" he complained.

"You can get a bird," I suggested, "or a fish."

Danny rolled his eyes, but he knew we could not risk breaking our landlord's rules. There was no way we would have been able to rent a house in our neighborhood on my budget if it did not belong to the church. We finally decided to check out the pet shop for something that could be kept in a cage or a tank, but my son was not thrilled. Fish and birds were neither cuddly nor cute in his eyes.

When we got there, Danny had the most wonderful idea; hamsters would be an excellent compromise to our dilemma. Their furry little bodies made them as cute and cuddly as a pet-loving boy could want, yet they were small and portable and living in a tank! He quickly picked out two, because as he put it, they would each need a friend.

Worried about the rate of reproduction, I quickly asked the sales person to double, then triple check, and make sure that both hamsters were boys. Several times he flipped both of the animals over to show us the tiny pink dots buried beneath their furry bottoms. "See, these are both males," he confirmed over and over again. I actually had no idea what I was looking at so I had to take him at his word.

Thrilled with his new purchase, Danny carried "Lenny and Squiggy" home in their tiny cardboard carrier. He put them into their new tank which was lined with fragrant cedar chips, and included a food dish, water bottle, and a squeaky exercise wheel. He also swiped a scrap of soft fabric from my sewing box so the hamsters could use it when they wanted to cuddle. This last addition was soon shredded to form a nest for the creatures.

Danny spent his afternoons carrying his little fluffy pets everywhere. In fact, it was not at all uncommon for me to feel an unusual movement from his shirt pocket when I hugged him.

Only a few months after their arrival, we discovered that either Lenny or Squiggy was not a boy. Three tiny naked and tailless hamster babies lay in the nest that their parents had made. Their black eyes were still shut tight when Danny discovered them, as they searched blindly for their mother's milk.

The next day, only two hamsters remained. Perplexed, Danny searched the floor and table around his tank, but there was no evidence of an escape or of the escaped animals. By that evening, no baby hamsters remained. My son was heartbroken. Being novices, we had no way of knowing that the father would eat his own babies, but we soon learned. The next time "Squiggy" became pregnant, Danny immediately built her a partition to separate the youngsters from their cannibalistic father. This litter fared better and we only lost one. I was not really sure that this was such a fortunate outcome. After all, I was now in the exact predicament that I did not want to be in the first place, with a growing number of hamster babies to care for and support.

Danny put his entrepreneurial skills to work immediately and began selling Squiggy's offspring to friends and neighbors. With dollar signs still ringing in his eyes, he began to calculate his possible earnings from the Lenny and Squiggy manufacturing company.

Unfortunately for him, and even more unfortunate for us, by her fourth pregnancy, Squiggy disappeared. We searched high and low, and would have considered holding Lenny accountable, but this time Squiggy's escape was obvious. We set out her favorite snacks to lure her back to the cage, but freedom was a much more pleasant option for her. The pregnant mama hamster never returned.

One day, we heard a noise in the upstairs wall. Then a few days later I found some droppings on the floor beside the spare room desk. Food was also mysteriously disappearing from the pantry. Our home was infested with rogue hamsters!

Next problem: How do you tell an adolescent boy he has to set traps for the animals he formerly called his pets? I soon discovered that even if I did the dirty work for him, Danny would go behind me and disengage the traps. I had to accept that we might never rid our home of Squiggy or her offspring but, by the time we moved from that house, there was no sign of them so perhaps they died from lack of food or other natural causes.

CAMP CHEROKEE

Nosoca Pines Ranch had been a fun summertime activity for Danny and Esther, but I soon discovered that our new conference had a summer camp of their own. Our first exposure to Camp Cherokee was during one of my teacher in-service trainings held on the campgrounds.

Nestled in the Adirondack Mountains only a few miles from the Olympic Training Center, Cherokee was a taste of God's handiwork here on earth. Situated near Gilpen Bay of Upper Saranac Lake in uppermost New York, the lake was cold in the mornings but soon warmed up so that we could enjoy the water. There were less than a handful of private residences and only one other campground using this area of the lake.

Tall Saranac trees swayed around the lake. Rustic cabins and activity buildings sat between the trees and pathways, both paved and unpaved, connected everything. These pathways proved more of a challenge to me than I had anticipated.

As usual, I was wearing yet another cast on my leg. For the rest of the summer, I had to navigate the uneven terrain with my bulky cast, while avoiding another accident—either one of my own, or one that I might inadvertently cause involving my fellow teachers.

A CLEVER LITTLE BOX

I learned that this would be my last year in Albany. Once again I petitioned for a trans-American move, and once again I was turned down. Instead of moving to the Sunshine State, we were moving to one of the coldest cities in America: Buffalo, NY.

When the conference decided to move me, Esther was already attending the academy and Danny was still in middle school. He had actually begun to attend a public school, although I really wanted him out of that environment.

Ella's roommate Sherri had married and had a beautiful baby girl by this time. My eldest daughter was once again living at home so she decided to make the move with us.

Being a single mother, I appreciated the way the church helped with the move. Though the conference paid for a moving company, our belongings now being significantly more, we needed to find extra bodies to help us move.

Uncle Charley, an elderly member of the Elmira church, was the first to volunteer. I stared in semi-shock at his stooped form standing on my front steps when I opened the door, fearing that he would do more to injure himself than to help. But Charley seemed to know his limits. He consistently chose the smallest boxes and avoided any that were marked "books."

Danny had other plans for our ancient helper. He positioned a very small corrugated cardboard box in a convenient spot that would catch Charley's eye. Then he stood back to watch the show. Sure enough, Charley headed directly to the box to load it into the waiting truck. Slowly, his lanky form folded as he stooped to pick up the package, his large fingers gripping the bottom of the box and his legs pushing against the ground to help him straighten up. But the elderly man could not stand. He pulled again but still could not move the box. After a third try, Charley gave up. Brushing his hands on his denim trousers, Charley looked at my son who was watching him with a mischievous grin on his face.

"Wad'ja do? Glue this box to the cee-ment?" Charley scowled in mock sternness at Danny.

"What do you mean?" Danny's eyes opened wide and innocent. He bent down and effortlessly picked up the box that Charley had been struggling with, set it into the open truck bed and turned back to face the older man. But Danny could not maintain his guiltless pretense any longer. He burst into giggles and opened the box to show Charley that it was packed with his workout weights. Fortunately Charley found it as funny as my son had, and the two of them joked about the prank for the rest of the afternoon. As the hours wore on, the truck filled, our home emptied and our lives prepared for a change. After that, though, Charley avoided any boxes that Danny tried to pass his way.

Figure 25 - Raya Directing Music, Danny Practicing Piano while Esther Reads

PART IX: BUFFALO B&B, 1982–1989

"... God shall supply all your need ..." Philippians 4:19

Once again, I found myself without a home for the first month. It seemed that this was becoming a habit for me. Until I found a permanent place to live, I moved into the school house and took my showers at the local health spa where I was a member. The church had a kitchen where I prepared all my meals, and my bed was a small foam mattress which I conveniently rolled up and stored in an empty closet along with a box of my clothing. This arrangement suited me fine. It wasn't the first time I had chosen such a simple lifestyle, and I would find out that it would not be the last.

But I knew I could not stay there forever. Ella would be the first to join me when she finally left her friends in Albany. She would not be appreciative of my Bedouin lifestyle. And when Danny and Esther had home leave from the academy, they would want more than a rolled up foam mattress to sleep on. I knew I needed to find a permanent home for myself and my children.

Although he was only in the eighth grade, I had sent Danny to live at the academy and attend the Adventist Elementary School within walking distance from his dorm. Our family friend, David Santos, was the boy's dean for Union Springs, and I requested special permission for these arrangements. This way Danny would be out of the way until I got settled.

Though we had always had a good experience with our landlords, I was tired of living in homes owned by others. I decided to call a realtor and every day, after school and after working on my lesson plans and grading tests and homework, he and I searched the neighborhoods for a house.

After more than a month, we found a tiny three-bedroom home only one mile from the church-school. It was perfect! The home had a long driveway and tall blue spruce trees which sheltered us from the busy street. Our home would be located on more than three acres of land, a portion of which was buried deep in the woods behind us. There were three McIntosh apple trees, a plum tree that we eventually had to cut down from its infestation of black rot, a cherry tree that blossomed snowy-white in the spring though never yielded any fruit, and a low-lying quince bush that served us only one quince fruit each season.

The edge of the woods was bordered with prickly raspberry bushes, their fruit so sweet that the children risked any amount of scratches and torn skin to retrieve it. Tall leafy maple trees were scattered around the property. The weather had started to turn cooler when I was doing my house hunting so these beautiful trees were a deceptive lure. Much later it proved to be more of a chore to rake and gather the leaves than it was worth to enjoy the vision of beauty.

Attached to the back of our home was a large screened-in porch which Ella decorated so we could relax there in the late summer afternoons. It also allowed us to enjoy a show of woodland animals, including deer, which graced the backyard. But the very best benefit of our tiny home would be ownership. I was purchasing this house with my own money that I had earned myself!

Before the home was officially ours, we ran into some glitches. The home inspector found that water had seeped into the basement and repairs would be needed. A trench was dug around the foundation and the surfaces touching the earth outside were covered with a weather-proof coating of sticky black tar.

Next, he discovered that the septic tank was overflowing periodically. We had to have it pumped and emptied before the bank would approve our loan. The thought of anyone working with someone else's waste being pumped out of a tank was sickening. More than once I wondered who would possibly take a job like that. But the pay must have been good enough because the septic tank was pumped and ready even before I signed the papers.

Finally, with all of the repairs completed, inspections passed, loan documents signed and approved by both the seller and me, we were ready to receive the keys to our new home. However, we ran into one more issue: I had purchased the home as a foreclosure, so the former owner had no interest in leaving his residence.

The young man had lived alone in that house for several years and refused to move out. I remember thinking it would take a bulldozer to get him to vacate my new home. The "bulldozer" came in the form of a very effective letter sent by my realtor citing the District Attorney, the Board of Real Estate, the local sheriff and a well-known real estate attorney. With reluctance, the man moved out and I could finally move in. During this dispute, I spent two-and-a-half months living on a roll-up mattress in the back of my classroom. I was more than ready for a room of my own.

When it was time to finally move in, Ella drove over from Albany. We were shocked at the state of the home. With all the furniture moved out, the dirt and grime was even more apparent than before. The sticky hardwood floors in the front room had a huge black mold spot that had been covered by the previous occupant's dusty, outdated area rug. Peeling paint flaked off in the tiny, under-ventilated bathroom. A sparkling texture coating covered the ceilings of every room, including the darkly-paneled and dimly-lit master bedroom which had a chandelier hanging in the middle of it. The kitchen floor, a dark brown laminate designed to look like someone wished it was parquet flooring, was now so old that gaps appeared where pieces had chipped off and bulges appeared where the flooring decided to make up for those gaps and chips.

The whole appearance of the house was as if someone had one afterthought but then got distracted by several other afterthoughts until finally he couldn't have possibly remembered the first afterthought that had started it all. But to me, my house was perfect!

Ella and I got to work scrubbing every single surface we possibly could. Windows began to sparkle and fresh paint gleamed on the bathroom walls, which we would soon learn needed to be repainted at least once every year, regardless of the ventilation fan Danny would later install. The laminated countertops needed to be scrubbed repeatedly all year long. Yet no matter what we tried, we could not polish that grimy old floor.

My new friend and fellow church member Gladys Rupenthahl arrived with a solution. She and Ella hoisted a large, electric buffer from her car and the tall, graceful woman soon had it buzzing around the room, sandpaper attached. Ella took a turn next until her own arms were numb from the vibrations of the machine and I took over. Well, I can honestly say that I tried to take over, but the large buffer, this time with only the buffing pad attached, was bigger and heavier than I was. It practically took *me* for a spin around that room before I gave up and passed the machine back to my daughter. After three passes, the ugly black spot still remained.

Had this spot occurred anywhere else in the room, it would have been disastrous, but in its own little corner, we decided to cover the spot with a large potted plant and pretend it was never there.

Just as we finished our thorough cleaning, the moving truck arrived and backed into our long driveway. Once again, we were able to rely upon our church members to help with the unloading of our prized possessions. This time I was sure to forewarn our helpers of Danny's little prank: expect a very tiny but very heavy box.

Ella pointed out where items should be placed, and I went around reminding people to bend their knees when they lifted. I am sure that all my warnings were greatly appreciated, although it worked Ella up into near hysteria when I gave her the knee reminder while I was supposed to be helping her lift something.

"Mother! You are already shorter than anyone else! When you bend your knees while you lift it actually pulls the furniture *down* and makes it *heavier!*" She complained until she finally sent me to the kitchen to unpack boxes and place those items into the cabinets.

When I resurfaced from that task, I started to make my rounds through the rapidly filling rooms.

"Ella, where's my exercise bike?"

"I threw it out, Mom. That was so junky."

"Oh Ella, that was a perfectly good stationary bike."

"Mom, the seat was torn, the chain was broken and the tension hasn't worked for months."

"I saw it," the truck driver said with a twinkle in his eye. "That thing wouldn't even make it around the block!"

Danny and Esther arrived for home leave at the end of the month to find the house completely arranged and everything in order. I had the largest bedroom in the middle—the one that had a chandelier in it until we took it down and installed a much more stylish ceiling fan. Ella had the back room. It was the smallest, but it was also the only one with its own heater. Since this room did not have a closet of its own, Ella bought several hanging racks and placed all her clothes on them. Her bedroom looked like one giant walk-in closet with only a small bed tucked into the farthest corner. Esther had the front bedroom. It was sunniest and Ella thought it looked the best with her white princess furniture in it. And Danny would either share my room or sleep on the old orange hide-a-bed couch in the den.

Ella had placed a cluster of candles of various heights on the small window between the living room and the kitchen. "Just like all the people we've known everywhere we lived, these are all different sizes, shapes and colors," she explained, and I loved it. Photos of our family at various stages of our lives graced the walls, as did the three paintings my Uncle Habib had painted while he was in Iran, one for each of my children. Everything felt like home.

MASTER'S DEGREE

I continued to spend my summers taking courses at the university while all the other teachers were traveling with their children. I was determined to obtain my master's degree one of these days. I had been working on my education so slowly, in fact, that it wasn't until I received a letter from Andrews University that I realized how much time had passed since I started my graduate work.

"The credits you received for your classes in 1970 will expire at the end of this year if you do not complete your graduate studies by May of 1982."

"May!" With the school year starting in September, it was impossible for me to take any classes then. So I resigned myself to the fact that I had only one summer to finish my master's degree in elementary education.

Danny spent that summer in South Carolina with Aunt Viola, helping out with her aged brother-in-law and swimming in Black River. Esther and Ella stayed at home. Ella had been working in telephone marketing and she got a part-time summer job for Esther with the same company. I was pleased with this arrangement since it prevented Esther from sleeping in until two in the afternoon.

By this time, the girls had made friends in town and spent every free afternoon swimming, listening to music, or just hanging out.

With my children occupied, I would have the whole summer to concentrate on my last semester of graduate school. As it turns out, that last term was my very favorite session ever. The last course I had to take was Teaching Physical Education to Elementary Students.

We went through the President's Fitness Award Program, which I had already learned several years before, and studied general health and wellness. But the best part came when our instructor brought out exercise tools designed to make physical education fun.

We had short wooden dowels with long, brightly colored ribbons attached to them and with these we learned several different exercises that had elements of gymnastics and ballet. Chinese Ribbon Dance was the newest rage, and by the time it was represented in the Olympics two years later, my students' families already thought I was a progressive teacher, although the "Hooked on Classics" music I used could be why the students preferred to play softball.

Graduation was just around the corner and I was much more excited than I thought I would be. Finally, at the age of fifty-six, twenty-two years after earning my BA degree while raising three children and working full-time as a teacher in four different cities, I would receive a master's degree. I called Ella and she arranged to drive with Esther to the ceremony that would take place on August 8, 1982 at the Andrews University campus in Berrien Springs, MI. Danny would not attend since spending time with his rich and generous Aunt Viola Baker seemed much more appealing.

Graduation day arrived with a flurry of activity. Graduates and their families scurried around taking photos, exchanging contact information, and giving out congratulatory hugs and well wishes. Parents and siblings posed for photos, newlyweds gave embraces of support, and all around me everyone was surrounded by loved ones. But where was my family?

Dr. George Keogh, my first Bible teacher from Middle East College, trotted past me on his way to the platform where his direction was needed. "Raya! What's wrong? You look like a lost lamb!"

"My kids haven't arrived yet and I guess I'm just feeling lonely," I admitted. Dr. Keogh, pressed for time, embraced me quickly with a prayer for their speedy arrival and then jetted off briskly in the direction he had been heading.

I stood in front of the administration building and scanned the crowd of joyous faces looking for Ella and Esther, but they were nowhere to be seen. Perhaps it was my parental worry that made me look so deserted, or maybe it was just that people were not used to seeing me standing in one place for such a long time. Before long, I was approached by another acquaintance. Dr. Larry Geraty, whose father had given me away at my wedding and whom I had known since he was just a teenager, was now a professor at Andrews. He also had the same question of concern.

"I'm waiting for my daughters, and now I'm starting to worry," I disclosed to him.

"Did you phone them?"

"Yes, but there hasn't been an answer at our house since last night, which is when they were supposed to leave."

"Did you check at the dorm?"

"They weren't there when I left just an hour ago."

"And they didn't call you?" His last question bothered me most. Surely Ella would have called unless something really bad had happened. Larry must have detected how uneasy his investigation was making me because he provided me with the best solution. "Let's pray for their safety." And he offered a few words of support before heading in the direction that now everyone seemed to be going.

The crowds in front of the administration building thinned out as families took their seats and graduates lined up for the commencement ceremonies. I had no choice but to join the queue. I waited toward the back of the line, still praying that my children would arrive quickly and safely.

The typical graduates were closer to Ella's age than my own, and everyone looked so young and joyous. I would be the oldest student graduating, with only one other woman coming close to my age. Only a few of my fellow students had married between getting their bachelors and master's degrees, and a handful more were expecting to marry afterwards. None that I knew of had accomplished their education while simultaneously raising adolescent children singlehandedly. Quite frankly, I should have felt old, but that thought had never crossed my mind.

At the moment, I just felt worried. Then my eyes focused on two dark haired forms moving toward the lineup and I gasped. They made it!

We quickly embraced as tears of joy and relief threatened my eyes. "You made it! Thank the Lord, you made it!" I wasn't sure if I was speaking out loud or to myself.

"I'm sorry, Mom!"

"It's a long story."

"We'll tell you all about it when you're through!"

"Just go now and get that diploma!"

Everyone's voices jumbled in my mind as I staggered back toward the line, receiving hugs from my fellow graduates, those who had seen me worry over the past couple of hours. We marched up to the stage, took our seats in the front rows of the audience and listened to the valedictorians and the keynote speakers.

After the stress of the morning, I was completely exhausted. Sitting front and center facing the podium, I could not concentrate on the ceremony. I had no idea if the speakers were longwinded or brief, or how relevant their speeches would be in my life. I only kept chanting in my mind, "Thank you Lord, for bringing them safely."

The story Ella and Esther shared with me had us all stunned. They had planned to leave Buffalo once Ella returned from work, but instead she found Esther at home, still unpacked and watching TV without a care in the world. It was late in the day when they finally got in the car and headed west. The goal was to drive in a direct line, from Buffalo into Canada, then back into the United States through Michigan. It made the most sense. Why drive through four states when you can just eliminate two by driving across a country border line?

However, Ella had not anticipated something in her plans: kilometers. By the time the girls had driven into Canada, it was already late at night. Esther, never being much of a co-pilot and having slept *only* 14 hours the night (and morning) before, became drowsy and crawled into the back seat. Ella, always in control, was at the wheel.

The speed limit was posted in kilometers per hour. Ella felt a twinge of worry. She had no idea how to calculate the difference between kilometers and miles, but she drove on. The dial of her gas gage dipped lower and lower, and Ella wondered when she would see the next gas station. In the distance she could make out a sign growing closer: Petrol 18 kilometers. "OK, I know that petrol is gas," she thought, "but how in the heck do I figure out how many miles is in 18 kilometers?"

As darkness closed in around the car and with no idea how to tell distances—where they were in relation to where they wanted to be—Ella made the executive decision to turn back around. Esther was still sound asleep in the back.

By one o'clock in the morning, the girls rolled onto the Peace Bridge between the United States and Canada. They had completely back tracked in order to regain familiar ground. Ella drove up to the brightly lit border patrol check. She was very familiar with the routine and her ID was in hand even before she rolled down the window. The young agent stepped out of his booth to peer into their car.

"What is your name?" he inquired.

"Ella Abadir," she answered, even though she had just handed him her driver's license containing her name and photo.

"Where were you born?" the officer asked.

"Egypt," Ella answered honestly, though she had never been asked that before.

"Wake her up," the young man gestured to Esther, still asleep in the back seat. Ella reached back to wake her sister.

"What is your name?" he continued his interrogation, this time directed toward my younger daughter.

"Esther Abadir."

"Where were you born?"

"Iran."

This last bit of information was just too much for him. One Egyptian and one Iranian in the same car? He must have believed that no good could come from that union. Without further questioning, the officer sent the girls inside the building for a secondary inspection where the same questions were asked and answered all over again, this time in front of a different audience.

"What were you doing in Canada?" the new officer interrogated.

"We were on our way to Michigan."

"Why did you feel you needed to go through Canada?"

"I thought it would be shorter."

The girls answered questions about how long they had lived in the United States: "All our lives." Where they lived now: "In Buffalo." Who they lived with: "Our mother and brother." Had they ever lived with or associated with any known terrorists or any persons who committed terrorist activities: "What? No!"

And then a long search was conducted to find the paperwork that Ella claimed had been filed for our family's naturalization some seven years earlier. Lotfy and I had been sworn in as citizens just before the divorce, and our new status was carried over to our minor daughters. Danny, being born in the United States, did not need to become naturalized.

Unfortunately, the paperwork could not be found. Without it, 15-year-old Esther and 21-year-old Ella had no proof that they were U.S. citizens. Esther huffed and rolled her eyes at the stupidity of the whole situation while Ella, bearing the responsibility for both girls, cooperated as thoroughly as possible. The girls watched in frustration as other travelers were served completed papers and sent away. Meanwhile my daughters had to wait in the cold, noisy room under the harsh yellow office lights.

"You are both illegal aliens," the agent finally said, brusquely thrusting a stack of papers at the girls. "You need to report on this date to a judge. If he approves, you will need to go to the Department of Immigration and

Naturalization. You will be tested on your knowledge of American history, geography and politics. If you do not appear on this date to be sworn in, you will be charged for jumping bail and you will each be sent to the country of your origin."

"But," Ella sputtered in shock, "but we haven't been there since we were born! We don't know anyone or anything about Egypt or Iran!"

"Then don't lose this form and don't miss your appointment." The officer turned away from the girls abruptly and proceeded to question the next person in line.

By the time Ella and Esther got in the car again, the sun was only one hour from rising and they were exhausted. But being more agitated than tired, Ella was able to continue driving to make it to my graduation ceremony. And when the hearing came, they both passed despite the minimal amount of studying Esther did compared to the hours Ella spent memorizing presidents, states, capitals, and anything else she could think of.

MAKING ENDS MEET

By the mid-1980s, Ella realized that she had been struggling in a variety of college subjects which did not seem to take her toward any clear goal. She decided to incorporate travel into her education. I showed her brochures from a variety of Adventist colleges around the world, encouraging her to think about them. She finally settled on Newbold College in Bracknell, England.

I purchased a $99 open-return ticket to London on People's Express. The airline ran such a thrifty business, making sure to let people know that the only food served on their flights was for purchase only.

Moving into the dorm, Ella found she had not one, but two roommates. Karen was from Canada. Drene was from London. My oldest daughter would be working on campus, earning enough to pay her tuition since her work permit did not allow her to earn spending money.

Adding up the cost of her education, airfare to and from England, and the little spending money I could send Ella, I quickly realized that her time in England was costing less than either of my other children's tuition in the boarding academy they attended. Still, the need to support three educations, plus the mortgage and monthly expenses was more than I could handle alone.

I searched and prayed for some type of assistance. I approached the conference with my financial situation, expressing my desire to educate my children in the Adventist system as much as possible. But everywhere I looked I was told that "Church-School educators get a discounted tuition for their dependents." Most people, coming from two-income families, could not understand the problems I was undergoing.

Then, somewhere through the Adventist grapevine, I heard about the Adventist Bed and Breakfast program. I called to find out more and was told that I could rent out a room in my home for any amount, and it would be listed in a directory available to all other members of the program. This way, I could earn an extra income from boarders and travelers, all of whom had been screened by the bed and breakfast directors. I immediately placed my name and address on the listing, found some extra bedding, and opened my home for business.

But who would want to go to Buffalo, New York, the capitol of nothing really great? It turns out that *many* people would. Close to the Canadian border and only a short drive from Niagara Falls, we found ourselves with a steady stream of visitors from around the world.

The first visitors arrived while all the kids were away at school. Every weekend, and even some weekdays, I kept my home lively with activity. Any time my presence was required at the children's school, I would merely decline guests. The situation seemed perfect.

When Danny and Esther were visiting for spring break or another home leave, we simply modified the sleeping arrangements. If it was only one young man, he could sleep on Danny's bed while my son slept on the couch. A married couple would do just fine in my room, while I shared Esther's. A family of three or four would take a bit more planning. I would put them in the family room, the parents on the hide-a-bed and the children on a cot on the floor. For some reason no one complained about the limited accommodations. Instead, they filled my guest book with praises on how we made them feel just like family.

Many years later, during the buildup of the Internet era, I planned a trip to see my cousins in Canada. My membership to the Adventist Bed and Breakfast organization had long since expired, but my fond memories of the experience had not.

"I want to find a bed and breakfast home," I said.

"Where's your directory," Esther asked me.

"Ella must have thrown it out during one of our moves," I realized, searching my bookshelves for the small yearbook that would have listed all the names and addresses. "Anyway, everyone probably moved from those places by now and that book would be no good. You can find anything on the computer. Why don't you look up the Adventist Bed and Breakfast in Abbottsford?" I must have sounded pretty certain that she would find it there, because Esther began her search online.

Only one listing for an Adventist bed and breakfast emerged, and that was in Africa. Esther finally talked me into trying out one of the non-Adventist lodgings. I looked over her shoulder at the images she brought up. Bright, beautiful lodgings, fully decorated rooms dedicated solely to the lodgers' needs and even bountiful online menus to choose from.

"I feel like we cheated your guests with our meager lodgings," Esther remarked.

"But no one complained," I responded. "Maybe they didn't know the difference." But still, many of our guests had traveled from all over the world, and most likely they had stayed in more than one other bed and breakfast. "Maybe we just got lucky," I guessed.

During spring break, a group of young musicians came to Buffalo from, of all places, the Soviet Union. I was so excited to take my children to listen to them perform. And when I found out that these young adults would need a safe place to stay, I mentioned my B&B to the director.

I was thrilled that the young man who was staying with us played not only the guitar but also the Balalaika. I explained the twelve-stringed traditional Russian instrument to my children, but it was not until they saw it firsthand that they could comprehend its complexity. Danny and Esther were as interested in the uniqueness of the young man and his culture as he was in ours.

"What do you mean his name is Sasha," Danny muttered. "That's a girl's name!"

"Not in Russia," I replied, explaining that Sasha is the nickname for Alexander. Fortunately, our guest could not understand our conversation.

I made it clear that these young people had been given an opportunity that no other Russian had been given since the Iron Curtain style of government had been installed. The Soviet Union did not want their nationals to be "contaminated" with Western ways. To keep them under control they told their young people that Russia had the best of everything.

The propaganda had not worked on most citizens.

We soon realized there were many things we took for granted living in the United States. "Blue jean?" Sasha asked, over and over, trying to get us to help him purchase anything denim. I explained to the children that certain things, such as blue jeans and bubblegum, were outlawed in Russia.

"How will he wear them if they are against the law?" Danny asked.

Sasha rambled off an answer which I translated to my children. "I guess they are not outlawed, just sold on the black market, so they're very expensive," I explained. Danny offered him a pair of his own jeans which he had outgrown. Sasha wore them everywhere after that, except to his concerts.

When Danny tossed a bag of popcorn into the microwave and turned it on, Sasha stared at the electronic box in horror, waiting for the expected explosion he was sure would follow the rapid popping noises.

Later, when Esther was using her electric toothbrush to get ready for bed at night, he gasped, calling me in to find out what harm my child was doing to her mouth.

Sasha once made a phone call to a cousin in the Midwest, shouting to make himself heard, not realizing that our lines of communication did not require that.

Just before his last concert, Sasha, with Danny petitioning for him, convinced me to take him shopping. I chose K-Mart, knowing the young man did not have enough money to spend at the mall. He wandered the brightly lit store, so amazed with the selection of goods that he did not pick up a single item.

Danny, on the other hand, found several things *he* needed. I headed to the cash register to pay for our items and told the boys to follow. By the time I had gotten through the line, Sasha was gone. We searched the store for over two hours, but he was nowhere. We were forced to go back to our home without him. How would we explain this to his guide and concert director?

Later we learned that Sasha, his director, and several other performers had all defected simultaneously that same day. I was stunned. Was life in Russia still that bad?

SUMMER MISHAPS

The summer of 1987 was filled with a variety of strange events. If what we are taught is true, then it's possible that my family underwent these challenges just to make us stronger.

It all started with Charley. Danny had spent the previous year with his father in Yonkers, NY. He had taken extra classes and helped Lotfy build a sub-basement under one of the apartments that my ex-husband claimed not to own. "Mom, I got you a present," Danny told me secretly when I picked him up from the airport. "But I can't show it to you now. I could get into big trouble!" Everything was a mystery and drama with Danny. I could only imagine what kind of trouble he had brought back with him.

The present turned out to be an albino ferret. I looked into those ruby eyes and instantly bonded with the little animal. "His name is Charley," Danny said, and I knew that the sweet, calm creature would be a very popular addition to my classroom.

Sure enough, the girls carried him around like a stuffed ragdoll and the boys built mazes from books and blocks for him to run through. Charley didn't seem to mind all his new friends. Yet by the end of the year, he was trying to make a break for freedom.

First, he snuck out of the classroom and into the church during worship service. Two of my students went chasing him down the aisle in the middle of Pastor Giller's sermon, and suddenly the fact that I had allowed what looked like a rodent to run free through the school became the topic of that sermon.

"Does he bite?" the students' mothers asked, eyeing him suspiciously.

"Oh never!" I promised. Charley was nothing like the ferrets many of the parents had heard of in the past. Though he could squeeze himself into the tiniest hole like his kin, he never bared his teeth and I knew he was far too gentle to ever bite or scratch. Still, Charley and I would be on probation with the parents and church, I was sure.

After that, I began to leave Charley home on weekends or take him places with me. One weekend I took him to the academy so I could visit Danny and Esther. We left him in Esther's room while we went out for dinner and sure enough, when we returned, Charley was nowhere to be found. Esther searched under her bed and dug through the clothes in her closet. Both places were extremely untidy, which I mentioned to her several times.

Suddenly, from down the hall we heard screaming. "What are those crazy girls doing?" I wondered aloud.

"Someone found Charley," Esther said with certainty. She rushed out of the room and banged on a door two rooms down from hers.

"There's a big white rat in here!" a girl shouted when she opened the door.

"He's not a rat. That's Charley," Esther said, shoving past the girl and her roommate. Charley's head was sticking out of a hole barely big enough for the furnace pipes that stuck out from it. True to his nature, Charley had found a way to navigate through the smallest possible route between the rooms.

After many similar attempted escapes, we knew to keep a sharper eye on Charley. Still, he seemed content to wander through the house while we did our chores. Whenever he slept, he preferred to curl up beside one of us on the couch. But during his wakeful hours, Charley wandered the house freely or stayed locked in our spacious screened porch.

Then one spring afternoon, while Ella was at work and Danny was home for the weekend, I decided to water the lawn. Most people in Buffalo attach a sprinkler head to the garden hose and let the system do the work for them. But I prefer the old-fashioned method of holding the hose, with my thumb pressed down just enough to send a fan of water out around me. This had been my light-diffraction and rainbow-making lesson to my students over the years, and I never tired of it.

As I stood in the warm sun, watching the spray of water turn into a fine mist, I noticed a white streak moving toward a small hole in the ground just beside the basement window. Where that hole led, I had no idea, but I feared we'd never see our pet again. "Charley!" I screamed.

Charley did not even hesitate. Instead, he continued to steadily creep toward the shade of the cool earth. I dropped the hose and broke into a sprint after the escape artist. One second I saw him running toward the hole and the next second I was flat on my back staring up at the blue spring sky. With the adrenaline surging through me I could not completely understand how I managed to fall down. I lifted my head to survey the damage and saw my foot twisted at an extremely odd angle from my leg. I was out of commission.

"Danny!" I screamed, "Danny, come quick! Come catch Charley!" My son came flying through the back door to find me lying on the ground.

"Mom! What happened?" he asked, kneeling beside me and cradling my head in his lap.

I lifted my head again but this time to look for the ferret, who for some reason was frozen in time and had not moved an inch since I fell down. "Oh Danny, it was awful! Charley almost got away!"

"Not Charley, Mom! I mean, what happened to you?" Danny asked again.

"I was chasing after Charley and, boom! I just fell down!" I explained. "Now, go catch Charley!"

"Mom, forget Charley! Your foot is badly broken. I have to call 9-1-1."

"First catch Charley, then call 9-1-1," I plea bargained.

Danny called the ambulance first and was still able to catch our pet, who had not moved. When the paramedics arrived, they loaded my crumpled body into the ambulance and rushed me to our nearby neighborhood hospital.

It was all downhill from there. The dispatcher of the closest hospital answered to say they were completely full. We would have to be redirected to another hospital. The paramedic called the next hospital while the driver re-routed us. That hospital was maxed out as well. We changed course again and were finally accepted at the downtown community hospital.

We then ran into another problem; the weekend traffic had started, and an accident was jamming the highway. Our ambulance crept along, lights spinning and sirens blaring but to no avail.

"Good thing I'm not dying," I muttered sarcastically, gritting my teeth against the pain.

Finally, I arrived in the emergency room and was ushered in to wait for medical treatment. Two interns entered my curtained space and introduced themselves. "What seems to be the problem?" the taller young man asked. Evidently some visual impairment prohibited him from noticing that my leg and foot looked like a staircase.

I explained my accident to them, still more concerned that Charley was a non-recovering run-away. Then I moved the blanket to reveal my badly broken ankle. One intern skillfully supported my foot and with a sharp movement, snapped my ankle back into position. I hollered out in pain and the other intern immediately began to scold the first.

"What are you doing? She needs to be anesthetized." But I hardly heard the rest. I passed out in a dizzy wave of pain and nausea and heard nothing until I awoke again with Ella staring down at me, many hours later.

My ankle had been too badly crushed for a mere cast to fix. Instead, I had to undergo an emergency surgery at 11 PM and had two metal plates pinned together to stabilized the bone.

The nurse came into my room to discuss my care with me and Ella. "The doctors want to send you home," she told us.

"That can't be right," Ella was shocked. "You just had surgery on a compound fracture. How will you get along?"

"We're sending her to physical therapy to prepare her."

"Mom, are you OK with this?" She was worried.

"Oh sure. I can't just sit in bed here and rot!"

"It's not called *rotting*, Mom," she said sternly. "It's *recovering*! There's a difference."

But that weekend the hospital had seen more accidents and illnesses than they were prepared to handle. They were in a hurry to open more beds for incoming patients. I was ushered down to physical therapy with Ella following close behind.

The therapist welcomed me in and placed crutches in front of my wheelchair. "Are you sure this is a good idea?" Ella asked with uncertainty.

"It's in the doctor's orders, not mine," the therapist answered, supporting my waist with a gait belt and hoisting me up. A sharp pain burned my ankle at the surgical site and I groaned out loud.

"Please," Ella begged, "this is hurting her!"

"She'll get used to it," the therapist replied. But I did not get used to it. A pressure was building up in my chest that was unbearable.

"I can't ..." I gasped.

"Yes, you can," the therapist persuaded me.

"... I can't ... breathe ..."

"Just try ..."

Without waiting for her to entice me further, I collapsed at her feet. Through the haze of another unconscious spell I heard someone shouting, "Heart attack!" And somewhere in my mind it registered that they were talking about me. There was a flurry of activity around me, but slowly I was slipping away.

I awoke in a dimly lit hospital room. Deeply drugged and with every part of my body in pain, it took me several minutes to remember where I was. A nurse walked in to check my vital signs, chatting about the scare I gave everyone the night before as if she was reminding me of the events at a fun party.

"Where is my daughter?" I asked her, groggily. I had the vague recollection of Ella being with me last.

"She just left a little while ago," the nurse replied. "But she was with you all night. You should rest now that you have the chance."

My mouth tasted bitter and felt like it was stuffed with cotton. "Can I have some water?" I asked.

"You're getting fluids from this IV," she said, although she took a moment to swipe a glycerin swab across my mouth, moistening it. I closed my eyes again and lay my head on the pillow.

"Tiny!" My son's booming voice burst through my trance, calling me by a nickname he had given me because of my short height of 4'8".

"Oh … Danny Boy! And Esther! Oh Ella, you brought everyone!" I was so happy to see my children. But I knew that Esther had been in Massachusetts attending college. I asked her how she got here.

"Mom, people are so nice!" she gushed. "I was at a conference when I got the call from the college to call home. When I heard you had a heart attack, I tried to get a flight out, but I didn't have a credit card. Some guy I never met before was in the telephone booth next to me and he just gave me his card number so I could book a ticket!"

"Thank God!" I smiled. "I am so happy to see all of you."

"Everyone's worried about you, Ma," Danny scolded me in his typical teasing tone of voice. "You've been causing lots of trouble, haven't you?"

The nurse scurried back into the room and jingled the cables attached to my arm and chest. "Your family?" she inquired.

"Yes. This is my son and these are my two daughters."

"Well, kids, whatever you're doing it must be right. Your mom's blood pressure just dropped and her heartbeat has stabilized."

"So that's good?" Ella asked, squinting at the monitor above my head.

"It's very good," she answered.

"See Ma?" Danny nodded with satisfaction, "We're good for you!"

THE UNWELCOMED VISITOR

While I was recovering from my heart attack, Ella bought me an adorable calico kitten that we named Red. He was sweet and affectionate and a great companion for my long quiet days at home. Although we still had Charlie, he was too independent to keep me company.

Ella was assured that Red was house trained when she bought him, and for the first couple weeks he did a great job of only doing his business in his litter box or outside in the yard. To make it more convenient for him, we would often leave the sliding glass door open to the backyard. Sitting with my legs stretched out on my worn den couch, I loved to watch his tiny orange ears peeking from the grass like a tiger cub lurking in the jungle.

One day, we found an unexpected brown pile of unmentionable material beside the big bean bag in our family room. Ella harshly scolded the kitten by rubbing his nose near the feces and sticking him outside to sulk. The next day we found another pile under the end table and the day after that we found one beside the couch.

Each time, Ella went through the routine of training Red to go outside by putting his nose near the poop and then sending him outside but with no luck.

"I think Red is sick, Mom," Ella said to me. "I'm going to take him back to the place we got him from so he can be examined."

But the next day, with Red gone, we found yet another pile of feces. I couldn't believe that little guy had made such a mess that feces kept popping up all around us. "Maybe it was Charley," Esther suggested.

But Danny came rapidly to the ferret's defense. "That's way too big to come from Charley," he pointed out, knowing that Charley had gotten himself into enough trouble that summer.

That evening, my pastor Dr. Giller dropped by to check on me. I sat reclining on the couch with my broken leg stretched out in front of me while he and I talked. The sliding glass door was open, just in case we needed to keep the air quality fresh after Red's "accidents." Dr. Giller was sitting on a dining room chair, which he had placed near me. He leaned forward to offer a prayer before heading out.

"I thought you said you sent your kitten back," Pastor Giller said, staring at a dark shadow in the corner of the room.

"We did," I answered, following his gaze. I was not quite sure where his comment was coming from. Just then, I noticed a small black form creeping out from behind the couch. "That is not my kitten," I told him.

"Possum!" we both cried out in unison.

We hollered for Esther to bring us a broom. Thinking we were afraid of a mere spider, my daughter came wandering in casually. She jumped to attention immediately once she realized what the commotion was really about. Standing in the farthest possible point away from the possum and stretching the broomstick across the room, she gingerly handed it to the pastor. He then attempted to sweep the possum toward the sliding glass door.

Dr. Giller was successful in getting the critter *to* the door, but once he tried to sweep the animal *out*, the possum grabbed onto the long draperies and swung back in. Once more the pastor tried to push him out without success. Three times we thought we had triumphed over our unwanted guest, and three times he leapt back in at the last second.

"Where is Danny, the trapper, when we need him?" Esther wondered aloud.

"Of course!" I exclaimed. "Get Danny's trap from the garage!" Large and safe, the live trap would be a perfect solution.

Esther set up the trap in the family room and baited it with a small piece of melon. Then we quietly waited in the kitchen for the possum to re-emerge. It only took a few moments before we heard the metal door clang shut. Finally, we had the possum safe behind bars.

Dr. Giller looked into the darkened backyard. "Do you want me to take him into the woods?" he asked tentatively.

"Oh no!" I exclaimed. "I want to show him to the kids in church first!"

"Of course you do," the pastor laughed. He was used to my steady stream of wildlife.

The students loved peeking into the cage at Pete the possum, but I warned them not to get too close. "He's not like Charley," I explained. Charley had been handled from a very young age, but Pete had lived alone in the wild all his life, except for the two weeks he had lived in our house.

After a couple days of show and tell, Esther begged me to release him. "He's not used to living in a cage," she said while watching my students drop cat food and carrot sticks into his cage. "Even if he's getting more food now than he ever did in the wild."

That afternoon, Danny carried the trap deep into the woods. Finding a spot near the Ellicott Creek, he opened the cage and watched Pete tentatively step out to freedom. And after that we made sure to close the screen door whenever we left the back door open.

AND MANY, MANY MORE

I was always pretty good at concealing my age, not that my appearance was exceptionally youthful. I started a family when I was 34 and turned grey so young that at one point people were calling Esther and Danny my grandchildren. It was more that I avoided answering the age-old question, "How old *are* you?"

Despite my best intentions, I had several people try to calculate, guess or pry the answer from me. I became pretty good at changing the subject whenever it would arise. Of course it was usually my students who were attempting to do the research. No doubt they viewed me as an ancient being who was still surprisingly able to hear, run and even eat without losing her dentures. Still, I never honored their inquiries with a direct answer.

This particular year, the Adventist Church was celebrating its 100th birthday. Although the General Conference was formed in 1863, the new church's leaders first met in 1889 which marked the real beginning of the Seventh-day Adventist church. By its centennial anniversary, it had become well known worldwide. The General Conference had planned festivities around the globe to commemorate this very special occasion. Even better for me was the fact that these activities would begin on *my* birthday! I felt as if the entire Conference of Seventh-day Adventists was celebrating *me*. Proudly I shared the news with my students the very day that I learned about it.

"Guess what, children," I grinned, peering into their faces during our morning worship that Friday. "This year, on November 1, our church is having its 100th birthday!" The students gasped, just as I had expected. One hundred years is a hefty number for a child whose age hasn't even reached ten yet. "And guess what else," I continued. "That is *my* birthday too!" They stared up at me in stunned surprise, the older ones stealing meaningful, sidelong glances at each other. I had never disclosed my birthday to them so it was easy for me to recognize their shocked expressions.

"Really, Mrs. Abadir?" Chris McCarty asked.

"Really, truly," I answered.

"A hundred years?" Beracah Sullivan pried. "How can that be?"

"Oh, believe me! A hundred years goes by fast!" I answered.

That day was exceptionally smooth going for me. All the students seemed to be in a cooperative mood. No disputes broke out during recess, everyone worked quickly and quietly in the classroom and Tyler, my naughtiest student, even offered to help clean the chalkboards and take out the trash, *willingly*, without it being part of a punishment.

The next day, on Saturday, I rushed into church—late again as usual. It's amazing that living only one short mile from the church did not help me make it in on time. It could be likely that I seemed to spend every waking moment in our church classrooms, and so I may have possibly moved a little slower than usual on Sabbath, but I really attributed the consistent delays to my teenagers who loved to dress right up to the last minute.

Mrs. McCarty, the mother of two of my students and one of my biggest parent helpers, was the church greeter that morning. She embraced me and asked how I was doing, searching my face intently.

"Oh, I'm fine," I said, attempting to breeze by, impatient to make it to my adult class before the lesson ended. But Helen was interested in more conversation than that. The young woman seemed to fidget and avoid any actual topic but still would not let me pass by. Her two children sat on the bench in the foyer peering up at me with great expectation. I half wondered why they hadn't made it to their children's class, but I was distracted by Helen's strange behavior.

"Is everything OK?" I finally asked her.

"Oh yes, fine really." She giggled self-consciously, cleared her throat, and then asked, "So, Mrs. Abadir, just out of curiosity, not that any of it makes a difference one way or another ..."

"Yes," I prompted her, still thinking that I was missing my Sabbath school lesson and could she just get to the point. I couldn't think of what was possibly on her mind since nothing eventful seemed to happen at school the previous week.

"I was just wondering," she began again, "how old *are* you?"

I laughed and gave my customary response, "Now, you know a woman will never tell her real age!" I got ready to distract her by chatting up the kids who were watching the whole conversation with unusually captivated attention, but her son, Chris beat me to it.

"Mrs. Abadir, didn't you tell us that you are almost one hundred?" he quickly asked.

"A hundred!" I gasped. "Definitely n--," but before I could finish my sentence I understood what had caused the confusion. The students had confused that my birth, November 1, had occurred the same year as our church had begun. A sudden insight on the student's exceptional behavior the previous day dawned on me. I laughed and shared the misunderstanding with Mrs. McCarty.

"Of course," she exclaimed, laughing self-consciously as well, "I never believed them!"

"Of course," I replied.

"I should hope not!" I thought to myself.

"I just couldn't understand why you would say that you were that old!"

"Well, let's just hope that none of the other students made the same mistake!"

But that was just too much to hope for. I quietly entered the adult class, the lesson well underway, and tried to sneak discretely down to my seat.

"Raya! Lovely you could join us," Jim interrupted his lesson to welcome me. "I understand you are going to be celebrating a milestone birthday soon!"

Well, *milestone* would be one way to look at it, although *gravestone* would be more likely if I really was as old as the students were saying. "Listen, I don't know what you all heard but ..."

"We heard you're going on one hundred," Kevin laughed. "You're doing great for your age!"

"I am *not* one hundred!"

"Well, we know that, or we never would have hired you," Jim chuckled. But the rumors had already circulated through the entire church.

Pastor Giller even stood up during the announcements to express everyone's excitement over our upcoming centennial church celebration. Of course, he had to put in his own good natured taunts about my age as well.

Long after my birthday ceased to be the sensational news around our church, my students continued to pry about my age. Suddenly the topic was of great interest again. As usual, I evaded the questions and changed the subject so everyone soon stopped asking.

It is not as though I was ashamed of my age. In my mind it was merely a number useful for legal documentation and nothing more. The point was a matter of principal. I had held out this far and I refused to back down and disclose my age now.

The school year continued and struggling students began to make improvements in their work. The class was blossoming. Having a multi-grade classroom my entire teaching career, I was well adapted to making the most of our integration. Joint Bible lessons were every day. Reading and math were taught daily, grade by grade, since those lessons could not be combined. For science and social studies, I alternated the days I worked with different grade levels. On alternate days, while I was teaching the upper graders, the younger children would review their lessons. While I was teaching the first and second graders, the third and fourth graders would be writing in their workbooks. This way each class was on the same subject at the same times. Older students were usually more independent and the faster ones would coach the slower or younger children. My classroom was well functioning and highly adaptive with each day flowing smoothly into the next.

On this year, we had received new textbooks in several of our subjects. Some changes and advances had been made, but overall the content was the same. For that reason, I was surprised when the fourth graders approached me during their independent math lesson.

"Mrs. Abadir, we need a calculator and none of us has one," Chris said.

"No," I declared, "you don't." Calculators were not necessary for the simple assignments they were working on.

"But the lesson says so," he insisted, thrusting the book in my direction.

"Let me see that," I peered over my glasses at the text book. Sure enough, the assignment was directed to teaching calculator basics. I could not believe it. When I had started teaching at the age of 24, calculators were not even a concept in people's minds. Even when they first were invented in the 1960s, they were so large and inconvenient that only businesses would use them. It wasn't until the 1970s that personal, pocket sized calculators had surfaced, and even then they were outrageously expensive and only performed the most basic calculations, so that it was cheaper and more convenient to just figure it out in your head. Having to teach calculator skills in an elementary school classroom was unthinkable to me.

"OK, fine," I relented. "There's a calculator built into my purse. You can use that one."

Chris walked toward my desk and the upper graders settled back down to do their work, allowing me to focus once more on the second graders.

In the classroom giggles were being muffled behind me. Now, every student goes through a period of his or her life believing their teacher has eyes behind her head. Many times I have wished this were so. Although it is usually easy to decipher when students are up to trouble without looking directly at them, sometimes it is more difficult to understand how exactly they are misbehaving. I craned my neck, trying to see.

"Tyler, sit down," I ordered one boy back to his seat. "And Chris, finish your work before you get up."

"Yes, Mrs. Abadir." More giggles, this time from the other side of the classroom.

"Girls, did you finish your math?"

"Yes, Mrs. Abadir."

"Then you can help the first graders with their homework." This time the giggles surfaced near the window seats.

"Boys, what are you doing?"

"Mrs. Abadir, how old are you?" Beracah asked. This was surprising since I thought I had finally put this old subject to sleep.

"If I guess how old you are, can we have a whole hour of recess?" Tyler interjected, before I could think of a way to dissuade Beracah from the subject. All the students were laughing now.

"No! Now sit down quietly." I answered. "What has gotten into you children?"

"Oh, just this …" Tyler held up my purse. Right beside the calculator, with the date of my birth clearly printed on it, was my driver's license. No more evading the subject. News of my age, all 60 years of it, spread so quickly around the church again. This time though, parents were not as quick to question me about it. After all, 60 was now the new 100, and that was just a little too realistic for anyone to joke about.

ESTHER'S WEDDING, 1988

Sometime during their college days, all three of my children worked as home health care aides. This had been a great way to fit work into their school schedules. Esther and Ella attended Buffalo State College and Danny began studying art in the community college.

Buffalo State had a unique schedule plan. On Tuesdays and Thursdays, for one-and-a-half hours during lunchtime, there was a campus-wide break. This meant two things: the cafeterias would be crowded on those days, and students had an opportunity to participate in clubs, fraternities or other activities during this time.

The high energy around the quad was irresistible to most students. My daughters, in school together for the first time since Ella had graduated from the eighth grade in 1976, were not immune to the appeal. They would meet with friends, have lunch, and sometimes take naps in the student lounge. But no matter how they built their schedule, they made sure they were on campus every Tuesday and Thursday.

One semester, Ella had the great idea of scheduling all their classes on Tuesdays and Thursdays. The girls could carpool together, leaving the rest of the week available for work, workouts, or whatever else they wanted to do. Esther, always willing to follow her older sister's lead, managed to cram as many classes as possible into those two days. Everything would be perfect.

Cupid, however, had other plans. Right before my children headed out on a white water rafting trip for their spring break, Esther met a young Muslim man named Nasser, who was from Palestine. Before that, she did not know much about Palestine or what was involved in the Islamic religion.

"You believe in God, right?" Esther asked him.

"Of course!" And that seemed to be enough for her.

I begged Esther to go slow. After living in Muslim countries, I knew the extreme differences between Nasser's beliefs and our own, although Esther didn't believe me. Then one evening, Nasser came to me and asked for my blessings on their plans to wed.

In desperation, I wrote to Dr. Keogh, my religion professor in Middle East College. He had been born to Adventist Missionaries in Egypt and had extensive knowledge of not only the language but also the Muslim religion. Dr. Keogh took it upon himself and corresponded directly with Nasser, letting him know of our beliefs. Nasser wrote back assuring him that he expected Esther to worship any way she pleased. When I pressed him further, worrying about my future grandchildren, Nasser also said that the couple had agreed to raise their family with a clear understanding of both religions.

Three short months after meeting, on the Fourth of July in 1988, the two eloped. After that, Nasser would always joke that he had lost his independence on Independence Day. I, on the other hand, would not accept that my sweet daughter had gone against all my advice not to marry a Muslim. Though I never tried to get between them, I refused to acknowledge the marriage without seeing a wedding with my own eyes.

Esther invited me to her apartment one afternoon while Nasser and his sister were in New York City. I arrived heavy hearted, although I have to admit I *was* bearing gifts. A wedding, even one I had not witnessed, was a fabulous reason to go shopping for crystal.

"Do you like it, Mom?" she asked, hoping for approval. Lacy valances, framed pictures, wicker chairs and plants filled the tight corners of the small space. They had done so much to turn the tiny, dingy studio apartment into an adorable home only four blocks from their school.

I sighed as dramatically as I could and sank down onto the couch. It was actually more of a couch segment, one of the three pieces of furniture left by her landlord. The other two were a kitchen table built out of an antique Singer sewing-machine base—pedals still intact in case she decided to hem a skirt during dinner sometime—and a hefty dresser with the face of one drawer missing. All the rest of the furnishings, meager though they may have been, were provided by Nasser. With no bridal registry, no wedding shower and no bridesmaids, the young couple had shopped at K-mart to round out the décor.

"Esther, how could you do this to me?"

"What?" she laughed. "I didn't do anything to you! I'm just showing you our place!"

"I can't believe you would live in sin," I pressed.

"Mom," she thrust a paper in my direction, "*this* is our marriage license. How can marriage be a *sin?*" But it was too hard to express all the turmoil I was feeling. I already had one daughter that had a failed marriage at such a young age, and now I felt I had another daughter making the same mistake. Esther still had the rest of her college years ahead of her, and I was sure she also had a nice Seventh-day Adventist boy waiting for her somewhere in the future.

"How could you do this to me?" I begged and pleaded.

I realized that my pain was conflicted with my feelings about several different things. First, there was the struggle about my own beliefs on marriage and how I was raised. Then there was the shame of what others would think, in particular, all our friends at church. Most importantly, there was the pain that Ella was going through. Ella and Esther had coordinated their entire work and school schedules. Now, instead of driving to school together, Ella made the commute alone while Esther walked hand in hand with her new husband. Rather than taking road trips together with friends, Ella coordinated smaller gatherings and Esther stayed home to make dinner. No shared lunches in the student lounge, no shared wardrobes and no more girls' night out. My daughters were going their separate ways.

That next semester, Ella and Nasser graduated from Buffalo State. Esther still had two years to go, but Nasser received a call from a family friend inviting them to work in his family business in Boca Raton, Florida. My child would be moving away.

While they were apart, Ella and Esther mended their differences. I took this opportunity to talk about my daughter's wedding with the Baptist minister who was renting our church on Sundays. My own pastor, as was the policy with all Adventist pastors, would not conduct the ceremony because Esther and Nasser were of different religions—*even* if they were already legally wed. When the Baptist pastor agreed to perform the ceremony, I eagerly called Esther in Boca Raton to tell her the good news.

"Mom, you *cannot* keep trying to control my life," Esther snapped.

"Oh Esther," I pleaded, "don't think I am trying to control things—I'm not! I only want to see you walk down the aisle with my own eyes! We have such a lovely church and I want my daughter to be married in my own church!"

"Mom, we're already married and a second wedding is way more work than it's worth. Besides, I really don't think Nasser has any interest in going near our church," she admitted.

"Why not? You're married no matter where the ceremony is held." But I continued to pressure her. I wanted a big wedding for her and couldn't believe they were really married until I witnessed it in my church. When she finally asked Nasser, he agreed. And so the date was set.

FROM WEDDING JITTERS TO DISASTERS

With my middle child miles from home, life seemed slower and quieter already. In the past, Esther and I had shared a car, so the immediate thing I noticed was that I now had the freedom to plan my schedule without worrying about when I needed to pick her up, or if she was using the car that day. I commented to my students about the change in the atmosphere at home. Lonelier was probably how I had phrased it.

A week later, one of the parents brought me a beautiful blue-eyed Siamese kitten from their recent litter. "To keep you company," she explained. I named her Tara, thinking the elegant cat deserved an equally elegant title. The precious feline worked wonders in helping to ease the empty space that my child had once filled. Yes, Esther had quickly been replaced by a cat.

That year, Ella, with the help of a good friend Louise Grabianowski, did most of the legwork as event coordinator for Esther's wedding. Esther gave a few opinions from her distant home in Florida, but it was Ella who secured locations, picked bridesmaids dresses, and interviewed photographers.

Finally, two weeks before the wedding, Esther arrived in Buffalo to enjoy her bridal shower, already planned and prepared by Ella and Louise. A week later, she picked up her husband from the airport and drove him directly to the tuxedo shop for him to try on the suit they had sent measurements for one month earlier.

It was there that the first two disasters struck.

As Nasser walked out of the dressing room, our attention focused on the disproportional quantity of skinny ankles beneath the cuff of his trousers, while his jacket sleeves hung down around his knees. The sales attendant stared in horror at the deformed alteration job. "What ape did you measure, Esther?" he demanded, playfully.

Esther immediately burst into hysterical laughter. "Hey, I measured you," she retorted, choking back the last of her giggles. "You must have had an abnormal growth spurt since I left Florida."

The salesman cleared his throat uncomfortably. "Excuse me while I look for our tailor," he said, scurrying out of the room.

When they had settled the matter, with the measurements taken by the well-practiced tailor this time, Nasser patted his pockets, searching for his wallet so he could pay.

It was then that the second disaster surfaced. Somewhere between Florida and Buffalo, Nasser had lost his wallet. They searched the car, hoping to find it wedged between the seats or fallen on the floor. But the wallet wasn't there. They rushed back to the airport and searched the baggage claim area, the hallways, and the bathroom that Nasser had used just before meeting up with Esther—no wallet. Finally he went to the baggage claim office to fill out an incident report.

Both Esther and Nasser were crushed. All their wedding-week plans ground to a halt as they returned to my home to cancel credit cards and apply for a new driver's license. This was not the type of stress one needed right before a wedding. Unfortunately, disaster would strike once more.

The day before the rehearsal dinner, a mere two days before her actual wedding, I was out searching for just the right headpiece for Esther. None of the tiaras she had looked at were the style she wanted. Esther had an image in her mind of a traditional, delicate crown to top off her simple gown. Unfortunately, all that the bridal stores were offering was the current late '80s fashion that looked more like an ivory-gilded sweatband.

Most brides would be frantic at the concept of walking bare-headed down the aisle but not my child. Somehow Esther knew that if she ignored a problem long enough, someone else would fix it for her—me in this case. As a last resort, I had walked into, of all places, an AMVETS thrift store. There in the window was an ugly, dingy, yellowed bridal gown, straight out of a Victorian-age JC Penney's Catalog. The gown itself was not what had drawn my attention. I wouldn't have wished anything like it on my enemy's daughter, but still, I couldn't help thinking that maybe this store would have a solution to our need.

The store had only two veils. One was on the mannequin bride in the window and was as dull and hideous as the wedding gown she wore. The other was hanging rather carelessly from a nearby hook. The headpiece was definitely crown shaped, although the strands of rhinestones decorating it were falling off in more than one section. The veil was so old it almost looked tan and had definitely been chewed on by some animal. "It's perfect!" I thought to myself.

I paid $2.19 for it and brought it home. All in all, it was an exceptionally successful day. I had even gotten my hair styled and had time to start a load of laundry before I left the house that morning. This also solved the need for giving Esther "something old."

I walked into the house wearing the lopsided tiara on my head, loudly singing the wedding march. "Dum dum de dum." Esther looked up from the dining room table where she sat in a daze.

"Oh Mom!" she stood up and stared at me in amazement. "It's *perfect!*" I noticed her eyes were filled with tears and I must admit, I was moved that my little thrift store find could make my child well up with tears.

"I know!" I exclaimed in full satisfaction. "I mean, it needs a new veil and we'll have to glue the beads back on, but ..." Before I could finish, Esther burst into tears.

"It won't be that bad, darling," I reassured her. "The glue is no trouble at all!" The sobbing continued. "I'll do it for you!"

"No, Mom, it's not the veil ..." But Esther broke down into freshly hysterical anguish, babbling incoherently through her waterworks. Ella walked in and at that moment I knew that something truly bad had happened. Ella's eyes were also puffy and red from crying and my eldest rarely gets as emotional as her little sister.

"It's Tara, Mom," Ella sobbed. "You killed her!"

"Killed my cat? But how?" It's true that I never had much luck with animals. While they are in my care, they know that they are loved and adored. Unfortunately, bad things just seem to happen to them. One bunny electrocuted himself chewing on my computer cords, and we had a guinea pig bake in the car even though we were sure that we left him in the shade. Lost cats, eaten birds—really anything could be expected. But still, Tara had been alive and following me everywhere right up until the moment that I left the house.

I could not have possibly anticipated the answer I received.

"Y-you, you dried her with the la-laundry," Ella stuttered, bringing on a fresh outbreak of tears from both girls. "I pulled h-her out of the dryer and she was s-stiff as a board." The washer and dryer were separated by an oversized double utility sink. The cat must have slipped into the dryer when I was pulling laundry out of the washer to load the dryer.

"Danny buried her," Esther sniffled.

"And I bleached out the washing machine and dryer," Ella gulped.

"Oh, my poor, sweet Tara!" Tears burned my own eyes as the three of us embraced. I was heartbroken for my precious cat and the misery she must have suffered. But there was no more time for mourning; we had a wedding to prepare for.

After all the tears were dried and the shock of our sweet dear Tara was set aside, I finally had my wedding, I mean Esther's wedding, witnessed by my very eyes.

One year and 19 days after their elopement, Esther and Nasser were married again. It wasn't exactly a renewal of vows—only our families and closest friends knew they had already been married—rather, it was a ceremony to soothe the mother of the bride.

END OF AN ERA OR START OF A NEW ONE?

The school in Buffalo was struggling. It seemed as if every week I was making a plea for donations to keep it running and the members were more than likely growing impatient with my constant fundraising efforts. That is not to say that our work there was not appreciated. In fact, I received a very charming recognition one Sabbath at church.

Louise Grabianowski, one of the parents, stood up to give the children's story. She began by talking about a teacher named Mrs. Ridaba who made learning fun for students by incorporating games and songs into their lessons. I thought, "Wow! I could learn a thing or two from that lady!"

Then Louise went on to tell about how two kids in her class weren't getting along, but Mrs. Ridaba helped them to treat each other respectfully. Now the girls not only were nice to each other, but they had become good friends. I must admit, I was impressed with this teacher. I made a mental note to ask Louise if she could introduce us. But there was more. "Mrs. Ridaba even invited all the students to her house for a slumber party. She fed them supper; they had a watermelon eating contest; they played hide-and-seek in the dark; and when it was time for bed she had a few funny surprises for each of them. The students had so much fun!" OK, now I knew I *really* had to meet this lady. She and I had a lot of the same interests and I was hoping she could teach me what some of her fun surprises were.

Then Louise had a surprise of her own. She turned to face the audience and said, "Ladies and gentlemen, I just want you to know that Mrs. Ridaba is right here, and we want to thank her personally." I twisted my neck around to see if there was someone unknown to me in the congregation that day. Maybe I could invite her to my house for lunch!

"This is how you spell the name," Louise held up a sign that said *RIDABA*, "but you'll notice that backwards, it spells ..." Louise turned the sign around and it spelled ABADIR. It took me a full minute to realize that she was talking about me. By the time I had recovered from the shock, all the children were showering me with long stemmed chocolate roses that Louise had made. I hugged each of them and thanked her profusely. But later, after the worship service was through, I admitted how stunned I had been.

"In all my years of teaching, no one has ever given me such a nice and memorable thanks." I told her. "I've been doing these things in every school I worked for, but none of it seemed to be noticed!" Louise tearfully told me what a difference I had made in her own children's lives, sealing the gratitude with an embrace.

Despite the parents' support and the students' enjoyment of our little school, I sensed that my time at Buffalo Suburban was drawing to a close. The school board announced that David, the upper-grade teacher, and I would be required to attend the next board meeting. I knew that the church could not support paying both of us.

As David and I sat in the hall, waiting for the board to make its decision, I began to pray. "Lord, I know You are guiding my life. If You want me to stay in Buffalo, I would be very happy. Two of my children are here and I have come to love this church family. But if it is Your will that I leave, that's OK too. I really want to go to California. So, if You want me to leave, please help me to be near to my family there, if it is Your will."

In my heart I knew I would be moving to a new school. After I left, the school closed for several years. Today the school is alive again with over 25 children, good Christian teachers, beautiful classrooms, a huge gym, a cafeteria and a school bus that my son Danny donated to the school in my honor.

By this time, I really felt that I belonged in California near my family there. I began to research openings by calling various conference offices and inquiring about their positions. I was willing to take any job, even if it required a pay cut, just to get my foot in the door. But the administrations there would not even look at my resume. "Buffalo is just too far to relocate you," one education director mentioned confidentially. "Why don't you look into some of the more central states first? Once you get that far, your options may open further."

That was the plan I was looking for. I jumped into action, calling on conferences in New Mexico, Colorado, Utah, and Arizona. I studied the job openings list that the General Conference sends out and went directly to the top official whenever possible. "I have heard about some positions available in your conference and I would like to come visit your schools," I told them, time and again. I scheduled interviews and tours of different schools. I looked up places to stay as inexpensively as possible, and I contacted churches to assist me with my tours. I was excited to reconnect with our former, precious church members, the McGills, who had previously moved to Colorado. They were more than willing to be my hosts and tour guides. My first stop would be Cortez, Colorado.

I flew to Denver, and Jan McGill met me there, fed me dinner, and let me rest in her home after my long trip. Early the next morning, almost before the sun was up, Jan drove me to the bus station and I was on my way to Cortez.

The bus trip from Boulder to Cortez took nine long hours over mountain peaks, down deep canyons and valleys, and around hair-pin curves. My stomach lurched and churned with each stop, each bump, and each turn of the road. As I finally exited the vehicle, stretching and aching, I realized that I had spent almost as much time traveling from one city to the next as it had taken for me to fly more than half-way across the United States. I sighed, discouraged. "I'll never be able to get my children all the way out here," I thought.

The chairman of the school board met me at the bus station and drove me even farther, to the tiny schoolhouse. Then, probably knowing that the distance and the crowded basement classroom were not appealing enough to entice an experienced teacher, he showed me the sights. We visited the ancient ruins of the Pueblo Indians. We viewed amazing homes built right into the mountainsides and, much to my desire, we shopped at the visitor center.

I was almost convinced that God wanted me in this beautiful part of the country when my host dropped me back off at the bus stop for my painfully long journey back to Boulder.

The other schools I visited during my job search were rather unremarkable. Still, I was willing to consider them as long as the job brought me closer to my final goal of California. However, the conferences were not as willing to move me all the way from Buffalo. If I were to make the move, God would have to open one more door.

I hoped and prayed and pleaded with God to find a way to send me to California. I discussed it with my children, describing the cities I had visited, making them seem as appealing as possible. But they were not easily swayed. "We have our lives here, Mom," Esther said. "I'm in school and Nasser is a store manager. We don't want to move."

"Will you at least visit me if I decide to go there?"

"Of course!" they each insisted. But I knew that once they made the long journey out West, they would be more likely to reconsider joining me for good.

I was at a crossroads in my life and just knew that sunny California, with its forward-thinking way of life would be the best place for me. I soon realized, however, that God was not as impatient about my situation as I was.

Figure 26 - Paintings by Uncle Habib. Top: Iran Brass Marketplace (for Esther), Bottom: Iran Rice Plantation and Woods (for Ella)

Figure 27 - Master's Degree at Andrews University

Figure 28 - Buffalo Suburban SDA School

Figure 29 - Ella, Esther, Danny, and Raya; Raya with Van Donated by Danny

PART X: ATHOL, MASSACHUSETTS, 1989–1990

"... Not by might nor by power, but by my spirit, says the Lord ..." Zechariah 4:6

I received a letter from the conference in 1989 that a teaching principal was needed in Athol, Massachusetts. On a Friday afternoon, I drove seven hours to check out my next new job located on Maplewood Avenue in Athol. The tall trees lining the streets and the mountains surrounding the modest town made me feel instantly at home.

This was the first time I would be moving to a new area without my family. All my children were settled in Buffalo, living together in my old home on Harris Hill Road. They were unwilling to make the move with me. I didn't mind though. That house was the first home I had purchased on my own, and as far as I was concerned, my children could live there forever—with or without me.

The next day, I went to the Athol church service. I walked into the large, dimly-lit foyer and was greeted by a kindly-faced gentleman. I introduced myself to him and his face instantly lit up with recognition.

"Raya Abadir! We've been expecting you!" Shaking my hand and introducing himself as the school board chairman, he quickly called to another woman who rushed off to bring the pastor.

Before the pastor arrived, a young boy came to meet me. "You're going to be the new teacher?" he asked, carefully sizing me up with his eyes.

"Yes, I am."

"I'm going to be in the sixth grade next year so I'll be in your class," he boasted, still scanning me from the top of my head to the bottom of my shoes. I was certain that if he had a measuring tape he would have used it to determine my exact height.

"Oh good!" I exclaimed. "What is your name?"

"Phillip," he replied. His tone indicated that he enjoyed the sound of his name, or at least the sound of his own voice.

"Well, Phillip," I said as the greeter ushered me toward the approaching pastor, "I'm pleased to meet you, and I'll look forward to seeing you again on our first day of school!"

The move was inevitable and, once I returned to Buffalo, I knew that I would have to decide which belongings I would transport with me and which I would leave in my home. I would not need much in Athol.

Just before I left Buffalo, I was in a car accident that totaled my Chrysler Le Barron. Although I was not hurt, Ella was mortified, but I was nonchalant. "I didn't like that car anyway," I admitted.

"You don't wreck a car just because you don't like it! Even if you hated it, you'll still need a car in Athol," Ella insisted. "How will you get to work from home?"

"It's, okay! I decided to live in the school, so I won't need to drive anywhere." I'd made the transition so quickly that I did not have a chance to look for a place to live. Once again, for the sake of convenience, I would live in my classroom until God revealed where he wanted me to be.

Esther and Nasser drove me back the seven hours to my new job. As we got into town, we found it had a library, a small grocery store, the public school, a fire station, a police station, and a YMCA. It had everything a small town needs. Then we headed toward the church school. I liked the location of the church grounds and was already making plans for all that could be done in that little rural town, though my children were not as enthusiastic.

"Mom, there's nothing here!" Esther was worried.

"We really can't leave you here by yourself," Nasser insisted.

"Nonsense! I won't be by myself! God is with me, and I will have all my nice church family around," I replied.

"God won't be driving you to get your groceries," Nasser challenged me. "You can't stay so far from civilization without a car!" It was true, if I wanted to go anywhere in Athol, I would have to walk for the time being.

"Everything is right around the corner," I stated. "This is a tiny town!"

Reluctantly, Esther and Nasser set up a cot behind some bookshelves for me to sleep on and stored my clothes nearby. The ceiling was sloped and made walking back there awkward, even for someone as short as I. Hopefully this would deter anyone from rummaging through my personal belongings.

To me, my room looked all set, but to my children's critical eyes, there was so much more that needed to be done. A heavy odor clung to one corner of the room, and Esther asked the school board chairman to examine the wall for dead animals.

"Really? You think there's a dead animal in here?" He asked, scanning a storage crawl space with his flashlight. None of us felt courageous enough to search it out ourselves. "I'll have the custodian look first thing in the morning."

Ella came to visit the following week, bearing a large box of black and gold document frames.

"What is all that?" I asked. If there is anything to buy, organize or decorate, Ella is on the job. She once filed all my photocopies so neatly that I spent the entire school year trying to figure out where they were. If I asked her if she had seen the purple ornamental dragon teapot that I had picked up from a flea market, or the masking tape and glass jar pencil holder Danny made in Vacation Bible School, she could pull them out of hiding in seconds by searching her very thorough card catalog for its exact storage space.

"I framed all your diplomas and awards," she replied.

"*All* of them?" I asked amazed. "What for?"

"I'm going to hang them up in your classroom, of course!"

"Ella, I don't need to have all those hung up," I insisted, "That is too much work for you!"

"Mom, if the doctors can hang all their credentials on the walls of their offices, why shouldn't teachers?" Secretly, I was pleased with the thought of displaying all my credentials for everyone to see. With a slight resistance, I allowed myself to be persuaded into using Ella's new decorations. After all, I wouldn't want her hard work and money to go to waste!

And I must admit that after the room was sufficiently decorated, the frames made my humble new home look much more impressively professional.

Ella had another surprise for me. Because I was living alone, she brought in a cage with a huge bow and a beautiful fluffy bunny to keep me company. I named him Midnight. He was good company in the evening and the school children loved taking care of him during the school hours.

When we were finished decorating, Ella and I took the same, short tour of the town which I had taken with Esther and Nasser. She had the same criticisms my younger daughter had about Athol.

"Mom! There's nothing here!"

"Oh no," I insisted. "I have a library and a YMCA. And there's a grocery so close I can walk to it, no problem!" Reluctantly, Ella left for Buffalo.

The nights seemed so long and dull without the noise I was used to from living with several young adults. I had set up a small black and white television in a corner of my little "room" for company and was taking advantage of the down time. The first time I called home I excitedly told Esther, "I bought each of you a present!"

"Mom, you have no car to go shopping," Esther challenged me. "How on earth did you buy us presents?"

I went on to describe this amazing new discovery of mine. "It's called the Shopping Network!" I explained. Now I could shop all I wanted, have it shipped directly to my children, and never even leave my classroom. Esther was not as enthusiastic about the concept as I was. Images of needless trinkets, polyester pants with elastic waists and cheap cosmetics filled her mind.

"Mom, next time you are tempted to turn on Shopping Network, *don't*," she instructed.

ANOTHER SCHOOL YEAR

My first day of school was crisp and clear. The foliage had begun to turn bright hues of gold, red and orange lighting up the tall trees around the church like flaming torches. Students filed up the steep stairs to the one-room school above the church and parents introduced themselves to me. Phillip was there, of course, and was still sizing me up with a hint of a challenge in his eyes.

There were twelve students spanning seven grades. The students settled in for morning worship. The most fitting song I could think to teach them was "There Were Twelve Disciples," and from that point on, I called them my twelve disciples.

There is not a lot of real work, in the way of studies, on the first day of school. Instead we played several orientation games, opening up the children's minds and attitudes and helping me to learn their names. I also ran through our daily schedule and what they could expect during each class. Most important were the classroom rules.

"What do you do when you have a question?" I asked the students.

"Raise your hand," the older students chanted, mechanically.

Immediately Phillip's hand shot into the air.

"Yes, Phillip?"

"What do we do if we have to go to the bathroom," he asked, causing all the other students to snicker.

"You raise just one finger," I suggested, off the cuff.

"Oh," one of the boys said, nodding his head thoughtfully, "you mean like going number one?"

"OK. Sure, like going number one," I agreed. Again, Phillip raised his hand. "Yes, Phillip?"

"What if I have to go number two?" he asked, and the children erupted into louder giggles this time.

"You raise two fingers," I answered, as if I had been asked that question a thousand times before. I knew that Phillip was not going to make my school year easy.

From our classroom window we could see a hill just beyond the church grounds. All morning long that peak called out to me. "Now kids," I said when lunchtime came, pointing to the hilltop, "we will hike that hill and eat a picnic lunch there."

The kids lined up enthusiastically for our hike. "No running ahead! You must always stay within my sight and the sound my voice," I instructed. "We'll be going on the buddy system so pick a partner and watch out for each other."

We marched, more or less single file, along a pathway and up the steep grade. The children scattered a bit at first, with the older ones going ahead of the younger students, until I called them back. Then again, they got ahead of us and once more I called them to return. As we neared the crest of the hill, everyone seemed to be dragging along at the same, slow pace. Only Phillip's sister, the youngest in the class, needed my assistance. We thoroughly enjoyed that meal once we finally reached the top. The children congratulated each other, scanning the horizon. Below us the church seemed so small, like a doll house, and the view was spectacular.

We finally arrived back at our classroom, barely half an hour before parents would be returning to pick up the students. Phillip collapsed onto the floor dramatically as he reached the top of the stairway. His cheeks were bright pink and all the children were flushed with fresh air, sunshine, and sheer physical exhaustion.

"Oh, Mrs. Abadir!" Phillip exclaimed. "When I saw you for the first time, I thought I could wear you out this year. But you wore us all out, *on our very first day!*" I chuckled, feeling proud of myself. And from that time on, Phillip would never really cause me any trouble, though I am sure he would have liked to if he thought he could get away with it.

READING, WRITING, ARITHMETIC AND REAL GOOD COMMUNITY SERVICES

"Know ye not that ye are the temple of God, and that the Spirit of God dwells in you?" 1 Corinthians 3:16

Twelve students plus seven grades within one small classroom equals a great deal of energy. I knew I had the choice to let that energy run randomly in circles all year long, or turn that energy into a useful project. I chose the useful project.

Because my students spanned such a broad range of ages, I needed to be able to maintain the interest of the older, more restless students while I worked with the easily distracted younger ones. I explained to the upper graders that part of their classroom requirements would be to fulfill community service hours.

We had a classroom discussion about the reasons behind our church's health message of vegetarianism as well as restraint from smoking and alcohol use. The children made posters to describe our health policies and used the information to write reports on healthy living.

The first community outreach programs we started were through the library. I introduced myself to the librarian and told her that my students could teach vegetarian cooking classes and good nutrition as well as direct a Stop Smoking program. She was excited to have such a young staff hosting these programs. Within a few weeks, she contacted the Athol Daily News and wrote a lengthy article about the services we would be providing. Fliers were posted in the library, and our programs were quickly underway.

In class, we found healthy recipes that were easy for the students to prepare in order to provide samples for our guests from Athol to enjoy. I made sure to point out the math involved in multiplying or dividing a recipe. We rehearsed talks on healthy living until each student could perform flawlessly. On a chilly autumn afternoon, we all walked to the library unsure of the audience we would find there. The students were excited to make their presentations in front of the community. Knowing that it would help things go more smoothly, I had bribed them with good grades for this project.

Several people filed into the room, interested in the message our students had. The children waited patiently while I introduced them. Then, one by one, each of the upper-graders took turns describing good nutritional elements: protein, carbohydrates, fruits, vegetables, dairy and water. While this was happening, the younger students mixed ingredients and served the samples to everyone attending. Given by any other presenter, the topic might have seemed stale. But when active young children deliver their speeches with such earnest enthusiasm, the reception is amazing.

When it was time to conduct the Stop Smoking program, we used a kit that I had owned since I first began teaching. The students prepared brief reports on the harmful ingredients in cigarettes, which the librarian had copied off for us to pass around. But nothing is as effective as visual tools. Using a three foot tall blow-up cigarette and the bust of Smoking Sam, whose cotton lungs turn black when he puffs on a lit cigarette, the students wowed our viewers with their presentation.

We passed around a variety of poisonous ingredients commonly mixed in with tobacco. Most people were already aware that nicotine was poisonous, and a few people had heard of tar and carbon monoxide being used. But learning that ammonia, cyanide, arsenic, and even DDT were found in cigarettes was enough to give pause to most smokers in the room. For ten consecutive weeks, the students shared their knowledge of cigarettes' harmful effects and shared ideas to help the participants quit their toxic habit.

Letters poured into the school from the community, thanking our students for their informative classes. Of the eight participants who started with us from the first week, one quit the class, but three others quit smoking. We were very excited for the three!

One Sunday spring morning, with nothing planned for the day, I set out on a walk around my neighborhood. As I was passing the fire station, I decided on a whim to stop in. I found several men in work pants and T-shirts, sitting around.

"Can I help you?" one young man asked.

"I am Raya Abadir," I introduced myself. "I am teaching in the Adventist church school on Maple Avenue, and I would like to speak to someone about a fireman visiting our school."

The captain quickly told me that they had just that type of program, and they would be happy to bring a fire truck to our classroom. We picked a date and time for the trip. "How many students will be there?" he asked.

"I have twelve students, grades one through eight," I answered.

"Twelve students in each class?" he inquired.

"Oh no," I chuckled. "Twelve students total." If the captain was surprised about the small size of our school he did not complain.

The firemen's visit was a huge success for our class. The students had been peeking out of the window all morning long in anticipation of their arrival. When the bright red truck rolled into our driveway, I could hardly contain them enough to have them walk out in an orderly fashion.

Wearing heavy yellow coats, pants and boots, the firemen discussed how to prevent a fire: "Never, ever play with matches. Do not leave candles unattended. Use a safety screen in your fireplace." Then they explained what to do in case a fire does start.

"Stop, drop, and roll!" they soon had the students chanting in unison as each child demonstrated this important safety maneuver.

"Right," the captain said. "And what do you dial in an emergency?"

"Nine-one-one!" The children shouted.

"That's right! That is the emergency phone number. Once you call it, stay on the line. A dispatcher will answer and figure out the best person to help you. Usually, a fire truck will be there, and sometimes also an ambulance or a police car."

"Is anyone allowed to visit the fire station?" Phillip wanted to know.

"Of course," one of the firemen answered.

"Do we need to be on fire first?" he insisted.

"If you are already on fire, you should not try to make it all the way to the station," a fireman said, trying to contain his smirk.

"But I'll tell you what," the captain interjected, "why don't you ask your nice teacher if she can bring all of you to visit us another day."

"Yeah!" The students' shouts shook the surrounding maple trees. I laughed. How could I say no to a reaction like that?

Now, being a single woman and getting to hang around with handsome, young, strong firemen, not once, but three times in a span of two weeks was a real perk in my mind. I'm not saying that that was what motivated me to take the students on another field trip, but it is worth mentioning.

The next week, with a healthy stack of twelve handmade thank-you cards, we set off on a short hike toward the fire station. The students climbed the steps into the great, red truck and put on the firemen's uniforms.

"This is heavy!" Phillip's little sister exclaimed. She was buried within the coat, which puddled around her feet.

"Mrs. Abadir! Up here!" I looked up to see all the boys standing at the top of the fire pole. My breath momentarily caught in my throat as I froze, anticipating them dropping through the hole and splattering on the cement floor. But they didn't fall. With one smooth movement each one jumped toward the pole and slid down to the ground.

"Try it, Mrs. Abadir!" Peter shouted.

"I don't think so," I declined. I could just picture my silk skirt flying up around my head and my feeble bones shattering beneath me. The mental picture was enough to keep me firmly grounded while my students stretched their wings.

The following Saturday, like most other weeks, the students stood up in church to tell the members about our community activities. Our presentations always started with the students performing a song they had learned in class and ended with their favorite memories. As they were excitedly telling the congregation about yet another activity, two very special guests were sitting in the pews watching.

After the service ended, a couple approached me and introduced themselves as Ruth and Harold Fagal.

"The Fagals?" I recognized that name.

"My brother was a Seventh-day Adventist television musical host for many years," he explained

"Of course!" I immediately realized where I knew the name from. William and his wife Virginia had entertained Adventist audiences ever since we first began broadcasting on television. "How can I help you?"

"Well," Harold began, "I work for the South Eastern California Conference, and I can't help but think that your talents are wasted in this small school. Every time my wife and I visit our home here in Athol, we see your students involved in so many community projects. Could you be persuaded to interview for some of the administration openings we have in California?"

Could I be persuaded! This man had no *idea* how long and how hard I had prayed to be moved close to my cousins in California. I could not believe the turn of events.

We wrapped up the school year with the usual exams, final projects and parties. But throughout it all, my mind was absorbed with the anticipation

of relocating. I announced the impending move to my students, and they generously sent me off with a fond and memorable farewell. Cards, homemade art, and bountiful hugs filled my suitcase and my heart. Crowning these gifts was a scrap book the children had made of our school year and events together. And on the last page they had cropped a photo of my head which they pasted onto a surfer's picture. "California, Here She Comes!"

Figure 30 - Athol School Activities

PART XI: SAN DIEGO, SURFERS, AND SUNSHINE, 1990–1992

INTERVIEWING AGAIN

"The heavens declare the glory of God ..." Psalms 19:1

Receiving the invitation to interview in California was, for me, like receiving an invitation to heaven. I had never had my choice of which school I would work for, and now I could select from not one, not two, but *five* different locations that needed a teaching principal.

One of the options I was given was Needles, California. I looked it up on a map. The tiny town was situated in the heart of the desert, almost on the border of Arizona. *No thanks*. I did not even go to look at that one. It would be too far from my cousins, and I had already had my fill of desert life when Lotfy and I lived in Egypt. Another of the schools immediately felt wrong just by reviewing their needs and my skills. I would interview for the remaining three.

I flew into Ontario, California and was met by Marilyn, the Elementary School Education Director. We drove past palm trees and rolling hills while I continually pinched myself, amazed that I was really going to work in California.

The first school we were visiting was in Palm Springs. For two hours in traffic through winding, mountainous roads, we journeyed. Have I ever mentioned how carsick I get? Marilyn chatted pleasantly with me, pointing out various bits of scenery which I was completely unable to focus on for fear of losing my entire airplane meal.

For some reason, this desert city had become a luxury vacation destination for California residents. This is something I had a hard time understanding; It had bitter cold in the winter and scorching heat in the summer. "But don't worry, it's a *dry* heat," I was told repeatedly. I was already suffocating within the first hour that I stepped out of Marilyn's car even though summer was just beginning.

The school was small and the entire yard was paved in cement. My interest in the location was quickly fading. I stayed that night in the women's dorm of La Sierra University in Riverside. I called my children and checked in with them, and I called my cousins to tell them that I was close by.

"What do you mean you don't have time to visit, Raya *jan*?" Akie pleaded with me, using the Persian word for "dear" as we all did in conversation. "I will come get you. Please come." But my itinerary was just too tightly packed.

"Don't worry Akie *jan*," I answered. "When I move here we will be able to spend every weekend together!"

The next location was Fullerton, CA. This would be closer to my family living in Hollywood. I was excited. Surely this would be the best location for me. I prayed intensely that God would lead me there. Scarcely looking around at my surroundings, I was already convinced that this would be my new home. But Marilyn did not want me to decide just yet.

"I have one more place I'd really like for you to see," she said. "El Cajon, east of San Diego, just had their principal step down to a teaching-only position for this coming year." She explained the situation as we drove two long hours toward the third school. I would be interviewing with several other teachers for this location in front of the school board panel.

I loved San Diego instantly, but my heart was set on moving closer to Los Angeles. Once again, already deciding that Fullerton would be the best location for me, I scarcely looked around the school. "If I ended up here, I wouldn't be disappointed, but Fullerton would be better," I thought. With five classrooms and even a kindergarten, the school was larger than most I had taught in.

I sat outside of the conference room in the hallway with two other teachers who were also interviewing for the position. I couldn't help but be reminded of losing my position in Buffalo the last time I had interviewed like this.

The older woman was about as full of self-importance as anyone I could imagine. Her husband was already working for the same conference and, in her opinion—which mattered to her very much—her name was already established in this community. She made it known to both of us that the position was going to her, and our interviews were just a formality. If I didn't immediately dislike her, I would have been relieved to let her take the open position.

On the other end of the spectrum, I was also interviewing against Melanie, a much younger woman. "This school would be the answer to my prayers," she confided in me. I loved her gentle spirit and the fact that she was proclaiming her desire for this location to serve God. I began to pray for her too.

Once inside the board room, I realized that I was not nervous at all. I told them about my qualifications and answered all their questions. Most of the board members wanted to know the standard information: the various locations I had worked and my preferred style of teaching. But some of the questions were more unusual. "If a child who was not your student was breaking a rule, how would you respond? Would you punish the child yourself, call the student's teacher, or ignore it? How would you respond to another teacher disciplining your students in front of you?" I began to suspect that some of the teachers had had conflicts with each other in the past.

When my interview was over, I had a surprise of my own. "May I make a suggestion?" I proposed. The board members nodded, dumbfounded. I mentioned Melanie and recommended her for the job. I knew I was headed for Fullerton and I did not want to give the position up to Mrs. Full-of-Herself.

"We will take your recommendation into consideration, Raya," the chairman said, "But to be honest with you, Melanie does not have the experience we are looking for. This school needs a leader that can withstand the various personalities we already have."

I stepped back into the hallway to await their decision. In my heart I continued to pray for Melanie, but when the doors reopened, Marilyn asked me to return. She stepped out to tell the other two ladies that they were excused. I think all of us were crushed.

The board members shook my hands and beamed at me. "Congratulations! We have chosen you to be our new teaching principal."

"Do you mind if I take some time to think about it?" I asked with hesitation.

"You may, of course," the chairman answered. "We wouldn't want anyone here who was not fully committed to our school."

Marilyn spoke up, "Raya, of all the schools we have in our district, I really feel that this one is best suited for you and that you are the most qualified for this position."

I went back home and reviewed my memories of each school. I wondered which one stood out in my mind as where God would want me. How would I know? I cannot possibly know what moved me to let go of the Fullerton school.

In the end, I went with El Cajon. The school was bigger and my responsibilities would be greater, an experience I knew I would embrace. The city itself was beautiful and still, travelling to Los Angeles would only be two hours. My California life was almost ready to begin. But first, where would I live?

CALIFORNIA, HERE SHE COMES!

As usual, God had everything under His control. Before I even set foot back in Buffalo, I received a call from the pastor of the El Cajon Church. "Is there any possible way to rent a place while I'm looking for my own home?" I asked him.

"Actually, an elderly woman in our congregation needs a roommate," he responded. "She is homebound, so some caregiving would be required."

"Oh, but I'll be working full-time!" I gasped. A caregiver sounded like a full-time job. I had seen the work my children did as home health aides in Buffalo while they put themselves through college. I also knew I should be realistic about the hours I would put in at school.

"Mrs. Faible is able to do most things on her own," he reassured me. "She prepares her own breakfast and lunch and bathes herself. She would just need help with the shopping and light housecleaning, and maybe cooking something for dinner too."

The opportunity was beginning to present itself in a much better light. "How much does she want for rent?" I asked.

"Rent? Oh no! She would exchange free room and board for her care," the pastor replied. "Even if there is not much work involved, it wouldn't be fair for her to ask you to do all that and still pay."

Free room and board? I could not even think of turning down that opportunity. "Sign me up!" I exclaimed, the wheels of my brain already in motion. I needed to do no more than pack my personal belongings before returning to my new hometown of El Cajon, California. I squeezed my children goodbye, loaded my car, and headed west.

GENERAL CONFERENCE SESSIONS

Before heading to California, I learned that Indianapolis, Indiana would be hosting the 1990 General Conference Sessions. The sessions only occurred once every five years and were an important political forum for the election of church officials. Delegates, pastors, teachers, and talented musicians came from all over the world to these meetings. It was an amazing cultural and religious affair for all those who attended, and I looked forward to the ten-day event and a break from my drive out west.

My car was packed as full as I could possibly make it with books, classroom supplies, clothing, food, my recently acquired bunny Midnight, her cage—which took up the entire back seat—and of course a new AAA TripTik®. As had been our custom when traveling, I woke before dawn and settled into my heavily-burdened automobile. I slowly picked my way west around Lake Erie and on towards Indiana.

A normal person driving the speed limit and stopping about two times for fuel and food could make the 500-mile trip in about nine hours. I, on the other hand, took closer to twelve-and-a-half hours with all the stops I made for, not only gas and food, but for occasional naps and to check on my rabbit.

By the time my car reached the conference area, it was after 7 PM. The sky was deepening and shadows were growing long as the sun began to drop for the day. I could see a row of automobiles lining the street near the entrance. I pulled in behind the last parked car under a shady tree where my bunny would be safe from the heat of the next afternoon.

I eased myself out from behind the steering wheel and stretched my achy back, kneading the pain from my lower spine and shoulders. "Thank you Lord for my safe journey," I thought. And then something detrimental happened. I tried to move my right leg, but it would not budge. A sharp, deep pain shot down from my hip to my knee. I inhaled deeply, unsure how I would walk up the steps to the conference hall. I tried stretching it, gently rubbing it, and shaking it out until my leg could finally bear weight. Although I suspected the cause, I didn't find out for sure until much later that the pain was caused by a pinched nerve. At this point, all I knew was I would never make it all the way to San Diego without further irritating my leg. I would need a traveling partner.

Most people go to conferences or meetings and come out completely overwhelmed with the quantity of information they hear. Years after the actual General Conference Sessions have ended, I can't remember one single thing I heard that week-and-a-half. I *do* remember the greatest lesson I took away from my experiences there: proof once again, that God truly does watch out for us, even when we have no idea we will need Him.

An example of God's care came almost immediately. I limped toward the wide arena steps to register myself for the weekend. "Raya!" A woman's voice called from the doorway. I squinted into the shadows forming as evening fell. Really, in this place, I could run into anyone from as far back as my years in Middle East College to a local church member I just potlucked with last week. Anything was possible. I only hoped that I would recognize whoever was calling me.

Somehow, even with these thoughts racing through my mind, I stepped confidently toward the voice until a familiar face appeared before me. "Caroline!" I was so pleased and amazed to see her. Caroline and I had been assigned as roommates during an educator's conference the year before, and our time together had been filled with long talks of wonderful anecdotes from our lives as teachers. I could not believe this blessing in being re-connected with her. We had not even called or written since the course had ended.

"Raya! When did you get here?" she asked, embracing me.

"Just now," I answered. "I just stepped out of my car, right this moment!" With thousands and thousands of visitors and delegates in one place, the chance of knowing the very first person I would run into was extraordinarily slim.

Caroline linked arms with me and ushered me in toward the registration tables, talking at the speed of light, just as she always had. "I hope your trip was comfortable. We arrived so quickly I hardly had time to tell two stories—and you know how I like to tell stories. I'm staying at the Holiday Inn," she gestured toward the side of the conference hall that was bordered with hotels and businesses, "with two ladies I met in Camp Meeting. Where are you staying?"

"Oh. Well, I guess I hadn't really thought that far in advance," I admitted. I realized that most people usually plan a place to lay their head down, while I just sleep wherever I find lodging. Somehow God always provides. "I mean, I did bring my sleeping bag with me," I quickly added.

"Well, that settles it then," Caroline rushed quickly into her conclusion. "You can stay with us, I mean we do have three people staying in my room already, but we have plenty of floor space for a tiny little lady like you."

"Are you sure your roommates won't mind?"

"Nonsense! We are all just sisters in Christ. How much trouble can it be?" And so I moved my overnight bag, my sleeping bag, and my small self into the hotel room with three lovely ladies. There is a text in the Bible that promises, "The beloved of the Lord shall dwell in safety." I couldn't help but feel that, once more, God had taken care of my shelter without my even thinking about it.

Morning dawned and my roommates and I reviewed the list of main programs and breakout meetings we could participate in. We grabbed breakfast from my stockpile of provisions and took off for the conference center.

It wasn't until our lunch break, with the sun burning high over the Indiana plains that I decided to check on my bunny. I walked out of the hall and down the broad steps where, just the day before I had run into Caroline. Squinting into the brightness of the day, I scanned the road for my automobile. But unlike the previous evening, today there were no cars parked along the road. I turned and looked at the doorway again. Yes, this was where I had entered, but where was my car? I turned back toward the road and, peering very skeptically at the tree that I had certainly parked under, I set off to investigate. No car. No road sign. No indication that I was not going crazy.

I headed back inside once more and inquired at the information booth. "I can't seem to find my car." I'm sure I sounded perplexed to the young lady working there.

"Well, it's easy to lose your car here," she admitted. "Our parking lot is so huge!"

"But that's just the thing," I said, "I didn't even leave it in the parking lot, I parked it right outside under that big tree."

"Oh," she looked mournful, "that's the problem then."

"What? What's the problem?" I demanded.

"That area is for loading and unloading only. There's no overnight parking allowed. Did you leave your car parked there last night?"

"Yes, along with all the other cars that were parked there."

"I'm sorry," she pushed a slip of paper with the name and number of a tow company on it. "Try this place," she suggested. "They probably have your car."

"But my *bunny* is in that car," I exclaimed as if that should magically bring it back.

"Oh my! Well, let's hope they moved your car to a shady spot," she answered with complete lack of concern before turning toward the next person seeking her information skills.

After successfully rescuing my car and bunny, I made sure to legally park in an appropriate spot for the remaining conference sessions. So, now that I had my room situated and my car and bunny back in my possession, I could concentrate on enjoying the festivities the rest of the week.

PARADE OF NATIONS

The first weekend of the conference included a fabulous Parade of Nations in which people from every country, dressed in their cultural costumes and carrying their national flags, walked the conference stage in a grand procession. Having so many nationalities represented in my little self, I always watched the Parade of Nations and thought, "Ooh! I should be up there!" Unfortunately, participating in a parade takes a good deal of preparation and foresight that a "just wing it" type of person like me does not naturally possess. For one thing, packing a national costume was the last thing on my mind, and no one really wants to see a parade of the latest outfit I bought at Sears.

During dinner our first night, as I sat beside my friends, I heard some people speaking across the table. "*Vy govoríte po-rússki* [Do you speak Russian]?" I asked, as my roommates looked on in amazement.

"*Da, da!*" one of the women answered, and we immediately engaged in a long discussion about life in the Soviet Union. She introduced herself as Tatyana and told of the struggles she and her husband were having as they tried to spread the word in their underground church in Russia.

"Please walk with us in Sunday's parade," she said as we embraced at the end of the night.

"Oh, I would love to!" I exclaimed. Then as I thought about it, I realized that it would not be possible. "I always wanted to participate in the parade, but I don't know. I left Russia when I was just a child and I don't have a costume to wear," I answered.

"Don't worry," Tatyana said, reassuringly. "We have so many members here from Russia that we will surely find something for you to wear!"

The very next day, I was proud and happy to march in the parade, not with Russia but with Uzbekistan. Although we never found any Russian outfit, I did have my own Uzbekistani folk costume so was able to participate with church members from the country where I was born.

CALIFORNIA OR BUST

By the end of the first week of the conference, memories of my long and already difficult trip began to resurface, and I decided to make a firm effort to find a driving companion. I made a sign using a disposable Styrofoam lunch tray I had been using to carry my food. I found a marker and in bold letters wrote "FREE RIDE TO CALIFORNIA to anyone willing to share drive time." I was quite pleased with my idea as I held up the sign for people passing through the conference doors.

"Hey, free ride to California!" people called and waved as they walked by me. "What a great idea!" or "I wish I could go there with you!" One couple, a husband and wife, did say that they needed a ride to California. "We would love to help you drive."

"Oh, I'm sorry," I admitted. "I'm traveling cross country because I'm moving there so my car is just too full for two people. I really only have one space left." They looked at me as if I was quite nuts, and probably were thankful to be spared the trip with what could potentially be a crazy lady. They shook my hand and went safely on their way.

But all afternoon no one else approached me to actually take advantage of my free ride.

On the last day of conference, I began to worry that I would be driving the remaining 2,500 miles alone. After breakfast I put up my makeshift sign, without any hope for success. Then a well-dressed young man and woman approached me. "Great, another couple," I thought, nearly ready to repack my whole car in order to welcome them aboard.

"Are you really looking for a driver to California?" the woman asked with a thick Hispanic accent.

"Yes, but unfortunately I only have room for one person," I answered, surprised to see that her face still brightened from my response. Speaking in rapid-fire Spanish and gesturing boldly, she translated for the young man. When he responded in equally speedy Spanish, the young woman turned back to me.

"Only my cousin Danny needs a ride," she answered motioning to the young man who accompanied her. "He is a pastor in Argentina and he wanted to visit his brother in Riverside, but he did not have any other way to reach there."

"Oh wonderful! And my son's name is Danny too! Can he drive in English?" I asked, actually wanting to know if he was authorized to drive in

America.

"Of course," she laughed. "He only can't speak it very well."

"Well that's OK," I answered. "I know six languages, although Spanish is not one of them, so I can communicate with anyone!" So with a new traveling companion, I was able to see yet another one of God's provisions on this trip.

The trip from Indiana to California went remarkably well for two people who spoke seven languages between them but no two the same. Danny's English was meager and he chose to drive the entire way himself. I was thrilled to be relieved of the duty. I turned my attentions instead to teaching the young man English.

"Apple?" I ask holding up a ruby-skinned fruit for him. Then I would repeat, "Apple. Aaaple. AAA-PEL."

"Do you want a drink?" I offer later, holding a plastic cup out for him. "Water … WWAAAATER." With each repetition my voice grew louder and probably ever more annoying. But Danny just smiled and accepted whatever I offered him, occasionally pointing to the map or motioning to the needle on the dash.

"Gas?" I wondered. "Do we need gas?" Danny smiled. "Gaaaas. GAAAAS." He drove the car to the nearest station and I ran inside to pay. That was only fair since he had taken on the entire chore of driving. Besides, I had the chance to do what I loved most: Teach! "Bathroom?" I suggested. "Do you need the bathroom? BAAATH-ROOM …" And so my lessons continued for 2000 miles.

If Danny was tired of my tutorial he never complained. When I grew tired of teaching, we sang hymns together, each in our own language, or I napped or read. But Danny drove the entire way, finally pulling into his cousin's home in Riverside, California. Danny's cousin offered to let me rest at their home briefly, but I was anxious to be on my way to San Diego. I could manage the last two hours on my own.

GETTING TO KNOW SAN DIEGO

I arrived at my new home with my pre-arranged roommate Mrs. Faible in El Cajon. She and I smoothly merged our lives into a well-functioning system. I had wondered what type of care I would be giving in exchange for free room and board but was quickly reminded what a blessing it was to have a great roommate. She was intelligent, well-read, widely traveled, and we had many of the same interests. Rocks, plants and animal specimens filled her home. I had never seen so many dolls, mirrors, and antiques outside of a museum in all my life. Mrs. Faible was more of a collector than I was!

I soon got right to work with the most important part of being a newcomer: making friends. That summer, I became friends with Marianne Esteb, one of the women in my church. Like me, she enjoyed outings to the world-famous San Diego Zoo, Sea World, and Balboa Park. She was also willing to live anywhere she was able to rest. Her current home was a large RV camper which she had parked in the school parking lot. Like a turtle, she used her completely mobile home for every need, including transportation. Thanks to her I was able to know more of the city than I ever would have on my own.

One of the things she did was take me to a Padres baseball game. At that time, I could not even imagine what a Padre would be.

"They are our baseball team," Marianne explained.

"Oh, baseball," I said, recounting my first week in the Yonkers School. We laughed and chatted and enjoyed our day in the sun watching the Padres. And in the end, I left there realizing that I still could not figure out that game.

EL CAJON SCHOOL

My school life, on the other hand, had its share of disappointments. Now, don't get me wrong. The school itself was just fine. It was other things that happened around me that crushed me.

Once all my possessions were unloaded from the car, I discovered that the beehive, which had been transported from city to city ever since Danny first discovered it in Albany, would not grace any corner of my new classroom. Each time I moved to a new city, a tiny bit of it would chip off. This time, the large waxen structure, beaten down by five days of transportation across the Mohave Desert, had finally melted.

The hardest part for me was that Danny had wanted to keep the hive in Buffalo. "C'mon, Ma," he implored, "that would look so cool in my room. You've had it long enough! Let me have it back."

"Oh Danny," I had promised, "I'll take it to San Diego and you can have it whenever you finally move there with me." Now the giant gift of nature was destroyed. I couldn't help but worry with guilt that if I had listened to my son, the beehive would still be whole.

❖ ❖ ❖

My new classroom included fourth through sixth grade. Even though the developmental differences in this age range were not well-suited to one classroom, the students were bright and lovely. They adored my bunny Midnight just as my students in Athol had. I had to set up a schedule for each child to take turns caring for the bunny, otherwise one child would monopolize our classroom pet, fights would break out, and no one would get any work done.

During one of my outings with Marianne, she approached a subject I had not even thought about. "Raya, I know your classroom grade level is not the easiest one …"

"Oh, they're alright," I said quickly. I would never admit that any class was beyond my capability.

"True, they are sweet children," she acknowledged. "But still, do you think you could benefit from having a full-time aide working with you?"

"Of course!" An aide could help the fourth graders while I work with the fifth and sixth, listen to students reading while I teach grammar, run off copies, or watch the playground while I make the lesson plans. I was fully capable of putting someone to work in my presence.

I ran the idea past the board. "The aide's mother actually wants to fund the position just so that her son James can build up his work experience," I explained. How could they refuse an offer like that? James came to work with me the very first week of school and proved to be a great blessing amid my misfortunes.

That week was an upsetting one at home. My elderly housemate became ill quicker than any of us could have ever imagined and was eventually moved into long-term care. I went about my life caring for her house, popping in and out of the nursing home to visit her, and believing that she would be back soon. Suddenly our cozy little home seemed cold and quiet without her.

That same week, two other tragedies, each one more heartbreaking than the last, would occur. It was a hot, arid September day when I arrived at school to find parents already waiting outside the office. Apparently the doors had not yet been unlocked. I jumped from my car and quickly ushered everyone in.

From there, my day went downhill. Our morning worship and song services were punctuated by silliness. When my students should have settled into their math lessons, they were hopping up and down from their seats. The heat seemed to bring out the most restless behavior in children.

"Mrs. Abadir, Mrs. Abadir," a frantic voice called to me from the back of the classroom.

"What now?" I wondered.

"Mrs. Abadir, where's Midnight?" Michael was searching the back of the classroom for my bunny cage.

"Oh, the bunny!" I exclaimed, rushing outside to my car. I had run out of the car so quickly that morning that I had forgotten all about the bunny. But it was too late. Although it was still early in the day, Midnight could not tolerate the intense heat of the morning. I slumped down against my car, placed my head in my hands and sobbed.

I knew I needed to compose myself before the children saw me, so I wiped my face on the back of my hands and brushed them off on my skirt. It was too late; fourteen faces peeked out at me from the doorway and windows of my classroom. I sighed.

"Children, I have bad news," I told them.

"No! Not the bunny!" Angela, my most dramatic child cried.

"He had a good life," Michael consoled her, patting her on the back. I thought of all the traveling Midnight had done throughout his short-lived life. I mean, he had made it all the way across the United States. He had endured a tow truck abduction, and in fact had even lived through a mild, though balding, experience with some electrical wires in Athol. Yet Midnight did not survive the typical September heat of Southern California.

All day long the children migrated toward the empty spot that once housed Midnight's cage. And the next morning I dragged myself back to school, ashamed to face the classroom without him.

As I approached the door, I noticed a white box propped against the wall outside of my classroom. Holes the size of quarters were cut into the side walls and a suspicious scratching noise drifted out from inside. Curious, I dropped my books and purse on the nearest table and opened the lid of the house-shaped box. A pair of pink eyes peered back at me from the center of a white furry face. The sweetest little bunny had come to make our classroom his home. "Snowball," as the children called him, seemed to fit right in from day one, and I never did find out who had left him there.

I wish I could have said that the tragedies ended with Midnight's death, but unfortunately something much worse was going to happen. While volunteering to repair the shingles of our school's new roof, our first grade teacher's father, Mr. Subsbury, fell to his death. The family struggled to come to terms with their deep and sudden loss.

I knew somehow we needed to change the energy of our little school. I assembled the teachers together for a meeting. "We are going to have a faculty worship service every morning before the first bell rings," I said.

In spite of the objections by some of the teachers, I knew that we needed God to be watching over us more now than ever before.

MISSING STUDENT

One morning as I was setting up my classroom for the day, the upper-grade teacher Neil Adams knocked on my door. "Raya, I have really bad news for you. One of my seventh grade students, Katrina, didn't come to school yesterday. When I called her parents last night they said she had left for school that morning but never came home!"

"What? Are you sure, Neil?" I was stunned by the news. I remembered the girl was agitated during the fire drill the week before. She had been stubborn and seemed angry during Mr. Adam's roll call. I hadn't thought to correct her. After all, she didn't do anything more than cross her arms and roll her eyes at us. Still, had I missed the warning signs somehow?

"How do you think a child just leaves the house without her parents knowing where she is going," I asked.

"I guess she walks to school every day," Neil answered. "So they expected her to come directly here."

The two of us sank to our knees to pray for the young girl. "Lord, Katrina is only 12 years old," I begged Him. "Please keep her in your care; protect her from all harm and danger and return her to the safety of her family."

All morning long, anytime the thought crossed my mind again, I continued to pray for Katrina. Finally, after lunch we received word of her location.

"Katrina is at her brother's house," Neil rushed into my room to tell me. Relief was radiating from his whole face. "She has been hiding there since yesterday. Her parents have agreed to let her stay as long as she continues coming to school. She'll be back tomorrow."

Once more we knelt down to pray, although this time it was with praise and thanksgiving.

Soon after that day, I had a conference with Katrina, her guardian brother, and her teacher. "What seems to be the problem?" I asked her.

"I hate how I'm treated at home," she snapped.

Neil and I exchanged glances. This was an awkward situation. On one hand, if there was some kind of abuse going on, we should find a way to protect the child from it. On the other hand, preteens very commonly sense that they are being wronged, just because they don't get their way. We all feel that way when we are young, yet we expect the next generation to be immune to those feelings.

"Tell me how you are treated," I probed. I had learned years ago that an open ended question would go much farther with this conversation than a leading one could.

"My stepdad is so mean," she began. "I can't stand him!"

"How is he mean?"

"He's just bossy. He's so, like, bossy and pushy and ... mean."

"How is he pushy?"

Katrina rolls her eyes. "I mean, he doesn't hit me or shove me around, ya know? Like, he just thinks he's my boss or my *dad* and he's not! I don't have to listen to him!"

"So, your mom and dad, your real dad, I mean," I chose the words carefully. "Are they the only people you have to obey?"

Katrina looked at me as if I were an idiot. "I know what you're trying to make me say, that I have to listen to my teacher or a policeman and the pastor and now my brother because he's going to be my guardian and all that but not *him*. I do *not* have to listen to *him*!"

"You're right," I admitted to her. "I really was going to point that out to you. I know you're too smart, so I won't try to fool you into saying anything you don't believe in." Katrina rolled her eyes again. "I mean, Katrina, your teacher, the police, your mom, and your brother all have your best interest in mind, so it makes sense that you should listen to them."

Katrina's arms remain crossed, and the scowl didn't leave her face, but from beneath a deeply knitted brow, she finally, curiously looked up at me.

"But don't you think," I continued, "that just like a policeman or your teacher or your brother, just like all of them, your stepdad, who buys your clothes and books, who pays for your food, who provides you with a safe, warm home—don't you think that he also has your best interest in his heart?"

"You can't make me go back there," she said with a hint of panic touching her voice. "My brother is my guardian now. I'm staying with him."

"Honey," Katrina's brother stepped in, "no one is going to make you go back right now. But in order to stay with me, you still need to show everyone that you are following some very basic rules."

"I know that! Do you think I don't know that?"

"Of course you know that," Neil said. "You're a smart girl—my brightest student."

At that moment, an idea struck me and I continued where I thought Neil was heading. "That's why we all think you are important enough to meet with, and to make sure that your time with us meets all of your expectations."

Katrina and I struck up a deal. She needed to finish all her assigned class work and then she could come to my room and help me with little projects. At first it was just erasing black boards and organizing paperwork. Soon I started to let her assist one or two students with their work.

Every day Katrina approached me, tentatively at first, then soon with more and more enthusiasm. Because she was required to finish her classwork, her grades went back up. Everyone began to notice the difference in her. Where she had been dark and brooding before, she was now friendly and patient with others.

"How did you know your project would work on her?" Neil asked me.

"I didn't," I answered truthfully. "But I think God did."

RAINY DAY

My first year in San Diego marked the fifth year of drought for this fine city. Lawns were dehydrated, gardens were dying, and the threat of brush fires hung in the air all through that autumn. To protect my car from the blazing sun, I often parked under the eucalyptus tree outside of my house, although when the full heat of the day raged, even that was not enough coverage.

One December morning I awoke before the sun had even risen. The sound of pouring water outside of my window puzzled me. Could there be a leaky sprinkler system or a broken fire hydrant? Dressing quickly and "gobbling down" my breakfast (all of which takes me over an hour, even at my speediest), I soon discovered the source: rain. But this was not just any rain. So much was coming down that I really did believe a fire hydrant was spraying directly over me. It was as if the heavens had turned on a faucet and the water was pouring—*flooding* really—over El Cajon.

I scrambled around for an umbrella, finally finding one buried in the back of Mrs. Faible's coat closet. I opened the front door and braced myself against the attack of water. I do believe the rain was actually propelling *sideways* toward me. When I managed to peer through the heavy downfall, I could not find my car.

Instead, parked under the tree where I was sure I left my vehicle was a brown, muddied, filthy hunk of metal. I pressed the alarm remote on my keyring and was surprised to hear the unfamiliar object in front of me beep to unlock. It wasn't until I got inside the vehicle that I recognized the interior as my own. The dust which had accumulated on the tree during five years of drought had washed onto, of all things, my car.

Once the rain stopped, I drove to the nearest car wash. The wipers, which I had never needed until this point, smeared a brown arc of mud and dead insects across my view. "Having fun four-wheeling?" the attendant asked with a smile as I paid for the service.

I actually didn't even understand what his question meant until James, my volunteer assistant, explained it to me when I arrived at school. "Four-wheeling?" I thought, "Is he kidding? I'm a middle aged woman! Did he really imagine that I was rolling over sand dunes in my tiny Honda Accord?"

A major problem well understood by educators in Southern California is the lack of large enclosed facilities to be used as shelter during bad weather, be it rain, snow, or tornadoes. Who needs a cafeteria when the children can eat in the fresh outdoors? Our campus did happen to have a gymnasium, so we made full use of it during lunch that afternoon.

Large though it seemed when only one class was using the gym for PE, today it was certainly cramped and noisy with the entire school running around inside at lunchtime. Suddenly, mid-game, one of the boys paused and his ears perked up, straining to listen. Slowly, more and more children stopped in their tracks, eyes growing larger and larger in wonderment. Above us, on the flat gymnasium rooftop, it sounded as if thousands of tiny hoofs were landing on our building. "Santa," one child whispered, staring straight up at the ceiling, hoping to catch a glimpse of the legendary sleigh.

"What is that?" Janine asked, perplexed by the day's climate.

"Look at the marbles!" one of the boys exclaimed, staring out of the glass doors. "There are millions of them falling out of the sky!"

"Hail!" I gasped. I had only seen hail once in my entire life. That was in Buffalo, one of the coldest cities of the Northeast. I couldn't understand seeing hail in sunny California! This day was just getting stranger by the second.

ELLA MOVES TO SANTA MONICA, CA

Shortly after I had received my invitation to go to San Diego, Ella began her quest to join me. At the time, she was an assistant manager for a jewelry store called Gordon's. Ella heard various store locations would be hiring from time to time. As soon as a position opened up in Southern California, Ella petitioned for a transfer.

"You'll never get it," her district manager warned her. "Corporate will never pay moving expenses for an assistant manager."

"Look, I don't need Corporate to move me," Ella replied. "I'll pay for the move. I just want to be sure I have a job once I get there."

Her boss promised to do what he could, but Ella knew better than to wait for him. She contacted every other Gordon's manager she had ever worked with, and together, they sent in an overwhelming report of praise for her. Ella got the job, but it would be in Los Angeles, two-and-a-half hours away from me.

Ella's trans-American trip could not have been any more different from my own. She packed everything she had into her tiny Honda CRX and, stopping only for fuel, drove continuously through to Lancaster, the home of one of my cousins, one-and-a-half hours away from her final destination. No rest stops, no scenic detours, and no picking up non-English speaking strangers to help with the driving. Needing every last penny for the down payment on her new apartment, Ella even spared expenses by staying in cheap motels and not purchasing any food the last several hours of her trip. For three thousand miles it was just Ella and the road.

I, of course, was thrilled to have one of my children living close to me. After staying with her cousin Haleh, Ella settled into her own apartment in Santa Monica and jumped right into her new position at Gordon's Jewelers.

CALL ME *BABUSHKA*

Our first Christmas in California in 1990 would be strange without all the snow and sleet that tormented Buffalo, even more so without Esther and Danny. So I was thrilled when the girls conspired to have Esther come out for a visit between Thanksgiving and Christmas just to celebrate with us a little bit.

Nasser owned a minimart in downtown Buffalo and put in long hours seven days each week so he wouldn't be able to get away. Besides that, his parents had been visiting from Jordan. Esther looked forward to the escape, and I looked forward to sharing my little town with her.

Of course, my version of sightseeing is to take my family to our church, our school, and the local Adventist-owned hospital. "These things are important, Esther," I insisted, dragging her to yet another church function. "You should know what wonderful things your church is doing."

"Mom, I came here to be with *you*, not your entire church," she would argue on the way home from helping in my classroom one afternoon. Fortunately for her, my friend Marianne was a much better hostess. She took Esther to Sea World, Balboa Park, and the Zoo, just as she had taken me, and later Ella, after her move.

I had noticed that Esther seemed to be less energetic than usual, but I thought it was probably due to jet lag or boredom, nothing to think twice about. It wasn't until a month after she returned to Buffalo that Esther revealed that she was pregnant. Having gone through two miscarriages earlier in their marriage, Esther was reluctant to share the news with anyone until she safely passed her first trimester.

My hearing of this wonderful news was quite a surprise. I had called my children to share some news of my own. "I just registered for classes to get my PhD in Education," I bragged. "Your mother is going to be a *doctor*!"

"Mom," Nasser laughed over the phone, "we have good news for you too. You're not going to be the shortest one in the family anymore!" I was thrilled! And that had nothing to do with finally being bigger than one of my relatives. I was *ready* to be a grandmother.

Precious Miriam was born in Buffalo on September 18, 1991. I had finally become a *babushka*. Not able to be there myself, I sent a huge package with dresses, blankets, tights and bibs. Esther later shared that she would have much rather had me there. "It was so lonely in the hospital all alone," she pouted over the phone as the baby made cooing, suckling noises beside her. Ella and I wished we could have been there too, but we made a commitment to call each other several times during the coming weeks for updates.

That Friday I had an appointment with my cardiologist. It was just a routine angiogram to check my arteries. "No problem," he told me, "This procedure has been done hundreds of times. It shouldn't take more than four hours, max."

Unfortunately, it was during this particular visit that we discovered I had an extreme sensitivity to anesthetics. It wasn't until Sunday afternoon that I was finally released from that "routine, four-hour procedure." I hadn't called anyone because, thinking I'd be driving myself home after four hours, I hadn't taken my phone book with me.

Gratefully, I pulled into my driveway late Sunday evening. I had spent a lonely weekend recovering at the hospital. Unlocking the kitchen door, I saw the answering machine blinking madly.

"Hi, Mom," Esther's voice, "Just checking in. You're probably still at school, so give me a call whenever you get home." Then a couple of hang-ups and Esther's voice again. "Mom? You really need to return phone calls! I tried calling earlier. Give me a call."

"Hi Raya, it's Marianne. Missed you at church today."

"Raya, this is Shirley. Since you're usually front and center in church I thought I'd tell you we missed you today."

"How nice," I thought.

"Mom," Ella's voice this time, "Esther said you're not returning phone calls. Is everything alright? Mom? Mom?"

"Oh my dear!" I worried.

"Mom," Esther sounded really panicked this time and I could hear Miriam screaming in the background. "Mom, call me back immediately!"

I guess I should have called my children from the hospital. The startling ring of the telephone brought me back to the present time. I picked it up, but Esther was shouting before I could even say hello.

"Where have you been all weekend? Why haven't you been answering your phone? Don't you know people are worried about you?"

"Oh my dear, Esther. How are you, honey?"

"Are you *kidding* me, Mother? I'm worried *sick*! That's how I am! Where have you been all weekend?"

"Well, I was in the hospital …"

"What? The hospital? Why?"

"Oh, it was nothing."

"Nothing? *Nothing?* You don't stay in the hospital all *weekend* for *nothing*, Mother! What happened?"

I explained that I went in for a routine angiogram. "I didn't tell you because I didn't want to worry you."

"Well that backfired, now didn't it?" she responded sarcastically. I received her instructions to get some rest now, with strict orders to carry her phone number with me at all times. "Someone should know where you are next time, Mom."

Somehow motherhood had turned my daughter into my parent.

SAN PASQUAL ACADEMY

At the end of my second year in El Cajon, I received yet another call from the conference. It was time for me to move again! Here I thought I had finally reached California, the goal I had been striving for ever since my divorce 16 years earlier, yet my administrators had other plans for me.

"You won't be leaving San Diego, Raya," the phone call explained. "There is a new position for a teaching principal at San Pasqual Academy. It's a single classroom school primarily for the children of the academy teachers. You are the one person who has had lots of experience teaching multiple grades combined."

I remembered seeing San Pasqual Academy on my many trips to the Wild Animal Park, one of my favorite places in San Diego. The academy was on a gorgeous, desert, mountain road leading to Ramona. There I had also visited a tiny, one room schoolhouse on the property that was now used just for historical purposes. Bright, lush orange groves surrounded the property.

Then I remembered how effortless a one room school could be. My two years in El Cajon had taught me that piloting multiple teachers could sometimes be more like babysitting your peers than leading and directing. I embraced the change and accepted the move.

The summer before I started at San Pasqual, I attended classes at La Sierra University. I had finally begun my journey towards my PhD. The class I was taking on Elementary Leadership had a very creative and inspiring professor. At the end of that summer, he told us to write an essay on what we could picture ourselves doing in five years.

I couldn't explain why it happened to me, but suddenly I was flooded with memories: sitting on the shores of the Caspian Sea, singing songs with the Kubrocks, listening to their stories, and finally my baptism. The Kubrocks would never have been in Iran that year if their plans had gone the way they had expected. They were supposed to go to Russia but were not granted permission by the government. Instead, they were stuck in Iran and had lost all their students except for one—me—and they had completely changed my life forever.

My essay would be easy. I wrote about my birth in Russia and our escape to Iran. I envisioned myself picking up where my own teachers had left off, heading back into Russia. Russia, which I had left in the middle of the night 50 long years before, had been a bleak, dark land, stripped of opportunity and void of God. But in recent years, the media was spreading the news that the Iron Curtain of Communism was falling. The United Soviet Socialist Republic would now simply be called Russia. A new president, new government, free trade and, best of all, God would be accepted into the new regime. I wanted so badly to be a part of that movement.

The summer ended, my paper was turned in and I made my move to a small condo in Escondido. This way I would be closer to my new school in San Pasqual. It was the second home I had purchased since my divorce. I must admit, I was once again very proud of my accomplishment. As expected, Ella swept in and helped me to turn two cramped bedrooms into a warm and sunny home. Neighbors welcomed me and introduced me to Marie, the other elderly lady in the building. Together we enjoyed an occasional cup of tea or an evening swim at the complex's pool.

Life settled into a comfortable routine for me as the school year got underway. The students at San Pasqual were bright and sweet and I loved the scenic drive onto campus. But still, continuously my thoughts kept turning toward the essay and my desire to return to Russia as a Missionary.

Esther had teased me more than once about having a direct line to God. Everything I asked for I got, she said. And I was asking, *begging*, every day that He would find a way to send me back to my homeland.

FLOCKING TO SAN DIEGO

That November Esther and Nasser brought my first baby granddaughter to visit me for Thanksgiving. Nasser felt the need to get away from his shop after *two* armed robberies, and he couldn't get much farther away than California.

Mimi, as she was nicknamed, was a bright-eyed, wriggling ball of joy. I filled the kitchen sink with warm water and bathed her brown little body, remembering how sweet and fun it was to take care of my own children when they were that small.

"Look at that tiny nose!" I peered at her perfect face. "I don't think my children had such little noses! I don't know how I'm going to get this tiny nose cleaned!" I was in love.

And the best thing about this visit was that Nasser had also fallen in love with San Diego.

"The mountains look just like Palestine," he said, driving me to work one morning.

"Good, why don't we move here then?" Esther teased from the back seat, knowing that ever since they had visited Los Angeles, Nasser had vowed he would never live in California.

"I could live here," he admitted thoughtfully. Esther was shocked. I was secretly thrilled of course, and now I had something new to begin praying for.

By March Nasser had sold his business in Buffalo and was staying with me while he looked for work in San Diego. One more prayer answered. Esther needed to finish the semester at Buffalo State College, so he left Esther and Mimi in Buffalo where she would pack up the family home for their transfer.

Because she had no family around to help with babysitting and she was not working, Esther cleared permission with her instructors to bring Mimi to classes with her. Large, intense, brown eyes and curly black hair peeked out from the baby backpack Esther carried her daughter around in. As a result, Mimi became known on campus as one of the youngest students.

Meanwhile, Nasser found a job almost immediately as a retail bakery manager. The hours were horrendous and he spent long days moving large sacks of ingredients, shuffling papers, and standing on his aching, tired, feet. Most difficult to manage was his time during Ramadan. Not only did he have to maintain his tough work schedule, but he did it all while fasting from food *and* water, sunup to sundown, for one entire month as his waist grew thinner and his eyes more sunken each day.

Otherwise, having a young man in the house was quite interesting. He and I shared the mealtime chores, mainly because he was more willing to eat his own cooking than mine but partially because our schedules were so random that whoever was home first was the one to prepare the meal.

"One of the General Conference workers called me today," I told Nasser during a meal. "He and his wife will be coming for dinner this Friday. What do you think I should prepare?"

Nasser wiped his mouth and stood up to start clearing away the dishes, although my plate had more than 90% of the food still on it.

"Depends," he answered.

"On?"

"Well, how much do you like these people?"

"Oh, I like them very much!" I answered. "I've known them ever since we lived in Egypt."

"In that case you shouldn't cook for them, Mom," he said, with a twinkle in his eye. "If you want to keep them as friends and they work for the conference who decides if you get to keep your job, you better be safe and don't prepare anything for them."

"Nasser," I objected, "I am a good cook!"

"Of course, Mom," he said, laughing as he picked up my plate to wipe underneath it. "We especially enjoy your cooking when we don't need to *eat* any of it. Do you remember the first meal you cooked for me?"

Nasser would not let me forget the very first time I cooked for him and a Lebanese friend, Nick. Although I had enjoyed *tabbouleh* immensely when I lived in Lebanon and attended Middle East College, I had never prepared it. I was confident that I was a Lebanese food specialist but Nasser and Nick, I later learned, were not impressed.

"Mom, trust me," Nasser wiped his hands on a towel, his clean-up chores finished, "if you like these people, you won't try to feed them."

I decided to make Russian borscht. That is the one meal my son-in-law could not criticize since it was never in his mother's cooking repertoire.

When Elder Neil C. Wilson and his wife Claire came to my house, we settled into a warm nourishing bowl of the hearty Russian soup. Catching up with my friends from the Middle East Conference was exciting to me. They had done so much as missionaries in the years since I had seen them last. "When will it be my turn, Lord?" I wondered.

My turn came sooner than I expected.

"Raya, have you ever thought of going back to Russia?" Neil asked me.

"Have I ever? Is he kidding?" I thought.

"I *dream* of going back there," I answered. "I have been feeling the pull more and more lately. I can just imagine what it would be like to go back and finish the good work my own dear friends, the Kubrocks, began when they met me."

"Well, I have an offer for you, but I'd really like you to think about it for a week before you give me your answer," Elder Wilson began. My heart was thumping so loudly I could hardly hear what I knew he was going to say.

"We would like you to be the Associate Director of Elementary Schools in the Euro-Asia Division," he said.

I could feel my mouth hanging open, as if I could catch his words in it. "I would *love* to!" I blurted out.

"Wait," he held up his hand to slow me down. "I want to explain the role to you so you can consider it."

"You can explain, but I already know I want to go!"

Elder Wilson began again, "You would be in our Moscow headquarters, although you would be responsible for helping to train the educators all over Russia and the Ukraine to open schools. We want the churches there to have a more Christian mindset in their teaching method. Coming from communist backgrounds, many of these teachers have very strict and rigid upbringings. We want them to learn to share not only Christian education with the students but also Christ's love."

"I accept!" I nearly shouted this time. I think I may have been bouncing slightly in my chair with anticipation.

"Well, Raya, I want you to really take time to think about it. Even though Communism has ended in Russia, the country is still very harsh. You won't have an easy time there."

"I don't have to think about it," I said enthusiastically. "I accept. Right now—I am ready to go!"

One week later, as promised, Elder Wilson checked back with me. By that time I had already told my children I was accepting the position. How could I do anything else?

Ella and Esther were both convinced that the KGB would get me. In their minds, grave dangers lurked in the former Soviet Union. But Danny had other concerns.

"How many weeks are you staying?" Danny wanted to know.

"Weeks? I'll be there four years!" I answered.

"Four *years*? No, Mom, you can't do that. You'll starve to death! We'll never see you again!"

"Danny," I replied patiently. "There are millions of people in Russia who are not starving."

"What are you going to do there?" he asked.

"I'll be the Associate Director of Elementary Schools in the Euro-Asia Division," I carefully repeated my lengthy title.

"Wow," Danny's voice was respectful. "Did they know what a tiny person you are when they gave you such a big position?"

I recalled the tall visiting pastor from my college years who had looked at all of the slightly built Middle Easterners assembled before him and declared that only tall people could be leaders. Yet, here I was, barely reaching 4'9" and would be in charge of opening elementary schools and training teachers across the entire former USSR.

"You know Danny," I replied, chuckling softly, "it is not by might, nor by power, nor by height that I go but by the spirit of God."

Before I left, Danny came to California for one last visit with me. Starting in Lake Tahoe for a ski trip with his cousin, Kian, he then traveled by bus to San Diego. I was at the bus station waiting for him.

"Is this the bus from Tahoe Lakes?" I mistakenly asked one of the bus drivers. The man just laughed, shook his head and pulled the lever to shut the door. I stood in the driveway with my hands on my hips. "Now how am I supposed to find my son in this big station?"

"Tiny!" I heard Danny's voice booming behind me.

"Oh, my Danny Boy," I turned to embrace him. "How was your trip?"

"Beautiful, Ma," he said, shaking his head in wonderment. "The snow was perfect, everything was perfect!"

"Maybe you'll want to move out here since you like it so much," I prodded, as I normally would.

"What's the use, Ma?" he said. "You're leaving anyway."

"True, but I'll be back before you know it."

"*If* you survive," he reminded me of his fear.

"Of course I'll survive!" I countered. "I'll be just fine. God is with me."

"I don't know if God can find you in that country, Ma," Danny worried. "Besides, I won't move here. I love Buffalo. And *if* I ever decided to move to California it would have to be up north. I love the snow, I love the changing seasons, and I love to ski."

Meanwhile, Esther had finished college so she and Mimi made their final transition to San Diego. Danny would be moving back into my house in Buffalo with some of his friends. His girlfriend, Susan, was not at all thrilled about the idea. Susan was from Buffalo's Little Italy and had lived in the city all her life. To her, visiting Danny in the suburbs seemed so far it was like traveling to another country.

MAJOR PREPARATIONS, 1992

In the months preceding my journey to Russia, I spent time traveling from church to church around San Diego County petitioning for help of any kind. I told my story of living in a country lacking more than a few staples of food, void of freedom, and without God. I talked to congregations about how it felt when I found God for the first time and that my own teachers had been banned from Russia. I shared my last university essay with them and the desire to return to my homeland to continue the Kubrocks' good work. Donations poured in.

The conference's amazing disaster relief organization (ADRA) would be transporting all my belongings to my new home. They provided an enormous crate that I could fill with anything I would need.

I sighed when I thought of leaving my homes in Buffalo and Escondido. "What do I need there, really?" I thought to myself. I would be staying in a fully furnished apartment so I didn't need to bring any tables, beds or even dishes and bedding. I took my clothes, my lesson books, which I would translate into new publications when I arrived there, my trampoline, and my stationary bike. The crate was not even filled a quarter of the way.

One day, after one of my many appeals in church, a couple introduced themselves as Elwin and Beth Dunn. "Raya, if you have time to visit our home, we may have some things that could help you," Elwin offered.

I followed them through winding, mountainous roads and over a long private driveway until we reached their home. Elwin opened his garage door and I walked in to their deep storage basement. Shelves lined the walls and were filled with five gallon buckets. Each bucket was filled with dehydrated foods—potatoes, peas, fruits, soups, and more, needing only boiled water in order to become a meal or even a dessert. Even dehydrated salads were available though I couldn't imagine how rehydrated lettuce would taste.

"Where did you get all this?" I was stunned.

"Well, we have friends who are Mormon," Beth answered. "They keep staples and dehydrated foods on hand in case of a crisis and they are happy to sell their surplus to us."

"We didn't know when we picked up so much of these supplies that we would be giving them away to such a noble cause," Elwin added humbly.

That wasn't the only donation of food I received. Another church member filled a shopping cart with rice, raisins and gallons of olive oil she found on sale. One parent donated five-gallon buckets of wheat. Not flour but un-ground, un-processed wheat kernels. Another student, whose father was in the Navy, told me I could find a personal-sized wheat mill in the military exchange. With fresh ground wheat and plenty of yeast, I could at least have bread there. There was also the parent who donated twenty pounds of legumes.

My tiny classroom became so full of miscellaneous *stuff* that I could hardly find room to work. Fortunately, the packaging company owned by San Pasqual Academy gave me dozens of their sturdy, cardboard boxes to transport the items more easily. Although I spent the shortest term of my entire working life at that location, I found that the church members embraced my upcoming mission with as much enthusiasm as I did.

All in all, five hundred pounds of foods met me in Russia but not until three months after I arrived. Though I am known to always travel with a surplus of food, I had never, ever, in all my life journeyed with such an enormous quantity of provisions.

And so, everything was arranged. I was 66 years old, certainly advanced enough in years to be retiring if I wished, but God and I had other plans.

Figure 31 - Marianne and Son James, Raya Holding Midnight, El Cajon School, Hail on Car, La Sierra University Roommate

PART XII: RUSSIA, 1992–1996

RETURN TO MY HOMELAND

"... Be not entangled again with the yoke of bondage." Galatians 5:1

After a long, tiring 15-hour trip to Russia, I finally arrived in my birth country. Being a naturalized citizen of the United States, I had to endure interrogation by immigration officials. "Why are you returning? Where will you be staying? How long will you be here?" I don't recall all the other tedious questions but I know I was there a very long time.

When I finally made it through immigration and found my luggage, I discovered my next challenge: searching for a taxi. Every time I gave someone the address, each taxi driver would give the same response: "I don't go there," or "Too far." Finally, I was able to bargain a $50 fare. Although the ride was only an hour away, it seemed like an eternity as the taxi drove further and further away from the airport. At one point, I was scared and didn't know if I would ever see my children again.

As we drove, I noticed that many things had changed since I was in the country of my birth. When I left Russia there were almost no cars and busses only ran during the daylight hours over narrow unpaved roads. Now hundreds and thousands of Russian-made cars zoomed over six-lane highways. The streets around me were dirty with piles of garbage on every street corner, vendors setting up their wares anywhere they desired, and men spitting globs of slimy mucus directly onto the sidewalks at my feet. My homeland had deteriorated to filth. Maybe I couldn't remember accurately the day-to-day life on the streets of Moscow from my childhood, but I was shocked!

Seeing my grey hair and wrinkled face, small children cried out, "*Babushka!*" I could hardly believe I was hearing someone call me that when my one and only grandchild was still too young to know what a *babushka* was.

My first three months in Russia would have been a struggle if I had not been so excited to be back. First of all, my crate of belongings was delayed until ADRA had a sufficient number of crates shipping to the same location. Having never dealt with the non-profit group from the receiving end before, I had no way of knowing when to expect the arrival of my crate.

Secondly, as seemed to happen every single time I moved or traveled, I had no place to stay. Headquarters were located in the Zaoksky Seminary, and since it was the middle of April when I arrived, the campus was already filled to capacity. But not to worry—as if I would. My director helped me settle into a nearby summer camp that the conference occasionally rented out.

I was the only one staying in this six-bed cabin. The winds of early spring whistled through the bare walls and my footsteps echoed in the empty room. Still, I was so thrilled to begin my mission that I could have jumped from bed to bed like a child.

"Breakfast will be served in the cafeteria at 8 AM," Kulakov, the son of my director stated. "Do you have any special meal requests?"

"Oh no, I love everything," I said. But then I thought better of it and added, "But maybe you should tell the staff that I am a vegetarian."

Early the next morning, which was really late at night if you consider that my body was still on California time, I bundled up in a brand new, red woolen coat I had just purchased for the journey and headed out the door for the cafeteria. I had barely stepped one foot outside of my cabin when, as if it had been waiting for me all night, a crow immediately released his droppings on my shoulder. I groaned in disappointment as I looked down at the white poop stain painfully obvious on my crimson coat.

Miserable, I hurried into the dining hall. Rows and rows of empty tables and chairs filled the long dining hall. For a minute, I wondered if I had actually overslept.

"Alloo?" I called toward the glow of light I saw in the kitchen. A plump, grey-haired woman with gold teeth promptly came out.

"Welcome," she smiled and greeted me warmly in Russian as she motioned to the hundred or so empty places in the dining hall. "Feel free to sit anywhere you like!"

"Look," I stopped her, turning my soiled shoulder for her to inspect. But her smile did not waver.

"It's good luck!" she insisted, nodding vigorously as she dabbed it away with a kitchen towel that I hoped she would then discard.

"How could bird poop be a sign of good luck?" I wondered. Perhaps it meant that nothing worse could really happen to me than to start the day with a bird using my brand new garment as a toilet.

"*Spaceeba*," I mumbled my thanks to her and sat nearest to the kitchen entrance where I could receive the food as soon as it came out hot and steaming.

She rushed back to the kitchen and returned with a fragrant platter of sardines. I was shocked. "But, I … I told them I was vegetarian," I stated, staring into her face. "I don't eat meat at all!" I used hand gestures and shook my head vigorously, worried that I wasn't sufficiently explaining myself in Russian.

The plump little face gave a gold-studded smile. "Don't worry!" she assured me, "This is not meat; it's fish! You know, *fish*? It swims in the water." She moved her hands from side to side in front of her, making the unmistakable motion of a swimming fish.

"I don't eat fish either," I explained. First a bird soils my jacket, and then a pile of fish soils my plate. Could nothing go right this morning?

I watched the smile of Ms. Golden Teeth drop from her face. "Well, we don't have anything else," she answered dryly.

"I'm sure that you at least have *kasha*," I suggested. The hot and hearty porridge was a morning staple that I had been dreaming about since I first heard I'd be returning.

"*Dah, dah*," she nodded vigorously, and her face brightened again, "We have *kasha*, but it will be a quarter of an hour longer." I examined the plate of tiny, bony fish and knew that to wait 15 minutes for a hot bowl of nourishing porridge would be a small price to pay.

TRAVELING IN MOSCOW

Once the conference moved me into my own apartment, a tall building centered at the heart of a Moscow community, I began to feel more settled. Every day I made my trek from my apartment to the office or anywhere around the city that my work took me, using the extensive metro system or one of the conference-hired drivers.

If the metro wasn't an option, I could choose from one of the many "taxi" drivers that could take me around town. I use the term "taxi" loosely because there were very few actual marked taxis in the city. Travelers in need of a ride could stand by the side of the road, point to the ground in front of them, and expect that a private individual who owned a car would stop to pick them up for a fee.

The metro system in Moscow was unique compared to any other train or subway I had ever seen. I recalled watching young men in Egypt dive onto swiftly passing trains to hitch free rides. In the Bronx, I was sometimes frightened for my life as I rode the bus and subway. But I had never experienced anything like the Moscow metro.

First of all, in a city where nothing is dependable and everything seems to function on a whim, metro trains would arrive at their stations exactly every three minutes to the second. In fact, to prove their punctuality, a timer hung above each platform ticking off the seconds until the next departure. The other remarkable characteristic of the system was how extraordinarily beautiful each station was even though the rest of the city was devastated. No one dared to drop a speck of garbage onto the platforms, although I once did see an old *babushka* holding her tiny grandchild over a trash can to defecate into it.

Most platforms were paved in granite or even marble. Several of them had distinctive sculptures and chandeliers that were kept polished and maintained by stooped, gray-haired ladies wearing scarves on their heads and aprons tucked under their sagging bosoms. The whole effect of city transportation felt like a cross between a noisy museum and an efficient underground rail system.

Once a year, tribes of Eastern European gypsies migrated to Moscow, filling the streets with entire families from infants to the elderly, who would swarm around passersby, smiling with golden teeth and begging for alms. When the begging didn't work, or even if it did, the gypsies would carefully slip a hand into a pocket or purse and rob the victim before they were even noticed.

I had been forewarned of the gypsies' skills as master pickpockets so, like many of the native Muscovites, I traveled the streets cautious of any potential thieves. That was why, during the evening's rush hour as I was returning home from work or errands or shopping, my arms overflowing with books and bags, I always clutched my purse tightly and protectively to my body.

One particular evening, I was guarding more than just my purse. Hidden deep inside it was my passport and $1000 with which I had intended to purchase an airline ticket. Unfortunately, when I'd arrived at the travel agency, it was closed. Fearfully, I returned to my home on the metro.

Standing near me at the metro platform was a blond, dark-skinned woman and her child. The doors opened and the pre-recorded voice warned, "*Ostaroshna* [Be careful]!" Passengers started to rapidly fill the train and somehow the woman and child were separated from each other as we entered, but only enough to wedge me tightly between them.

"What are you doing?" I snapped in Russian as the two pressed closer and closer to me.

"My greatest apologies," she smiled with her gold studded grin as she moved swiftly away. That's when I noticed that her white blond hair had roots which were black as night. Something about her gestures discomforted me, but I couldn't put my finger on it.

I arrived at my station and I dragged my weary body up four flights of stairs to my apartment. As I *should* have expected, the cramped, urine-smelling elevator was unexpectedly broken that day.

I finally dropped my bags onto the floor and set my purse on the table. But something was wrong. My purse felt too light and sounded empty. I picked it up again and this time stared in horror at a deep, long, gash across the front of it. My heart sank like a boulder had smashed into my gut. The woman's face and mismatched appearance flashed through my memory. "They were gypsies," I thought. "My cash! My passport! What will I do if that gypsy took them?"

I turned my purse upside down, but only a few slips of papers with my scribbled notes fluttered out. I felt faint with fear. I had seen how the bureaucratic red tape in former Red Russia could tie people up for years. How would I replace my passport and my hard-earned money?

Hopelessly, I looked inside of my empty purse. The zipper inside caught my eye. Could it be? I knew I had stashed everything in the main compartment of my purse, but I tugged the zipper open anyway. There, tucked safely inside the smallest pocket of my bag was a familiar small manila envelope. With shaking hands, I opened the envelope and found all the money and my documents safe and sound. I whispered a prayer of thanks, not even sure how God had pulled off that miracle.

LOST IN TRANSLATION

One of my first duties in Russia was to play tour guide in a city that I still scarcely knew. That would not be a problem for me. My conference assigned a driver, Andrey (Russian form of Andrew), who would take us anywhere we wanted to go so I didn't really need to know my way around. All I needed to do was to be the translator for visiting missionaries and for my Canadian associate. To me, this basically meant negotiating cheap ticket prices. Bargaining was my forte and the conference directors must have discovered that very early.

For most events at that time, there were two prices. While a Russian might pay one ruble, equivalent then to about five cents in American money, a foreigner would pay $25. The difference was preposterous! I couldn't let our guests be robbed like that! Everyone would be watching the same show regardless of where they were from.

My conversational skills were excellent despite what the Russians really thought. Being back in my birth country brought me great pleasure, especially being able to converse in my native language again. In one of the churches I visited, I was asked to translate when my associate addressed a group of teachers. I remember walking up the stairs to the platform and hearing giggles behind me. Once I reached the top step and turned around, I found that a stray dog had followed me all the way up. Where he came from or how long he had "tailed" me, I did not know, but now I was faced with having to get rid of him.

"Shoo," I scolded, fanning my hands at him. The dog jumped out of my way but then, wagging his tail, jumped right back. His eyes sparkled with joy and his tongue flopped with drool. I sighed and turned toward the microphone that was set up for me.

"I guess he wants to help me translate," I said in Russian to the uproarious laughter of the congregation.

"Can we begin, Raya?" Dr. Mayden asked me in English.

"*Dah*," I answered him, a bit flustered, which of course only made everyone laugh more.

Dr. Mayden and I quickly moved into a comfortable rhythm where I translated his words at every pause. Throughout our speech my canine friend sat by my feet, just happy to be near me.

After the talk was finished a woman rushed up to me, "You did so well!" she praised. "I understood every word!"

"Thank you," I paused, "But I *was* speaking Russian. Of course you should understand me!"

"I know! But you were speaking *old* Russian!" she laughed. "I haven't heard that vocabulary spoken for at least 50 years!"

I had always prided myself on being fluent in Russian. Now I realized I sounded foreign—even in my mother tongue!

After that day, I began to pay closer attention to how others spoke, and I realized that I *was* fluent in Russian. Although in the old days, only pure Russian was allowed, the new Russian language incorporated some French and a *lot* of English. I would scarcely need to translate at all!

JUST FOUR WEEKS

One day during my first July in Moscow, I arose early as usual for work. After wasting time around my apartment, I realized the morning was getting away from me. I needed to get ready for work. I stepped into the shower and turned on the faucet, then screeched as ice-cold water splashed over me. I jumped out of the shower, trying to catch my breath, and waited for the water to warm up. I waited and waited and waited. Finally, I realized that the water was just *not* going to get warm. I struggled back into my nightgown and robe, and quickly went to knock on my neighbor's apartment before anyone saw me.

The door burst open and a very wrinkled face peered out at me. "I'm sorry to bother you," I said, "but do you have any hot water? Mine seems to be turned off."

A smile beamed across her face. "Why no!" she exclaimed gleefully, as if I had asked her if she would mind sharing a million dollars with me. "The whole building is turned off!"

"The whole building? For how long?" I questioned in amazement.

"Just four weeks," she said, happily. "Maybe less, but usually it lasts the whole month. Yes," she was pleased to agree with herself on this matter, "plan on four weeks."

This tiny woman didn't seem to be the least bit bothered that she would be walking around soiled for thirty days! "But-but how will we bathe?" I inquired.

"Why you go to the bathhouse, of course!" she answered.

"A public bathhouse? In Russia?" I couldn't have been more thrilled. From the window she pointed to a small, darkened doorway a couple of buildings away from our apartment and assured me that I could bathe there. I thanked her and rushed back to my apartment to collect shampoo, a bathing suit, and a towel—everything I would need at the bathhouse.

Moments later, I arrived at the bathhouse and steam flowed out as I opened the door. I blinked to adjust my eyes to a dimly lit room. An old matronly cashier squatted on a stool just inside.

"How much is the entrance fee?" I asked.

"How many hours are you staying?" she asked.

"*Hours?*" I gasped. "I only want to take a shower and leave!"

"One Ruble," she grunted, although by the deathly look she gave me, I felt as if I had said something entirely inappropriate and offensive.

I handed her the change and attempted to push past her when she thrust a fist full of long, stripped willow branches into my hands. I stepped back and shook my head, unsure of what she expected me to do with them. She rolled her eyes, crossed her arms, and waited for the next victim to walk through the doors while I entered like a scared mouse.

In the first room I saw bags of women's belongings lining the wall and assumed I had found the changing room. I quickly pulled off my street clothes, put on my swimsuit and slid into the steamy inner room.

"Whisss snap, whisss snap, whisss snap!" a hypnotic rhythm greeted me as my eyes adjusted to the even darker room. Perhaps twenty or more women sat along the benches, whipping themselves with the willow branches. At least I knew that the woman at the door didn't have plans to beat me. She just wanted me to do the job myself.

Every eye rose to stare at me as if I had arrived wearing nothing but my birthday suit. That is because *they* were all wearing nothing but their birthday suits. In my swimsuit I was extremely overdressed.

"She thinks she is going to swim in the beach," one woman scoffed in a whisper as a bathhouse worker continued to beat her with a long strip of willow. I ignored her remark. I was not about to swim publically in the buff!

"What are you doing with those things?" I pointed to the willow branches. Now that I had been identified as the outsider, I did not hesitate to ask silly questions.

"They are for increasing your circulation," one lady answered, offering her own, sweaty branch for my beating pleasure.

"No, thank you," I answered, backing away until I found my way to the swimming pool area and finally to the showers.

Later that day, I decided to try, at least once, the willow branch. I must say, it felt very invigorating. And, since we are instructed to do as the Romans do when in Rome, then the same could be said for the Muscovites in Moscow. Yes, I eventually became comfortable going there in the nude too.

That month, the bathhouse became a second home to me. I had to go there every day in order to bathe. The funny thing was that I rarely saw the same women twice.

THE BOLSHOI

Within Moscow's city center, just outside of the Red Square, I desired to see a performance in the Bolshoi Theatre. Distinct memories of my years going with Uncle Habib to watch his wife Zina dance filled my mind every time we passed the giant pillars.

"I've never gone," one of the British women working in the office admitted.

"Are you kidding?" I was stunned. "It should be mandatory to see the ballet, even if only once before you leave here!" From that time on it became my mission to take everyone I knew to the Bolshoi. Thus, just as I did when I was a little girl, I got to see every ballet, every opera, and every concert that was performed all season long.

One week, ten visitors (five couples who were in Russia from the General Conference in Washington, D.C.) came to our office. They wanted to see a program at the Bolshoi and that evening *Swan Lake* was playing. What luck! To watch a Russian ballet performed by Russian dancers in the Bolshoi was a unique experience for our guests.

"We have to arrive ten minutes before the show starts to purchase our tickets," I instructed.

"Ten minutes? Are you sure?" everyone asked repeatedly, afraid that we would miss out on the performance altogether.

"The box office never opens. All the tickets are sold, sort of underground, from hand to hand," I explained. "Really only one or two hawkers buy the tickets, then sell them on the streets." The new "open market" in Russia mainly meant that anyone with friends or connections could maintain a monopoly over the goods they wanted to sell. Russians called it freedom, but I called it the Russian Mafia.

"Don't you think they will sell out?" one of the men asked.

"Oh no!" I waved the thought away. "They sell the tickets very expensively all day long, but when they see they have some left before the show starts they drop the price down."

Ten minutes before the show started, as planned, I walked around the promenade alone, looking for the hawkers. I had given strict instructions to my friends to act as if they didn't know me. If the boys heard them speaking English, the price would immediately be increased.

Of course, I was able to get tickets for everyone, but it was difficult to find eleven seats together. Three couples sat close to the orchestra pit. The show would be larger than life for them. The two other couples would sit farther back, but still with excellent seats. I gave them my opera glasses to share.

Since there were no single seats on the first level, I climbed the narrow stairs up, up, up to the third balcony level. By this time the show had started and I had to carefully climb over seated viewers, trying not to step on feet or knock them with my purse. This was not an easy task on the third level of the Bolshoi; the higher you climb, the smaller and tighter the seats become until you are practically sitting on the lap of the person next to you. At that level you are so high up you have to either squint at the tiny figures twirling across the stage or use binoculars to see the actors closer.

Finally seated, I smiled at the young lady sharing the seat with me. Surprisingly she smiled back, obviously forgiving me for all the commotion I had caused, and handed me her opera lenses. "I just saw this last week," she whispered. "You enjoy the ballet."

"*Spaceeba*," I answered, gratefully.

During intermission she introduced herself to me as Raisa. "Why, that's *my* name too!" I answered in surprise. (Raya is a short form of the name Raisa.) As we chatted, we realized that we had even more in common. In a city that was so packed with high-rise buildings, we were *neighbors* living in the exact same community. *And* we both worked for a school system. *And* we were both without husbands.

"You are such a lovely lady. Why are you alone?" I asked her.

"My husband passed away from lung cancer last year," she answered. "His elderly parents live with me and I take care of them now." Somehow I am one of those people who can talk to someone once and learn their whole life's story. Raisa disclosed to me that she was suffering from depression and had slipped out of the house for two hours just for some freedom. I thought of all the people in Russia who drowned their sorrows and frustrations in a bottle of Vodka, and I was impressed that she would choose such a beautiful venue. At the end of the ballet, we exchanged phone numbers and agreed to keep in touch. I know that many people do that: jot a phone number on a piece of scrap paper and promise to call but never do. But Raisa was not like that. She phoned the very next day, and we got together nearly every day after that. She quickly became like family to me. I shared promises of hope and healing from Bible stories and she helped me with chores around the house, never coming to visit without bringing some treasured trinket she purchased that day.

"She's like the daughter I never had," I told Esther over the phone one day.

"Mom," she corrected, "you already have *two* daughters."

"Oh! Well, of course!" I replied. "I mean she's like the *third* daughter I never had." Even though my kids loved to tease me about my new daughter, they were happy that I was creating a family for myself so far away from home.

I invited Raisa to church with me and she devoured the words of the pastor and biblical messages. Daily she called me to share some passage she had just discovered. Within weeks of her first sermon, Raisa was teaching God's love in her own Sabbath School class.

FAMILY MATTERS

One evening I received an unusual call. "*Eta* Raisa Mikhailovna?" a woman's voice called me by my paternal name.

"*Dah*," I responded tentatively, wondering how she knew me. Most of the contacts I had in Russia up to that time were through the conference and none of them used the formal greeting for me.

The woman introduced herself as Lena. She told me she was married to my cousin, Nadir. He had been born in a concentration camp after his family—my mother's sister, Galya, her husband, and their 10 month old daughter—were sent there on suspicion of espionage in the 1930s. Although my own father had died in a similar concentration camp, Nadir's parents survived 25 years of imprisonment until the entire family was released. By that time Nadir was 20 years old.

This woman, whom I had never heard of in my life, knew the entire story. And she knew the names of all my aunts and uncles. *And* she knew that my father had died in Siberia, my brother left for Iran with my paternal aunts and uncles, and my mom and I left Russia years later to follow them.

She knew way too much. She had to be who she said she was. The only other explanation would be that she was part of the KGB. It was still soon enough after the fall of the Iron Curtain, and I knew that not everyone in Russia was happy about religious freedom, so it seemed appropriate for me to be cautious and concerned for my safety.

"How did you ever find me?" I asked as politely as I could.

"I had to leave Baku," she explained. "Being a Muslim country, it was becoming too dangerous there for me. I am Armenian and, they assume, Christian so I moved to Moscow. My husband Nadir had to remain in Baku where he has a job. I'm living in a one room apartment with my sister and her teenage son."

This is just a side note, but when someone from Moscow says their family is living in a one room apartment, don't be misled into believing that they have one bedroom, with a living room, kitchen and bathroom. No, that would be luxury. Rather, a one room apartment means the family *either* has a bedroom *or* a walled off living room in an apartment that they have to split with at least one other family. The bathroom and kitchen are shared spaces. In Lena's case, she was very fortunate to be staying with her sister and nephew, rather than with a larger family or strangers.

"So, I thought I would research our families," Lena continued. "You know, with the Red Cross …"

"The Red Cross can do that?" I asked surprised, "Really?"

"*Dah, dah,*" she answered. "I knew you had left for Iran, but I had heard you left there for the United States. How did you get back here to Moscow?"

I chose my words carefully, telling her as much as I dared about my new mission work for my church.

"Please," she begged, "I want to meet you. Can you visit my home?"

I feared this had to be a trap. "I work during the week," I apologized. "Maybe you can come to the Community Clubhouse on Saturday. I will be there for my church service." I figured that I would feel safer in the presence of my coworkers.

We made arrangements to meet at the main entrance before church started. I discretely asked several of my Mission friends to stand beside me just in case she was not who she claimed to be. I told Lena what I would be wearing and she told me how to recognize her, but we needn't have exchanged that information.

"Raya!" A lovely, dark haired lady exclaimed, sweeping me into an embrace. "I would know you anywhere! You look exactly like your mother's picture!" I hoped this woman was not KGB. I was beginning to like her already.

Lena and I sat side by side through the sermon. With tears streaming down her face, she devoured the message of love, faith and caring that the pastor was preaching. Although Lena came from a Christian descent, she had been raised in a Moslem state of a communist country, where freedom of religion was not permitted. Lena had never before sat through a sermon like this one.

Within four months she was baptized standing amongst the other new believers in the murky waters of the Moscow River.

For some reason, when the conference sought out living quarters for those of us who would be missionaries, they found two-bedroom apartments (that is, two bedrooms, a living room, a bathroom and a kitchen all for one person or one family). What may have seemed like tight quarters to Americans was considered spacious accommodations to the Russians. It seemed so silly to me that Lena was cramped in a tiny room with her sister and nephew while I had an entire apartment to myself. Lena moved in, and for two years she and I lived together in my spacious two-bedroom apartment.

DIAPER MINISTRIES

One evening, Lena watched a documentary on the television while I shuffled papers in my own room. The segment was about a woman raising birds—tons of them—in her one room apartment. Cages filled every corner of the room and in each cage sat and screeched a colorful, tropical bird while her baby boy sat on the hard, wooden floor, watching the TV screen with fascination.

"Raya, come and look at this woman," Lena called to me. She didn't have to ask twice. I love television, but even more entertaining than ordinary television was Russian television. You never knew what you would see!

As the cameraman zoomed in for a closer look at the birds pecking around the child, a stream of urine spread out from beneath the baby boy. I was mortified. "Why didn't she put a diaper on that child before the cameramen arrived?" I asked, completely shocked.

"Diaper?" Lena laughed in surprise. "We don't *have* diapers here!" I was certain she must have misunderstood my Russian, so I explained again, using animated hand gestures to describe the location a diaper would be placed on a baby. Still she shook her head.

"Rayichka, believe me, we don't have anything like that here."

"Then what do mothers do with their babies?"

"They toilet-train them," she responded rationally.

"That would explain why the woman I saw at the metro station was holding her baby above a Metro garbage can to defecate," I thought to myself.

Since I had been in Moscow, I rarely saw people with babies. Young children were not common on the streets either. However, after that television eye-opener, I made a point of seeking out those who might have children.

If I had known before I left the United States that potatoes, cabbage, onions, and beets were staples in Russia, I never would have wasted the space in my crate with dehydrated versions of them. Instead, I would have filled it with diapers. When I finally found a young mother who claimed to have disposable diapers for her baby I wanted to laugh. The item was barely larger than a sanitary napkin and was covered with a stiff, waxy paper.

Obviously the Russians were not going for maximum absorbency when they designed that one!

From that point on, I contacted some friends in Buffalo and San Diego, asking for donations of diapers—lots of them. When the question, "Do you want disposable or cloth?" came up, my answer was a prompt and resounding, "Yes!" We would take whatever was offered to us.

One of the Escondido church members had a service that picked up soiled cloth diapers from peoples' homes and then returned the articles freshly washed, clean and white. As more and more of his customers switched to disposable diapers, he found that the volume of unused cloth diapers exceeded the demand for them. "Take as many as you can," he offered to our pastor's wife, "My warehouse is overflowing!"

That crate, sent once again through ADRA, came filled to capacity with diapers rather than dehydrated foods. To make room in my apartment for all the diapers, I knew I had to get rid of the unneeded potatoes, cabbage and beets. I found a janitor cleaning up around my apartment. "Thank you for your hard work," I told the old lady, presenting her with a tall bucket of dehydrated vegetables. Her face lit up and she thanked me profusely for the simple gift. Soon word spread to other workers and nearly every day someone would knock at my door asking for the wonderful soup ingredients. They did not know that they were helping me as much as I was helping them!

As I unloaded the giant crate, Raisa and Lena lined the packages of clean white cloth diapers along my bedroom walls, around my bed, and stacked them until they reached the ceiling.

I sighed, staring at the imposing partition. "I will never be able to get rid of all these!" I told them.

"You will," Raisa told me with great confidence. "I have an idea!" And thus began my diaper ministries.

First, we sorted all the diapers into sizes and approximate ages to match. Then we bundled them up into stacks of twelve and included pretty diaper pins, a plastic panty, and a slip of paper with the name and address of the nearest church and my own phone number in case they needed a diaper refill. Once the packaging was complete, it was time to take care of delivery.

Raisa and I kept a few bundles of diapers in our purses and set out on any given day to wander through the parks surrounding the apartment buildings until we caught sight of some young mother pushing a baby carriage.

"Oh! How cute!" Raisa would exclaim with sincere pleasure.

"How old is your baby?" I would ask. Then the reply would come that the baby was three, six, or eight months, and I would remark, "Congratulations! Your baby just won a diaper set from our church!" The mother would look at me skeptically as I thrust a hefty white package at her.

In Russia everyone expects that if a stranger offers you a gift there are strings attached. I could almost read the question in her eyes, "What do you want from me?"

When the mothers realized I required nothing in return, they began to warm up, asking questions and chatting a bit. Several would come to church the next week and they would smile shyly or greet me enthusiastically. Many more would never be seen again. Regardless, we were exposing these mothers to a new way of taking care of their babies and keeping them clean. Other workers in the office thought it was a great idea and grabbed a few bundles for their own neighbors' children. Lena carried reams of the packets with her whenever she would travel back and forth to Baku, and soon everyone seemed to be interested in our new ministry. Before I had ever hoped, my wall of diapers had diminished. But in its place was built the solid foundation of new friendships with Jesus and with each other.

I should also note that these diapers were not only appreciated by the young, new mothers. Old ladies in the church were thrilled to have such soft, white "kitchen towels" to replace the ragged ones they had been using. Although I had to ration the quantity I gave out to our matriarchs in order to keep the majority for my diaper ministries, I must admit that giving even the simplest of gifts to those who were already active in God's service went a long way in fueling their needs.

THE EVANGELISTIC EXPLOSION

Our little Diaper Ministry was not the only evangelical move we were making that year. All over Russia and the other newly independent provinces, evangelistic meetings were being held. Gatherings ranging from as few as a handful of participants to hundreds began to spring up in every major city.

I enjoyed my duties translating books for the new church schools to use. Of course, we had official translators who could convert an English word into a Russian one, but more important than that was the transliteration— putting meaning into the words of our new school textbook, *Naouka E Zdarovia* (*Knowledge and Health*).

But everything didn't always go as planned. For one thing, the Orthodox

Church was not happy to have newcomers introducing their faith to the citizens of Russia. Every time we left our meeting halls, signs were posted by the Orthodox Church leaders: "Russians have always been Orthodox and Russians will always be Orthodox. Yankee, Go Home!"

In Moscow, we had launched a two-month series of seminars known as the Mark Finley Crusade. Although posters and billboards covered the city streets and the radio was advertising the event for us, we began to see what it was like to do business in the former Soviet Union. Two weeks into our seminars, we were told that we couldn't continue meeting in the Kremlin Hall where the crusade was being held. The space was needed for another purpose. In a flurry of activity, we rushed around thinking we would now have to find a new venue. But Finley was not so easily dissuaded.

As each of us in the office huddled in prayer to help us get through this new obstacle, Mark Finley contacted the man who had arranged the rental. "We have a contract," he reminded the man, producing the document. "In other parts of the world, people do not take back their contractual agreements without good cause. I had assumed we were dealing with a trustworthy organization here!" How could anyone argue with that line of thinking? Especially when Russians were struggling to catch up with what the rest of the world was doing!

With no further delay we were reinstated in our original assembly hall and the convention proceeded. Busloads of people arrived each day and, after attending ten days of seminars, the attendees could take home their very own free Bible in Russian. Before the end of the crusade, our Russian churches were pleased to have successfully baptized *thousands* of people craving to learn about a loving God.

Since Russia was usually frigidly cold, most of these baptisms were held in public swimming pools we rented for this special occasion. In warmer weather, we were able to gather around the muddy waters of the Moscow River for an old-fashioned, revival-style baptism. It was in these very same murky waters that I tearfully watched my own family members and friend, Nadir, Lena, Larisa, and Raisa, dipped down to wash away their old lives and reveal new lives in Christ Jesus.

Later, during one such baptismal service on the northern peak of the Volga River, we were shocked as two soldiers came running toward our assembly, shouting some indistinguishable words. Several of the pastors braced themselves for what we were all sure would be trouble. Anything was possible on Russian territory and we were dangerously close to some military barracks. The men waved their arms and continued shouting as they ran nearer and nearer to the water's edge until, to our amazement, they ran directly *into* the water.

"We want to get baptized," their words were intermingled with their gasping breath. "Baptize us too! We will never have this chance again and we want to be baptized together!" Clasping each other firmly, they nearly danced out of their skin in anticipation as the pastors from Australia deliberated. In the end, with a firm grip on the shoulder of each young soldier and invoking the blessings of the Father, the Son, and the Holy Spirit, the pastors dunked the soldiers' heads in the river.

That was not the last of the amazing spectacles we would witness on the shores of the Volga River. Despite the fact that we had only enough baptismal robes for the people who had previously committed to the service, several other women showed up, begging to be baptized. We broke the sad news to them, that we were not prepared to perform the service on them that day. They would have to come another time. The women were not discouraged. Instead, there in public they began to strip down to the slips beneath their dresses. "We will never have this chance again," one woman insisted, echoing the words we had previously heard the two young soldiers say. Each woman rose, teeth chattering from the frigid waters as bystanders covered them with thick woolen blankets.

As more and more eyes were opened from the blinders that had been created through generations of communist rule, the SDA church grew from one tiny building in Moscow with only 20 members meeting in secret to thirteen enormous "churches" (rented former Soviet clubhouses), each one serving up to 500 members every week. The largest one, the International Church, was preached in English and translated into Russian. This Church was a great draw for the younger population of Moscow as they sought to learn anything they could about Western ways.

OPENING SCHOOLS, OPENING MINDS

My biggest task as Associate Director of Education of the Euro-Asia Division was to open new schools and inspect those currently running. I held in-service meetings to train teachers, much in the same way that I had attended those same classes when I was a teacher in the United States. I remembered how it felt to learn new skills and the pleasure I had when I took my lessons back to the classroom with me. Now I was sharing my knowledge with other eager teachers. My life had truly come full circle.

The first time I entered a school in Moscow, I immediately noticed a huge difference between American classrooms and those in Russia. For one thing, all the children were seated at their desks, hands folded in front of them and eyes facing forward. When I entered, the teacher gave a command and every chair was instantaneously emptied as students leapt to their feet and stood at attention. I stifled a smile at their military-like behavior.

Throughout the day, I listened as teachers sharply reprimanded their students, harshly shaking fingers under the children's noses. I pulled aside, first one teacher, then another, then even more, and patiently tried to teach them that severe brow-beatings were not tolerated in American schools. I knew how much Russians liked to imitate Westerners now that the Iron Curtain had lifted. "When you talk to your students," I instructed, "speak with love and patience. Don't wag your finger at them. If you need to, take a deep breath before you correct, so that your words will not be hasty. Sandwich your criticism between two compliments."

The women really did try to follow my direction. But often the deep breath only fueled their words of anger. In one school, a teacher stood with her back to her classroom while I spoke to her. I noticed her shoulder shaking repeatedly and might have mistaken her for having a tic if I hadn't realized that she was shaking her finger at her students behind her back where she hoped I wouldn't see.

Another thing that surprised me as I traveled and worked around Russia was how *old* the elderly were. Women retired at 55 from menial jobs which would not have been difficult to continue. Many were surprised to find that I was still working late into my sixties.

At first I was working with the Baltic States of Estonia, Lithuania, and Latvia. I enjoyed visiting these schools with Dr. Grimaldi, one of the visiting dentists from Southern California. Everything was clean and classrooms were well organized. Respect for teachers ran deep in the Euro-Asia states. Soon, however, the Baltic States joined the European Division and these schools were out of my sphere of influence.

MURMANSK

It was summer and I had a new assignment. I was to visit a tiny province, far north of the Arctic Circle, known as Murmansk. If it were winter, I would be subjected to total darkness throughout my stay there. Because it was summer, I endured days of endless sunshine, although the weather was still not warmer than about 60 degrees. Since it was so close to the North Pole and bordering Finland, I expected cold weather and the beauty of nature.

When I boarded the small and smelly Aeroflot plane, I had no way of knowing what I would find once I arrived. A church member had produced the deed to a building we allegedly owned there and had wisely held onto that slip of paper for 70 years! I was going to help establish a school now that the church was getting back on its feet.

I arrived at the church grounds and was shocked beyond my imagination. During the communist rule our church had been confiscated and was being used, of all things, as a horse stable. Although repairs had begun two years prior, signs of the years of damage were still evident in the trampled floorboards and blackened walls.

Neighboring Finnish Seventh-day Adventist church members had already arrived, bringing building materials and muscle to help the Murmansk members remodel their church. Due to the language barrier, this was no easy feat since in Murmansk, the people spoke only Russian. Also, because it was so far from most amenities and supplies, work went slowly and there was still quite a bit of work to do before completion of the church.

Between training new teachers and performing my other tasks in Murmansk, I would take walks to the beach of the Arctic Ocean. I had lived in cities on each end of the United States and had swum in the Atlantic and Pacific Ocean as well as various smaller seas during my travels around the world. I couldn't wait to see the northern-most ocean of which our little planet boasts.

Chunks of ice sloshed at the shore although it was already July. I would not be swimming in these waters! As I stood staring out at the blue-grey waters, I was shocked to see two middle-aged men, dressed only in their swim briefs, drop their towels and step into the icy water. One man swam out so far that he looked like a small black dot moving farther and farther away. The other man swam out several paces, and then swam quickly back.

"How do you *do* that?" I asked him, as he scrubbed his pink skin dry.

"Oh, it is not so easy," he answered, "but if you just do a little bit every day, before you know it you are so used to how it feels that you almost even *need* to keep doing it."

"Kind of like prayer," I thought, recalling my own journey with God. After so many years, I found myself almost constantly in prayer.

That Sabbath, I stood before the church congregation telling them the story of a young Russian-born girl (me) who had escaped to Iran and eventually to the United States and was back again, doing God's good work. Just as their neighborly love and dedication had warmed my heart, the Finnish people sitting in the service were thrilled with my story. "Please come back with us and speak at our church," they begged. No one had to ask *me* a second time. I was always happy to travel someplace new.

Cramming ourselves into the tiny car of one of the visiting church members, we headed toward Ivalo, Finland. Our trip would take about three hours. It amazed me that in the United States I could travel three hours and still be in the same state yet there I was driving to another country. I was excited to be on this surprise journey with newfound friends. As was my travel custom, I had filled their car with essential road-trip snacks.

At the border we explained the reason for our trip and presented our documents. This was where we encountered a major setback. The border patrol officer flipped through our paperwork, calling us each by name so we could signal who we were before he would stamp them. My documents he reserved for last. "Who is Raya Abadir?" he asked.

"I am," I answered briefly. My children had a fear of crossing the border with me since I tend to say too much, giving away my foreign born status. This time, I was in my birth country. What could go wrong?

"Your passport is expired," he told me simply.

"Oh really?" I had left the United States in such a flurry of activity that I hadn't realized how little time was left on it and I hadn't even begun the renewal process yet. I explained this to him. It seemed simple enough for me.

"You cannot enter Finland on an expired passport," he stated.

"But it is only for the weekend," I reasoned.

"I am sorry, but you may not enter. You need to go to the embassy and renew your passport before you can come back here."

"The embassy? *Moscow?* But I am here now," my logic was clear enough to me. "Surely you can just let me enter for the weekend. I'll take care of my passport once I am back in Russia," I persisted, but his authority was stronger.

"Sir, is there any way we can sponsor her?" one of my new Finnish friends offered. "We are willing to keep her under our care for the weekend and return her on Monday to Russia."

"I cannot authorize that," the young man stated. "Take these papers into the office and ask there."

I breathed a sigh of relief thinking we would be on our way again in just a matter of moments. But at a border crossing, a matter of moments can take a really long time. More than three hours later, and only after the office had received an invitational note from the church of Ivalo, Finland, were we finally back on the road. I apologized profusely to my travel companions, but they graciously brushed my worrying aside.

"We are happy to have you share your story this weekend," they assured me as we completed our trip.

As I spoke that weekend in church, I was overwhelmed with the members' sincere interest and support of our work in Moscow. A fast, deep friendship developed as soon as they voiced the words of true friends, "What can we do to help?"

FINLAND

Because Russian medical health standards were so poor during the early '90s, the conference gave us instructions to have all non-emergency medical procedures done at the Seventh-day Adventist Hospital in Finland. When it came time for my annual health exam, I looked forward to returning to the beautiful, snowy country and reuniting with my Finnish friends. Unfortunately, the medical facilities were in Helsinki, which was on the southern border, far from my friends in the east. As an alternative, I made arrangements with the church in Helsinki to speak on Sabbath.

The church office made a reservation for me on what I came to call the "Cheap Hotel": an eleven hour, overnight train ride from Moscow to Helsinki in a tiny, cramped compartment shared with one other traveler. Even on the trains, the Russians maintained their tradition of severely starched sheets and pillowcases.

I spent the night preaching to whomever shared my compartment, starting with my usual icebreaker question, "Are you a believer?" and ending only after the steady, bumping rhythm of the train put us to sleep.

In the morning, after our stale food box was delivered for breakfast, the conductor announced our arrival at Helsinki. I embraced my traveling companion and we emerged from our sardine-can quarters. Blinking in the bright, morning sun, I looked around. On every side of me, the city was busy since it was rush hour. Friday morning here was just as busy as Friday morning anywhere in the world.

A realization settled over me; for the first time in my life, I had absolutely no idea where I was. "I need a phone," I thought, logically. I pulled out my Finnish contact's number and glanced around for a phone booth that I knew should surely be close by the train station entrance. I spoke six languages and I knew how to spell telephone in all those languages. It should have been easy for me to locate a public phone.

I approached a young lady who apparently worked for the train station. She spoke only Finnish. I hadn't expected to hit *that* road block. I looked around me and sought out a passing businessman, again, no English and no Russian. I had no way of communicating with these people. I will say that despite our inability to understand each other, the Finnish people were very friendly. A small crowd of well-meaning locals had gathered around me and were all desperately trying to help me out.

Finally, a young man approached who spoke broken Russian. "I have this telephone number," I told him, thrusting the scrap of paper at him, "but I can't find a public telephone anywhere."

The young man brought me to a small red box, about the size and shape of an American mailbox and pointed to the word above its door, *puhelin*. "Telephone," he said, smiling at me.

My first surprise was that the word "telephone" which looks like the word telephone in almost every other language was so *foreign* here! But even more surprising was that, at just about four feet, nine inches, I was probably the only adult in Finland who could fit into the tiny box.

Soon, I had arrived safely at the conference headquarters and was settled into a beautiful guest room on the second floor of the office. It didn't take long for me to get acquainted with the neighborhood streets. I was surprised that though it bordered Russia, Finland's stores were bright, clean and generously stocked. I wasted no time filling several bags with foods I had not eaten in months, as well as some I had never seen before.

During my translated speech at church the next day, I made a suggestion. "I don't know anyone here yet," I said at the conclusion, "but I would love to see the sights of your beautiful city if anyone would like to take me around."

One of the young men who heard my story invited me as well as another visitor to have lunch with him at his island home. "Sounds wonderful!" I exclaimed. I was glad that I had bought so many goodies the day before. I brought along a variety of crackers and spreads to share during the meal.

"There's not much to see there," he said in his poor Russian as we boarded a small dinghy and jetted across the icy waters to his home. But what a surprise I received as our boat neared the pebbled shore. Only three homes stood on the island: one was his uncle's, one belonged to his mother and one was his.

"Your family owns this whole island?" I gaped in amazement.

"*Dah*," his young face crinkled into a smile. "It's small enough for us."

We settled down to a simple meal. Everything we ate including everything I brought with me, had to be ferried across the water, so I understood the generosity that went into the dinner. The island seemed like paradise. Although there was no electricity and no plumbing, it was just perfect.

Or was it? Later, before I retired, I asked to use the bathroom.

"It is outside," my host told me, pointing to the patio door.

"An outhouse?" I asked in dismay. My stomach lurched at the thought of squatting unsteadily over a small, smelly hole in the ground. I had visited too many public outhouses since arriving in Russia and I knew the worst of what to expect. Still, what could I do if I had business to do?

Holding my breath, I pushed the white-washed, wooden door open and stepped inside. I could feel the pulse on my forehead. "How long can I hold my breath?" I worried, finally expelling it in a whoosh. But then, I breathed in and was not knocked over by the foul odor I had expected. "Maybe I am just used to the smell now," I thought. But really, no one can ever get used to that smell!

"Your bathroom is so clean!" I exclaimed to my hosts as I went back into the house. "I wonder why they can't do the same thing in Russia."

"Ackh! Nothing is as bad as the Russian outhouses," the son said, shaking his head in disgust. "We only put sawdust down and then sweep it out," he explained as he waved his hands toward the fragrant forest they owned on their island. "Keeps away the smell *and* the germs."

The people from Finland tried everything possible to educate Russians on improving their lifestyles. With help from the Adventist Church, small neighboring cities were getting cleaned up and improved upon one at a time.

Sawdust in the outhouse was not the only unique experience I had in Helsinki. During this same inaugural trip, one of the church members offered to drive me around the city to see the sights. Beauty was everywhere I looked. I marveled at the tall Scandinavian cathedrals standing next to modern buildings. There were acres and acres of green grass, along with flowers and trees that created park settings for residents to lounge in. Even dogs had their own parks, something that I had never seen anywhere else in the world.

As we drove further away from the business section of the city and its cobblestone streets, quaint little red barns and churches dotted the countryside. Finland was truly a beautiful country. But my most favorite memory of all was as I stood on the wooden boardwalk near the beach. I watched in amazement as stout women, wearing scarves on their heads and toting long handled brushes, scrubbed away at something.

"What are they doing?" I wondered aloud.

"That is how they clean the carpets," my tour guide told me.

"What an ingenious idea," I thought to myself, and decided to practice it as soon as I arrived back at my living quarters.

"I noticed that the guest room rug was kind of spotted with dirt," I mentioned to my host. "Maybe I should bring them here so I can scrub them like those Finish housewives are doing."

"We can take care of them for you," he quickly answered, obviously amazed at my forwardness.

"I am happy to do it," I exclaimed, and I really was! First, because I wanted to give back to the friends who had so hospitably welcomed me to their beautiful city, but also because I just couldn't wait to try it out!

The next day, one of the church ladies brought a bottle of detergent and told me that it was safe for the environment. This was a concern since the soapy water would be running down into the sea. She also had a couple of brushes for us to scrub with. After washing and rinsing the rug, we carried it to a huge wringer and wrung the excess water out. Then to my surprise, we hung the rug in a sunny area and took off to more sightseeing. In the evening when we returned, my guestroom rug was clean and dry, ready to go back to its place on the floor.

On one of my other trips to Helsinki, I walked into the headquarters office and greeted the ladies just before they left for the day. I always tried to arrange some time in my schedule so that I could address the congregation on Sabbath and fill them in on the work we were doing in Moscow. By this time I had come to know the workers fairly well.

"Raya!" they welcomed me enthusiastically, "Why don't you come to the sauna with us tonight?"

"Is it far?" I asked. I would hate to inconvenience anyone in taking me all the way back to my guestroom. But still, I knew I would hate it even more if I had to miss the chance to visit a sauna.

"Far? No!" one of the ladies exclaimed, "It is right down the stairs in the basement!"

"*Downstairs?* Really?" This was too good to be true. I have never worked or lived in a building that housed a sauna right in the same structure. Soon enough I had changed into my swimsuit, which I was glad I always kept on hand, and joined them as we walked down the stairs and opened a small wooden door to reveal an even smaller wooden room that was stifling hot. Just the way I like it! I made a mental note of bringing this idea back to the States with me, but realized I couldn't exactly justify every office building in "75 and sunny" San Diego having its own sauna.

It turns out that once again I didn't need that swimsuit of mine. That's another thing that is done differently in Finland. Just like the bathhouses in Moscow, no one feels the need to cover up. "Women and men soak separately, of course," one of the ladies explained to me. "Except in their own homes they do whatever they like, I am sure."

THREE GENERATIONS

Although I was enjoying my time in Russia immensely, I did miss home. A couple of times I visited the United States briefly, usually for additional medical care and sneaking a quick peek at my family, but then had to hurry back to Russia almost before the jet lag wore off. Meanwhile, my children were a world away and I had a granddaughter growing up without me.

"I'm sending you all tickets to come visit me!" I exclaimed excitedly on the phone with Danny one day.

"No thanks, Ma," he shot me down.

"But why, Danny Boy?"

"I am not going to some communist country to be searched and tortured by the KGB, Ma," he gave his usual, sarcastic response.

"Oh Danny," I pleaded, knowing that a part of him was only kidding, "there is no more communist country and no more KGB!" But kidding or not, Danny would not be easily persuaded.

I tried Ella next. "Ella, would you like to come visit me here in Russia? I'll pay," I quickly added before she could turn me down, too.

"OK!" After Danny's rejection, Ella's quick response took me by surprise.

"Really? Because I'll bring you and your brother and sister out here. Everyone!"

"Why not?" she answered. Ella was always up for a trip. Having studied in Canada as a young teenager and in England as a college student, she became a world class traveler at an early age.

I left it up to her to persuade her siblings. Esther didn't need much convincing and even agreed to bring Mimi along. Even though Danny would not come, I was really looking forward to some family time.

Since one of Ella's best friends lived in England, she decided to stop there first before arriving in Russia. Esther and Mimi would come straight here, but then leave to meet Nasser in Jordan. Fortunately, their arrival times were only a day apart and the airport was about an hour away from my apartment and office. But I was not worried. By this time I had my wonderful driver Andrey who took me anywhere I needed to go in Moscow for about $20 a week. With one dollar being worth about 5000 rubles in 1993, his salary was four times greater than the average unskilled worker so he was very happy to be at my beck and call.

On the day before Ella was supposed to arrive, I was called out of a meeting to get an emergency phone call from Lena's daughter, Lala.

"*Tetya* Raya, your daughter is here and she is at the airport waiting for you!"

"What? But Ella is not supposed to come yet!" I knew this for certain.

"Not Ella, Esther!" Lala corrected me. I argued that Esther wasn't due in until Tuesday.

"*Tetya* Raya," Lala said patiently, "today *is* Tuesday."

There was no time to send Andrey all the way out to the airport. Traveling with a baby was hard enough and Esther had already been waiting an hour for me to pick them up.

In a mad scramble of activity, Lala and I arranged a ride with the taxi stand which had let Esther use their phone to call us. The woman running it was probably the only person in the entire airport who spoke English and had noticed Esther, with a worried expression on her face, pacing around carrying a baby and four giant suitcases.

Once Esther arrived safely at our apartment, thanks to the directions Lala had given earlier, I begged Esther's forgiveness.

"It's OK, Mom," she answered dryly. "I'm used to being forgotten in this family. But I never thought you could forget your own *granddaughter*!"

"How much did they charge you?" I asked. I couldn't help myself; Russians ask the cost of everything.

"Only twenty dollars," she replied nonchalantly.

"Twenty dollars! Esther, are you sure?"

"Yes, but I gave him a tip, too, so twenty-five."

"Twenty dollars is more than he makes all month! You shouldn't have paid that much!"

"Well," she argued, "if I wasn't left all alone and forgotten I wouldn't have had to pay him anything, now would I?" I couldn't exactly debate with that logic, but knowing that he was paid about 125,000 rubles for that ride made me sick to my stomach.

Esther did not care much and changed the subject by proudly waved a street map at me. "The driver gave me this," she said pointing out various spots (all in Russian) that were marked on the map. "And it even has the Russian Alphabet!" she added. "I practiced on my way here."

I groaned. How could *my* child worry so little about money? I turned my attention instead to Mimi. She had grown so much since I saw her last. Only nine months old back then, she was now almost two years of age.

"Mimi," I cooed at her, "you are so cute!"

Her dark little eyebrows hung over eyes that were even darker. "No!" she snapped and Esther stifled a giggle.

"Mimi," I said gently, looking for a common ground with my granddaughter, "I am your mommy's mommy."

Mimi only yelled louder. "No!" she snapped again, this time shaking her little fist at me. This generational gap was going to take some getting used to.

Once Ella arrived safely—and Esther was sure to point out repeatedly, that I had picked up her older sister from the airport *on time*—we could get down to business with some sightseeing.

"Who wants to go to my office in our headquarters?" I sang out happily. I could entertain them there while I worked, so this seemed like a perfect plan to me.

That same day, I managed to take my girls to my office, the church, and our medical clinic where physical therapy and dentistry were being performed by American standards. Beyond the physical benefits, patients received spiritual healing as well at both clinics. The girls and I ate lunch together in the clinic cafeteria: steaming, savory cabbage stuffed with whole grains and legumes (recipe at end of chapter). Mimi tried only one bite and then refused to eat any more.

On our way home Esther complained that Mimi hadn't eaten more than two bites of food since they had arrived. Although she was not normally a picky eater, we had not found a single item of Russian food that she could tolerate. I suggested that we get off the metro an exit early and find something for her at the hotdog stand there.

Now, I am sure that these days Russians have gotten used to Western travelers and most likely have signs posted in various languages. But in 1993, the only way to know where you were going in Russia was to be able to read Russian. All Russians could read; the illiteracy rate was very low. People read books in the streets, on the metro, in lines, and most likely at home.

We stepped off the train at a station where I would lead my girls onto a connecting train. "*Frusenskaya, Frusenskaya,*" I mumbled as I carefully scanned the signs telling which line would take travelers to various destinations. Although I searched carefully, I couldn't find the connecting train we needed. "Oh no!" I groaned. "We're lost! I can't find *Frusenskaya!*"

"It's right there, Mom," Esther pointed.

"No, it's nowhere and we're lost now."

"Mom," she said impatiently pointing to one of the signs, "It's right there. It's the second name on that list."

I looked again. "Oh," relief flooded over me. "You're right! It *is* right there." Happily, I started to walk toward the connecting train, but then I paused. "Wait a minute! How did you know that said *Frusenskaya?*"

"I told you," Esther said marching toward our destination, "I studied the alphabet on the map my taxi driver gave me!" Ella and I stared at her in amazement.

"You mean you just looked at it *once* and you can read now?" Ella asked in surprise.

"Not exactly once," Esther admitted. "I mean, the trip did last an hour and I reviewed some of the letters when I got up this morning." She looked at my wary expression and added, "I told you, you should have taught me Russian when I was seven. I would be fluent now."

On day two, when I tried to take them back to headquarters with me again, my girls refused. "Mom, we did not come all the way over here to watch you work," Ella stated.

"But, what will you do?" I asked. I needn't have worried. Ella had already researched all the famous sights around Moscow as well as some of the less-traveled areas that only locals knew. Before she had even picked up her plane tickets she had an itinerary made up for the entire week. And now that she knew that Esther could read the signs, the two of them, as well as Mimi, were a happy threesome shopping and sightseeing all day without me.

Ella quickly learned how to say, "*Skol'ko eto stoit* [How much is it]?"

which was a very important phrase when you are haggling in the art shows and markets for souvenirs. And Esther learned how to read Mimi's favorite words: *morozhennoye* (ice cream) and "hotdog," which needed no translation.

Mimi was not always the happy traveler. Used to the comfort and safety of her car seat, she was terrified on the streets of Moscow. The trains were too loud and Andrey's driving was much too reckless for Mimi's peace of mind. After the first day of trying to buckle her into a car seat that had no safety restraints, we abandoned the idea and stopped dragging the car seat around. Mimi bounced along on the seat between her aunt and her mother, holding on to their arms with all her might, her dark eyes wide open in fear.

Since Ella was a world-class traveler, she came prepared with some of her travel staples: a medicine kit, comfortable shoes, and an entire suitcase full of candy. I am not even exaggerating when I say that. Ella and her boyfriend, Cyrus, were in the habit of taking treats to Mexico for the children whenever they traveled there. It was her intention to appease her sweet tooth and still be able to give little candies to the Russian children that we would meet on the streets.

As I mentioned earlier, small children were rarely seen in the streets around Moscow. The neighborhood playgrounds stood empty most of the time and Mimi's stroller was typically the only one we would see. I am not sure if parents just managed to keep their children indoors all the time or if a whole generation had been eliminated by Communism's depressive nature. The only children we usually passed on the streets seemed to be Russian gypsies—and you do *not* want to encourage *them* to come near you by giving them gifts.

Now, Ella had a desire to be the most popular auntie for her little niece. She knew *exactly* what she was going to do with all that extra candy; she was going to share the entire suitcase-full with Mimi. However, Esther and Nasser had a strict one-sweet-a-day rule that worked very well for them. Ella had been ordered to abandon her "favorite auntie" plans for the sake of her niece's health. Still, she couldn't let all that candy go to waste.

"Sshhh! Don't tell your mommy," Ella would whisper, popping some M&Ms into Mimi's mouth. Honest Mimi would then go immediately to her mother, tilt her head back, with mouth wide open, and show Esther what her auntie had given her.

"Ella, you can't be giving her so many sweets," Esther scolded. But older sisters do think they know more than their younger counterparts.

"It won't hurt her," Ella insisted with a shrug more than once. "You guys are too strict anyway. How am I supposed to be the favorite auntie when you won't let me spoil my niece?"

By day three of Ella's favorite auntie tricks, combined with the lack of sleep we were all getting due to the Russian "White Nights of Summer," Mimi had become a constant ball of motion. One evening, we all sat in my living room as I tried to entertain my good friends, Charlie and Charlene. Although it was almost 11 PM, the sun was just setting but would shortly rise again before 3am. All the excitement was too much for little Mimi who bounced off the walls, couch, floors, and, I'm fairly sure, even the ceiling a few times.

Ella stared at her niece, an astonished look glazing her eyes. "What is *wrong* with her?" she demanded. "Mimi never acts like this at home!"

"That's because at home she doesn't have her favorite auntie stuffing chocolate and chewing gum into her mouth constantly," Esther responded smugly. From that time on, Ella kept her sweets securely locked away, giving them out only to Russian children she would see.

I, on the other hand, continued to try and win my granddaughter's affections by using my own tactics. "Mimi," I would say sweetly, "your mommy is my baby. She was in my tummy!"

But Mimi's response was always the same. "No!" she would snap, once again shaking her tiny fist at me. I tried everything: singing Russian songs to her, playing peek-a-boo, buying her a scrawny, bluish-grey chicken to make soup out of, but still, nothing could make Mimi agree that I was her grandmother.

Since we hadn't found many children on the streets of Moscow and the newly enlightened Ella realized that a constant diet of candy and *Frusenskaya* hotdogs was not the healthiest for her niece, we needed a way to get rid of all those extra sweets.

Esther tried baking some of it into a cake mix I had purchased at one of the expensive, commercial import shops, but the directions were in Russian. "Mom, can you read this to me?" she asked, pushing the box toward me.

"I thought you could read Russian now," her sister challenged her.

"I may be able to sound out the letters," Esther replied, "but that doesn't mean I understand what I'm reading."

"Why don't you try," I urged her. "You know the words for most foods." The teacher in me always made my pupils try to read.

Esther stared at the words on the box. "Um ... eggs? Milk ... butter ...?"

"You're just guessing!" Ella complained. "You already know those things would go in a recipe!"

"Maybe, but guessing wouldn't get me the right quantities."

In the end, although tasty, the cake did turn out rather dry. Of course we didn't know if we should blame my temperamental oven, the poor quality of ingredients, or Esther's inadequate Russian skills. Still, we had hardly finished any of the candy Ella brought.

"You can take it to church with us on Sabbath," I suggested. We had a large congregation and people actually brought their children there. Plus, it wouldn't seem as weird for my daughters to be handing out goodies to the families I knew personally as it would if they were giving candy to strangers' kids on the streets.

That week my daughters saw that we did in fact have children in Russia. Mobs of little boys followed them around everywhere shouting, "Sneakers, sneakers!" Ella looked down at the pumps both girls had on. "But we're not wearing sneakers," she wondered aloud.

"I think they're trying to say Snickers," Esther laughed. And from that day on, Ella's name at our church became "Snickers."

Mimi was good natured for the rest of her trip, although we did realize that she missed her father. Her favorite book those two weeks was *Animal Daddies and My Daddy*. She made her mother read it at least twice daily. And every day she would sit in my living room, on her car seat and say, "*Baba, Baba* [informal Arabic word for father]," while looking up at us with her unhappy black eyes.

I had found a little black stray kitten and gave it to Mimi. She loved it and played gently with it for hours. Alas, even this fury, treasured gift was not enough to win the affections of my granddaughter.

We soon discovered that the Russians were not too excited about having my family here in Russia. Of course, my friends loved my daughters as did my cousin's wife Lena and her daughter, Lala, who had recently had a son named Orchan. But in general, my children were outsiders. Their clothing, nicely made and better fitting than anything the Russians had, gave them an obviously Western look. Their dark hair and eyes made them *chornaya*

(black) unlike most Russians who were blonde and blue-eyed. Though they carried a baby with them everywhere as gypsies typically did, they sported no gold teeth. The Muscovites didn't know what to make of them.

Museums seemed to give us the hardest time. There would have been no problem if I were willing to pay the visitor's price for the entrance, but I had to prove, if only to myself, that my Russian was good enough to get the local's ticket prices everywhere. If Esther stepped out of my sight for even the shortest time, one of the docents would try to kick her out.

On the last day of their visit, I sat sad and weary on my couch while Mimi played with my little black kitten. "Come here, Mimishka," I said, gently grabbing her hands before she had a chance to protest. I tugged her toward me until she was standing on my feet. I began to bounce her to the rhythm of some of the same Russian children's songs I had tried out earlier in their visit. My granddaughter laughed and squealed as I tossed her into the air, catching her on my lap.

"Mo, Mo!" Mimi urged me for more fun, so I continued the whole game all over again. Truthfully, I was exhausted, but nothing can wake a person up like her grandchild's giggles.

When our game was finished I looked Mimi in the eyes and reminded her, "Mimi, your mommy is my baby!"

"Yes," Mimi nodded, smiling up at me.

"She was in my tummy!" I added. This time, my granddaughter hugged me fiercely as only a two-year-old can. Since that day we have had a special grandmother-grandchild bond.

DANNY GETS MARRIED, 1993

While in Russia, I received wonderful news from Danny. He and his girlfriend Susan were going to get married. Although Susan had been in his life for quite a long time, since they had met after I left Buffalo, I did not have a great chance to get to know the stylish, petite ballet dancer my son had chosen as his wife.

Over the years, I visited Buffalo several times and, each time, Susan would invite us to dinner. Her mother Rachelle was an excellent Italian cook so I would usually go to their home and share an enormous meal. Rachelle was my first and only exposure to St. Joseph's Day—an Italian's excuse to indulge in non-stop food! Sometimes Esther or Susan's father Bob would join me. But no matter who was with us, we left feeling stuffed.

"I'll call my Buffalo pastor right away and make sure the church is available on that date, Danny!" I offered with excitement when Danny called to announce the wedding.

"No, Ma, don't worry about it," he said. "We're getting married in the church where her parents were married."

"Her parents? But aren't they Catholic?" I asked with dismay.

"Yeah. So?" he replied brusquely.

"Danny Boy, you can't be married in a *Catholic* church," I insisted. "You need to be married in a *real* church."

"Oh Tiny," he replied with amusement in his voice, "don't you go worrying about which churches are real or not real."

I stood my ground, but so did he. In the end, the two were married in a beautiful Catholic church downtown. They did make sure that both our pastor and the priest officiated. At least I had that much. And I was really too excited about the whole trip to think about how to change their plans.

My cousins travelled from California for the wedding, as did Ella and Esther.

"Bring Mimi with you!" I begged Esther when she called me in Russia.

"Mom, I can't!" Esther insisted. "I can't drag a two-year-old 3000 miles away for just one weekend!"

"But I want to see my granddaughter!"

"Who would watch her while we are in the wedding, Mom?"

"I will!" I offered readily, but we both knew that, for the mother of the groom, that would not be feasible.

Upon my arrival, Danny and Susan took me to my first home. Although it would be their first home together, it would always be *my* home and I was thrilled to be back.

I unloaded my bags into the spare bedroom, feeling a little displaced to be considered a guest there, and looked around. Everything was so different now that Susan and Rachelle had redecorated. The first things that had to go were the heavy draperies framing the window. I dragged a chair into the room and struggled to remove them.

"Raya, my mom and I were up until midnight working on your windows! What did you do here?" Susan asked later when she saw the changes I had made.

"Oh Susan," I complained, "the room was too dark. I just wanted to let in the warm, healthy sunshine. Sunshine has vitamin D, you know." The draperies were left off for the duration of the visit but Susan did not seem thrilled with my efforts.

Susan and Rachelle did a beautiful job on the wedding. During Mass, when the bride and groom stepped over to kiss their families and offer the greeting, "Peace be with you," Esther and Ella whispered into Danny's ear "You better be good to her!" And with that Susan was christened as a new sister into our family.

A SHOULDER TO FALL ON

My last year in Russia, I had a young architect named Marozova living with me. Together, she and I were working on translating a vegetarian cookbook during the evenings where we spent many hours reviewing recipes and converting the best ones from cups to liters or grams.

One wintery Sabbath afternoon, with no work to do for the day, we headed out the door to visit another church. Even bundled as I was in long johns, stockings, a Sabbath dress, and my warmest, red, woolen coat, I couldn't get used to the frigid air. Twenty-nine degrees below zero feels pretty cold no matter what you wear! We hurried along the sidewalk as fast as we could, anxious to get into the shelter of the metro station.

I should have expected it but did not notice the slick layer of black ice that coated the snow on the bottom-most step. Before I knew what was happening, my face was down in the snow. I must have tried to catch myself because my arm was extended out from beneath me at an awkward angle. I didn't notice any of this because the breath had been knocked out of me and I was too busy fighting for oxygen.

By the time I could gasp for breath again, it was to scream out in pain. Always the speedy thinker, Marozova flagged down a taxi driver and helped him to move my helpless body into the car. Every jerky bump was agonizingly painful as we sped down the street with me crying, "Ow! Ow! Oh, be careful," and Marozova shouting, "Hurry! Oh hurry! Faster, please," until we finally skidded to a stop in front of a nearby medical clinic.

Throughout the ordeal, my roommate's name, Marozova, ran repeatedly through my head and it wasn't until later that I realized the irony of this. Her name means *frosty*, just like the sidewalk that took me down.

As I approached the clinic doors, fear gripped me. I realized I was entering a Russian medical facility and worried what fate might greet me there. "I can't stay here," I hissed in English so no one else would understand me, grabbing Marozova's arm and pulling her toward me. "I'm only supposed to get my treatments in Helsinki!"

"Raisa Mikhailovna," Marozova soothed me as best as she could, "this is an *emergency!*"

I dropped my head back on my pillow and squeezed my eyes shut in defeat, sure that the Russian staff would leave me worse than when I arrived. And then, as if an angel emerged, I heard a very American voice speaking with no trace of a Russian accent, "Mrs. Abadir? I'm Dr. Brown."

I dared to peek my eyes open. The voice came from a man wearing a white lab coat and carrying a stethoscope around his neck. "You're American?" I sighed in relief through pain-clenched teeth.

"Yes," he answered smiling, "and you look like you've dislocated your shoulder."

"You're American and you're a doctor?" I wanted to be sure.

"Yes," he laughed. "Now, I want you to relax, I'm going to give you some pain medicine."

"No!" I shouted, as I cringed from the sharp twinge in my shoulder. "No pain medicine … can't take it … makes me sick …" I remembered only too well that it had taken me two days to recover from anesthesia during an angiogram some years back.

"OK, no pain medicine," he assured me, "but then you'll just have to promise to relax so I can reset your shoulder." I slowly exhaled to show him that I was relaxing, then inhaled slowly again, then exhaled, managing a forced smile in Dr. Brown's direction.

With a painful pull, a push, and a tug, my arm was back in its normal position and the pressure was gone from my chest again. I murmured a shaky thank you and the color began to drain back into Marozova's face once more. I hadn't realized how worried she had been for me.

"Now," the doctor said, issuing my discharge orders, "I'm no orthopedic physician, so I can't guarantee you anything, but you should be fine if you are very careful. You'll need to keep this arm still and close to your body for at least four weeks—no lifting, no pulling, or pushing with it."

I was so relieved to be treated by an American doctor that I just kept saying "Yes, doctor. Oh thank you, Dr. Brown!"

"Be sure to come back and see me if you have any problems," he instructed, sending me on my way.

I really did plan on being careful, and for one whole week I was. Lena bandaged my arm close to my body so that I wasn't tempted to use it and Lala checked on me every hour or so if my roommate was out. Every day Raisa visited me, sharing some of her groceries and even prepping the herbs and vegetables so I didn't have to wash or chop them myself.

Two weeks passed, and I returned to work. After three weeks, I was feeling much better every day. Exactly one month from the day of my fall, I was sure that I had completely recovered.

From the first day I saw my bathroom, I knew the giant Russian bathtubs were not made for my short legs. This enormous, porcelain tub challenged me even more while I was injured. I was fortunate that Marozova was there to help me during the worst of my pain, but as I got better, she told me she had made plans to go to Ukraine. I would be by myself except for the visits from Lena and Lala.

For one whole month I had sat on the edge of the tub, slowly swinging my legs around until I was *in* the bathtub. One day while I was rushing to get ready for work, I let my defenses down and decided to step completely out of the bathtub. In a split second, I slipped and fell—of course—on the same arm. This time Marozova was not around to help me.

Although the pain was excruciating, I knew what to do. I pulled one of the baggy dresses over my head that I had worn while recovering and dragged myself down the steps to the street to hail a cab. "*Clinica*," I gasped to the first driver who stopped for me.

"Lady, there's a million *clinicas* in this city," he said. "Which one do you need?"

Unfortunately, I have never been good with directions. I had to have the taxi take me all the way to the metro station where I had originally fallen before I could direct the driver to the correct medical clinic so I would find my American doctor.

Dr. Brown came rushing into the exam room to check on me. "Mrs. Abadir, I am so sorry," he said. "I feel responsible for this ... perhaps I just didn't set your shoulder right." Though I tried to lessen his worries, he told me he was sending me to a Russian Hospital.

Now I knew I was in trouble. I begged and pleaded for him to just set it himself, but he was adamant. "Don't worry," he assured me as he ushered me toward the door, "I will stay by your side the whole time."

The hospital had a very good system for taking care of their patients. I was checked in, then Dr. Brown and I waited and waited—and waited. The sun set and still we waited. We talked about his family, my work, and of course religion, but still we waited. Somehow, through my pain and anxiety, I managed to fall asleep at the Russian hospital.

I awoke surprised to see, not Dr. Brown's face, but one that was totally unfamiliar to me. "Dr. Brown!" I called, frantically, dodging away from this strange man in a white lab coat. "Where's my doctor? I want Dr. Brown!"

"Your precious American doctor is not here," the man sneered in Russian. Then boom! He stuck a needle in my arm and I immediately felt myself lose consciousness.

I awoke again, this time in a dark room. "Dr. Brown ..." I called out again weakly.

"There is no Dr. Brown here," a nurse hissed as she too sent a shot of drugs into my system. I didn't know it until later, but I was out for three days. During that time, my friends from the Seventh-day Adventist clinic in Moscow and my family stopped in to see me, but all I was able to do was mumble incoherently. When I woke up at last, flowers filled my room and Raisa sat in a chair beside me.

"Raisa Mikhailovna," she said gently, "you had us all worried! We thought we lost you!"

"They drugged me," I mumbled, struggling to get up before I was "treated" with another round of medication. Here I traveled the world telling young people the downfalls of drug use and in just three days I had more morphine pumped into my system than an elephant needed.

EGGCELENT EMUS

While I was in Russia, another baby joined our family. Precious Rema was born as bald as a basketball to a very proud big sister, Mimi. Photos of a dimpled and beautiful baby arrived for me to enjoy from far across the ocean. I just had to get back and visit my family.

During each of my trips back to the United States, I traveled around to various churches in New York and California, just as I had before I left for Russia the first time. As before, I made sure to secure some pulpit time so that I could promote our work in Moscow.

After visiting a church in Ramona, California, a man came up to me and introduced himself as Dr. Larry Grimaldi. "Would you like to visit us for lunch?" he offered. "I have something I think would be of interest to you that you could take to Russia when you return." Never one to pass up lunch with newfound friends or a gift for Russia, I happily accompanied Larry and his wife to their home.

Ramona was about 40 minutes away from my home in Escondido where I was visiting Esther and her family who were living in my condo during my absence. From the Ramona church, we traveled an hour-and-a-half going right past my home to Hemet, California. I couldn't believe that anyone would travel so far to attend church, and was even more surprised to find out that Dr. Grimaldi traveled the same distance every day to work as a dentist in a little town called Julian, famous for its apple pies.

I have to say, I was pleased to learn that he was a dentist. Having my teeth checked was on my to-do list while I was home in the States. I made a mental note to call his receptionist that coming Monday.

Meanwhile, we walked around the grounds of his ranch, looking at all his strange and beautiful animals. The giant emus ran around on long legs while they stretched their hose-like necks toward the ground. Awkward birds like those make a person of faith feel that God has a great sense of humor!

"I have a business proposition for you," Dr. Grimaldi said as I laughed at the silly antics of a nearby chick, larger than any baby bird I had ever seen.

"Oh sure!" I said, before I even knew what he was proposing.

"I have a friend who can send me ostrich eggs," he began. "Can you find an artist who can paint on them?"

"Certainly!" I agreed again, this time knowing that I could fulfill my end of the bargain. Russia had plenty of artists. Children's talents were nurtured and developed from an early age to foster the most amazingly creative people I have ever met. On every street corner one can find an artist or tradesman selling his merchandise. Dr. Grimaldi and I sealed our deal. We immediately began counting our enormous eggs, planning how to spend all the money we would be making from our venture.

That week, when I secured a dental appointment with Dr. Grimaldi, I made sure to tell the receptionist that the doctor needed to know I was coming. "He's bringing me some ostrich eggs," I told her, "and I'm coming from Escondido, so I don't want to make two trips."

On the morning of my appointment, Esther nursed the baby and dressed both girls for our early trip to the dentist in Julian. While I finished eating my breakfast, Esther rushed around the kitchen to start chicken stock for that evening's supper. She proudly showed off the new stainless steel pots that her husband had just bought her, filling the largest with water, onions, celery, carrots, and spices before adding one huge, plump chicken.

I giggled when I saw the healthy, pink bird, recalling a joke I had heard recently in Russia:

A Russian chicken and an American chicken were plucked and sitting in the kitchen, waiting to be cooked. "Ha, ha!" the American chicken laughed at the Russian bird. "Look at you, your skin is so blue and your legs are so scrawny. I am pink and plump and healthy."

"Oh yeah?" countered the Russian hen defensively. "Well, if you're so great, then why is it that you were murdered while I died of natural causes?"

Esther was not amused by my story. "Mom," she said, appalled, "please don't joke about the food I'm going to eat!" She turned the stove on simmer and waited, quite impatiently, for me to finish eating so we could go.

"I just have to brush my teeth," I said, finally rising from my meal.

Esther rolled her eyes. "Here goes another 45 minutes," she sighed, turning up the heat on the range. "This meal is going to be cooked before we even get out of here!"

I ignored my daughter's complaints and rushed off to take care of my pearly whites. The running water drowned out her shouts of "Let's go, Mom! Come on, you're going to be late!"

Emerging from the bathroom I glanced at my watch. "Oh my dear! We are going to be late!"

"What do you think I've been trying to say, Mom?" Esther complained. "And you promised Mimi a donut, too. I guess we'll have to stop on our way back." Mimi loved her cream-filled donuts. I'm pretty sure it was the first word she learned how to say and I loved watching her eat them.

"Oh no, Esther," I insisted. "I would rather be late than make my beautiful granddaughter wait for her donut!" I rushed Esther and the babies out of the house, calling Dr. Grimaldi's office on my way.

Once Mimi's tummy and round little cheeks were all filled with her morning donut, we were finally on our way. I had forgotten how much more time everything took with small children. Esther's minivan climbed along the winding, narrow roads toward Ramona and Julian, twisting and turning as the mountain took us higher and higher.

Esther smiled at me. "Well, we got off to a late start, but when we get to Julian I'm going to pick up one of those famous apple pies for tonight's dessert and we have-" her voice broke off suddenly and she gasped, "My soup! I left the pot of soup on the stove!" She grabbed her cell phone from me and dialed her neighbor's house. The phone's beep indicated it was out of range. Frustrated, she dialed again, but, being so high up in the curvy, mountain roads she could not get a signal.

We were crawling along one of the main streets in Ramona before we finally got a cell tower signal and Esther was able to call our neighbor. This was one of the times that we were grateful for my "skill" in locking myself out of every house and car I ever owned. As a precaution, I had left a key with my neighbor, Marie, who was now Esther's neighbor. Since we were unable to reach her, we contacted another neighbor who walked over to Marie's house to get the key. By the time they opened the door, according to their story, smoke came billowing out. They called us back to say that everything was fine, although Esther's meal was completely burned.

We finally arrived at the dentist much later than expected. Awaiting me, just as he had promised, was a case of empty ostrich eggs. I couldn't wait to get back to Russia and start on our project.

Evening had settled over the neighborhood by the time we returned home. We could see the kitchen curtains blowing through the open window as we approached. We did not need to get very close to smell the scorched meal that filled the entire condo. The smell was so bad that everything—all the way to the closets upstairs—still smelled like burnt soup when I returned two weeks later from a trip to New York. Even worse than the smell was Esther's disappointment in ruining her brand new cooking pot. "I know the set was expensive," she mourned. "And we just don't have the money to waste on disposable pans."

I assured her that I would fix it. Sadly, even after soaking the pot for three days, the inside remained black and the base had peeled away from the bottom in a wavy pattern, looking nothing like the original cookware.

Returning to Russia with only two of the ostrich eggs damaged, I discovered that finding an artist was more difficult than I had expected. The girls in my office told me that the street artists would not be able to help me since they were not used to painting on curved surfaces. "You need an architect if you want someone to paint on eggs," they explained. I couldn't imagine how I would be able to afford to pay architects; their salaries were so much higher than typical street vendors.

Once we quickly solved that problem by hiring student architects, we soon discovered that the oil paints would not adhere to the eggs' smooth finish. Additional steps were needed to keep the paint from sliding off which would have ruined the hard work of the artists.

When the first batch of painted eggs was ready, Dr. Grimaldi joined me in Moscow to pick up his merchandise. But he did not come empty handed. Dr. Grimaldi had also intended to visit the schools in my division during his visit. Aside from brining more of the fragile eggs, his suitcase was almost entirely filled with papers, pencils, rulers, glue, chalk, and even an entire case of crayons that my son Danny had donated. Dr. Grimaldi presented these supplies to teachers as we traveled from Zaoksky seminary to Tula Seventh-day Adventist Church School and all around Moscow.

Also nestled amongst his luggage was an emu egg. Slightly smaller and much more delicate than its cousin, the ostrich egg, the emu egg broke immediately in the artist's hands. Dr. Grimaldi and I agreed that we wouldn't try to transport any more of the fragile shells.

The artist I contracted replaced the broken emu shell with a block of wood which he had turned into an egg shape. On it, he painted a perfect portrait of my curly-haired, black-eyed Mimi. I was thrilled to have the heirloom treasure—one which I could not break—smiling up at me!

In the end, our cost to paint the eggs would be $30 each. It was hardly a bargain and Dr. Grimaldi quickly realized that between transportation, storage, loss, contracting an artist, and returning the painted orbs, hopefully undamaged, we would have to charge over a hundred dollars for the sale of each egg just to make a profit. Gifting the eggs seemed like a much more valuable use of the unique souvenirs. Not that the artwork wasn't worth the money; it really was! Perfect paintings of St. Basil's cathedral decorated the large eggs while others showed minute horses pulling tiny carriages with passengers in an 1800s view of Red Square and the Moscow River. The pieces were beautiful and I agonized about caring for them until I had taken them safely back to the United States.

GENERAL CONFERENCE SESSIONS, UTRECHT, NETHERLANDS

We have this hope that burns within our hearts,
Hope in the coming of the Lord.
We have this faith that Christ alone imparts,
Faith in the promise of His Word.
We believe the time is here,
When the nations far and near
Shall awake, and shout and sing
Hallelujah! Christ is King!
We have this hope that burns within our hearts,
Hope in the coming of the Lord.
~Wayne Hooper – written for 1995 General Conference Sessions

While I was in Russia, our church was having its General Conference Sessions in Utrecht, Netherlands, so off I went. Since I had been born in Uzbekistan, I would be wearing an Uzbek costume and representing the country, although technically I was considered a General Conference Delegate from the United States.

It was here that I found out that our precious physical therapy clinic in Moscow would be closing for good. Up until this time, we had maintained the clinic and had a great number of very high ranking and wealthy Russian patients who appreciated the high standards of our dental clinic and physical therapy services. Unfortunately, as often happens in a country where bribery has more worth than skills, a shady Ukrainian man had been left in charge who had neither medical nor business experience. For months before the General Conference Sessions, he had been running the clinic into the ground.

After the sessions were over, several of the other Euro-Asia division workers and I decided to use our vacation time to travel to France. I was thrilled at the chance to see another European country. We hopped on a tour bus provided by the conference and headed four-and-a-half hours towards Paris.

As we approached, I saw sights of the city that I had only seen in movies or pictures. It was like a dream to be there in person. I couldn't wait to take pictures of my own.

But as usual, I had taken too many photos during the General Conference Sessions. I had expected this so came prepared with many extra rolls of film, but now my camera batteries were dead. There I was, standing in the middle of one of the most photographed cities in the world and I couldn't use my camera. No problem though, right? How hard could it be to find AA batteries in a major metropolitan city?

After struggling with directions and my awkwardness with the language, my friends and I headed to Lafayette, a department store that was popular with the tourists and had employees who could speak a variety of languages.

I explained my problem to an unemotional cashier who picked out a package of four batteries and rang me up.

"One hundred twenty Francs, please," she declared.

I stared at her in surprise. I looked down at the camera—and I must admit I had to pick it up and look under it to see if she was charging me for a wedding ring or a microwave too. "Why so expensive?" I asked, stunned.

Having lived in Russia for four years, I was used to haggling, but I knew that even I couldn't get the price down in a store like Lafayette.

"You have to take the conversion rate into account," she explained, still very unfriendly.

"Oh … well, I only have dollars. How much is it in dollars?" I asked.

Our sales girl punched a few buttons on the register and glanced dryly at me again. "Thirty dollars," she answered.

"Thirty dollars? *Thirty dollars?*" There was no way I heard her correctly. "Are you sure? I've never heard of spending *thirty dollars* on four AA batteries!"

"That is the price," she answered. I seriously considered not buying the batteries, I really did. But that would be like telling a baby to go without his milk or an addict to go without his drugs or a vampire to go without blood. OK, I have a problem when it comes to photos, but I still couldn't get over the price. In the end I was glad I bought them, but never again! I vowed that next time I would bring an entire suitcase of film *and* batteries, just in case.

Like any other tourists, we walked around the city snapping pictures of the Eiffel Tower, the Arc de Triomphe, the Louvre, and Notre Dame Cathedral. We ate in a tiny street-side café, as much like locals as we possibly could, while we chatted away in Russian. It was here that we soaked up Paris sunshine and planned the rest of our brief day.

"Let's take a ride down the Seine," someone suggested. Forgetting my tendency toward severe motion sickness, I readily agreed. Still, I hesitated as we approached the *Bateaux Mouches* (tour boats) which would carry us down the river and back to our docking point. But fortunately, this one time, I did manage to keep my lunch down as we traveled the river listening to the tour guide tell us in French, over a poor speaker system, about the various sites along the way. It didn't matter though. We were just happy to have the break from work in such a beautiful city.

All too soon we boarded the bus again, with dusk settling around us like a blanket, and drove back to the Netherlands where I would find my way back to Moscow and my traveling companions would return to the Ukraine and other provinces.

"OUR LITTLE BROTHERS"

I received a call from my cousin, Adileh, that she and her mom would be visiting me in Russia. I was eager to see my California family and share Moscow with my dear Auntie Sara who had so generously shared her home with me when I had first moved to Iran as a teenager.

On the first night of their visit, we stayed up late, chatting like schoolgirls. Adileh had never been in Russia before and Auntie Sara spoke excitedly about being back again.

I went over the itinerary I had made for their stay. We would visit all the important places around Moscow, especially the Kremlin and the Bolshoi. We would also attend services at our church, of course, and I had already showed them where I was stationed at the district conference offices. I didn't stop to think that, not being Adventists themselves, these items might not interest them too greatly. I also suggested that we take a train ride to the beautiful city of Leningrad (Saint Petersburg).

"I want to go to Astrakhan," Auntie Sara quickly interrupted my plans and list-making. Usually so calm, I was surprised to hear her speak up. "I want to visit my home," she said quietly this time.

"OK, *Tetya* Sara," I said, staring from her to the envelope on which I had scratched all my notes and back to her creased face, glowing with anticipation, "we will go to Astrakhan!"

That night over dinner, as we chatted with Lena and Lala about our new plans, Lena suggested that we visit her husband's sister in Baku. I had not seen my cousin Toma since she was only 10 months old when her family was taken to a Siberian concentration camp. I should point out that neither Adileh nor Auntie Sara was directly related to Toma, only through marriage, but we were all up for the adventure.

Touching the sea and surrounded by mountains, Baku was beautiful. Gone were the narrow, dusty, cobbled streets from my childhood memory. In their place were modern buildings and highways. I had a distinctly vivid memory of nearly drowning in these waters when my Auntie Galya was trying to teach me how to swim decades ago. Somehow the trauma didn't affect me as it should have. I still love the water!

"What is that?" I asked my driver as we passed a tall tower facing the shoreline. It seemed out of place and rather old looking among all the newer city structures.

"That is *Devichya Bashnya* [the Maiden Tower]," he answered. He was obviously proud of the ancient building, although he, like anyone else we asked, could not give us a clear picture of why the building was so important to them. Someone did mention a story about a king's young daughter throwing herself from the top of the tower into the waves below. Still, its significance seemed overrated to me. Perhaps because Baku is in a wealthy oil country and had added so many contemporary buildings in order to keep up with current times, the residents were just happy to have *any* reflection of history around.

Toma greeted us with a cheery, dimpled smile and an enormous embrace. She chatted happily about her parents, her childhood, and what little she knew of me and my life. Together, we rolled up our sleeves and made *paramacha* (fried Russian dumplings, similar to *pirozhki*).

While we ate, Toma asked Auntie Sara about her family history. When she realized their heritage, Toma told us she knew other Askarnias (referring to Sara's family name) and she planned to introduce us to Gulara and her mother.

The next day it was arranged and we all drove to what appeared to be a dangerous street, not far from Toma's house. As we walked in from the outside corridor, we found a long, luxurious table set with so much elegant china and crystal stemware that the table was invisible beneath it all. There were homemade *pierogis*, savory pastries, fruits, and such an abundance of desserts that I felt as if we were standing in a bakery.

As usual, I always tried to combine my travels around Russia and its bordering countries with visits to the local schools and churches. After lunch, I left Adileh and Auntie Sara to get acquainted with my cousins while I set off to mingle with the Adventists. I was pleased to find that Baku had an active church community with many highly educated young members. I encouraged them to consider opening a church school and, happily, later saw them at many teachers' in-service meetings that I hosted. Although truthfully, you never know with Russians if they are attending because they are blessed by the program or if it is because they are being treated to free food and board upon their visit.

Gulara was a lovely and talented young mother. Her daughter, who clearly seemed to have suffered from encephalitis as a child, hung back shyly while we visited together. Five energetic women can be quite intimidating for a sheltered juvenile.

"You are not married?" I asked Gulara, bluntly.

"I was," she explained, her eyes flicking quickly toward her daughter and back to me again, "but he did not want to take responsibility when our child was born." I understood the impact his selfishness would make on her life. She was sweet and beautiful, with so much to give to a relationship, but I knew that in their culture, having a child would make it difficult for her to remarry.

Gulara and I hit it off right away. And her daughter, Nigar, couldn't stop hugging me. I was immediately smitten. I invited Gulara to work in our dental clinic and she soon followed me there.

The next day, Auntie Sara, Adileh, and I boarded a train headed to Astrakhan, my auntie's home town where I also grew up. We sat in a small semi-private compartment room and settled down to the steady rhythm of the train. In just two short days, we had visited so many new family members that we were all exhausted. My eyes began to droop as I relaxed into my bunk bed.

Suddenly, I snapped them open. "Maybe I should warn you," I began tentatively peeking through the curtain to see what my cousins' response would be, "I haven't found any place for us to stay when we get to Astrakhan."

"Don't worry!" Adileh said in her usual merry response. "We will find a hotel somewhere." I nearly choked. I am not one to spend good money on a hotel when we have Adventist church families all over the world who are happy to meet another like-minded individual. Nonetheless, I had to admit that although I searched the conference directory before we left Moscow, I hadn't found any Adventists in Astrakhan.

When we stopped at the first station, the cabin door creaked open and a man stuck his head into our room. "Yes?" I asked impatiently.

"That top bunk is mine," he said, indicating the empty bed above me.

I looked at him carefully, up and down, trying to measure his strength with my eyes. "That depends," I said, "are you safe?" He burst out laughing in spite of my attempt at intimidation.

"Yes," he held up a small music case, thumping on it gently. "I am a music student in Astrakhan," he smiled at me.

"Welcome!" I smiled back. "Maybe you can tell us where to find a good hotel when we get to Astrakhan."

"Hotel?" he asked, scratching his head. "We don't have a single one, but you can stay in the Conservatoria Dormitory with the students," he offered. I didn't give my cousins a chance to disagree. I had spent every summer of my adulthood living out of college dormitories while Lotfy and I put ourselves through school. I had become quite used to the experience.

That is how it came to pass that we found ourselves walking into the lobby of the women's dorm. A petite, young girl showed us to our room. "Here you are," she smiled at me, pushing the door open to reveal a scurry of brown, flat cockroaches crawling away from the light that beamed into the room.

Auntie Sara stepped back a pace, clinging onto Adileh's arm. "We can't stay here," I protested. "I mean, they're going to crawl all over us all night long!"

"Oh no," the young girl assured me, attempting to calm my fears. "We just draw around the bedposts like this …" She pulled a piece of chalk out of her pocket and sketched a thin line on the floor around each of the bedposts. "The bugs will not bother you now!" she promised.

"Are you sure?" Adileh asked skeptically.

"Of course!" she said as she bounced away down the hallway.

"Do we trust it?" Adileh asked me.

"Do we have a choice?" I replied. I don't know how the roaches knew not to cross the line, but they didn't. We slept all night, barely trusting to close our eyes completely, but not one cockroach touched a single hair on our heads.

The next morning, the three of us headed downstairs to see what we could find in the kitchen to eat. From the hallway we heard happy voices from young women along with the sounds of water running and pots banging. I pushed the door open and our mouths just dropped. *"Devochki,"* my Auntie Sara scolded the women, "there are bugs everywhere!" The women looked up from their work to the walls that seemed to be alive and moving on their own.

"Nonsense!" one young girl brushed our concerns aside, "Those are just our little brothers!" We stood there in disbelief.

We managed to force a simple meal of porridge down, but not until we over cooked it to, hopefully, destroy any lingering germs. Then we ate and headed out the door.

Auntie Sara was stunned with all the changes around town. We took a taxi to her old neighborhood where she looked around, searching for any trace of familiarity. Not one single item showed evidence of the past. All the single story homes that my auntie had once lived in were torn down, and in their places were tall high rise buildings. "Where is my home?" she asked, over and over again as she looked around the street she once walked on.

"What did you expect?" Adileh asked gently, placing her arms around her mother's thin shoulders.

"Not this," my eighty-year-old auntie admitted. "This makes me feel so old!"

INDIA

While I was in Russia, several couples from the Zaoksky Seminary attended Spicer Memorial College in Pune, India as part of an exchange student program. A delegate was needed to check up on the students since the Euro-Asia Conference was responsible for them. Of all the people the seminary president had to choose from, he selected me. I should have probably been honored by this assignment, but looking back I figured out that, when faced with the question, "Whom should we send?" they decided that Raya has had a tough life, so she can handle whatever happens in India.

Tatyana was a Russian-American girl working in the clinic at that time. Whenever I was sent on an assignment she used my travels as an opportunity to journey with me. I enjoyed the company and, like me, all these experiences were new for this young woman who had grown up in America.

Once our plane arrived in Delhi, Tatyana and I visited the Taj Mahal on our way to Spicer Memorial College. This white palace, with its gleaming orbs of gold, was possibly the most beautiful building I had ever visited in my life. I was stunned to hear the story behind it and wondered, "Who would ever think of building a castle for a wife who had already died?"

We stood facing the long pool with two low-lying structures on each side and watched as little black monkeys hopped from tree to tree, feasting on coconuts. Of course, watching them made me hungry. It's a good thing I never travel without emergency rations. We fueled up before our long trip to Pune.

The train to Pune was crowded with young Indian men. For seventeen hours we bounced along, watching small villages and forest sights zoom in and out of view outside our window while we chatted with the other passengers. Everywhere we traveled, we met people who were curious about the new Russia now that the Soviet Union had fallen.

"What do you do in Russia?" one young man asked me. I loved giving the answer. It gives me great pleasure to quote back a title that is longer than I am tall.

"I am the Associate Director for the Euro-Asia Division of the General Conference of Seventh-day Adventists," I would tell anyone who wanted to know. My answer was always immediately followed by their inevitable follow-up question, "Yes, but what kind of *work* do you do?"

I spoke proudly of the work we did, opening church schools and supporting new churches around Russia, the Ukraine, and other Baltic states. The men were courteous and friendly, making Tatyana and me feel like celebrities in our dirty, cramped train, all the while stuffing wads of something into their mouths and chewing, chewing, chewing.

I asked one of the men about their chewing. "Tobacco," he answered, smiling with reddish teeth gleaming beneath his brown face. He showed us how he wrapped a pinch of tobacco leaves in a red beetle-nut leaf before stuffing the small mass between his cheek and mandibles. I couldn't believe what I was seeing. Here I was, the biggest advocate of stop-smoking programs, getting a lesson on how to chew tobacco.

"That is no good!" I finally exclaimed. "That tobacco has so many *poisons* and you are putting them right into your *blood* system!" He nodded and smiled, listening intently as I chastised him with suggestions on how they all could be cleansed of this bad habit. The young men graciously accepted my instructions, never acting as if I was wrong in assuming that they would want to quit.

Leaves seemed to be the theme everywhere we went in India.

When we arrived at Spicer Memorial College, there were some important officials visiting the campus. To honor them, we sat on mats on the floor of the balcony, under a canopy of palm trees and stars, and feasted on a banquet served on, of all things, banana leaves! It amazed me that a meal so simple could feel so decadent.

Unfortunately we were traveling around the country during the hottest time of the year. September in India is hot, sticky, and full of mosquitoes. Regardless, the campus was beautiful with lush greenery everywhere we looked.

I visited with our students to make sure that they were content and that all their needs were being met. But I found that they were extremely under-challenged in their new college. "We already learned everything they are teaching us," one young lady complained.

"Is there any way we can study in America?" her husband asked. Everyone wanted to go to America. After so many years of listening to Soviet propaganda, the Russians had finally discovered that there actually were much better places in the world than their own country. India was not one of those places.

I promised the students that once I returned to Moscow, I would check into the possibility of having them transferred. But unfortunately, because of meager funds in the Euro-Asia division, we were not able to send the students to the United States. Instead, I secured enrollment for them in one of our colleges in South Africa.

During one of our days in India, the social studies professor took his class to the Gate of India in Bombay. "Would you like to come along with us?" he invited me and Tatyana. Of course we did!

Along the way, one of the students passed out plastic bags filled with fragrant, sticky curried rice. Inside the rice was one hardboiled egg for each of us to lunch on. Even with the simple service, my mouth watered with anticipation for the spicy meal I knew I would be eating. The others all dipped their hands directly into the baggies and popped fistfuls of rice into their mouths. Tatyana and I just looked at our bags, helpless. In the past, whenever people were eating a slice of pizza or a chicken leg and apologized for eating with their hands, I would dismiss them by saying, "It's OK. God made fingers before the fork!" But this was not a slice of pizza. This was sloppy, sticky rice, drenched with curry sauce. Gratefully, I accepted the plastic spoons that someone dug up for us so we were able to enjoy our meal.

We bounced along until our bus came to a sudden halt on the side of the road. There was a flurry of activity as all the young men on board jumped off the bus, popped open the hood, and used their curried-rice hands to work on the engine. In under half-an-hour, the engine hood slammed down and all those young men, newly grimy from dirt and grease, jumped back on board and we were on our way again.

The lush green canopy gave way to tall buildings while the narrow road opened to a busy highway. Filth and slums trailed up the mountains behind the city skyscrapers. People living in cardboard boxes sent their children to press us for money. Snake charmers and trained monkeys performed for the tourists, demanding tips.

Despite the poverty all around us and the muddy foul waters backing up to it, the Gate of India was an amazing sight to see. This free-standing structure faced the Indian Ocean, historically the welcome post to the country.

In India, it seemed like everyone from the highest officials to the simplest street vendors spoke some English so it was relatively easy to communicate. On the other hand, the locals would quickly show their unhappiness with you for not giving them alms or tips. We were grateful to be back on our bus and returning to the clean, beautiful campus.

One day I visited the tiny elementary school that was associated with Spicer Memorial College. This schoolhouse was used by the student teachers as they worked toward their accreditation. I stood in front of the narrow classroom, with its bare walls and cool tile floors. Squatting on the floor in front of me was a classroom of about twelve smiling, brown faces. These children did not seem to notice or mind that they had no chairs to sit on; the naked floors were good enough. Although the children spoke English in their classroom, I was a newcomer and very strange to them. I sang songs with them, teaching them new, simple choruses which they had never heard.

In the middle of all the Indian children were fair-haired Anna and Konstantin Morar. I knew them well since I had stayed with the Morar family in Tula, Russia in 1993. Their parents were now students at Spicer Memorial College so the children were able to attend the elementary school.

TURKEY

A Favorite Hymn:

He's able. He's able. I know He's able. I know my Lord is able to carry me through.
He healed the broken hearted and set the captive free.
And made the lame to walk again and caused the blind to see.
He's able. He's able. I know He's able. I know my Lord is able to carry me through.

One summer, my friend Tatyana and I decided to use our two week vacation to visit Turkey. She had booked a room overlooking the sea. I could not believe I would be swimming in the Mediterranean Sea just as I had done during my years in Middle East College.

Our room was on the fourth floor of the hotel—no elevators, of course. And the sea was probably the same number of steps from the hotel's lobby to the shore. Every day we walked 120 steps down to the main lobby, then another 120 steps down to the seashore where we swam, sunbathed, and picnicked for hours. Needless to say, all this walking, swimming and climbing was an excellent, though not restful, way to spend our vacation.

On one of these trips to the sea, I began a conversation with a family there. All my life I had told my children and my friends that I spoke six languages, Turkish being among them. Since coming to Turkey, I had already discovered that Turkish here was a world away from the Turkish I had learned growing up with parents from Azerbaijan. Although I could understand what people were saying, they could not understand me unless they also spoke Russian or Azerbaijanian.

Fortunately, my newfound friends also spoke Russian. "What is your name?" the husband asked as he greeted us.

"This is Tatyana and I am Raisa," I said.

"What?" he looked astonished. "Did you say Raisa? You have to come see our store, Raisa! You will love it!"

I knew immediately I would love his store. I mean, I love any store that I can shop in, providing it is not like the empty ones in Russia.

Now, I am not accustomed to climbing into the back seat of a stranger's car, but I had already heard from my associate director and his wife that the Turks were extremely generous and hospitable. Because of this, I happily jumped into our new friends' car and dragged Tatyana in with me.

We drove up the windy road, past our hotel, and into the cobblestoned city. All along the way the husband showed us points of interest as he was practically bouncing in his seat with anticipation. His wife also chatted happily with us, taking a sincere interest in our work.

It wasn't until our car came to a stop that I realized what his excitement was all about. There, in 18 inch letters over the doorway of his store was my name—Raisa.

"Oh!" I exclaimed, jumping out and gazing up at the gold and red letters. "What could be better than a store named after *me* in Turkey?"

Another shopping experience I had in Turkey was while buying some fruit from a street vendor. I tried to bargain with the salesperson so he asked me, "Where are you from?"

"I'm from Russia."

"Russians never bargain!" he exclaimed.

Just then, a Russian man walked up and said, "Give me one kilogram apples, one kilogram peaches," continuing with a long list of items. He pulled out a wad of $100 bills from his pocket, paid, and left.

I turned back to the salesperson, "He did not work hard like I do to earn all that money. That is the difference!"

HOMEWARD BOUND

In 1996 my four year contract with the Euro Asia Division came to a close. It was finally time to return to the United States for good. There would be no more third-world countries, traveling through dirty streets, or struggling to secure food. But that also meant fewer new experiences, new friends, and new discoveries. Part of me was elated that I would soon be reunited with my family. Part of me was fearful that I would grow stagnant without my daily adventures. What lay ahead for me, only God knew.

Recipe for Stuffed Cabbage (*Golubtsy*)

For the cabbage rolls:	For the meat filling:
1 medium head cabbage	2 Tbsp clarified butter or olive oil
2 cups chicken stock or water	1 medium onion, finely chopped
3 Tbsp tomato sauce	2 medium carrots, shredded
4 cloves garlic, finely chopped	1 lb. ground (minced) beef
1/4 cup lemon juice	1 cup long-grain rice, cooked
salt to taste	salt and freshly ground black pepper
plain whole-milk yogurt or	1/2 tsp ground allspice
sour cream for serving	2 Tbsp chopped fresh parsley

Directions:

Preheat the oven to 350F.

To make meat filling, heat clarified butter or oil in a frying pan over medium-low heat. Add the onion and fry until soft, about 7 minutes. Place in a bowl with beef and remaining filling ingredients. Mix well to combine.

Core cabbage and place whole in a large pot of boiling salted water. Cook just long enough to soften leaves, about 10–15 minutes. Drain in a colander and cool under cold running water. Carefully remove the leaves.

Cut thick ribs from larger leaves, then halve the leaves; keep smaller leaves intact. You will need 14–16 leaves. Use leaves and trimmings to line a deep saucepan.

To make the rolls, place a generous tablespoon of meat filling at base of each leaf, roll one turn and tuck in sides to contain filling. Roll firmly to end of leaf.

In a saucepan over high heat, bring the stock and tomato sauce to a boil. Add the garlic, lemon juice and salt. Cook for one more minute.

Arrange the rolls in a large pot, pour the sauce over the top. Cover and bring to boil. Place in an oven for about 45–50 minutes.

Serve the rolls hot or warm. Serve with yogurt or sour cream.

Figure 32 - Baptisms in Russia

Figure 33 - Raisa with Raya at the Bolshoi, Dr. Grimaldi with Family and at SDA Clinic, Raisa

Figure 34 - Aunt Sara and Cousin Adileh; Raya with Sara; Toma, Nadir, and Raya; Nadir, Raya, Lena; Lena Holding Orkhan, Nadir, and Lala

Figure 35 - Visiting Paris, Rega-Estonia, Building Church in Odessa, Ukraine

Figure 36 - Baku Church, Gladys Kubrock and Raya Selling *Matryoshka*; Aprons, Dolls, and Brooches; Children in Kiev, Ukraine

Figure 37 - Morar Family, Raya's 60th Birthday, Mother's Day at the Lake, Produce Line in Russia

Figure 38 - Pyatigorsk University Classroom, Teachers' Potluck in Tashkent

Figure 39 - Zaoksky Seminary Students, Seminarian Housing, Zaoksky Church
(SDA Members Re-constructed the Old, Donated Church)

Figure 40 - Director of Ed. Harry Maden, Associate of Ed. Raya, and Secretary in Russia; Raya Speaking in Chernivtsi; Raya Teaching Ellen White's Stories to Children

Figure 41 - Raya Translating in Russia, Raya Speaking in Kiev

Figure 42 - Murmansk Church (Summer), Bus to Murmansk (Later Winter Trip),
Sledding Near Murmansk

Figure 43 - Raya with Kazakhs in Murmansk, Baptism in Arctic Ocean

Figure 44 - Raya in Finland

Figure 45 - Ella with Mimi, Mimi and the Kitten, Esther and Mimi

Figure 46 - Speaking at Escondido SDA Church, Danny's Wedding

Figure 47 - SDA School in Netherlands, SDA Conference - Uzbekistan Delegates

Figure 48 - SDA Conference Parade in Netherlands, Raya with Russian Bible, Netherlands Station

Figure 49 - Taj Mahal, Indian Artisans

Figure 50 - Anna Morar (top) and Konstantin Morar (center) in Pune Indian School, Indian Schoolchildren, Raya Speaking at Spicer Memorial College in India

Figure 51 - Raisa Store in Turkey, Owners of Raisa Store, Steps to Mediterranean Sea in Turkey

PART XIII: UNITED STATES, 1996–1997

HAWAII

"... Eye has not seen, ear has not heard ..." 1 Corinthians 2:9

There is a voyage that every person needs to experience at least once in a lifetime, a voyage to a lush, green paradise of beautiful sunrises, tropical waters, and warm, sandy beaches. That journey is a trip to Hawaii. In 1996, Ella gave me the best birthday gift of my life when we went on this trip together.

Now, typically Ella and I are not the most compatible travel companions. Ella wants to see local hot spots and historical sites, and I want to see all the Adventist church schools and hospitals. While I want to do everything economically, she just wants to do everything—period! If any opportunity for an SDA speaking engagement could be included in my trip, it would be as close to perfect as I could get.

Despite our differences, Ella and I had a fabulous time together. You can't help that when you're in paradise! Our trip began in Maui where we stayed in an A-frame guest house. This house had several benefits for us. First, it pleased the church goer in me because it was owned by a Seventh-day Adventist church school. Even better was the second benefit: we got the beautiful accommodations for the best price ever, $15 a night! Even Ella couldn't refuse that kind of deal.

Ella rented a car and, using our handy AAA TripTik®, drove us all around the island, pointing out the various landmarks and destinations. We took the winding scenic road to Hana and scaled a path leading to majestic waterfalls. This fulfilled Ella's desire to do everything possible.

With all the money we saved on lodging, we decided to do a little island hopping. Our trip continued with a short flight to the island of Kauai, appropriately known as the Garden Island. If we were pleased with the price we got on our Maui accommodations, we were even happier with the price we got in Kauai where we stayed for *free* at my friend Marianne Esteb's condo. Anywhere you go on Kauai is beautiful. But these condos, with their doorsteps practically touching the beach, couldn't be more idyllic. Once more, Ella acted as a tour guide taking me all over the island to show me the treasures she had researched for our journey.

Have you ever seen waterfalls that towered sixty feet into the air or gazed at Kauai's Sleeping Giant or adventured into a cave by boat to see intensely colored coral reefs? Every size and shape of creatures swam by me, mocking me for not having an underwater camera with which to capture them.

Our final destination was Honolulu on the island of Oahu. We found everything much more readily available and less expensive on this island since it was the main airport hub of all the islands. I always love shopping for needless, dust-collecting, touristy things that let your loved ones know that they were missed. Honolulu's big city made this so much easier.

Once again, we were extremely fortunate with lodging on Oahu. One of the conference pastors let us stay in his home while his family was away on vacation. We really couldn't have planned that any better.

BACK TO ESCONDIDO

In 1996 I returned to my life in California and found that I had no job. At the age of 70, I had very few prospects of employment, but still, I was not ready to retire. I thought of the Russian women I had met, retired at the age of 55 and hobbling around like old *Matryoshka* dolls. I knew that I would not be happy if I did not have a purpose.

I visited the Escondido Adventist Academy, only two miles from my condo. Working there seemed to be a perfect solution, except that there were no teaching positions available. The only option was to be a substitute when needed.

I also found that in my absence, I was not the only one who had matured. Esther's girls were now growing up, and needing more attention. Meanwhile, Esther had decided to continue her education and was working as a physical therapy aid. If I were available to babysit it would help her out. I decided that a substitute teaching position *would* suit my needs to keep busy.

I usually substituted for the early elementary school grades, first through third, but once subbed for the hockey instructor, watching a gym full of sweaty, barbarously-dressed boys push and shove each other as they chased a hockey puck from one end of the gym to the other. That was a new experience for me, since I had never even *seen* a hockey game before that week.

Although I was able to work and be near my family, I did not feel fulfilled. It wasn't until later that year that a phone call revealed a new chapter which would be starting in my life very soon.

A church friend from Buffalo, Dr. Una Underwood, called to tell me that she and her husband had started an English Language school in China. Because China was a communist country, the school itself was not affiliated with the Seventh-day Adventist church. Things in that school had progressed to the point where they were in need of another teacher. I thought of my four wonderful years in Russia and jumped at the chance to continue my missionary endeavors on a more covert level.

As I expected, my three children were not thrilled to hear that I was leaving again so soon. Once more, I was headed for foreign lands and once more they were uncertain of the outcome.

"Mom, who are these people you'll be working with?" Danny asked me.

I simply answered, "Just some church friends."

"You know that you can't even breathe a word about God in China, right Mom?" they all prompted me. I knew that when it came to my God, I would not keep silent. Although I never said so in words, my children knew that as well. People were being tortured for preaching God's word in several communist Asian countries at that time, but I was sure that with God, everything would turn out fine.

Figure 52 - Rema and Mimi in Uzbek Hats, Raya with Mr. Oster, Raya and Ella in Hawaii, Mrs. Oster with Raya

PART XIV: CHINA, 1997–1998

CHINA

"Troubles may come and troubles may go,
We trust in Jesus, come weal or woe,
Are we downhearted? No! No! No!"
from a song by Robert Harkness

When I arrived in the Hebei Province capital city of Shijiazhuang, China, I was given the same warning in my contract. "No teacher shall discuss any religious matters within the school premises or with any student at any time. Violators will be subject to immediate suspension and their contract will be terminated." If we broke the rules in any way, the school would be at risk of closing and the directors fined, or worse, imprisoned. I was going to have to be very careful when I taught my students about God. After all, I didn't think He would make a way for me to go that far unless he wanted His word spread.

At my first day of class, I smiled at a sea of adult students who had all previously taken English in some form or another during their schooling. These students were highly educated as engineers, lawyers and professors. They knew English vocabulary extensively and their spelling was perfect—better than mine in fact, since I have always spelled phonetically which gets me into trouble about ninety-eight percent of the time. Their problem and my challenge was that they needed to perfect their pronunciation and conversational skills. We had two months to complete the challenge.

"I am Mrs. Abadir," I told them. Whatever I said was instantly displayed to them on their individual monitors through the miracle of cutting-edge voice-recognition software.

"Meesa Abadee," they repeated in unison.

"Very good," I continued.

"Vayee gool," they mimicked.

I cleared my throat and went on, "I will go around the room and have each of you tell me your name," I suggested.

"Tao Mei Ling," the first girl said.

"Fa Xui Li," came the next name.

"Lee Feng," was a boy's name.

"Zhi Peng!"

"Miahua Huang!"

Each person shouted a name out to my increasingly bewildered face. There were fifteen names in all, none of which I could recognize. I had always struggled with my students' names, even when they were tidy little English names that I had heard for twenty years of my life. I needed an easy solution to keep these names straight in my mind.

"I want you geev to us Amelica name," one girl suggested. The translation took a moment to sink into my mind.

I paused, processing the meaning of her words. "I want you to give us American names," I corrected.

"Yes!" she beamed at me, smiling emphatically. All around her students nodded their heads.

"Repeat it correctly, please," I insisted. If they were going to learn English, they may as well start now.

"I want you to geev us Amelica name," they chorused.

"American-n-N names-s-Z," I corrected.

"AmericaN nameZ," they chanted.

"OK, you," I pointed to the first girl whose name I had already forgotten, "you will be Ella from now on." As I spoke the name, it displayed on everyone's computer and the newly christened Ella copied the name happily into her notebook.

"Era," she repeated out loud.

"Yes, Ella. That is my oldest daughter's name."

"Aaah!" everyone sighed, nodding their heads and smiling at the great honor I bestowed on the girl who sat closest to me.

"You are Esther," I said pointing to the next girl. "That is my other daughter's name."

"Danny," I pointed to the boy sitting front and center. "Danny is the name of my son." The new Danny was obviously pleased to be the namesake of his teacher's son. Now I had run out of children to rename my students after. This was no problem since teaching elementary school for almost forty years had provided me a collection of more than enough names.

"Brian, Lisa, David, Pam," I continued around the room, assigning names that were displayed automatically for the students to see and copy. Every two months I would get a new set of students and, after that class finished with these names, they would be passed on to the next class that came along.

SOMETHING'S BUGGING ME

Everywhere I traveled around the world, I found good and I found bad. Cities had varied from spotless and pristine, such as St. Petersburg, to various levels of dirtiness. In Cairo I had witnessed so much dust and so many insects that I sometimes felt Moses' curses on Pharaoh still existed. In Moscow I was overcome by the stench of people even as they passed me on the streets. In India the homeless seemed to be taking over urban neighborhoods.

China had air pollution so heavy, we could almost cut the haze with a butter knife. I asked the students if they knew why the smog was so dense in their city and found out that a former ruler had demanded a good portion of the trees to be chopped down and used for coal during a fossil fuel shortage.

I had not noticed this before because our school had a small border of trees surrounding it. After that time, whenever I left the school building, I began to notice the bare streets and lack of trees. Many times people wore masks while walking around the city or riding bikes. No birds sang in the streets, although admittedly, I didn't know if that was because the birds had nowhere to live or because they had all been eaten. I had quickly discovered that the Chinese ate anything that moved.

With the school term in session, I was accustomed to opening the windows to circulate the air before starting class every day. One morning, a faint humming sound drifted up and into the room. By lunch time, the noise had risen to the level of a chainsaw buzzing. Even after I closed the windows the sound seeped through.

"What *is* that?" I asked, exasperated and exhausted from the constant sound.

"Crickets," the students exclaimed gleefully. Obviously the noise was annoying only to me. Surely they were mistaken.

"We have crickets in America," I argued, "and they do not sound like that." But the students insisted, even describing the insects to me.

The trees outside were alive with the whirring of transparent wings on these two-inch-long, green creatures. Chinese crickets were as unusual to me as the language. But as disturbing as their noise was to my throbbing head, my students didn't seem bothered at all. "They bring good fortune. It is lucky to have them here," everyone insisted. But all they were bringing me was a headache.

One day, Lynn, an attractive young student, brought her six-year-old daughter to my class with her, stating that the child's own school was on holiday that week.

I didn't mind. I was quite used to having children around me, and Asians typically have very well-behaved kids. The two of them stayed behind after all the other students left for the day, and I enjoyed playing and chatting with the little girl, thinking of how my own grandchildren, so far away, would be when they reached that same age.

As we walked down the stairs together, I could already hear the increasing sound of crickets on the other side of the walls. I braced myself for the noise I would encounter outside and pushed the door open.

Immediately, one beautiful, jade-colored cricket landed at our feet. Now, my first thought, having collected various insects from around the world all my life for my classrooms, was, "How can I catch this thing?" But in the very next second, the little girl snatched it up and popped it in her mouth.

I felt the wind momentarily suck out of me. "Poison!" I gasped, even as the squirming insect legs wiggled into the child's grinning mouth. I cringed from the crunch, crunch, crunch of the girl's teeth on the green exoskeleton. "She's eating a bug! A bug!"

"Yes," Lynn assured me with a nod and a smile, "crickets are good— tasty!" And at that moment I feared that she would grab another flying insect and prove it to me.

"Why do you eat crickets if you think they bring you luck?" I asked astounded. Actually, there were a million other *why* questions I could have asked, but that was really the first one to pop into my head.

"They bring good health, too," Lynn stated.

"But how are they lucky if you are eating them?"

"Oh," my student said with a laugh and a shrug, "they are going to die anyway."

That was my first encounter with Chinese insects. My next experience would be even more unexpected.

❖ ❖ ❖

I slept on the fifth floor of the school building. One night, my screen window was broken by the wind. I was tucked into my bed all alone, sleeping soundly until a whirring, buzzing noise woke me up. It was louder than any of the crickets had ever been. In fact, it was so loud it could have been right in my ear.

I sat up in bed and touched my ear for verification. Sure enough, I could feel the back end of something wiggling around in there. I thought I would faint as a queasy feeling washed over me. I had something alive in my ear, but no one was around to help me.

I carefully examined my well-stocked first aid kit. I always travelled prepared: Band-Aids, useless; tweezers and scissors, too dangerous; matches, no way! I whispered a prayer before I finally settled on a cotton ball soaked in rubbing alcohol and applied it to my ear until the wiggling and buzzing stopped. That bug must have gotten drunk from the alcohol. Next came the difficult process of trying to knock it out while keeping my brains intact.

Finally, the bug fell out. But it was not any bug. It was a fat, ugly, shiny, brown beetle. I screamed in disgust, tossing the creature into the garbage. In all the months I lived in China, I never saw a beetle similar to the one that invaded my ear.

The only other thing on the fifth floor besides my bedroom was the cafeteria. This area was used during the school day for all the teachers and students who brought their own meals with them. Our kitchen in the cafeteria was staffed by a vegan cook so all our meals were completely vegetable-based. There were no animal fats, no dairy, and no eggs. This was tough because I love eggs. But I was told that since we couldn't verify what source the eggs or meat came from—the Chinese do eat anything after all—it was just best to remain vegan.

Since students brought their own food, Dr. Underwood insisted that no meat was carried into the school. Anything else was fair game so the Chinese students would noisily slurp bowls of noodles and broth. I've never been much of a pasta person, so I didn't concern myself with their meals. However, Dr. Underwood would see the mounds of white, slithery noodles and mutter under her breath, "Ha! Colon cancer," as if the processed flours were instantaneously making their way through the students' intestines.

The Underwoods munched on seeds and nuts by the handfuls to make up for their protein requirements, but because of my age, my teeth were not as capable of breaking open most shells. Instead, I opened them with a nutcracker and ground them into nut butters.

NOTHING BUT THE TOOTH

Like all Chinese kitchens, ours had no oven. Instead, buns were steamed atop a large boiler with holes in the lids and lined with a towel. When the buns emerged, fully cooked, there was no crust and crust was my favorite part. One of the other teachers had brought a toaster and an electrical converter back from the United States. We sliced the steamed buns and toasted them up, but the buns came out as hard as baked clay.

Worse yet was that the school had no elevators and my classroom was on the second floor of another building. Every day for lunch I had to climb the stairs, then hike back down five flights and back up another two to my classroom for afternoon sessions. Then I'd climb back up for dinner and, since I usually went out with one of my students in the evening, climb back down to the first floor where one of them would pick me up. Finally, I would climb up one last time for bed.

With all this activity going up and down the stairs all day and without bread, my favorite staple, you would think I would have lost weight while I was in China. But, as usual, the weight I came with was the same I was destined to leave with twelve months later.

Before I resigned myself to toastless, crustless bread, I really did give toasted, steamed buns a fair try. After all, I do love my bread. Unfortunately, this toast was so hard I would get sores in my mouth for a week after eating just one slice. I actually broke two teeth on the dry buns. Stubbornly, I still tried it occasionally, just pleased with the concept of *eating* toast.

Sometimes I would soak the bread in my hot tea or soup, creating a mushy, pasty sponge. Once I discovered how sturdy the bread was, I imagined the possibility of scrubbing the bathroom tile with it, but I abandoned that idea for fear of the dry toast being too abrasive.

Soon enough, when a pain in my mouth refused to heal, I discovered exactly how tough these crispy bricks were. I thought I was suffering in silence, but many people began to ask if I was okay every time I ate or drank anything. Finally, sensing I had endured enough pain, my students recommended a dentist. I had no immediate intention of visiting a third-world health professional, but as the swelling and pain persisted, my determination weakened. I finally gave in and "Nancy", one of my students, drove me to get relief.

I quickly discovered that my doctor spoke no English. Fortunately,

Nancy agreed to wait with me. She wanted to learn English very badly, so this student took every chance she could to guide me around the city. Once, I had even visited her parents' home, discovering that she must have come from a wealthy family. They had DVDs before I ever saw them in the United States. I once described the silver disc that we watched *Titanic* on to my daughter who, of course, knew exactly what I was talking about.

While Nancy described my pain to the dentist, I looked around the exam room and found it filthy and disgusting. I also noticed that the doctor's greyish, spit-splattered lab coat seemed to match his office decor. My trance was broken when a man walked into the room and shook hands with the dentist. They chatted for a few minutes while I sat there waiting for my exam.

When the man left, my dentist turned back to me, picked up an examining tool, and prepared to look in my mouth. But I was quicker than that. I clasped my hand over my mouth and shook my finger at him. The dentist gave me a confused look until I demonstrated washing my hands and pointed to the sink. He smiled and nodded and, after complying—three times with soap, I noticed—he returned to my side.

"Your tooth is abscessed," he explained to me through my student. "There is a very bad infection and I need to do a root canal." I thought of the clean, sterile dental offices I visited in the US and wondered if I would survive this ordeal.

"I am allergic to some anesthesia," I worried.

"I won't be using anesthesia," he assured me. I was sure I heard incorrectly. Something must have been lost in the translation.

Once again, shaking my head "no," I used hand gestures to represent a gas mask covering my mouth and nose. "He said he will not use gas," Nancy repeated. I tried another motion of injecting something into my mouth and shrugged my shoulders uncertainly. "He will not use any medication," my student assured me again as the dentist explained everything to her in Chinese. "He specializes in root canals and does it all without drugs."

"A root canal with no anesthesia, no medication at all? How could this be?" I wondered as I settled back into my chair, watching the doctor suspiciously, still sure he misunderstood me.

But one hour and no drugs later, I immerged from my seat with absolutely no pain at all. Had I not witnessed it with my own eyes and mouth, I would have not believed it.

That tooth never bothered me again. Once I returned to the United

States, I showed the results to my regular dentist, explaining the whole story. It's funny how people assume that if an old lady tells them something amazing, it must somehow be imagined.

The American dentist examined my mouth carefully stating that the work was very good. "It's a perfect root canal," he admitted, showing me my x-rays. I repeated that the Chinese dentist used no drugs in the procedure. "Hmm, yes," he nodded, although every feature on his face showed his skepticism.

TURTLE TO GO

Since anything that moved was fair game for restaurant chefs to cook, the Underwoods recommended that we maintain our vegan lifestyle outside of the school as well as inside.

Chinese restaurants are somewhat of a do-it-yourself experience. Storefronts displayed their meaty goods as well as an array of vegetables and pots of grains to add. Chicken legs hung as decorations in the windows and a variety of fish and crustaceans swam in giant tanks awaiting their demise.

Once patrons made their selections, the ingredients were brought to the table in a boil-your-own-soup fashion. It still seems amusing to me that people pay money to prepare their own meals, but I guess it is all part of the culture.

One evening one of my students, a nuclear engineer, invited me to dinner with his friends and his five-year-old daughter Mei-ling. I soon learned that even the wealthiest homes had very small kitchens with no ovens. As a result, our dinner would not be at his house but at a restaurant.

One of my greatest challenges when eating out was to clear the air— literally. In China most people smoke, which is fundamentally against every health belief I have. I faced this obstacle by carrying a small "No Smoking" sign with me everywhere I went. The simple illustration, a lit cigarette with a barred circle through it, is generally universally understood without any translation necessary.

I entered the restaurant and requested an all-vegetable dish. I was then seated with my five companions. I made it a habit to keep my back to the wall so on this day I was able to face the majority of the restaurant guests. Two young men at the table closest to me were enjoying a smoke with their meal so, using my most pleasant expression, I caught their eye and held the little sign up for them to see. The young men smiled courteously at me and put out their cigarettes.

I then turned my attention to the other tables around me, even having to get up to tap a man sitting too far away to notice my sign. One by one, all the patrons put out their cigarettes with a polite smile. As long as that sign remained on my table, not one person relit their cigarettes. It amazed me that Chinese were so courteous to the elderly, even to the point of refraining from cigarettes when prompted.

With the climate control in hand, I turned my attention to the pot set before me. In the center of our table sat a large pot of boiling water where I would cook my meal, much like a Japanese restaurant may have hibachis. As a vegan, I could not even have the meat broth that was normally used. The meat dishes that everyone else had ordered were prepared in the kitchen away from the patrons' watchful eyes.

That night I learned that the Chinese have more varieties of rice than I ever thought existed. I saw white rice, brown rice, black rice, red rice and yellow rice, which I recognized as not rice, but millet. Passing up the noodles with Dr. Underwood's warning of colon cancer still ringing in my ears, I dropped a variety of vegetables and rice into my pot and stirred it with anticipation as dish after dish of prepared foods were brought out of the kitchen for my host and his friends.

One dish in particular caught me by surprise. An entire boiled turtle was passed around the table as each of the men plucked a leg off and noisily sucked on it. *Noisily* is the only way to eat Chinese food, I learned, since slurping, chomping, and smacking were all signs of appreciation to the chef.

By the time the headless, footless turtle arrived at Mei-ling's end of the table it was an empty shell. The little girl looked at the carcass and burst into tears.

"Poor thing," I thought. "She must be horrified to see the men eating that cute little reptile." But I was wrong. The only thing that bothered Mei-ling about the men eating those turtle legs was that they did not save any for her.

My host rushed the waiter back into the kitchen with the order for another whole turtle, this one packed to go. As we left that evening, my stomach full from millet-rice soup and theirs full of animals I could only imagine, Mei-ling happily clutched a box with her snack for the following day.

A HISTORY LESSON

I found that the easiest way to strike up a conversation with others was to ask questions about their own beliefs and history. One day I asked my students about the sights I saw on the street. On every corner, wisps of smoke drifted up to the sky. "What are they burning?" I wondered aloud.

"That is money for our dead ancestors," one of the young men answered.

"They are burning *money*?" I gasped. No wonder there was so much poverty in this country.

"Not real money," he clarified. "It is special money, joss paper that we buy to burn at holidays. The smoke carries the currency up to our ancestors."

"And what do your ancestors *do* with this burnt money?" I asked curiously.

"Well, they spend it to make their deaths more comfortable," he explained.

"Hmmm," I thought carefully before replying. "So you believe that the dead can use this burnt paper for things they need?" My student nodded enthusiastically.

"I see," I began carefully. "Well, I believe that once we die, we are not gone, just sleeping. My belief is taken from the Bible. The dead know nothing." The students gave me a confused look and with a little more explanation, they appeared to understand my point. I learned quickly that people of every nation take comfort in believing that their ancestors' spirits live on.

Another day I found myself telling the students about my daily Sabbath School lesson readings. "I am going to tell you about King Nebuchadnezzar." I began the story of a man who could not recall a disturbing dream. When none of his wise men could tell him about his forgotten nightmare, he threatened death until a simple prophet of God, named Daniel, told him not only the meaning of the dream but all that the king could not remember.

My student, Daniel, beamed triumphantly at the sound of his pseudonym. "This is a history lesson," I told the students when one of them objected to me naming Daniel's God. "Everything I tell you can be found in this history book," I said as I held up the Bible for my students to see. From that time on I was able to tell them any stories I felt were appropriate, by calling them history lessons.

❖ ❖ ❖

Since we were not supposed to worship publicly, I usually spent Sabbaths in our school with the director and our four other teachers. Occasionally, we heard about secret underground churches around town and visited them by invitation.

These "churches" were held in people's homes and we arranged to arrive one at a time to avoid suspicion. One family member would lead the service and the hymns (sung by them in Chinese and by us in English). These services brought a sense of comfort to us all.

Although we could not openly invite our students or any other Chinese to worship with us, we did offer free stop-smoking programs and additional tutorials to them, all of which were conveniently held on the Sabbath. Occasionally a student or two would attend our services, which was always a source of joy for us. No matter the result, we were at least able to plant the seeds of God's love in people who may not have otherwise heard about Him.

THE EMPEROR'S ARMY & THE CHINESE MOVIE STAR: SHIYAN, CHINA

My student Nancy was always ready to worship with us or act as our tour guide. The more time she spent with me outside of school, the better her English became, and it was evident to all of us.

One weekend, Nancy offered to take any interested teachers on a tour of Shiyan. Betty wanted to go because she knew an elderly couple who lived nearby. I didn't know anything about that city except that everyone told me I should not leave China without visiting it. Therefore, I would not miss it for anything. There were no other takers, so Betty and I made plans for the trip with Nancy.

While we waited for our bus, a large, smelly, but thankfully functioning vehicle, I stood on a grassy hill overlooking a park. Young children were gathered there, playing without any supervision that I could see. Ever the school teacher, I climbed down from the hill and grabbed the hands of two of the smiling children.

"Now kids," I instructed, "let's play a game." I sang songs and we all danced and skipped, holding hands in a large ring. "Here we go looby loo! Here we go looby light," I sang while the kids giggled and bounced around me.

No adults came to check up on the youngsters. "How about another one?" I suggested. The children obviously knew no English at all, but still they smiled up at me and played along. We played "Skip to My Lou," "Patty

Cake," and "Ring around the Rosy" until I was exhausted, but still the children were left alone. Finally, something in the trees above me caught my attention. I looked up and saw a cameraman high above our heads, recording the whole thing.

"What is going on?" I asked, confused. The man climbed down from his perch and handed me his business card.

"Song Li Video Productions," he translated for me. "I record this film," he explained. "We not know anyone come, start to play with students, but I keep on filming."

"You are making a film? For what?" I asked, amazed that I had managed to intervene unintentionally. "And more importantly, how can I get a copy?"

"Film for Chinese movie," Mr. Song explained. "I give copy you." he promised. We exchanged contact information, and I did eventually get that copy, but because of the difference between American and Chinese technology, I was never able to view the recording which was later lost in one of my many moves.

Although both cities are in the Hebei Province, travel from Shijiazhuang to Shiyan by public transportation can take up to 15 hours, even with the least number of connections. By the time we arrived at the home of Betty's friends, we were more than happy to be off a moving vehicle.

The house itself was not extravagantly decorated; the walls and tables were all simple slabs of polished wood. But covering every wall were brightly painted posters of familiar Biblical scenes: Mary and baby Jesus, the crucifix, creation, as well as several depictions I had never seen like Jesus overlooking the Great Wall of China. I was amazed that this couple did not fear for their safety since displaying the paintings obviously disobeyed national anti-religious rules.

Betty introduced the elderly couple as Jie and An Long. Jie was the artist who had painted all the religious pictures. "Where did you hear these stories?" I asked him. I knew of one other place where I had seen evidence of the ancient biblical chronicles. It was, surprisingly, at the first Buddhist temple I had visited near the Great Wall. I recalled a lovely, feminine looking Buddha reclining on a pedestal outside of the temple. This caught me by surprise. "I thought Buddha was a man!" I said to my tour guide who explained that every Buddha I would come across may look different from another.

Jie explained in broken English that he was a Seventh-day Adventist and had been creating calendars with Bible pictures on them for many years. "How many have you made?" I wondered.

But he simply smiled and nodded, "Yes, many."

After we had filled up on a homemade Chinese meal and heard stories of their lives, Jie drove us to our hotel room. The next day we were in for an adventure that we had no way of expecting.

We took a short cab ride to the museum, built over an excavation site. Now, I've visited many archeological sites in my life. After all, I'd lived in countries with some of the deepest historical roots. But I had never seen anything like Qin Shi Huang's Army.

In 1978, farmers had unearthed some terracotta statues while trying to dig a well. At that time, the excavation had just started, and all these years later it was still underway. It will probably still be going on by the time this book is published. Every imaginable military figure was represented in this clay army: over 8,000 soldiers as well chariots, horses and various other items that were buried to protect the Emperor in the afterlife. The features varied from soldier to soldier and the expression on every face was unique. I find it difficult to describe the minute details of each figure and can only say what was said to me: "You just have to see it for yourself!"

HONG KONG IS FREED

Every day the students and the media began to grow more and more excited. Since 1842, Hong Kong had been occupied by the United Kingdom, but now in 1997, this tiny country was about to regain its freedom and independence and be handed over to the People's Republic of China.

On June 30th, every eye in mainland China and many others around the world watched an extravagantly elaborate parade as British soldiers, diplomats, and politicians made their respectful exit from Hong Kong. I was impressed that the end of a century's colonization could happen in such an orderly fashion. No battle had to be fought. The agreement had simply expired and England walked out gracefully.

Not one of the current residents of this densely populated country had ever known Hong Kong before the British rule. Over seven million people residing in an area of just over 1000 square kilometers had lived under the rule of a country that was more than 10,000 kilometers away.

Ironically, even after it was returned to mainland China, Hong Kong maintained a different political system from her parent country. Because of this, when Ella, her boyfriend Cyrus, and his sister Zari decided to visit me, the four of us were able to go to Hong Kong, while not one of my Chinese students was granted the permission without a Visa.

I traveled south to meet up with Ella, Cyrus, and Zari in Shanghai where we would continue our journey by train. That night we all sat down to dinner in one of the city's restaurants, chosen carefully by Cyrus who proclaimed, "Looks alright to me! You can always tell a good Chinese restaurant by the number of Asians eating there!" Everyone was excited to dig into traditional Chinese cuisine. Everyone, that is, except me since I had been eating nothing *but* traditional Chinese for the past eleven months.

"I am completely vegan here," I warned my guests. "We don't eat any animal products since we don't know where they come from."

"I know exactly where their animal products come from," Cyrus joked, "from animals!"

I tried to explain that we just don't eat *all* animals, but Cyrus was having too much fun teasing me and Zari was willing to go along with his lead. Ella and I chose the vegan soup pot (rice and millet in a bland broth) while Cyrus and Zari studied the menu, written entirely in Mandarin. In the end, Cyrus made his selection by blindly pointing to a random item and smiling up at the waitress.

"What did you order?" Ella asked him.

"I don't know," he admitted with a laugh. But when his food came, Ella was the one laughing. Meat, clinging to the tiniest bones I have ever seen, swam in a fragrant sauce.

"Cyrus, you have no idea if those bones came from a bird or a rat," I warned him.

"Or a lizard!" Cyrus chimed in excitedly, while shoveling spoonfuls of the sauce onto the rice and into his mouth. Obviously, my warnings went unheard. He finished the entire bowl himself while Zari helped Ella and me to finish our rice-broth soup.

"Really, Raya," Zari said, tasting a bite of her brother's meal before it disappeared, "his was better."

That night we climbed aboard a "cheap motel," as I liked to call the overnight trains, and headed for Hong Kong. Ella, who had a sensitive stomach and difficulty sleeping while traveling had an entire pharmacy of over-the-counter products. She took her standard Tylenol PM, which was just the right amount of sleep aid to help her sleep through the noisy, bumpy train. As a typical Abadir, I can sleep in any position while traveling and therefore needed no such assistance.

Even so, about one hour after falling asleep, I awoke from the bathroom light beaming into my eye. "What's wrong?" I asked Zari, drowsily.

"Cyrus is sick," she said, "and I can't find Ella's medicine box." The sound of Cyrus vomiting from the bathroom confirmed her diagnosis.

I searched through Ella's suitcase but found no medicine box. Soon, Zari joined in her brother's illness, although whatever was bothering him was not nearly as powerful in her system. Every thirty to ninety minutes, Cyrus was bowing over the potty hole to throw up and occasionally Zari would join him. Every time they got up, I went through Ella's suitcase, searching for medication, but I found nothing.

Finally, just before arriving at the border check, Ella's alarm sounded. Drowsily, she turned it off and pushed herself upright. She blinked in confusion at the three of us, already up.

"What?" she demanded in sleep-blurred annoyance. "What's wrong?"

"Oh Ella, darling," I rushed into the story, "where are your medications? Cyrus is so sick!"

"Sick?" she asked as Cyrus scrambled, once more, into the bathroom. "From what?"

"From whatever he ate," I said. "I knew those little bones were poison."

"Forget that!" Zari commanded, still looking green. "We need your medications!"

Ella scrambled to her carry-on bag, tucked beside her on the bed, and immediately found a nausea remedy for each of them to take. I knew that after the one night aboard the "Train from Hell," I would have no problem convincing Cyrus to remain a vegan for the rest of the trip.

After our train to Xi'an, we flew to Hong Kong. Ella, Cyrus and Zari had single entry visas to return to mainland China. They did not realize that by leaving the mainland to go to Hong Kong, they needed multiple-entry visas. We had to stay in Hong Kong for three additional days until they received another visa to re-enter China. Shopping in one of the world's most popular cities and all its conveniences made the days fly quickly. We also visited Victoria Peak every day, which was the highest point on Hong Kong Island. From there, we enjoyed breathtaking views of one of the world's most spectacular cityscapes.

RETURN HOME

When the end of my contract came, I was thrilled to receive my stipend for a return ticket home. After Ella and her family left, I was on the phone every day making plans for my return. I could not wait.

I'm not saying that I hated my time in China; that would not be accurate. There was just so much that I was looking forward to: my home, trees, and the ability to eat anything I wanted without fear that it may have once been an alley cat or a gutter rat. Most importantly, I could not wait to see my seven-year-old Mimi and four-and-a-half-year-old Rema.

When I returned from China, I had hoped that Mimi and Rema would be equally excited to see me again. I was not disappointed. Mimi, who just a few years prior would not even admit to being my granddaughter, greeted me with squeals of excitement, nearly jumping out of her father's arms. Rema, who was a tiny toddler at the time, quickly became my constant companion while her parents worked and her sister went to school.

When my plane landed on American soil, I almost cried. "That was the most difficult year I have ever spent," I admitted to my children as we sat around the dinner table in Esther's home.

"Does this mean your travel bug has been cured, Mom?" Nasser asked.

"Oh yes," I stated, "I have no interest in going anywhere for a long, long time."

Figure 53 - Raya with Jie and An Long, Jie's Art, Jie's Grandson

Figure 54 - Raya with Chinese Children

Figure 55 - Raya with Chinese Students

Figure 56 - Stop Smoking Session, Chinese Students

Figure 57 - Raya Touring China

Figure 58 - Chinese Students on Bicycles, Great Wall of China, Chinese Grocery, Raya in Chinese Cheongsam

PART XV: UNITED STATES, 1998–2001

HOME-SCHOOL TEACHER

"Then shall the king say unto them, 'Come, ye blessed of my father, inherit the kingdom prepared for you ... For I was hungry and you fed me, I was thirsty and you gave me drink, I was a stranger and you took me in ...'" Matthew 25:34–35

Two years later, memories of my previous travel hardship had long been forgotten. "I am going to Cambodia," I told Esther.

"Cambodia!" Her surprise was more than obvious. "Mom, you were tortured by your time in China and now you want to go to *Cambodia?*"

"Oh," I assured her, "this will be different."

"Different how, other than the fact that it is even *more* third-world than China was?"

"I was so lonely in China," I explained. "I didn't know anyone there."

"Who could you possibly know in Cambodia?" she asked.

I had recently met a missionary couple. After hearing Julie and Scott Griswold speak in church one day, I'd approached them with stories of my own travels. We sat for hours, exchanging memories until Julie finally asked me what I was really hoping to hear. "Mrs. Abadir, we need a teacher for our children while we are working in Cambodia next month. Would you like to travel with us?"

"Would I?" I thought. They didn't have to ask twice. Before they could even think about how much trouble they were getting into by traveling with a 75-year-old woman, I had my immunizations and health check-up taken care of and my plane ticket purchased. My missionary work would continue but not until I'd made another significant move.

CHARMANT DRIVE HOME

When I returned from China, Esther and Nasser convinced me to sell my condo. The transition from a condo to a one bedroom apartment had been quite a setback to my self-esteem. They explained that my home in Escondido had almost doubled in value, but the market would not continue to go up forever. Also, they wanted me to consider that most of the neighbors I was close to in Escondido had moved away or, like our precious friend, Marie, had died.

After the sale of my condo was finalized, Nasser proclaimed it a "good deal" for me. Even so, the whole process of moving felt surreal. This would be the first time since I was an independent woman that someone other than me was deciding where I would live. Although I would not have any type of temporary living arrangement like I had in past moves, I felt like my whole life was torn out from under me.

Every box of books that Esther donated to the Friends of the Library book sale was like pulling teeth out of my mouth. And every bag of clothes and household items we gave to my neighbors to take to their extended families in Mexico was like a painful removal of my nails or my hair. And that didn't even include the things that Ella was sneaking off to Goodwill. I was crushed and I made sure to let everyone know about it.

"You are giving away *everything* that is important to me," I complained to Esther.

"Really, Mom?" my child wanted to verify. "*Everything*? Because I thought that maybe being close to your daughter and the only two grandchildren you will ever have might be important to you."

"But this is my home, Esther," I reminded her. I had worked hard to earn a living and purchase property as a single woman in Escondido.

"Your new home will be closer to us in San Diego, Mom. You're not getting any younger and this way we can be with you more often."

I still had plenty of stamina left in me and I was not going down that easily. I tried every stall tactic I could think of, including having a salesman from a cremation company sit down and explain—in detail—the benefits of his services to me.

"What do you think of this program, Esther?" I called to the kitchen where she was wrapping glasses for the move.

"Are you kidding?" she asked me, appalled. "I am up to my ears, packing for your *move* and you want me to give you advice on your *funeral arrangements*? I don't even want to *think* about you dying!"

"Well," I sulked, "you know that *you* were the one who said I'm not getting any younger."

❖❖❖

Ella and Esther arrived on the big day to direct the movers and decorate my new apartment in La Jolla, just 10 minutes from the coast. That evening, with the majority of my boxes unpacked and the first decorations up on my walls, Nasser and the girls brought dinner for us to share.

"Wow!" the girls smiled at the arrangements. "This is so cute, Grandma!" I had to admit that every time I downsized, my decorations and collections were more noticeable.

Mimi found my exercise ball and immediately started bouncing on it while Rema skipped happily around my tiny living room, not much different from the condo I had just left. From there she leaped into my tiny kitchen. To me it was much smaller than the one I had moved out of, but to her it was just fine.

She skipped happily to check out the bathroom and we heard the echo of her voice exclaiming, "This bathroom is *huge!*" Indeed, it was a bit bigger than the half bathroom that had been downstairs in my condo. I didn't bother explaining that there was no other bathroom, no upstairs.

Up to this point, everything in this apartment must have appeared to be just about the same as the downstairs of my condo. Rema finally skipped into my bedroom. She walked out slowly, looking confused.

"Where is the *rest* of this house?" she asked as her mother stood behind me motioning frantically for her to please be quiet.

"Well, Rema," I explained with exaggerated patience, "your *parents* did not want me to have a big house so your father sold it."

"It's just ... *gone?*" she asked bewildered while Mimi began to tear up.

"What about all our neighbors?" my older grandchild sobbed. Their mother tried to calm them, but my good granddaughters let everyone know that they shared my sadness as we said goodbye to the first home of mine that either of them ever knew.

JUST BEHIND THE TEMPLE

My first self-appointed task, after moving into my new apartment and right before leaving for my mission trip to Cambodia, was to get to know my neighbors. This I managed to accomplish in a number of ways. First, I hung out at the pool and hot tub that belonged to the apartment complex. Second, I invited the grandkids to hang out with me at the pool and hot tub. Third, I brought lots of snacks when I hung out at the pool and hot tub with my grandkids.

The buildings I lived in were populated with college students, and you would be surprised at how fast you can make friends when you feed the youth. Of course, I did not do all the giving. I allowed my neighbors to do for me as well. Having all those strong young men around was great when I needed someone to take my groceries to my apartment or open a stubbornly stuck window.

The only other senior I met was Tamar, a woman who lived with her disabled adult daughter. Tamar was great about filling me in on all the happenings around the neighborhood. Together, we attended many bingo games, yoga classes, and parties.

There was another building in the neighborhood that intrigued me. Every day, in order to get to my home from shopping or socializing, I had to pass an enormous white temple that looked like a castle out of a fairytale or maybe Disneyland. One Sunday, dressed in my best attire for church, I decided to stop in at the temple and worship with my neighbors.

"Can I help you?" I heard a man approach me before I had even locked my car.

"No, thank you," I smiled at him and started to walk by. "I am just going inside."

The guard stepped out to block my path. "Are you a member here?"

"Oh no," I answered, "I am a Seventh-day Adventist and I live just behind this beautiful temple. I like to get to know my neighbors and would like to see inside it."

The guard explained that the temple was used only for weddings, funerals, and other celebrations. It isn't a church. He asked me if I would like to go to their church and invited me to fill out a visitor's information card. I took the card and filled it out, inviting the guard to my church.

The following week, two young men in starched white shirts and neckties stopped by my apartment and invited me to their neighborhood church. "Is it going to be in that beautiful temple?" I asked.

"I'm sorry, ma'am," one young man said. Evidently that is the first phrase they teach in Mormon conflict resolution. "But we would love to welcome you to our smaller chapel."

"I am a Seventh-day Adventist," I declared. "I go to church on the Sabbath. That is Saturday. Why don't you come to my church with me?"

"I'm sorry, ma'am," he said shortly before ending the visit. From that time on, I received monthly phone calls or visitations from the church, inviting me to various activities. I took advantage of these opportunities to talk to them about Jesus' love and to invite them to my own church.

Figure 59 - Raya and Family Visiting with Cousins in LA

PART XVI: CAMBODIA, SINGAPORE, MALAYSIA, 2001

CAMBODIA VIA SINGAPORE

"... God, who began good work within you, will keep right on helping you ..."
Philippians 1:6

With a rush of last minute activity, the Griswolds and I were finally ready to depart for our short mission in Cambodia, but first we would make a brief stop in Singapore. Two children, two adults, and a senior citizen on a seventeen-hour flight may sound daunting to some, but the children Nathan and Joelle were well behaved and their easy-going parents made the long journey fun. We rested, played games and, true to my entertainment standards, sang lots of children's songs.

At last we arrived in Singapore, tired but happy. The Asian Division President, Will Kormand, and his wife Dorothy greeted us. As we drove to their home in their car, I was stunned to see the glorious city. Singapore was spotless. No smoking or gum chewing was allowed on their streets. Dorothy informed us that violators would be fined one thousand dollars!

The Kormand's tidy home was an excellent representation of the city, only more welcoming. We arrived to the scent of freshly baked bread and the most delicious, home-cooked comfort foods I've ever eaten.

While our visit in the Kormand home was brief, we crammed what time we had with more sightseeing than I had done the entire year I was in China. We visited the Sri Mariamman Hindu Temple and, on my very favorite expedition, let birds perch on us at the Jurong Bird Park. What an amazing display of feathered friends that was!

Since moving to California, my favorite flower has been the proud, orange-headed bird of paradise. So when Dorothy directed my attention to the birds-of-paradise, I expected to see plants. Instead, I saw a beautiful, brown bird with white tail feathers draped around its body. More than once in this lovely city, I rediscovered the creativity and beauty of God's incredible universe!

THE THREE-MONTH TOUR: PHNOM PENH, CAMBODIA

With every possible tourist attraction in Singapore examined, it seemed there was nothing left to do but continue our intended purpose of returning to Cambodia. Actually, only the Griswolds were returning because this was their second trip.

The first time they had been there, they fell in love with and adopted a young orphan boy they named Steve. Because of the immigration laws, the Griswolds had to leave without him until he was 18 but promised him they would return. In the meantime, they were paying for his education and living expenses. The Griswolds' children, Joelle and Nathan, had chatted happily throughout the plane ride telling me stories of their bigger and much browner brother.

I never expect to be chauffeured in a limo when I travel. I have taken every known source of transportation (even a donkey and a camel when I was in the Middle East, although that was just for fun). I have very simple tastes. It is not that I would have rejected a limo should one appear, but any taxi or shuttle bus would suit me just fine. So I wasn't surprised that no limo pulled up to meet us at the airport. But no taxi or shuttle bus did either. Instead, two young boys rode up to us on bicycles. Mr. Griswold negotiated in his broken Khmer and then motioned for us to approach.

We did approach, although I have to admit I never expected to actually get *on* the bike, luggage and all. Sometimes when you are in a situation, you take on the Nike slogan: "Just do it." You don't even think before acting. Other times, like when you are a 75-year-old woman in a skirt carrying two suitcases and a purse and contemplating riding a bike, you notice every thought that crosses your mind. Not me! I jumped right on without a second's hesitation.

In an instant we were zipping along, my driver in front and me clutching tightly around his waist with Joelle wedged between us. It wasn't until I made my very shaky dismount, falling into a knee deep puddle that I remembered my doctor's strict warning ages ago: "Give up the bicycle! If you manage another break to your leg you will be lame for life!"

"I could have been crippled!" I gasped under my breath. But the kids and adults alike were too busy untying suitcases from all around the bikes to really hear me complain.

Let me tell you, you really get to see the countryside from the back of a bicycle. There were only two paved streets in Phnom Penh. One that went from the airport to the king's palace and the other one that leads from the king's palace to the train station. That's it! What more could they want? Nothing else around us was developed at all. Giant trees with huge, exposed roots grew along the road, but nothing else was along the road except those trees.

The war-ravaged country was the poorest I had ever seen. Even when I visited India the slums did not seem to suffer as much as this place. Still, little children played in the muddy street. Although it had been over 30 years since the Khmer Rouge had battled in the land, we could still see people with injuries from occasional landmines detonating. People had so much hatred for injuries which would never heal; the adults bore hatred that would last for generations. There was nothing that felt pure or natural, just poor and dirty.

Even though our two-story mission building was more or less protected from the anger of a broken country, what we saw outside the walls would be embedded forever in our memories.

Our own home was fully furnished: tiled floors, beds, tables and chairs. We even had a complete kitchen. The rest of the mission was very modest. Most of the ladies sat in clusters on the floor while they worked. For church services, we sat in rows on bare benches listening as Mr. Griswold spoke from the pulpit. Occasionally, our services were held outside on the ground.

Everyone took their shoes off when they entered the church. Even the preacher, up on his platform, preached in bare feet with a shoeless translator nearby.

Once we landed in Cambodia, the Griswolds' adopted son, Steve, came to live with us. Steve enjoyed practicing his English every day, and we enjoyed how he brought laughter and hugs into our mission home.

Work started, and immediately we were thrust into our routine of teaching. The Griswolds would be teaching mothers and children from the abuse shelter, and I would be teaching Nathan and Joelle. Because of this, most of the time it was just the kids and me. We incorporated the three R's (readin', 'ritin' and 'rithmatic) with our little songs and stories and games.

Unlike other mission trips I'd attended that had been fully funded by the conference, I was paying for this trip out of my own pocket. I received no stipend account this time around, and it was fine with me.

Looking back, I see how fun and carefree my role was. Mr. and Mrs. Griswold definitely had the bigger job, helping broken women and children to heal themselves and accept God's love when the only thing these families knew was pain. Meanwhile, the Griswolds taught them skills they could earn wages with through Crochet Ministry. For hours the women would sit, cross-legged under the shade of trees, chatting happily with each other while their fingers wove fine, cotton thread into everything from large tablecloths to tiny doilies, crosses, and angels using delicate, intricate designs.

Each time the Griswolds returned to the United States they would bring boxes of these beautiful, lacy creations back with them to sell at a fair market value before sending the mission all the proceeds of their hard work.

Traditionally, Cambodians are Buddhist. In fact, I'm fairly sure that many of the women that we served maintained some of their Buddhist beliefs. But in church we sang, prayed and praised God together in unity.

One thing that everyone, Buddhists and Christians alike, told me I must see was the Angkor Thom Buddhist Temple. One of the other mission workers decided she wanted to see the Bayon Temple as well, so we took a day off and traveled the short distance together by bike, of course. This time, I managed not to fall off during dismount.

Once in Angkor Thom, we climbed a high mountain (no easy feat for a 75-year-old woman who sweats profusely in the damp, tropical weather) until we finally reached the summit to find an enormous four-faced Buddha tower outside of the temple. With four faces, one looking in each direction: north, south, east, and west, this Buddha was said to be "all-seeing," and "all-knowing." I, of course, could not resist telling other tourists that the only all-knowing god was the one true God.

Rain, rain, rain! Sometimes all day and night we listened to the earth's song. Mud puddles of all sizes seemed a constant presence. When the sun would shine, the Cambodian skies were beautiful against the greens of the jungle. Still, it was so humid that regardless of how I would dress, I was drenched in sweat and was reminded of those muddy puddles. I was fairly certain the people here had no sweat glands because I seemed to be the only one who suffered in a constant state of dampness.

Everywhere I looked the children were playing in these mud puddles. Once I saw the most beautiful twin girls laughing and splashing around in a barrel of rainwater beside their toothless mother.

"Your girls are so nice!" I told her as I patted them on the heads. "Can I adopt them for my son and daughter to raise?" The woman smiled wearily and nodded, obviously understanding *none* of what I was saying. Still, I wished more than once that I could have adopted every one of these beautiful, bronzed children and given them a better place to live.

TALK ABOUT VALUE

On our last day in Cambodia I went to a bank and gave the teller a five-dollar bill to exchange for the equivalent in *riel*, the currency there. I had been enchanted by the beautifully illustrated *riel* with their bright, vivid colors and I wanted to show some of it to my grandchildren when I returned.

"Fi ... oh-too?" the teller asked me.

"What?" I demanded.

"Fi? ... Oh-too?" she asked again, this time more slowly. I had never heard of a "fi-oh-too" in all the time I spent in Cambodia.

I spoke even more slowly, raising my voice in case she had a hearing problem. "I JUST WANT RIELS FOR MY DOLLARS. CAN YOU CHANGE IT FOR ME?"

"FI? OH-TOO? FI? OH-TOO?" She insisted.

"What is 'fi-oh-too'?" I asked, exasperated.

"You wan fi ..." she held up a 500 riel bill, "... oh too?" she held up a 200 riel bill.

"Oh," realization sank in and the teacher in me came out. "Five. Or-r. Two," I enunciated clearly so she could learn the correct pronunciation.

"Fi-oh-two," she repeated again. "Wachu wan I gib yoo."

I could see my lesson was going nowhere and I needed to make it to our farewell dinner with the Griswolds. "Anything is fine," then, seeing she didn't understand me I repeated again. "ANY-THING."

The teller turned her back to me briefly. She counted up a stack of bills before turning back. Then she handed me the largest, newest, prettiest stack of money I could ever hope to own.

"What is this?" I demanded.

"Yo money," she answered simply.

"For five *dollars*?" I was in awe. "I get *all* this for five dollars?" How could I have lived for three *months* in a country where my money would go so far, and yet not buy *anything?*

I hurried out of the bank, almost feeling as if I had robbed it, and definitely afraid that I would be robbed if anyone knew I had so much money on me. My first order of business was to buy anything I could with that money.

I walked onto the mission campus and saw a group of mothers crocheting under the shade of a tree. "Of course!" I thought to myself. "If I buy some pretty things from them, I would also be giving back to the mission!" I love having a really good excuse to shop *and* having a pocket full of money to shop with. I haggled with the smiling ladies who were so pleased to assist me that more than once they tried to just give me the items for free.

Thrilled with my final selections, I hugged all the campus women and wished them farewell. I knew I would not see most of them the next day before we returned to Singapore.

TRAVEL TROUBLES

On our last night in Cambodia, we decided to treat ourselves to a little celebration. We ate in an Indian restaurant that people had raved about. I realized very quickly that some people do not have a clue what good food really is. Either this restaurant was not as good as everyone claimed, or it was having an extremely bad night. As if to verify exactly how terrible this place was, by midnight we were all sick from something we ate.

The children and I seemed to be hit especially hard by the stomach illness. I spent the night crawling toward a bucket which was soon filled from the return of my dinner. Before I could recover, dawn began to light up the morning sky.

With a groan, I dragged myself from bed and dressed for the journey to Singapore, but I was greeted by sounds that people had risen even earlier than I did.

By 6 AM, I believe that every single ADRA worker in Cambodia filled our tiny apartment to see us off. Parcels and letters were shoved into our already crammed suitcases with requests to deliver them to family members back in the United States. I scrambled upstairs to carry fruits down for all the visitors. After all, I was never too sick to forego my duties of hospitality.

When the hour arrived, Mr. Griswold finally came to usher me out. "Raya," he announced, "our van has arrived."

"A real van! Finally, a bit of civilization!" I thought. My assessment quickly changed as I watched every one of the workers pile into the van to accompany us to the airport. I soon decided not to expect civilization of any kind until my feet landed on American soil.

Sadly, Steve was unable to travel with us due to government adoption regulations. The Griswolds would be able to bring Steve to the United States after he was 18 years old, should he wish to live with them.

I don't think I have ever been so happy to see an airport in all my life—well, maybe except when I had left China. My time in Cambodia was very enjoyable, but the poverty of Cambodia combined with the remains of my illness was enough to make me ready to return home.

I escorted the children into the Phnom Penh Airport where Mrs. Griswold had me entertain them while the adults settled our flight arrangements. Never one to travel light, I had my carry-on suitcase and a backpack with me, as well as all the carry-on items for the kids. Mr. Griswold asked for my ticket and passport. I stared at him blankly for a moment.

"Raya? Your ticket?" he prompted me again.

"Just a minute," I said, lugging my carry-on, my backpack, and my suitcase to the counter. I began to shuffle through my bags. "OK, here's my passport, my license, my wallet ..." I searched every inch of my belongings, but I could not find my ticket. Here I was, a self-proclaimed world traveler, and I somehow misplaced the most fundamental thing I needed to travel with. "Oh Mr. Griswold! I'm sorry!" I exclaimed. "I was so sick last night that I have no idea where I put it."

"It's OK," he said patiently, "I'll see what we can do without the ticket." I could see by the poor man's pale face and tired eyes that he felt as badly as I did. We were all ready to be on our way. In fact, ready does not describe how we felt. Desperate was more like it. We all knew how unreliable Silk Air was when it came to their travel schedule. An 8 AM flight could mean 8:00, 8:30, 9:15 or even 5 PM. People crowded the airport waiting for promised flights that had not yet taken off and to pick up visitors who were long delayed. We did not want to risk having to catch the next flight out.

Five hundred dollars later, Mr. Griswold had settled the matter by purchasing a new ticket for me. Meanwhile, since the plane could not depart until we were aboard, it was delayed on our account, or should I say, on *my* account.

I threw my backpack over my shoulder and watched our luggage get carted toward the plane. Still exhausted from battling my food poisoning, I could not wait to be in my seat.

By the time our plane landed in Singapore, we were all feeling a bit better. Mr. Griswold pulled down our belongings from the overhead bins, handing articles to each person. "Raya, where did you put your carry-on?" he asked me.

"Don't you have it?" I asked.

"It's not up here."

"Didn't you put it on the luggage rack?" I suggested, hopefully.

"Raya, I'm sorry," he said patiently, "I didn't have it at all." Truthfully, I did know that it had only been in my possession, but it was wishful thinking that made me ask. I can be rather protective of my things when I travel and I usually like to keep everything crammed under the seat in front of me.

Mr. Griswold looked through his luggage receipts, just to be sure. Five receipts: one for my suitcase and four more for each of the Griswolds. We stared at each other with a sudden realization that I had left my carry-on luggage beside the ticket counter.

I'm sure that everyone was anxious to be back at the Kormand's home where we were guaranteed a delicious meal, free from food poisoning. Instead, we stood in a long line to report my missing bag.

The customer service manager was a Christian man named Joshua who was thrilled to hear that we were missionaries. As happened so often in my life, I felt a rush of satisfaction that "membership has its privileges." He quickly refunded Mr. Griswold's money for my lost ticket and then went on a telephone search for my lost luggage.

After several phone calls to Silk Air in Cambodia, they finally told us they found my luggage without a single trace of identification on the outside. "Well," I defended my carelessness to Mr. Griswold, "I didn't *expect* to leave it behind."

When we finally dragged our sick and exhausted selves back to the Kormand's home, our one-and-a-half-hour travel time had been stretched into *five* hours and I still would not have my luggage until the following day. To make up for it, we were greeted by the warm, rich smell of freshly baked banana-bread muffins and cinnamon rolls that Dorothy was pulling out of the oven. None of us had eaten more than a few weak bites since the previous evening, so we enthusiastically enjoyed Dorothy's delicious baking.

Once my delayed luggage finally arrived, we took a short monorail ride onto the Sentosa Island resort and entered a virtual fantasy land, traveling into other worlds of the deep ocean. We swam in warm, clean waters, watched varieties of fish swimming in the Underwater World, and were under-impressed by a *pink* dolphin show. I couldn't help but comment that our own dolphin shows in San Diego were much more exciting, but we certainly had never seen such a unique variety of the sea mammals before!

When we returned to mainland Singapore we felt revived by our adventures on Sentosa. From there we traveled to the Night Safari where we walked through jungle-like paths viewing hundreds of fascinating animals. My personal favorites were the fishing cats and the fruit bats. Later that night we rode the tram which took us all around the park and ended, of course, at the gift shop. Somehow I displayed an enormous amount of willpower and walked out with only one little T-shirt for each of my grandchildren.

MALAYSIA

Our last day in Singapore was the Sabbath. We spent the day at church, staying for a potluck with all the locals. The remainder of the day was spent resting before our trip.

Late that night we climbed into our "cheap motels" and traveled to West Malaysia. Although the rumbling, rocking train was noisy and uncomfortable, Nathan and Joelle were such good travelers that we didn't hear a single complaint from them all night long.

Once our train stopped, we disembarked and immediately climbed aboard a river boat that would take us to the world's oldest rainforest, the Taman Negara. What an amazing display of God's creations!

We used rope ladders to scale the highest trees until our heads were just barely under the brush of the canopies. Only one person could walk across the bridge at a time. Every five meters another person could enter, but we had to move as carefully as possible so as not to upset the person ahead of us. The adventure was breathtaking; it was as exciting as I imagined walking on the tops of the trees would be.

Finally, after what seemed like days and days of adventures, we all crawled from exhaustion toward our hotel. Only, this wasn't a typical hotel.

Certainly, we hadn't seen accommodations like this in the United States.

Our room, which we all shared, had only two tiny beds in it for all five of us. Joelle and I climbed into one bed while Mr. and Mrs. Griswold and Nathan climbed into the other. A more uncomfortable night has never been spent. If those children were any bonier, they would have been armadillos or spiny lobsters or something equally painful to cuddle with.

Evidently, we adults were no more comfortable to them. By morning, both children had slipped almost entirely off the beds and were practically on the floor. So went our last night in paradise before returning to home sweet home!

Figure 60 - Raya with Griswold Family, Coconuts in Cambodia, Adopted Son, Steve is on Right between Mr. Griswold and Joelle, Cart in Cambodia, Rope Bridge in Malaysia

PART XVII: UNITED STATES, 2001–2006

ON MY OWN AGAIN (WELL, ALMOST)

"... But as for me and my house, we will serve the LORD." Joshua 24:15

Akie, my cousin's wife, called to tell me that her youngest daughter, Sheila, was accepted into University of California, San Diego. She was taking summer classes and the dorms would be closed.

"Why don't you let her live with me?" I offered without another thought.

"Oh Raya," Akie hesitated, "are you sure?"

"Of course!" I was beginning to get excited at having my cousin's daughter around. Now, according to Persian customs, when anyone offers you something, you must refuse no less than three times before accepting. In this case, I already knew that I was in Akie and Que's will as the caregiver of all of their children should anything happen to the parents. With that fact she could hardly patronize me with false refusals. The deal was set and Sheila moved in.

I spent three wonderful months with sweet Sheila as my roommate before fall classes began and her friends pulled her into the dorms with them. Because of our time together, I think we developed a special bond that has never been broken. Even after she moved out, Sheila and her boyfriend Navid would come and visit me from time to time. It was so wonderful to attend their wedding in 2011.

Once I was on my own again, I really began to notice my aches and pains. Complaints about my knee or my back seemed to increase almost daily. When my children pointed this out to me, I grumbled about the stairs I had to climb every day. Even though, technically, I lived right on the lower level of my apartment building, my car was parked in an underground garage. To get to the pool required another several steps. I began to agonize over each step.

My misery was further provoked when my neighbor Tamar told me of a better apartment she had found for herself. "This one's less money Raya," she promised. Even if I had wanted to move, there were no other apartments available in her complex.

THE SINGLES CRUISE

To alleviate my pain, I needed a distraction. A trip to Hawaii seemed like the perfect thing. I had already been to Hawaii twice, once with Ella and another time for my cousin Asal's wedding. This time, my trip would be with a group of singles from my church and we would be taking a ten-day cruise. Our travels would take us to four different islands.

I didn't know anyone on the trip, not that it bothered me one bit. For the most part one goes on these adventures with the expectation of making new friends. I was seventy-something, so it's not as if I was expecting to find romance, but I knew that new friendships were waiting to blossom.

Even so, I would not have guessed that the majority of those traveling in our group would be *attached*. Within our group of over fifty "singles" only *five* of us came without a boyfriend or girlfriend along. Of those five, only one was a man, and boy did we shower him with attention!

One woman from our group, Raquel, spoke Spanish but had a distinctively different accent. "Are you Russian?" I asked her finally.

"Why yes, Raya!" she exclaimed, telling me that her family had both Russian and Argentinean heritage, and that they had immigrated to the United States. We swapped contact information and stayed forever close after that trip.

Coincidentally, Esther and her family would be on Oahu the same week that we would dock there. Her husband Nasser had business on the island. I couldn't wait to meet up with them and introduce them to my new friends. I called Esther's cell phone—imagine the technology—from the ship and attempted the arrangements. Of course, having communication technology and actually being able to communicate with your children are often two very different things.

I left a message on her cell phone of the date I would be in Oahu, but there was no way she could call me back; shore to ship calls were tricky. So I tried back, updating my messages periodically. Finally, I reached her.

"Where are you staying, Esther?" I inquired.

"I might be sightseeing and not at the hotel when you arrive, so you should call me on my cell and I will come and meet you."

"But Esther, I just like to know …" I persisted until she told me. We made arrangements to meet at the Pearl Harbor Memorial.

"Mom, you need to call me on my cell so that we can adjust our schedules if we need to find you!" she asserted. I had a better idea. I decided I would surprise her by showing up at their hotel.

I arrived at their hotel only to discover that my family had already left to do their sightseeing. I left a message for them in their rooms and waited in the lobby for them to return.

Eventually, I wandered over to the plaza adjacent to their hotel village. Confined to purchasing the limited items on the cruise ship, I was desperate for a greater shopping experience. I was sure I couldn't have been there for more than half an hour, yet somehow when I returned to the lobby and found that my children had still not returned, I had only half an hour to return to the ship. My entire day was wasted without seeing Esther's family.

Once I returned to the ship I called Esther's cell phone again. "Mom, where were you?" she demanded. "We waited in a long line at Pearl Harbor Memorial, forever, but we kept walking around to look for you."

"Oh, right," I murmured. "I guess I forgot about Pearl Harbor. I went to your rooms, but I couldn't find you there."

"You couldn't find us because you wanted to meet at the Memorial," Esther reminded me.

"Well," I replied, brightening up again, "at least I got to do some shopping!"

ONCE A TEACHER, ALWAYS A TEACHER

When I returned to San Diego, an old Russian friend of mine, Peter, told me about the apartments he had moved into. "So clean and new and very cheap!" he told me any time we spoke. I knew I had to see them for myself.

The apartments had everything I needed: a pool and community room, onsite laundry, and parking right outside my front door. Best of all, everything was brand new! In fact, many of the houses and apartments around this apartment were still being built and the road ended just past the apartments. I was instantly sold on the new apartment. Soon Esther and Ella helped me through another downsizing project to further remove garments and articles I had purchased in the year I'd spent on Charmant Drive.

"No more shopping, Mom!" Esther commanded.

"But Esther," Ella pointed out, "you get to inherit all the stuff she has no room for any time she moves."

"That is *exactly* why I say, 'no more shopping, Mom!'"

My first day out at the pool of my new apartment, I noticed a young boy sitting near the gates. It looked like he wanted to get into the pool area.

"Don't you have school?" I asked, but the boy just stared at me without speaking. I studied his features and suspected he was Afghan or Iranian.

"What language do you speak?" I asked in Farsi. His eyes opened wide.

"Farsi!" he exclaimed. After very little persuasion, he told me he was from Afghanistan, as I had suspected, and was already home from school.

"How interesting," I thought, "Peter speaks only Russian and this family speaks only Farsi. I wonder if there are other non-English speakers here."

"Tell your mother I can teach her English if she wants to learn," I offered, instinctively.

The next day I met more Russians. After that, I met a Mexican family, a Chinese couple, and a Persian couple. "Really? What is this place, the United Nations?" Every day more and more people knocked on my door asking for English lessons. Soon I couldn't squeeze them all into my tiny living room.

Finally, I went to the office with a request. "Rosie, can we please use the community room twice a week?" I asked our apartment manager.

"You have to apply every week and a leave a $50 deposit each time you need the room," she answered abruptly, barely looking up from her work.

"Rosie," I reasoned, "this room is empty every Tuesday and Thursday. If we are going to use it weekly, why should we do all those administrative things? Why can't you just reserve the room for us on a regular basis?"

"Write a proposition about the number of residents and non-residents who will use the area, the hours you are requesting it for and how much you will be charging," she answered hastily. "There is still a $50 deposit every time you use the community room."

"I'm not charging anything," I stated when I turned in the proposition. "This is voluntary and we're not serving any food or drinks. Can't you just wave the deposit?" Rosie fought us every step of the way, but in the end she agreed to let us use the space.

One day as she walked through the common area to her office, Rosie saw we had quickly outgrown the few couches in the community room. The next time she came to me, she brought a white board, ESL books, folding tables, and twenty-five folding chairs for us to use. "You and your students just need to set them up and put them away when you're done," she instructed. And so my career as a volunteer ESL teacher began.

"I'm feeling well again!" I happily told my children one day. "I don't even have time to think about my aches and pains so they have all just gone away!" Teaching and helping my neighbors was occupying all my time.

I began to drive groups of friends to church with me and to their "adult day care," as they called it, a senior community center where they received food, classes, and entertainment, all completely free. "As a visitor you have to pay, though," the director told me. "And you would never be able to join."

"Really? It's free for them, but *I* have to pay?"

"They are on Social Services," she explained. "You don't qualify."

"Wait," I tried to understand. "You mean that I worked for twenty-six years in this country, paid my taxes, helped my community, and I don't get to benefit from Social Services, but these people came from another country, never worked here a day in their lives, and they do?" I already knew that many of these same families paid half of what I did for rent, even though they lived in larger apartments.

"I'm sorry, Raya," she said. "Those are just the rules. You are getting pension and Social Security. However, if your income level drops, you can re-apply."

I knew that wasn't going to happen. So I kept helping my friends with their needs, and they repaid me in flowers, baked treats, and foods they were able to get from Social Services.

One day I received a notice that my rent was going to be raised by $100. "Are you kidding me?" I challenged Rosie. "I'm already paying more than any of the other residents."

"I'm sorry, Raya," she attempted to dismiss me, "Those instructions came from Corporate."

"Then I want to speak to Corporate," I stated. "I am already doing so much around here. I don't think I should have to keep paying more."

I spoke to the CEO, telling him about all the neighbors I was helping and about the classes we had been having. After researching, he discovered that, in fact, there was a large number of non-English-speaking residents.

"OK, Raya," he said, "we still have to raise your rent, but you will be reimbursed the $100 as payment for all you do. Sign the contract with Rosie on Monday."

"This means you're an employee," Rosie stated, handing me a Windwood Village Apartments T-shirt which I wore with pride. And so, in my retirement I began to earn the lowest teacher's salary I had ever had in my life: one hundred dollars a month!

CAR TROUBLES

While living at the Windwood Village Apartments I started to have a series of car troubles, not that I didn't already have car trouble. I mean, just putting me behind the wheel of a car could be trouble, although I would never admit it.

After I came back from Russia, my auto insurance, which I had continued to pay for the four years I was away, wrote me a letter congratulating me on my good driving record. I was even refunded $100 for having no tickets or accidents during that period of time. Any time my children complained about my driving, I proudly showed them my AAA letter. No amount of reasoning from them could convince me that my record was so clean simply because I had not been behind the wheel all that time. I had proof of my excellent driving capabilities signed by the American Automobile Association. Who could argue with that?

My first car problem came about because of all the new roads being built in Carmel Valley where I now lived. Every morning I would leave my house and by evening the new construction had me completely rerouted so that I couldn't find my way home. Once, Esther was waiting to meet with me at her house. From the time I called her and said, "See you in twenty minutes," to the time I finally pulled into her driveway, two hours had passed.

"Where have you been?" Esther asked in a panic.

"I got lost, Esther," I replied patiently, although I was as stressed as she was. "There *is* a road that goes from your house to mine, but there are *no* roads from my house to yours."

Even more confusing was trying to drive at night. I had trouble making out street names and directions as the sun went down, not that I would let a little thing like *vision* keep me off the roads. So I was surprised to see police lights behind me late one evening as I pulled out of a parking lot.

"Is there a problem officer?" I asked as sweetly as possible.

"Ma'am, you are driving on the wrong side of the median," he said sternly as he looked into my eyes. "Have you been drinking?"

"Certainly not!" I exclaimed. "I never drink!" Then I remembered my little trick of acting as pathetic as possible so I could gain some sympathy from the officer. "Oh!" I said in my most pitiful voice, "I am just new here and I don't know these streets too well and it is hard for me to see."

"Well, ma'am," his stern voice had softened somewhat so I thought my trick was working, "I don't think you should be driving anymore tonight if you can't see."

"Oh! But I have to get home! How will I get home?"

"Is there someone who can come here and drive you home?" he asked. I thought of my daughter who lived six miles away.

"No, sir, I don't know anyone in this city." There was no way I would let *her* know I had been pulled over by the police. Esther already treated me like she was my mother.

"Well then," he looked troubled, "I'm afraid I'll have to drive you home myself and have your car towed and impounded."

"Towed!" I gasped. "Oh! Oh no!" I struggled to dig my way out of this mess. "Come to think of it, I do know someone nearby." I unwillingly gave him Esther's number and tried to listen in on their conversation.

"This is Officer Sweets from the San Diego Police Department. Do you know a woman named Raya?"

"Yes! She's my mother! Is something wrong?" I cringed at the sound of panic in her voice coming through the officer's cell phone.

"Your *mother*?" He looked at me with concern and then dropped his voice cautiously. "She is fine, but she appears to be disoriented," he said. "She was driving on the wrong side of the median and didn't seem to know where she was." He talked like he thought I was a crazy person rather than a helpless old lady. "And she didn't seem to remember that she had a daughter in town."

"Oh great. She will never let me live this one down," I worried.

Unfortunately, Esther was not the only one who came to pick me up; it was her *entire* family. The girls stared out the window at their grandmother detained by the police. "Why did you tell Nasser?" I whispered to my daughter.

"Mom, I can't drive *two* cars at once! And we couldn't leave the girls home alone."

We received strict instructions from the police which included losing my ability to drive at night. The policeman gave his business card to Esther. "I should have impounded her car," Officer Sweets warned, "and if she drives at night again, I will."

I think Esther began to chalk my tires after that time because if my car was moved even a fraction of an inch at night, she knew and threatened to call Officer Sweets.

One afternoon I finished shopping and just wanted to unload my car before returning to Esther's house. They say you should never shop while you're hungry. Evidently you should never unpack groceries while you're hungry either. I became distracted by all the tasty things I had purchased and I began to eat some grapes. The grapes led the way to a sandwich, which I made for myself.

Crash! I heard the sound of metal hitting concrete outside of my door and I went running out to find a young man standing beside my car, which I had left running since I was planning on being inside just long enough to unpack. Beside him at his feet was the bike he had been riding.

"Are you OK?" I asked, startling him.

"Yes," he answered. My car did not appear to be hit by his bike, so I couldn't understand what had caused the crash.

"What are you doing here?" I demanded.

"Nothing," he said. Then he added, pointing to another residence, "I'm just visiting those people over there."

"Then go," I commanded, watching as he picked up his bike and pushed it to the apartment he was visiting. I went back inside to finish putting away the goods I had purchased, leaving the key in my car.

A few minutes later, I walked back out to go to Esther's house.

The boy was gone. The bike was gone. My car was gone. I stared at the empty space for a full minute before I could react.

"Police!" I shouted. "Police!" I ran inside and dialed 911. "Someone stole my car!" I yelled to the dispatcher. Soon the chaos sent several of my neighbors outside. "I've been robbed," I moaned.

"Did you have any belongings in it?" the officer asked me when he arrived.

"*Everything*," I sighed. And it was true; I tend to keep a little bit of everything in my car just in case of an emergency. I counted off all the items I could think of. "Sneakers, gym bag, dress shoes, notebook, bible ..."

"Anything of value?" he interrupted me. "Any cash?"

"Oh yes!" I remembered my purse sitting on the front seat. "A lot!

Maybe fifty, sixty …"

"Thousand?" he feared.

"No, dollars," I corrected him. He wrote up the report, seeming rather unimpressed by my low-value loss.

Everyone—my family and neighbors—pitched in to help me get around while the insurance company looked at the claim. Finally, they closed the case as a loss. With San Diego so close to Mexico, it was not unusual for people to have auto thefts cross the border. Because of this, the insurance company did not expect to find it so they gave me a check for what it was worth.

Four days later, with a new car in hand, I received a call I did not expect to get. "Your car has been recovered," the insurance company said. "You will have the choice of keeping your refund check or your car, but either way, you can go see it at the impound."

Recovered is not what I would call it. Evidently, the car was found abandoned on a dead-end street. It had several new dents and a broken side view mirror. The seats looked as if two people had been sleeping on them. A glass pipe for crack cocaine and a few discarded clothing items were shoved under the seats, although my purse was long gone. I could never feel comfortable in this vehicle again.

That wasn't the last time I would lose a car though. A few years later I dropped off my car at Sears for a tire rotation. Since the mall was in the same parking lot, I decided to do some shopping while I waited for my car. Four hours, two blouses, a pair of shoes, and a lunch later, I walked back out. By this time the sun was setting and the mall was closing. I had difficulty making my way through the parking lot in the little daylight that was left.

I walked to the nearest parking spaces where I usually left my car and looked around. I walked up and down the closest aisles that were marked "Handicapped." Esther once told me that if I had no arms and no legs I *still* would not be truly handicapped. I'm far too indomitable to fall into that category. Even so, I did love my handicapped parking spots, and as soon as my doctor gave me the go-ahead for a placard, I never drove into an ordinary parking spot again!

But how could a car just disappear? I flagged down the first security guard that drove by. "Excuse me," I called, "I can't find my car!" The guard had me hop into his cart and we drove up and down the aisles over speed bumps and around cars. But mine was nowhere to be seen. The security guard had me fill out an incident report before he called the police to take me home. My car was stolen again. I couldn't believe it.

Three days later I received a phone call from Sears. "Mrs. Abadir? This is just a courtesy call to remind you that your car is ready."

"My car?" I searched my mind to comprehend what he was saying.

"Yes, ma'am." he added. "It's actually been done since Monday!"

"Oh my dear!" I exclaimed. "I reported that car stolen! I completely forgot I left it to be repaired!"

AN OPEN HEART

The time had come for me to travel again. I was getting restless at home, regardless of how much fun I was having. Still, as much as I wanted to go, go, go, I was just tired all the time.

Danny called one afternoon and found me napping again. "Mom! What's wrong?" he demanded with worry in his voice.

"Nothing, Danny," I assured him groggily, "I'm just resting."

But I realized I was resting almost every afternoon and even the simplest tasks felt like work.

Around the same time, a couple from my church introduced themselves to me. "We are going to do some mission work in Romania, and we would love to have you with us," Rodica said. "You have so much experience in translating books and opening new schools, it would be a blessing if you could go."

"Of course I'll go!" I exclaimed without a second thought. Already I could feel my energy picking up again.

"You will not!" Esther reprimanded when I told her. "You are almost eighty years old! You can't go running off to third-world countries!"

"Mom, why don't you go for a checkup," Ella suggested. She had also noticed that I was more tired lately. "If your doctor clears it, I see no reason why you shouldn't go."

I wish I could say that the only trouble I had while I lived in Carmel Valley was car trouble.

I sat in Dr. Effron's office chatting away to him and his assistant. "It seems that retirement has brought out the worst in me," I complained. "I mean, why else would I be tired all the time? I just know that I'll feel so much better once I am doing mission work in Romania."

"Romania!" he exclaimed. "Raya, I know you have been all around the world, but you are simply too old to be going to third-world countries."

"But, Dr. Effron," I reasoned, "I need to be busy. If I don't keep working, I'll go crazy! And I would be going with some very dear friends who are young and healthy and can take care of me!" I didn't tell him that I had just met these very dear friends the day they invited me to work with them.

"I'll tell you what," he bargained, "I don't like the fact that you are so low in energy now." Dr. Effron had been my cardiologist since I moved to San Diego, and in the twenty years that he had known me, he had seen me at my strongest. "I suspect you may not be getting enough oxygen pumping to your heart. Let's do a simple angioplasty. If everything looks clear, I'll say OK to your travels. But if not, you'll have to stay here."

I didn't like the idea of checking into the hospital, even as an out-patient. But my doctor assured me that he would be supervising the procedure himself and the longest it would take, if I needed an angioplasty, would be four hours.

Two-and-a-half months and a six-bypass, open-heart surgery later, I finally left the hospital.

"Six bypasses!" Esther exclaimed in surprise. "I never knew there was such a thing!"

"This has been a remarkable day," my surgical nurse answered.

"She is a remarkable lady," Ella added.

For those whose life's journey has never carried them through such an extensive surgery, let me paint a picture of what an open heart patient goes through. First, they have to cut an incision from your throat to your navel. Next they use a circular saw to split your sternum so your ribcage can be pried open. After that, they dump an entire bucket of ice into your chest. This, believe it or not, is intended to *help* you by making your heart *stop* beating! As if this invasion is not enough, the doctors then pull veins out of your legs and use them to gift wrap the whole ensemble.

When Dr. Effron made his rounds, he was grave. "You will *not* be going on any more mission trips," my cardiologist told me sternly. I had every heart complication I could possibly encounter. But in the end, Esther's friend Jan brightened my mood and told everyone they kept me so long because all the nurses saw how much fun I was.

Over two-and-a-half months I got to know every nurse, doctor, volunteer, janitor, and lab technician at the hospital. And they got to know everything about me including all my allergies (no matter how much I'm hurting, *don't* give me pain medications unless you want me to throw up all over you) and how giddy I would become from a blood transfusion.

There's not a lot you can hide when you're wandering the halls in a surgical gown! Not only was I subjected to wearing the ugly garment, I also had to push around a Wound VAC (Vacuum Assisted Closure®), an important machine I was attached to by an unsightly cord for the purpose of cleaning out the hematoma that occurred when my angioplasty refused to close up.

In spite of my setbacks, there were many good times in the hospital. I learned to play golf, do crafts, and, especially fun for me, visit the hospital lobby's gift shop.

Finally, a social worker walked into my room while Esther was visiting as she usually did. The worker came in with the happy news that I would be leaving soon. I could hardly believe it.

"Where will you be going when you leave?" the social worker asked.

"I'm going to my home," I announced happily.

"She's going to *my* home," Esther announced to my dismay.

"No, Esther, you've done too much already. I can go to my own home."

But the social worker was already on my daughter's side. "If you live alone, I think it would be much better to stay with her a while."

"I think you just don't want me going to my home because you killed all my plants," I pouted. Esther was not born with my green thumb for plant care, so I anticipated empty pots when I would return.

We read through the tedious paperwork and instructions on my post-surgery care. A homecare nurse was assigned to me. On her first visit with me at Esther's home, the nurse asked all the standard questions: my name, age, and insurance.

"She's going to be 80!" Esther said, incredulously. The thought had taken me by surprise, but my daughters had already started to plan a birthday party for me.

"When are you turning 80?" the nurse asked as she examined my driver's license carefully.

"In two months!" I answered proudly.

"Honey," the nurse said, shaking her head, "you haven't been in the hospital that long. Your ID says you were born in '26."

"Yes," I acknowledged.

"Well this is only 2005—you don't turn 80 for another year!"

I honestly don't know if we were relieved to postpone the party plans for a year, or disappointed. There were days when I was sure I wouldn't make it through another year.

THE SAFER ROADS

Shortly before I was admitted into the hospital for my angioplasty, I had been in another fender-bender. When I was comfortably settled into Esther's house to continue my healing, she dropped another blow on me. "Mom, the DMV has revoked your license," she showed me the letter.

"What?" I exclaimed. "Why would they do that? I have a perfect driving record!" I searched for the AAA letter as proof.

"Mom, you do *not* have a perfect driving record," Esther corrected me. "You haven't had one since 1994 when Andrey was doing all your driving for you! Now is the time you will just have to give up your car."

"Never!" I exclaimed, scanning the letter for a loophole I knew I would find. "See here?" I happily pointed to the letter. "I can go in and be retested, then they'll give me a new license." But it wasn't that easy. In a complete reversal of roles, Esther began coaching me on my behind-the-wheel skills.

"Turn left, Mom … no left, LEFT! OK, pull up beside the car ahead of you and let's practice parallel parking." The monotonous drills and stressful repetitions continued day after day until the date of my driving test.

I sat nervously waiting for my turn to be called. Esther was reading a book next to me, and I looked around the DMV at all the other new drivers.

"Boy! I can't believe all these teenage drivers!" I whispered to Esther. "If I was the examiner I would feel nervous about so many young people driving on my streets!"

Esther giggled and looked up from her book long enough to pat my head condescendingly. "Tiny, did you ever think that maybe these teenagers are looking at you and thinking, 'Check out that old lady! If I was the examiner I'd feel nervous about an old lady like her driving on my streets!'"

I had to laugh in spite of myself, but I sobered up quickly. "Esther, don't speak such nonsense!" I scolded. "You should be praying for your mother to pass!"

"I did pray," Esther retorted.

Nevertheless, when the results came in, I did not pass. The examiner took Esther aside, as if she were my mother, and listed off all the reasons why he had to fail me.

We solemnly returned to the car. "You weren't praying!" I chastised Esther.

"I did pray," Esther said again.

"Then you were praying against me!" I insisted.

"No," she answered with a playful smile, "but I did pray that God would do whatever He felt was best."

Over the next few months I tried out for my license again, and then again. Each time Esther and I had the same conversation.

The night before my last driving test, I sat in my prayer meeting group. "Please pray for me," I told my friends as I looked around the room. "I have to take my driving test tomorrow and if I don't pass, I will never be able to drive again."

Everyone looked at me sympathetically. "It's so hard to give up your independence," my friend Beth empathized.

"It's not just for me," I insisted. "I do so much for others when I am able to drive!"

Despite the prayers, I still did not pass the next day. When the DMV finally told me I had run out of chances, I was devastated.

"This must be God's will," Esther said as we quietly drove home.

"How can this be His will?" I asked. It just didn't make sense in my mind.

"Well, Mom, if you are driving, you take your friends everywhere. You help so many people and everyone gets a little bit of you."

I nodded emphatically.

"But if you're not driving, the roads will be safer and we will all have you around longer," Esther reasoned. Which is how it came to be that, months before my 80th birthday, I finally gave up driving. At least I didn't have to give up my independence yet. I managed to recover and was able to return to teaching English at my apartment complex.

FALL FROM GRACE

By 2006, I was becoming more and more unsteady on my feet, although I was the last to recognize this newest trait of mine.

Ella and her friend Jennifer called to say they were stopping by my apartment late one Sunday afternoon on their way from Mexico back up to Long Beach. I looked around my lived-in home and knew it wouldn't pass Ella's high standards. In a panic, I rushed around, picking up discarded sneakers and straightening bookshelves. I finished just as the girls were arriving and needed only to take the trash to the dumpster.

"Be right back!" I called over my shoulder to the two startled ladies standing at my doorstep. Looking back, it would have made so much more sense for me to just have one of *them* take out the trash. But I wanted them to feel welcomed, not worked.

In a hurry, I dashed back up the walkway, cut across the garden, and tripped on the pavement. The next thing I knew, the sidewalk was rushing up to meet my face. Instinctively, my hand flew out to protect me, but even then, I landed head first into a terracotta strawberry planter, right at the feet of my daughter and her very alarmed friend.

"Mom! Are you alright?"

"... No ..."

"Mom, Mom!"

"... Ice ... I need ice," I groaned, as the two young ladies helped me to my feet and into my open doorway. Ella stepped around me, filling an ice pack and applying it to my face. I felt as if my head had been used as a punching bag.

"I'm going to take you to the hospital," Ella said.

"No," I replied, "I will be alright. Just let me rest for a few moments."

"I called Esther and she's on her way," Ella agonized.

I let out an incomprehensible grunt. It was painful to even talk.

"I can't find the Tylenol so you'll have to take this aspirin for the pain," she instructed, popping two small tablets into my mouth and handing me a cup of water to wash them down. "There ... you'll be better soon," she promised.

But I wasn't better. I felt worse every second, and neither the ice nor the aspirin did anything to alleviate the pain. "Sick ... feel woozy now ..." I managed.

Poor Jennifer looked on helplessly. This was not the way I wanted to welcome guests. I usually made an enormous meal that no one would eat, and I would tell jokes and stories and beg them to stay longer. But on that night, it was all I could do to just keep my swollen eyes open.

"Did you eat dinner?" Ella asked me.

"No."

"Oh great. You can't take aspirin on an empty stomach." She searched through my refrigerator. "Here," she put a cup of yogurt into my hands, "this will coat your stomach and you won't feel nauseated anymore."

I could tell Ella was getting nervous, and I'm sure we were all relieved when Esther finally walked in. "Mom," she gave me her customary greeting whenever I felt horrible, "you look like crap!" Normally I would scold her about using bad language, but tonight I didn't even have the strength for that.

"Don't worry," Ella soothed her sister, "I think she's just trying to get attention. You know how she is." Ella recounted the whole story for Esther.

"Mom may be blowing it all out of proportion, but there's a bruise that's visibly spreading on her face—probably because the aspirin is a blood thinner—and all her other symptoms are way too close to those of a concussion," Esther decided, pulling me out of my seat.

"What are you doing?"

"I'm taking her to the ER," she said.

"No ER. I hate it …" But Esther ignored my pleas as she whisked me into her car and sent her sister to take her friend home. "I know you guys have a long trip back. You can go. We'll be fine. Call when you get home and I'll fill you in."

By the time we arrived at the hospital, I was throwing up, and there was blood on the icepack I held to my face, although we never could figure out where the blood came from. Half of my face was purple from the rapidly growing bruise.

An intake nurse sitting at her desk jumped up when we walked in. "What did you do? Who did this to you?" She eyed Esther, assuming the worst. Suddenly, my daughter must have realized how bad the situation looked.

"Mom, tell her the story!" she hissed in my ear as I spit more blood into the napkin.

"No one did this. I did this. I fell," I mumbled to the nurse who sat back down but would not remove her sharp glare from Esther.

After four hours shivering in the chilly emergency room (really, do they have to keep it so cold?), I was admitted into the hospital with a concussion. "This is why I hate coming to the ER," I complained to Esther. "When they see me coming, they keep me here forever."

"Well, Mom," she answered dryly, "as cute as you are, that's understandable. But in this case they are keeping you here because the x-rays show that you have a concussion, a fractured cheekbone and a broken wrist."

Esther updated her sister Ella on my condition. When she heard the report, Ella drove back from Long Beach to make sure I was okay.

By the end of my stay, three of my front teeth fell out as well. I couldn't afford to lose any more teeth; now I only had six left! Of course I blamed that on the hospital as well. Don't get me wrong. I love that hospital! I now volunteer there three times a week, and I am very proud of the services we provide for our patients—for our *other* patients. I just don't like to *be* one of those patients.

On the day I was finally discharged, there was a party going on in my hospital room. Our neighbor Robbie was there with her son Justin and Esther's friend Jan (who made it a point to visit whenever I was hospitalized), as well as two of the nurses I volunteered with after my open heart surgery.

I was released into Esther's care and would be staying in her home again while I recovered. On the way there, my daughter made a mental checklist out loud: "Dinner, dishes, write my agenda ..."

"I will wash the dishes for you," I volunteered.

"No you will *not!*" Esther snapped. "You will sit on the couch and be served, as you should be!"

I sighed, deep and long, with self-pity. "What's the use of living if you can't be useful?" I groaned.

"You can be useful again when you're well," she softened a bit. "Even your son-in-law who is half your age rested for two weeks after his recent concussion!"

A NEW DRIVE

One of the Persian couples to whom I was teaching English grew a deep attachment to me. Parviz, the husband, warmly called me Miss Raya and his wife Fareshteh wanted to go anywhere I went. I had long before realized that my English classes could be enhanced by taking my students to church with me. Parviz gladly drove us, although he made every excuse to avoid the church if he could.

Now that I could not drive myself, Parviz began to drive me around other places as well. In return, I attended doctor visits and other appointments with the couple, translating as they needed.

"Mom! You're taking advantage of their kindness," my children scolded me. "You can't force them to be your taxi service!"

"I'm not forcing anyone," I insisted. "They love to drive me around! Besides," I added, "you do understand that I help them too."

But they didn't understand. Not until Niloo, the younger daughter of Parviz and Fareshteh, spoke to my daughters.

"I am so thankful for Miss Raya," she said warmly.

"*I'm* so thankful for your *father!*" Esther replied. "He has freed up so much of my time by driving my mom everywhere."

"Oh, he loves it!" Niloo insisted. "He said to me, 'I finally feel like a human again. I finally feel like I am contributing to society!'"

"See?" I said smugly, "I told you!"

THE BIG 8-0 CELEBRATION

Toward the end of 2006, I faced another hike in my rent. It wasn't that I couldn't afford to pay the difference; it was the principal of the thing. I believed that I should have a grandfather clause to protect me from price increases. I began to seek out yet another move. But before I went anywhere, I had just one more thing to do there. That year, with cousins, neighbors, students, friends and my precious family around me, I was finally able to celebrate 80 years of my God-given life.

What a wonderful birthday party it was! Not only was I surrounded by my church friends and neighboring students, my dear cousin Akie drove over three hours from LA to be there. She truly surprised me by bringing her daughter Fedra and Fedra's two precious sons, Darius, who was one-and-a-half, and Cameron, who was only nine months old. Danny and Susan came all the way from Buffalo, NY. Together with my daughters, they catered a delicious Persian meal for the guests. Ella arrived with a beautiful, huge cake, topped with fresh fruit. Esther, Mimi, and Rema were all great help during the party. They put a pink crown on my head and treated me like a queen. It was a night to remember!

There has never been a dull moment in my life. When I moved from my apartment, I was reminded of the theme song from the 1960 General Conference Sessions. I started singing, "Up there is my home, my home, blessed home. Far beyond the sun!"

Esther asked, "Mom, did you make up this song?" Later she found the lyrics on her smart phone.

I don't know when my Lord is going to come or when I will leave this world, but my only desire is to be ready to see Christ's coming in glory as the King of Kings and the Lord of Lords. I want to hear the angels and saints singing the Hallelujah Chorus from Handel's Messiah, "And He shall reign forever and ever." Amen.

Figure 61 – Raya's English Lessons at Windwood Village Apartments, Mitra and Lida, daughters of Abraham in Iran, Que's Daughter Sheila and Raya, Abraham's Daughter Roya Visiting Raya in Buffalo, NY

Figure 62 - Raya in Hospital after Surgery with Ella, Esther, and Former Elmira, Student Lisa Gordy; Danny with Raya before Surgery; Two Former Bronx Manhattan Students: Grace (3rd in Row 1 of Class Photo) with Raya; Ella with Ruthie (3rd in Row 3) and Raya

EPILOGUE

"When we do the best that we can, we never know what miracle is wrought in our life, or in the life of another." – Helen Keller

I am looking forward to my 90th birthday in another year. Shortly after my 80th birthday, I moved in with Esther and her family in their home in San Diego. Esther and Ella were concerned that, with my degenerating bones, I would continue to stumble and might hurt myself permanently. I of course blame my shrinking body and osteoporosis on the lack of calcium and poor nutrition I experienced as a child in Russia during the Great Depression. I thank God I am able to continue to take care of myself.

I am so blessed to have had my son Daniel help me financially over the past few years. Ella fills in by helping with all other needs from new clothes to getting a pedicure. I enjoy visiting them in NY every summer and seeing my dear friends in the church there. I also enjoy my children's visits to California every year.

It is wonderful to live with my loving daughter Esther and her family. I have enjoyed watching my two granddaughters grow. When they were younger, I helped Esther by babysitting them. Now they drive me when I need to go to the drugstore or need a ride to the pool.

I swim three times a week at the Jewish Community Center. They have a wonderful large heated outdoor pool and because of the mild temperatures, it is open all year. I also started taking Japanese Brush Art classes there and enjoy gifting my friends and family with my art. My bedroom wall has my paintings from the floor to the ceiling. During art class, I have met several people from other countries and usually stay after the class so I can teach them English. My passion is teaching, thus I will never retire!

On Mondays, Wednesdays, and Fridays, I also work as a volunteer at Scripps Memorial Hospital in La Jolla. Because Esther's home is close to the hospital, they provide me with free transportation on the days that I volunteer. With all my trips and falls, my long stay at the hospital after my open heart surgery, and routine doctor visits, I feel at home at this hospital and am proud to contribute and help where needed. They have a wonderful cardiac treatment center where heart patients, as well as diabetics and those with pulmonary disease, can exercise while being monitored by the nursing staff. After my volunteer work, I exercise there as well.

I love my forward thinking Tierrasanta Seventh-day Adventist Church family in San Diego. Their traditions are much more liberal than the way I raised my children. I enjoy our free-spirited church services and my caring, spiritual family.

It took Esther and me almost four years to write this book. I had a deep desire to have a memoir for my children and grandchildren, to share my travels, challenges, and God's blessings with others, and to encourage the youth of the world to follow God's guidance in every aspect of their lives. I can now close this chapter of my life.

I look forward to God's next challenge for me.

Figure 63 - Family Trip to Cancun: Danny, Susan, Ella, Rema, Esther, and Mimi, Morar Family from Tula, Russia, visiting in US with Esther, Rema, Mimi, and Raya

Figure 64 - Raya with Japanese Brush Art Teacher Takashi (center), Raya with Scripps Hospital Nurses: Chris, Glen, Lauren, and Mara

HOW TO FIND OUT MORE:

- For questions, contact me on Facebook:
  - ○ Raya Abadir.
- What is the Seventh-day Adventist Religion and Education?
  - ○ www.adventist.org
- How can I help the Adventist Development and Relief Agency?
  - ○ https://adra.org
- Where can I find detailed information about Adventist Colleges?
  - ○ www.adventistcolleges.org
- Is there a list of Adventist High Schools?
  - ○ www.mundall.com/erik/academies.htm
- Is there a list of Adventist hospitals?
  - ○ www.sdahealthcare.org
- How can I find out more on the Adventist quit smoking plan?
  - ○ http://www.breathefree2.com/

Made in the USA
San Bernardino, CA
13 January 2017